Gender and the Work-Family Experience

Maura J. Mills, Ph.D.
Editor

Gender and the Work-Family Experience

An Intersection of Two Domains

Springer

Editor
Maura J. Mills, Ph.D.
Departments of Psychology and Management
Hofstra University
Hempstead
New York
USA

ISBN 978-3-319-08890-7 ISBN 978-3-319-08891-4 (eBook)
DOI 10.1007/978-3-319-08891-4
Springer Cham Heidelberg New York Dordrecht London

Library of Congress Control Number: 2014947532

Printed on acid-free paper

Springer is part of Springer Science+Business Media (www.springer.com)

For my parents, Chris and Ellen, and for my husband Matthew, each of whom have shown me different aspects of the work–family interface throughout varying phases of my life thus far. And most especially for David, my beautiful son — my biggest work–family challenge to date, but also my most rewarding.

Foreword

It is an exciting time for work and family research! The field has been exploding with growing numbers of scholars identifying themselves as work–family researchers. Unlike previous decades, work–family conflict and positive work–life spillover are now core constructs used across many fields of research. A recent Google search in April 2014 of the terms "work family" yielded 2 billion six hundred and thirty million results! Growing appreciation of the importance for work–life well-being is recognized and valued in many societies around the globe. Many countries around the world from the USA to the UK to Sweden to Singapore are starting to create work–family research and practice groups. As an example, as the first formally elected President of the Work Family Researchers Network, I helped convene its second ever international conference. Over 1000 scholars and policy makers from over 33 countries met in June 2014 to share work–family research in New York, USA. Work–family scholars build on the work of WFRN Founder Jerry Jacobs of the University of Pennsylvania, the Alfred P. Sloan Foundation, and the seminal work of thought leaders such as Rosabeth Moss Kanter (my former dissertation committee member, now at Harvard University), and many other luminaries.

Despite this progress and growing interest in the work–family field, many questions remain regarding work and family research. Despite thousands of studies, the work–family field is still in its relative infancy compared to other scholarly research domains, and faces epistemological challenges. Common measures and ways of conceptualizing work and family are still under discussion (Kossek et al. 2011). Disciplines continue to dispute how best to understand this growing phenomenon. A recent *Wall Street Journal* article reports that use of workplace flexibility policies seems to have leveled off and stigmatization still faces those who work in different ways from the mainstream, even if strong performers. Such debate suggests that core knowledge and ways of knowing and understanding the work–family nexus are still in flux. More importantly, organizations, individuals, and societies are continually discussing how to best address the continuing chasm between work and family, as solutions are unclear. Despite the increase in availability of work and family policies and the acceptance of work and family in our popular zeitgeist, reports show a vast majority of members of society—regardless of whether they are male or female, single or married, old or young, working or not—reporting increasing work–life stress. Having access to workplace flexibility is another growing aspect of work inequality, as occupation, class, and gender stratification remain potential hurdles to flexibility and work–life supports.

I believe that a key reason for these persistent issues is that theory and research on gender and feminism are generally not well-integrated with traditional psychological work and family research. As an illustration, many work–family researchers under-examine how gendered workplace and societal experiences inherently relate to work and family relationships. Yet it is undisputed that those who grew up in poverty are likely to have been children raised by single mothers. Experiencing a glass ceiling, limited career opportunities, and self-limiting career ambition are all linked to gender discrimination. Women continue to face stigmatization for a host of reasons related to maternity, patriarchal-based stereotypes, and lack of access to flexible jobs that allow caregiving and breadwinning to be aligned. Theories of gender, gender role norms, and gendered work and societal cultures are also under-discussed in the work–family field. When gender is discussed in many work–family studies, it is typically framed mainly as a variable reflective of biological sex differences or a quantitative moderator of an outcome. However, such a narrow view of gender overlooks cultural and social science underpinnings.

Maura Mills' exciting book, *Gender and the Work–Family Experience: An Intersection of Two Domains*, begins to address these gaps by assembling an interesting collection of papers. Several cross-cutting themes that help advance the integration between gender and work–family research were apparent across contributors' works.

Theme 1: Increase the range of gender diversity in samples and tailor research to specify the gendered nature of contexts. A number of contributors argued that our existing research of work, family, and gender linkages is limited theoretically and empirically by not studying a wider range of gender-diverse samples in specified cultural contexts.

For example, Sawyer, Thoroughgood, and Cleveland (Chap. 5) build on intersectionality theory (Crenshaw 1989) to examine the ways in which multiple forms of role identity such as LBGT and work and family identities interact and combine to create unique social experiences. They argue that LGBT discrimination fosters gaps between the work and family domains, forcing a separation boundary management strategy for LGBT employees. They also make the interesting case that current measures of work–family conflict do not fully capture unique LGBT needs such as identity-based conflict.

Nomaguchi and Milkie (Chap. 9) argue that most work–family conflict research overlooks individuals in the context of the quality of their coupled relationships, which are shifting in gendered expectations. Using a national sample of dual-earner heterosexual couples, they examine how wives' and husbands' inaccuracy in estimating the other partner's level of work–family conflict may shape couples' relationship quality. They find that that over half of couples overestimate or underestimate each other's work–family conflict based on how they believe women or men "should" feel. Specifically, men's overestimating their female partners' work–family conflict is related to better relationship quality, while women's underestimating their male partners' conflict is related to poorer relationship quality.

Moving to the cross-cultural level, Rajadhyaksha, Korabik, and Aycan (Chap. 6) note the lack of systematic variation in cross-cultural and institutional values regarding gender ideology. They contend that more research is needed that includes broader cultural views of gender and linkages between the work–family interface. Scholars need to go beyond examining mere biological sex differences to examine cross-cultural value patterns in gender role attitudes. Micro-level frameworks of individual gender and gender role ideology should be meshed with macro-level cultural gender values assessing gender egalitarianism and gender inequality in order to foster multi-level research.

Rosiello and Mills (Chap. 13) observe that shiftwork is another understudied occupational context that is gendered and has work–family implications that differ by gender. While it remains disputed whether more men than women engage in shiftwork, as this may vary by occupation, men are more likely to work overtime and weekends than are women. Rosiello and Mills also note that shiftwork has negative work–family consequences, limiting time to dedicate to family or caregiving, have a social life, and increased likelihood of experiencing negative health problems linked with schedule unpredictability and lack of schedule control.

Mitchell, Eby, and Lorys (Chap. 7) encourage researchers to examine gender as a "downstream" antecedent of the ways in which negative spillover from work to family unfolds in gender-unequal domestic contexts. They argue that the mechanisms underlying within and between sex and gender differences in emotion and behavior must be examined in specified contexts such as the persistent inequality in domestic household division of labor. Gender-unequal contexts shape the mechanisms and unfolding of the work–family spillover process, emotions, and response. For example, women in unequal contexts may adopt different coping behaviors, choices, or goals, and may have access to varying job and family demands and resources. Mitchell and colleagues also make the interesting argument that demonstrating negative emotions related to work and family is not always dysfunctional but rather may mobilize the use of effective coping strategies to reduce negative spillover such as pursuing greater domestic household equality.

Theme 2: Develop new frames to focus on within- and between-group gender differences in work–life inequality. Several contributors pointed to the need to develop new constructs to examine work–family inequality, despite progress. Work–family experiences provide a window into the persistence of work–life inequality across gender and other minority subgroups in society and the workplace.

Cleveland, Fisher, and Sawyer (Chap. 10) develop the notion of *work–life equality,* which they see as a critical form of equality for well-being. They identify the paradox that while educational attainment and labor force participation have evened out across genders, women continue to not only devote more time to family caregiving but also to housework, family, social, and other meaningful functions than do men.

Frevert, Culbertson, and Huffman (Chap. 4) point to another form of work–life inequality; the growing linkage between work–family experiences, race, and class.

Noting the persistence of existing research to overemphasize the work–family experiences of professionals and white women, they highlight the double jeopardy of gender and race in regard to work and family experiences. Minority women's work–family experiences significantly differ from those of white women largely due to continued lack of equal opportunity access to managerial and professional job structures, which have greater job autonomy and access to work–family supports systematically available in professional jobs.

Stanfors (Chap. 17) takes a national institutional comparative perspective to understand occupational inequality for women in fast track professions. Using data from Sweden and the USA, Stanfors shows that although the Swedish public policy goals are to provide supports to alleviate work–family conflict for all workers, this goal is not achieved equally across professions and genders. For instance, she found that even though the USA and Sweden have very different levels of public supports for work and family, women doctors in both the USA and Sweden are more likely to have higher fertility rates than academics and lawyers in their countries. This suggests common occupational tradeoffs transcending variation in national cultural values and institutions.

Given the growing feminization of poverty, Odle-Dusseau, McFadden, and Britt (Chap. 3) conduct an integrative review of the poverty, gender, and work–family literatures. They note that due to the sex segregation of lower income service jobs, women are more likely to fill these jobs and experience work–life inequality. Lower wage secondary market sector jobs have more demands and fewer resources, thereby impeding one's ability to advance to better jobs and garner more work–family resources for effective management of work and family demands. This gap leads to greater likelihood of experiencing work–family conflict, lower levels of work–family enrichment, and ultimately poorer health outcomes and quality of life for low income workers and families.

Lucas-Thompson and Goldberg (Chap. 1) look at generational differences in social orientation toward work–family egalitarianism in division of labor in the home, and a trend reverting back toward gender inequality in young adults' work–life behaviors. They note the paradox that despite possessing more gender-egalitarian values, the younger generation entering adulthood is behaving in ways that are inconsistent with their professed values about gender. Their explanations for the gap in aligning ideas and behaviors related to gender are persistent societal ambivalence about maternal employment, the stigmatization of fathers reducing or ending work to stay home with children, and the continued scarcity of resources to help new mothers jointly manage employment and caregiving. They cite data from the Pew Research Center (2013) showing that while marriage and parenthood limit women's time spent in paid work and career advancement, these same factors are associated with greater work involvement.

Theme 3: Adopt new language, constructs, and refined frames to advance more nuanced understanding of gendered images of work and family. Several authors proposed new terms to refine gendered images of work and family. Clark, Belier, and Zimmerman (Chap. 16) focus on the interesting sample of "women workaholics." They encourage work–family researchers to apply the notion of competing devotions coined by Blair Loy (2003) to help reframe work–family conflict as a moral dilemma involving competing work and family devotions.

"*On demand jobs*" is another new term that is being suggested to replace face time as a form of virtual accessibility. Grotto (Chap. 11) discusses how executive, managerial, and professional jobs have the paradox that while they have job autonomy built into their positions, they are facing a new form of face time—being available "on demand." On demand jobs are defined as jobs that necessitate individuals to be constantly available and accessible to employers and clients during nonwork hours. Moreover, responding on demand is a virtual visibility strategy as a means to demonstrate loyalty.

"*Work–family guilt*" is explored by Korabik. In Chap. 8, she argues that women always feel as though they are cheating their husbands, children, and themselves. Korabik believes that women are more likely to feel and express work–family guilt than are men.

Theme 4: Increase the incorporation of men, masculinity, and masculine work contexts in work–family studies. Calling for deeper study of men's experiences in work–family samples, Munn and Greer (Chap. 2) observe the paucity of studies on men's work–family experiences, particularly in the USA, and observe that the prevalent conceptualization of the "ideal worker" is gendered. Our post-industrial society seems to see women as in greater need to overcome the ideal worker stigma. Research on work–family breadwinning stereotypes needs to incorporate how work–family conflicts affect whether men and women are seen as "ideal" workers. Interestingly, however, studies show that men who sought to use workplace flexibility practices are likely to be deemed poor "organizational citizens," less committed to work, and possessing "undesirable" feminine traits. Such a reaction is unfortunate as men and especially fathers are increasingly more committed to family not just for financial roles, but also emotional and caretaking roles.

Sprung, Toumbeva, and Matthews (Chap. 12) examine how gender influences awareness of, access to, use of, and outcomes associated with work–family policies. In general, women are more aware, have greater access to, and use of policies. Both men and women face stigma for using policies, but contexts and processes may differ. For example, a higher proportion of women than men are more likely to experience positive outcomes when using flexibility. However, supervisors may differentially encourage or tolerate men's versus women's usage of such flexibility policies. As such, Sprung et al.'s interesting chapter suggests that gender is very important for understanding work–family processes and outcomes related to workplace flexibility policy usage.

Huffman, Culbertson, and Barbour (Chap. 14) develop the notion of "gendered occupations," which can be defined as an occupation that society associates with a particular gender. In doing so, they focus on one of the most stereotypically masculine workplace contexts in which to examine work–family relationships—the military. They develop an interesting model and discuss how work–family conflict may differ in the military as opposed to in the civilian context due to the dominant gender of the personnel and more importantly due to the arguably gendered job demands. Examples of the latter include going into combat and hazardous work zones, high schedule unpredictability, lack of flexibility and schedule control, and heavy travel demands and deployment away from family, thereby limiting opportunity for family involvement while increasing work–family stress.

Jean, Payne, and Thompson (Chap. 15) focus on another gendered occupational context: that of science, technology, engineering, and mathematics (STEM) fields. STEM jobs are often embedded in organizational cultures that are more supportive of men and masculinity. Although many factors create a “leakier pipeline” for women as compared to men in STEM, work–family challenges remain an under-addressed critical factor impacting the recruitment and retention of women in such domains. National and individual initiatives countering gender stereotypes and barriers are needed to address this STEM gender gap.

Overall, Mills’ edited book includes many interesting chapters that break new ground and offer new perspectives on linkages between gender, work, and family. It is a creative collection of perspectives that will enhance scholarly and practical understanding of gender and the work–family nexus.

Ellen Ernst Kossek, Ph.D.
Basil S. Turner Professor of Management
Research Director, Susan Bulkeley Butler Center for Leadership Excellence
Purdue University, West Lafayette, Indiana, USA

References

Crenshaw, K. (1989). Demarginalizing the intersection of race and sex: A black feminist critique of antidiscrimination doctrine, feminist theory, and antiracist politics. *University of Chicago Legal Forum,* 139–167.

Kossek, E. E., Baltes, B. B., & Matthews, R. A. (2011). How work–family research can finally have an impact in the workplace. *Industrial and Organizational Psychology: Perspectives on Science and Practice, 4,* 352–369.

Pew Research Center (2013). *On pay gap, millenial women near parity-for now.* Washington, DC: Pew Research Center.

Preface

As I begin writing this preface, I am sitting at the hospital waiting for my husband to emerge from day surgery. Such is the life of a work–family juggler—and we all do it. The irony of this has emerged at every corner throughout the development of this book, beginning when I submitted the book proposal the night before leaving for my honeymoon—which was already a year delayed as a result of inflexible post-wedding work schedules. The challenge of being a successful work–family balancer becomes even heavier once one begins a book on the topic—and yet perfect success in both domains still always seems fleeting to me—and to most.

This almost ubiquitous struggle was highlighted by the plethora of enthusiastic and positive responses I received from across the globe when I initially announced plans for this book and was soliciting chapter proposals. While many submitted chapter proposals, many more took the time to contact me about how very much needed—and long overdue—this book was, and to communicate their deep hopes for its impact on research and practice, as well as on general societal awareness of the issues at hand. Further evidencing this interest in and relevance of the book's topics, when I accessed my university's library to find the 'competitive' books of similar topics while researching for the book proposal, I was informed that all but one of the books were checked out, indicating the high demand for information regarding work–family issues, and pointing toward the universal tensions that we all feel between these domains.

Why This? Why Now?

As suggested by the above anecdotes, the current zeitgeist—both in the field and also in popular culture—is ripe for a book thoroughly addressing the intersection of these domains. In light of the recent media coverage garnered by Yahoo CEO Marissa Mayer's controversial announcement regarding work–life policy changes at the company, in addition to the recent publication of *Lean In* by Facebook's Sheryl Sandberg, this seems the ideal time for a comprehensive, research-based, and interdisciplinary work addressing the various aspects of the intersection of the work–family and gender[1] domains.

Although work–family research and policy are becoming more widespread, comparably little research has examined possible gender differences or similarities between male and female employees in terms of work–family conflict, its antecedents, and its outcomes. In an attempt to account for this research gap, the chapters comprising this book explore various aspects of work–family conflict for both genders, as well as offering comparisons between the two in terms of career and gender perceptions, the conflict experience itself, and the consequences of such conflict, among other considerations. This is crucial because with gender-stereotypical ideologies shifting, women are taking on more demanding work roles, and men are taking on increased home responsibilities. This is the case not only in so-called traditional families, but also as divorce rates increase and as homosexual couples adopt children, forming nuclear families of their own. As such, work–life conflict arguably becomes as much an issue for male employees as it has traditionally been for female employees.

Nevertheless, despite these shifting gender roles and family constitutions, many organizations—not to mention national policies—are not adapting accordingly. Consequently, male employees with substantial home responsibilities may not be receiving the support they need from their organizations, and likewise female employees—who are increasing their participation in paid work but also still absorb the majority of household duties—may not be receiving sufficient support either. In response, this book, in part, responds to criticism suggesting that neither research nor practice has kept up with these changing gender roles insofar as examining or managing work–family conflict for males as well as for females, and for shifting family structures. In an attempt to contribute toward filling this gap, this book incorporates various chapters which collectively impact how work–family research considers employee gender as the field moves forward. Each chapter is grounded within the work–family research literature as well as gender-role literature, and each addresses a unique but related consideration of work–family conflict in regard to employee gender and/or gendered jobs.

For Whom?

I like to think that the issues explored herein are relevant to everyone, to varying extents, as well as to society as a whole. Nevertheless, the book is likely to be more relevant for some individuals or purposes than for others. For instance, this book is ideal for use as a text or reader in an upper-level undergraduate or graduate-level

[1] It should be noted that, for simplicity's sake, throughout this book the term gender is used to refer to biological, anatomical sex, as opposed to the gender with which one psychologically identifies. The latter is usually, although not necessarily, redundant with anatomical sex, a consideration overlooked by assumptions of biopsychological equivalence.

seminar-style course. Beyond more traditional textbooks that focus on outlining definitions and the like, this edited book takes a critical and in-depth approach to a representative variety of issues surrounding the work–family/gender intersection, thereby yielding opportunities to spur students' critical thinking for class discussions, debates, and dialogues. Further, this book is also likely to be of interest to researchers in the fields of work–family and/or gender, who I hope will find it to be a thorough and representative consideration of issues surrounding the intersection of these fields of interest. As such, this book serves as potential fodder for future research ideas and recommendations, as well as giving a comprehensive, research- and theory-informed discussion of various issues surrounding these domains.

The End of the Beginning

As should be clear by now, given the increasing interest in these issues as of late, in addition to new and important zeitgeist shifts in the field and in society as a whole, there is a very real need for an up-to-date, comprehensive book evaluating them from various perspectives. The unique and comprehensive collection of chapters included herein together offer an updated assessment of these topics in light of their various facets and with an eye toward both depth and breadth. My greatest hope for this volume is that it will serve as an updated, interdisciplinary, and comprehensive resource in these domains, giving both a voice and a research-based justification to those currently entrenched in the struggle, and in the joys, of the work–family interface.

As I finish writing this preface, I am 9 months pregnant and furiously trying to tie up as many work-related loose ends as possible before this little one makes his appearance. Nothing could be more fitting, and the irony of it has not been lost on me throughout my work on this book. Indeed, it is a funny thing, loving both your children and your job in a maternal, protective, enjoyable—and yet frantically overworked—type of way. Both bring some of life's greatest joys, proudest moments, and most frustrating struggles. Neither lets up during or makes way for the other. And yet somehow, someway, we do it. And we love it. Because this is the life we have made and chosen for ourselves, and we would not have it any other way (despite what we may think when we're awake in the wee hours of the morning consoling a crying child while sketching out the upcoming day's work commitments in our foggy minds). Keep at it, mothers and fathers and employees everywhere. This is life.

Maura J. Mills, Ph.D.

Acknowledgments

It goes without saying that an edited book does not come to fruition through one person alone. It took the hard work and dedication of many wonderful people who believed in the importance of this work, who saw value in the cause, and who each viewed the topic from a distinctive and worthwhile perspective, contributing something uniquely theirs. My editing of this book is merely the vessel through which their hard work is disseminated. As such, I would like to thank all of my chapter authors for their continued commitment to this project and their intrinsic belief in the importance of this compiled work. It very literally could not have been done without them.

In a similar vein, I would like to thank the two very wonderful women at Springer Publishing with whom I have had the pleasure of working throughout this process. It is worth emphasizing that this book would not exist without Sharon Panulla, Executive Editor at Springer. Were it not for her attending one of my conference symposia on this topic, and approaching me afterward with the request that I undertake this venture, there would be no book at all. Subsequently, Sylvana Ruggirello, Assistant Behavioral Sciences Editor at Springer, was indispensable in navigating the publication process and ensuring that my chapter authors and I had all the information we needed in order to produce a quality work. Both of these women have made this process a pleasure, and I thank them for that.

Finally, I would be remiss in a book about work–family were I not to acknowledge my own family. Thank you to my mother, who sacrificed the frequency of our phone calls throughout my work on this book, and to my father, who instinctively knew that what I needed most was simply space and time, and who quietly gave me both without my having to ask. Thank you to my husband for setting up a wonderful home office for me, complete with dreamy extra-wide double screens, which greatly facilitated those times when I "needed" five or six windows open at the same time. And finally, many thanks to my baby for sacrificing many hours of prenatal yoga and the like so that I may complete this venture (and similarly to my dog, who endured many substantially abridged walks during my work on this book!).

My greatest appreciation goes to each and every one of the aforementioned individuals who contributed to making this book a reality. It exists because of you.

Contents

Contributors

Zeynep Aycan Departments of Psychology and Management, Koç University, Sariyer, Istanbul, Turkey

Joseph Barbour Department of Psychology, Northern Arizona University, Flagstaff, AZ, USA

Angela A. Beiler Department of Psychology, University of Georgia, Athens, GA, USA

Thomas W. Britt Department of Psychology, Clemson University, Clemson, SC, USA

Malissa A. Clark Department of Psychology and Institute for Women's Studies, University of Georgia, Athens, GA, USA

Jeanette N. Cleveland Department of Psychology, Colorado State University, Fort Collins, CO, USA

Satoris S. Culbertson Department of Management, Kansas State University, Manhattan, KS, USA

Lillian T. Eby Department of Psychology and Owens Institute for Behavioral Research, University of Georgia, Athens, GA, USA

Gwenith G. Fisher Department of Psychology, Colorado State University, Fort Collins, CO, USA

Tonya K. Frevert Organizational Science PhD Program, University of North Carolina at Charlotte, Charlotte, NC, USA

Wendy A. Goldberg Department of Psychology and Social Behavior, University of California, Irvine, CA, USA

Tomika W. Greer Department of Human Development and Consumer Sciences, College of Technology, University of Houston, Houston, TX, USA

Angela R. Grotto Department of Management and Marketing, Manhattan College, Riverdale, NY, USA

Ann H. Huffman Departments of Psychology and Management, Northern Arizona University, Flagstaff, AZ, USA

Vanessa A. Jean Department of Psychology, Texas A&M University, College Station, TX, USA

Karen Korabik Centre for Families, Work and Well-Being, University of Guelph, Guelph, ON, Canada

Anna Lorys Department of Psychology, University of Georgia, Psychology Building, Athens, GA, USA

Rachel G. Lucas-Thompson Department of Human Development and Family Studies and Colorado School of Public Health, Colorado State University, Fort Collins, CO, USA

Russell A. Matthews Department of Psychology, Bowling Green State University, Bowling Green, OH, USA

Anna C. McFadden Department of Psychology, Clemson University, Clemson, SC, USA

Melissa A. Milkie Department of Sociology, University of Toronto, ON, Canada

Maura J. Mills Departments of Psychology and Management, Hofstra University, Hempstead, NY, USA

Melissa E. Mitchell Department of Psychology, University of Georgia, Psychology Building, Athens, GA, USA

Sunny L. Munn Department of Leadership Studies, Dwight Schar College of Education, Ashland University, Ashland, OH, USA

Kei Nomaguchi Department of Sociology, Bowling Green State University, Bowling Green, OH, USA

Heather Odle-Dusseau Department of Management, Gettysburg College, Gettysburg, PA, USA

Stephanie C. Payne Department of Psychology, Texas A&M University, College Station, TX, USA

Ujvala Rajadhyaksha Department of Business Administration and Economics, Saint Mary's College, Notre Dame, IN, USA

Ryan M. Rosiello Department of Psychology, Hofstra University, Hempstead, NY, USA

Katina B. Sawyer Department of Psychology, Villanova University, Villanova, PA, USA

Justin M. Sprung Department of Psychology, Luther College, Decorah, IA, USA

Maria Stanfors Centre for Economic Demography, Lund University, Lund, Sweden

Rebecca J. Thompson University of Baltimore, Baltimore, MD, USA

Christian N. Thoroughgood Department of Management and Organizational Development, Northeastern University, Boston, MA , USA

Tatiana H. Toumbeva Department of Psychology, Bowling Green State University, Bowling Green, OH, USA

Lauren M. Zimmerman Department of Psychology, University of Georgia, Athens, GA, USA

Part I
SOCIETAL INFLUENCES & ENTRENCHMENT

Chapter 1
Gender Ideology and Work–Family Plans of the Next Generation

Rachel G. Lucas-Thompson and Wendy A. Goldberg

1.1 Introduction

Over the last several decades, the gender disparity in the work force has been declining, as evidenced by findings that women now make up approximately half of the work force (Bureau of Labor Statistics 2010). Women's employment is vital to the national economy and to the well-being of their families (Joint Economic Committee Majority Staff 2010). In addition, the gender gap in education has not only narrowed but reversed: in the USA, women now receive almost 60 % of 4-year college degrees (Becker 2010). Most Americans (62 %) endorse the idea that both husband and wife should contribute to family income (Pew Research Center 2010), but ambivalence remains about the effects of mothers working, particularly while children are young (Sylvester 2001). Most Americans think that men should be economic providers for their families: Two-thirds of Americans say that in order to be ready for marriage, a man should be able to financially support his family, while only one-third say that about women (Pew Research Center 2013). Due to increases in egalitarianism over time, American attitudes toward gender roles were expected to widely embrace egalitarianism by this time; instead, changes in gender-role attitudes appear to have leveled off, or stalled, since the mid-1990s (Cotter et al. 2011). The stalled attitudes correspond to the slowed pace for maternal employment since the 1990s, the persistent though narrowed wage gap (Cotter et al. 2011; Joint Economic Committee Majority Staff 2010), and the less-than-equal amount of time that dual-earner married men and women spend on housework (Bianchi et al. 2006).

R. G. Lucas-Thompson (✉)
Department of Human Development and Family Studies and Colorado School of Public Health, Colorado State University, Campus Delivery 1570, Behavioral Sciences Building Room 419, Fort Collins, CO 80523, USA
e-mail: lucas-thompson.rachel.graham@colostate.edu

W. A. Goldberg
Department of Psychology and Social Behavior, University of California, Irvine, 4564 Social and Behavior Sciences Gateway, Irvine, CA 92697, USA
e-mail: wendy.goldberg@uci.edu

M. J. Mills (ed.), *Gender and the Work-Family Experience*,
DOI 10.1007/978-3-319-08891-4_1

Following the birth of children, it is rare for men to reduce or end their work outside the home; in the USA, only 3 % of families with children younger than 15 have stay-at-home fathers (e.g., Kreider and Elliott 2009; Townsend 2002). In the USA, most women with children are employed outside the home (Bureau of Labor Statistics 2012); 34 % of employed mothers are their families' sole wage-earners, and over half of mothers with children under 18 work full-time (51 %; Joint Economic Committee Majority Staff 2010). However, in dual-earner families, fathers spend more time on paid work while mothers spend more time on housework and childcare (Pew Research Center 2013). Moreover, many married women in the USA delay their return to work following childbirth and/or reduce their work hours to balance work and family (e.g., Kaufman and Uhlenberg 2000).

Longer parental leave policies would help dual-earner and single parents spend more time at home before re-entering the labor force. Federal parental leave policies in the USA provide up to 12 weeks of job-protected, unpaid leave (see the 1993 Family and Medical Leave Act), which extends to up to 24 weeks of combined unpaid parental leave for two-parent families (Ray et al. 2009). Although some states provide paid leave, parental leave policies in the USA are modest compared to the extended, paid leave policies found in the European Union and in most industrialized nations around the world (Ray 2008). Extended paid maternity leaves sound like an ideal policy for employed women but Dex (2010) suggests that maternity leave policies can "give with one hand": By reinforcing traditional gender divisions, generous maternity leave policies can impede women's long-term career potential by encouraging them to be out of the labor force, which in turn limits their career earnings and advancement opportunities. Cross-nationally, longer leaves are associated with a lower proportion of women in the labor force (Hegewisch and Gornick 2011). As such, there are serious financial and advancement costs to women and families when women curtail their employment to raise children (e.g., Barker 1993; Drobnic and Witting 1997; Hochschild 1989; Machung 1989). A number of countries (e.g., Australia, the Scandinavian nations) have taken steps to encourage men to share primary caregiving of infants by stipulating provisions for paternity leave and/or parental leave that can be divided (Ray 2008).

While strides are being made in the sharing of child care, the equitable division of housework has lagged behind (Parker and Wang 2013). Many theorists have argued that division of labor in the home is a particularly important context for understanding gendered behavior (e.g., Brines 1994; Coltrane 1989). From the perspective of gender theorists, the allocation of housework is a "symbolic enactment of gender relations" (Drobnic 2010, p. 241). Within the home, even adults who endorse gender equality continue to divide domestic labor and decision-making in traditional ways (e.g., Bianchi et al. 2000; Franco et al. 2004; Himsel and Goldberg 2003; Hochschild 1989). The household division of labor remains gendered (Parker and Wang 2013) even though men are doing somewhat more housework and women are spending less time on housework than in the past (Bianchi et al. 2000, 2006).

When women work outside the home and carry the weight of the "second shift" (Hochschild 1989), they often experience negative mental health consequences (e.g., Moen and Yu 2000). At work, the status of motherhood may elicit negative evaluations for women workers, particularly those in high-powered occupations (Ridgeway and Correll 2004), thus giving pause to young women who plan to combine a demanding career with family. Considering the career advancement and mental health ramifications of inconsistencies between gender role attitudes and behavior, coupled with stalled behavioral change in the domestic sphere, insight into whether these gendered patterns are likely to continue can be revealed by studying the views of the generation transitioning to adulthood.

In the current chapter, we review past research on the plans and strategies that adolescents and emerging adults (defined as the age period roughly from 18 to 25, Arnett 2004, 2007) have for managing work and family responsibilities, and what factors account for individual variability in these plans. In the face of empirical and theoretical arguments that ideas about gender change in important ways across adolescence and young adulthood (e.g., Galambos 2004; Hill and Lynch 1983), and that it is in adolescence that individuals first begin to decide how to balance work and family (e.g., Corder and Stephan 1984), we also present new data from two studies that examine these issues in two age groups, one in mid-adolescence and the other college-aged, i.e., in emerging adulthood. Attention in these studies is given to examining the work–family plans and expectations of the participants. The theories of planned behavior (e.g., Ajzen and Fishbein 1977) and reasoned action (e.g., Ajzen 1991) include intentions as one of the few and primary predictors of later behavior, and support for these theories has been demonstrated across a wide range of behaviors (see for reviews: Ajzen 1991; Eagly and Chaiken 1993). Although expectations of future plans can be criticized for being a far from perfect representation of future behavior (Fishbein and Ajzen 1975), there are several lines of research indicating that expectations do predict later behavior in terms of educational attainment, risky behaviors, and childbirth (e.g., Harris et al. 2002; Sewell and Hauser 1980).

In the first study, the Adolescent Study, participants were 15-year-olds ($n=101$; 49.5% female) from one site of the NICHD Study of Early Child Care and Youth Development, a sample that was primarily (66%) European American with significant Hispanic American representation (18%); adolescents came from families that were mostly middle-to-upper-middle class. Adolescents' families were recruited at childbirth from selected hospitals based on a conditional random-sampling plan that was designed to ensure the sample reflected the economic, educational, and ethnic diversity of the area. Adolescents provided the information described below during a visit to their home, and received payment for participation in the larger study during which these data were collected.

In the second study, the Emerging Adult Study, participants were undergraduates ($n=343$; 69% female) from three diverse colleges/universities across the country; a small liberal arts institution in Wisconsin ($n=92$), a commuter university in Chicago, IL ($n=76$), and a large research university in California ($n=175$). As a result, the college sample was heterogeneous geographically and in terms of socioeconomic status and ethnicity (42% European American, 30% Asian American, 12% Hispanic American, and 16% other or multiple ethnicities). College students averaged 20.35 years of age ($SD=1.59$; range of 17–24 years). Students provided the information described below during a visit to their classrooms, and received extra credit for participating.

Across studies, participants provided background/demographic information and completed a 24-item scale that assessed their gender ideology (Wenzel and Lucas-Thompson 2012). Their expectations for work–family roles were reported in terms of how much/whether they planned to work after marriage but before children ("I will not work outside the home," "I will work part-time," and "I will work full-time") and after the birth of children ("I will not work outside the home," "I will work part-time," and "I will work full-time"). Participants also indicated how they anticipated dividing childcare responsibilities ("I will be the primary care-taker," "My partner will be the primary care-taker," and "My partner and I will share care-taking equally").

In data analysis for both studies, gender differences in work and caregiving aspirations were examined; in addition, using bivariate correlations, chi-square analyses, and ordinary least squares regression analyses, associations were examined among gender ideology, work aspirations, and plans to divide caregiving responsibilities. Before presenting the results of these studies, we review prior research on the work–family plans of the generation coming to adulthood.

1.2 Adolescents' and Emerging Adults' Plans for Managing Work and Family

Research focusing on how young individuals expect to manage work and family has primarily focused on work aspirations. Social changes that picked up steam during the 1970s and 1980s have led to many young women planning to continue to work after having children (e.g., Baber and Monaghan 1988; Boushey 2008; Dennehy and Mortimer 1993; Goldin and Katz 2008; O'Connell et al. 1989), but many other young individuals plan to replicate the gendered pattern of their parents' generation in terms of men, but not women, planning full-time employment when they have young children (Goldberg et al. 2012). More recent cohorts of women expect future employment (Goldin et al. 2006) but typically both young men and women expect that wives will dramatically reduce (or end) their work outside the home when children are born (de Valk 2008; Weinshenker 2006). In addition, by high school, concerns about balancing work and family are already on the minds of young women, including choosing occupations that will allow a work–family balance that they desire (McDonald et al. 2011; Hardie and Hayford 2012). In contrast, young men do not engage in the same planning process (Hardie and Hayford 2012), or report expecting that family life will be a far second to work life in their adult years (McDonald et al. 2011).

Expectations about work before and after children are clearly important to include when investigating how emerging adults expect to deal with gender issues. However, other expectations need to be considered as well, including how individuals transitioning to adulthood expect to divide or share child-rearing, and how and whether work expectations are related to expectations about child-rearing (e.g., do emerging adults who expect to share child-rearing expect both partners to work equal hours?). For instance, a robust finding is that adults are often inconsistent in terms of behaving in line with their gender ideologies, in that even those with egalitarian ideals continue to divide household tasks in traditionally gendered ways (e.g., Bianchi et al. 2000; Franco et al. 2004; Himsel and Goldberg 2003; Hochschild 1989). Therefore, it is likely that emerging adults may also display inconsistencies in their expectations about balancing work and family.

Traditionally, work–family arrangements are most likely to become more gender-typed after the birth of children (e.g., Goldberg et al. 1985). Following the birth of children, it is rare for men to reduce or end their work outside the home (e.g., Kaufman and Uhlenberg 2000; Townsend 2002); indeed, emerging adults who become fathers plan to work more hours once the baby is born (Goldberg 2014). However, in the USA, most women with children under six years are employed outside the home (61.6%; U.S. Census Bureau 2011), and over half of mothers with children under 18 work full-time (51%; Joint Economic Committee Majority Staff 2010).

1.2.1 Findings from the Adolescent and Emerging Adult Studies

Results from our new studies confirm many of the findings from past studies, but also extend knowledge about how contemporary adolescents and emerging adults think about balancing work and family in the future. For example, among those adolescents and emerging adults who reported that they want to get married, men and women had similar aspirations for paid work after marriage and before children, with most expecting to work full-time (see Figs. 1.1 and 1.2). However, among those who hoped to have children someday, when asked to think about work aspirations after children are born, plans differed between males and females, χ^2s$(3)>25.34$, *ps*<0.001. Young men by and large expected to be employed full-time when they become parents, whereas a sizable number of women did not expect to be employed or expected to be employed part-time (see Figs. 1.1 and 1.2). Interestingly, however, the majority of both male and female individuals reported that they planned to share caregiving equally with their partner (although more women than men reported that they planned to be the primary caregiver of their children; see Fig. 1.3).

An interesting difference between adolescents and emerging adults was revealed in the links between employment aspirations and child-rearing plans. Specifically, for adolescent girls, their plans to share caregiving equally with future partners were not related in predictable ways to their expectations about work status after children were born, $\chi^2(4)=3.40$, $p=0.49$. Among girls who indicated that they will share caretaking equally with their partner, 23% reported that they will not work for pay outside the home, 51% reported that they will work part-time, and 26% reported that they will work full-time. However, among emerging adult women, these work and family aspirations were significantly related to each other, $\chi^2(6)=18.10$, $p=0.006$. College women who planned on being the primary caregiver were more likely to report not planning to work outside the home (42%) or planned to work

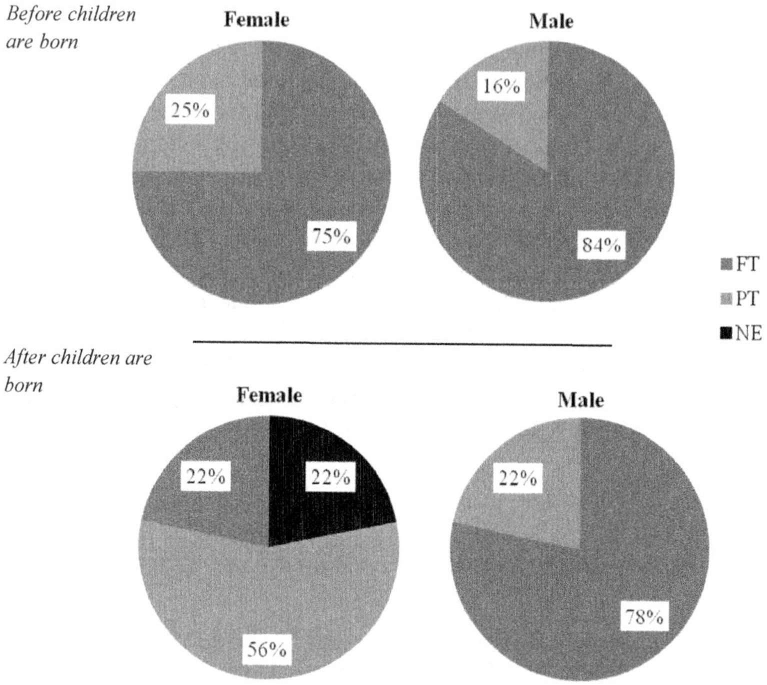

Fig. 1.1 Gender differences in work aspirations before and after children are born. (Adolescent Study)

part-time (38 %) than to report planning to work full-time (21 %). In contrast, college women who planned to share childrearing responsibilities equally with their partners were more likely to report plans to work full- (37 %) or part- (51 %) time than to report planning not to work outside the home (11 %). Compared to adolescents, emerging adults may be displaying plans that are more consistent across work–family domains because they are more cognitively mature, because they are further along in the process of identity exploration, because they are more likely to have a steady partner, and/or because they have had more time to think about work–family issues. This pattern, though, is in line with suggestions that increasing age predicts having more family- and work-related goals (relative to education- and friend-related goals; Salmela-Aro et al. 2007).

Overall, these new results combined with past studies suggest that a large number of adolescents and emerging adults expect to manage work–family commitments in much the same traditional, gendered way as the generations that have come before them in terms of the general pattern of women continuing to assume more housework and family care responsibilities than men (e.g., Dennehy and Mortimer 1993; O'Connell et al. 1989) and less paid work involvement after having children (Kaufman and Uhlenberg 2000, Townsend 2002). Despite changes in rates of employment and education that reflect increasing gender equality (e.g., U.S.

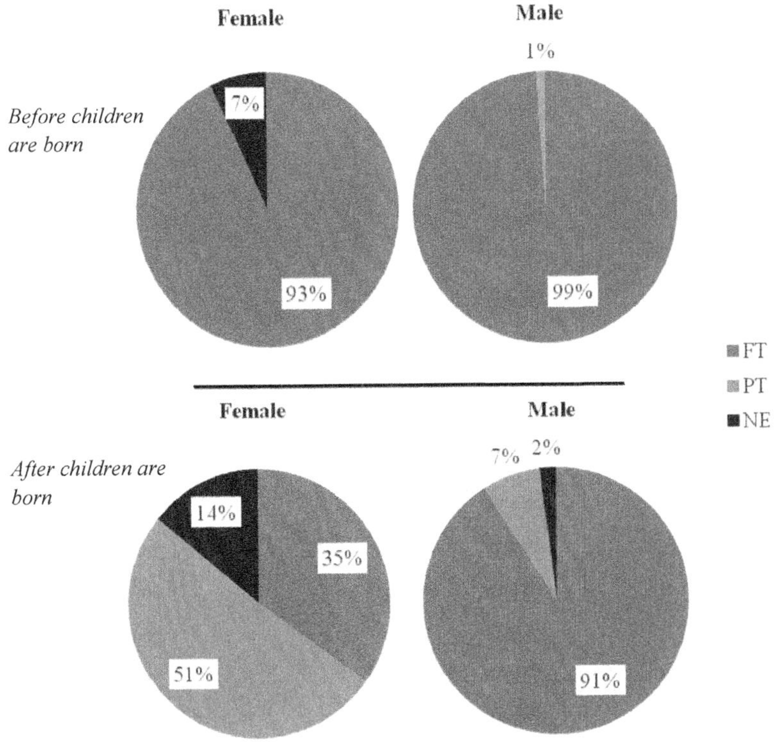

Fig. 1.2 Gender differences in work aspirations before and after children are born. (Emerging Adult Study)

Department of Labor 2010), college students still seem to hold stereotyped notions about the work competence of mothers (Fuegen et al. 2004) and exaggerated stereotypes about the negative consequences of maternal employment for children (Goldberg and Lucas-Thompson 2014). Therefore, the pattern of mothers being employed but working less than full-time (Kaufman and Uhlenberg 2000) may continue to be a common strategy to manage work–family commitments, despite more equal participation of men and women in the workforce (U.S. Department of Labor 2010).

Similar to results of studies with adults (Bianchi et al. 2000; Franco et al. 2004; Goldberg et al. 2012; Himsel and Goldberg 2003; Hochschild 1989), adolescents and young men and women are also demonstrating idealized expectations for gender equality. Across gender and age, most participants reported wanting to share childcare equally (although a small sub-set of women plan to be the primary caregiver), but the majority of young women plan to work part-time or not at all after having children. The expectation seems to be one of sharing child-rearing while following a traditional gendered employment pattern, the "transitional" pattern that echoes findings of adults; endorsing gender equality while behaving unequally (Hochschild 1989). However, unequal does not equate to unfair in the eyes of

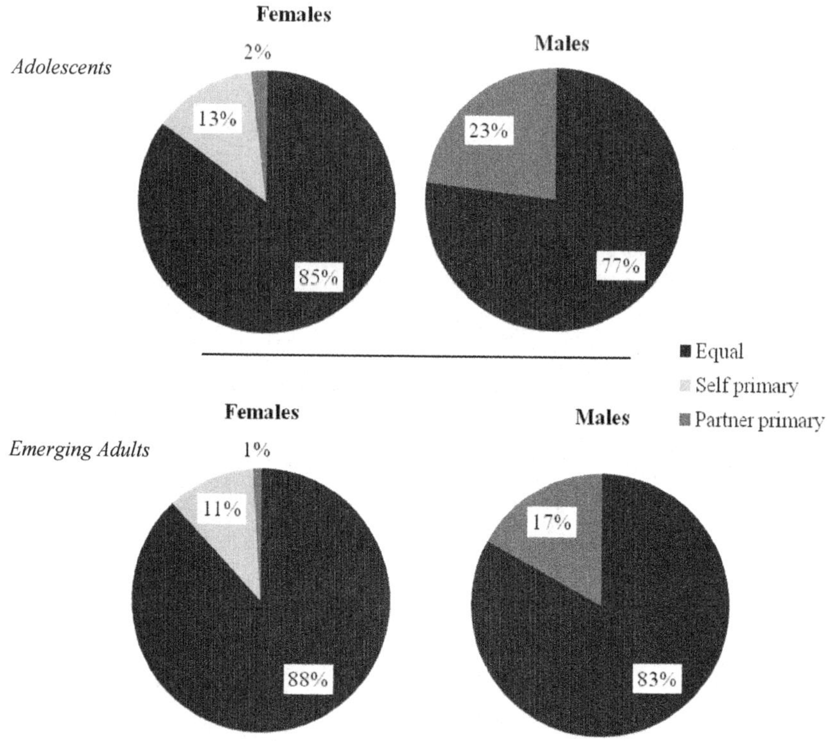

Fig. 1.3 Gender differences in plans to divide childrearing responsibilities

married women of different gender ideologies using differing comparative referents (i.e., "relative deprivation theory"; Greenstein 1996).

If the future behavior of these adolescents and emerging adults matches their expectations, the next generation may perpetuate some of the gender inequality in the workforce that persists today, despite the greater equality in labor force participation overall (U.S. Department of Labor 2010) that includes a narrowed wage gap (Pew Research Center 2013). Reduced labor force involvement when women become mothers can mean longer time to promotion and lower lifetime pay as well as economic hardship for their families (Drobnic and Witting 1997; Machung 1989). Despite these potential costs, some researchers have commented that this pattern may still be "the most rational plan for those who value both career and family" (Weinshenker 2006, p. 885), given the meager institutional and policy support given to parents. What is perhaps most troubling, though, is the potential that these young adults will make decisions to reduce or end employment without being aware of the long-term consequences. Indeed, the finding in the current study that young women expect to share child-rearing equally but follow a traditionally gendered employment pattern suggests that their plans may not be fully informed or "rational." However, these new data suggest increasing consistency in work–family plans once youth reach college-age. To sort out which factors explain this apparent developmental shift, longitudinal studies are needed, as is a closer look at individual differences in work–family plans.

1.3 Individual Differences in Plans to Manage Work and Family

1.3.1 Demographic Differences

There is consistent evidence that women's employment rates as well as their work–family values differ based on culture and ethnicity (Orbuch and Eyster 1997): Caucasian and African American women typically return to work sooner after the birth of a child than do Asian and Hispanic women (Han et al. 2008; Laughlin 2011). From a developmental perspective, parental ideas about gender and work–family balance are shaped, in part, by ethnic and cultural values, and parental ideas in turn influence children's expectations, aspirations, and values (Eccles 1994). It is not surprising, then, that there is some evidence that ethnic differences are reflected in adolescent and emerging adult work–family balance plans. For instance, research in the Netherlands has found that ethnic differences extend to the work–family plans of adolescent males and females (de Valk 2008) and research in the USA has found differences in the plans of Asian and Caucasian college students (Goldberg et al. 2012). Other family characteristics also appear to shape the types of expectations that adolescents have for balancing work and family in their future. For instance, coming from a religious family, or a family with lower levels of parental education, is related to more traditional work–family balance plans, particularly for girls (de Valk 2008).

Theoretically, one of the most important characteristics shaping children's ideas about balancing work and family is whether or not their own mothers worked while they were young. Working mothers provide positive role models for combining work and motherhood (Greenberger et al. 1988), and role theory predicts that children, particularly girls, of working mothers will be more likely to make nontraditional career choices and have greater levels of labor force attachment, and research generally supports this argument (Alessandri 1992; Eccles and Hoffman 1984; Hoffman 1980; Weinshenker 2006). There is some evidence that same-sex parental models are most important for adolescents in terms of expectations about their own work behavior, and other-sex parents are important for adolescents' expectations about their future partners' work behavior (Wiese and Freund 2011). Young women who had working mothers have more positive stereotypes about the effects of (particularly full-time)employment on several domains of child development, differences that appear explained, in part, by differences in gender ideology, attitudes about the benefits and costs of maternal employment, and work values (Goldberg and Lucas-Thompson 2014). Less studied are young men's experiences of having an employed mother, but these childhood experiences are relevant for them, too. For example, greater participation in household chores has been observed among married men whose own mothers were employed during their childhood (Gupta 2006).

1.3.1.1 Findings from the Adolescent and Emerging Adult Studies

Results from the new studies presented here suggest that there are many ways in which having a working mother does not appear related in predictable ways to the work–family plans of adolescents and emerging adults. For instance, for college-aged men and women, plans about dividing or sharing caregiving did not appear related to maternal work history. In terms of one's own employment plans, adolescent boys were more likely to report plans to work part-time after the birth of children if their own mothers had stayed home rather than worked for pay while they were children, an unexpected finding that deserves further investigation. More expected was the finding that adolescent girls of mothers who did not work for pay during their childhood were much less likely to report planning to work full-time (0 %) than part-time or not at all, particularly after the birth of children. In addition, female (but not male) college students were more likely to report planning to work full-time (41 % vs. 18 %) after children if their own mothers had been employed when they were young. Therefore, although sharing of childcare was not related to one's own mother's employment, it appears that adolescent girls and emerging adult men and women are more likely to report plans to reduce work hours after the birth of children if their own mothers were not employed. Other research indicates that college students' beliefs about the costs and benefits of maternal employment for children are linked to whether or not their own mothers were employed during their childhood (Goldberg et al. 2012). In line with role theory, it seems likely that a mechanism of transmission of gendered ideas, gendered behavior, and inconsistency between the two may be in part due to what children observe their own parents do.

1.3.2 The Importance of Gender Ideology

Social role theory was developed as a means to explain behavioral similarities and differences between men and women (Eagly 1987; Eagly et al. 2000). From this perspective, beliefs that people have about the genders are formed from observations of the roles that men and women occupy. Gender differences in personality and social behavior reflect the gendered division of labor around paid work and domestic work and the gender hierarchy for power, status, and resources (Eagly et al. 2000). Importantly, social role theory views gender roles as dynamic and open to change as the typical work and family roles change in a given culture (Eagly et al. 2000).

Consistently, gender ideology has emerged as an important contributor to the nature of the plans that young individuals make for their future work–family balance.

Gender ideology refers to a set of attitudes about the appropriate roles, rights, and responsibilities of men and women in a given society; traditional ideologies ascribe distinctive work and care roles for the genders whereas egalitarian ideologies endorse equal provider and care roles for the genders (Hochschild 1989; Kroska 2007). Gender ideologies can be thought of as "factors that frame the strategies of action an individual sees as possible" (e.g., Davis and Pearce 2007, p. 250); they reflect the extent of an individual's support for gendered and separate spheres of paid work and family work (Davis and Greenstein 2009). Gender ideology has been linked with a range of gender-relevant behaviors across the lifespan, including marriage, timing of first birth, division of household labor, educational attainment, and labor force participation (see Davis and Greenstein 2009 for a review). Furthermore, considering gender ideology can inform our understanding of the work and family decisions that young adults make (Davis and Greenstein 2009).

Research indicates that egalitarian and traditional gender ideologies formed before adulthood are associated with decisions about future occupation and education. Young men are frequently reported to hold more traditional attitudes toward work and family roles than do young women, but the mean differences can be small and there is substantial variability within each gender (Kerpelman and Schvaneveldt 1999). Adolescents, particularly young girls, who endorse more egalitarian gender ideologies also espouse more ambitious educational and career aspirations (Davis and Pearce 2007; Eccles 1994). In addition, a more egalitarian maternal (but not paternal) gender ideology is associated with adolescents' less gendered work–family balance plans (Weinshenker 2006).

There are several mechanisms through which gender ideology early in life can exert its influence on future plans. They include girls' and boys' internalization of societal norms about their abilities and the value placed on the expected roles for their gender (Correll 2001; Eccles 1994), and adolescents' attitudes about how men and women should balance work and family (Davis and Pearce 2007). This evidence suggests that young men and women with more traditional ideas about gender will anticipate work–family arrangements that are more gendered than those of less traditional men and women. However, much of the data concerning young peoples' extent of work expectations and gender ideology were collected in the 1970s (e.g., Corder and Stephan 1984). Constructions of gender have dramatically changed since that time (e.g., Bolzendahl and Myers 2004; Thornton and Young-DeMarco 2001), as has the demographic composition of the USA. Therefore, an updated examination of the relations between gender roles and work expectations is needed in a culturally diverse sample.

1.3.2.1 Findings from the Adolescent and Emerging Adult Studies

Consistent with past research (e.g., Kerpelman and Schvaneveldt 1999), the results from our new studies suggest that in both adolescence and emerging adulthood, young women were more egalitarian in their gender ideology than were young men. Interestingly, gender ideology was associated in ways that theory would predict with the work–family aspirations of emerging adults, but only very rarely with the work–family aspirations of adolescents. For female (but not male) college students, those who reported more egalitarian gender ideologies were more likely not to want to get married, $r = -0.14$, $p = 0.031$, but were no less likely to report wanting to have children, $rs < |0.13|$, $ps > 0.11$. This finding suggests that marriage and having children are not as intertwined for contemporary young adults as they once were. In addition, gender ideology was associated with plans about dividing caregiving responsibility for both male and female emerging adults: a more egalitarian gender ideology was associated with plans to share caregiving responsibilities, associations that remained after adjusting for ethnicity and income. In addition, for women, there was a significant association between gender ideology and work aspirations after children, controlling for demographic variables: more egalitarian ideologies were associated with plans to work full-time relative to part-time.

For adolescents, particularly adolescent boys, gender ideology was largely unrelated to work–family aspirations. More specifically, gender ideology was not related to adolescents' plans to get married or have children, $rs < |0.06|$, $ps > 0.67$. For boys, gender ideology was not related to plans about work after children or dividing caregiving responsibilities. For adolescent girls, a more traditional gender ideology was associated with more traditional expectations about who will raise children (e.g., women being the primary caregiver). This association remained significant after controlling for ethnicity and family income.

By definition, gender ideologies reflect whether individuals support gendered separate spheres or shared spheres of paid work and family work (Davis and Greenstein 2009); however, for young adolescent and emerging adult men and women, there were many ways in which work–family role behavior appears independent of reported ideas about gender roles. There was some evidence that work–family expectations were related to gender ideology, particularly for adolescent girls and for the sample of college students. Some researchers expect the liberalization of gender role attitudes to continue apace (e.g., Bolzendahl and Myers 2004; Brooks and Bolzendahl 2004), but others claim a plateau or reversal since the mid-1990s (Brewster and Padavic 2000; Cotter et al. 2011; Thornton and Young-DeMarco 2001). Our findings with circa 2007–2009 data can be seen as consistent with the latter position and with studies that found women to be more egalitarian than men (e.g., Bolzendahl and Myers 2004; Brewster and Padavic 2000; Galambos 2004; Goldberg et al. 2012; Steil 2000). In addition, for female adolescents and college students, a more traditional gender ideology was associated with expectations for more traditional caregiving arrangements. Across developmental periods, then, gender ideology seems to be particularly important for ideas about who will take primary responsibility for children.

The stronger associations between gender ideology and work aspirations in the college student sample compared to the adolescent sample could be due to several factors. First, the comparatively smaller sample of adolescents had less adequate power; therefore, the non-significant associations between gender ideology and work aspirations could be due to limited power to detect small effects rather than non-existent relations. Second, it is possible that the college students - for whom decisions about balancing work and family are more imminent and who have had more time to explore their identities - may display behavior that is more consistent with their ideals (Arnett 2007). They may also be more realistic about the challenges of managing work and family.

1.4 Conclusion

On a societal level, we are witnessing the reversing of the gender gap in higher education, but a stall in the progress toward egalitarianism in the home and workplace. Looking at the plans and behavior of adolescents and emerging adults, we do not find seeds of renewed vigor in the move toward egalitarian gender roles. Why is the generation now entering adulthood behaving in ways that are inconsistent with their ideas about gender? One potential reason is the difficulty of successfully aligning ideas and behavior related to gender (Sjoberg 2010), particularly with societal ambivalence about maternal employment (Sylvester 2001), disapproval of fathers reducing or curtailing work to stay home with children (Nock 1998; Townsend 2002), limited parental leave policies (Ray et al. 2009), and scarce allocation of resources to help new mothers reconcile employment and caregiving. Marriage and parenthood exact a toll on women's time spent on paid work activities, including career interruptions, whereas for men, marriage and parenthood are associated with more work involvement (Pew Research Center 2013).

Although the new studies presented here provide important current information about gender equality and gendered behavior, there are several limitations of note in addition to the power issue mentioned above. The adolescent sample was also mostly middle- to upper-middle-class and from one region of the USA; however, the college student sample was diverse geographically and in terms of socioeconomic background. Demographic differences between the adolescent and college samples (e.g., proportion Asian American, socioeoconomic status) could have contributed to differences attributed to age cohorts. Utilizing samples of different age cohorts is important for gender and work–family issues (e.g., Corder and Stephan 1984; Galambos 2004; Hill and Lynch 1983), and along with samples composed of diverse cultures/ethnicities, strengthen the generalizability of our findings.

The new data presented in this chapter were from cross-sectional studies. Needed are longitudinal studies that could illuminate the factors that might explain the apparent developmental shift from adolescence to college such as greater experience with romantic relationships, more time spent contemplating work–family balance, and more mature cognitive and long-term planning abilities. In the current study, participants reported their plans for future employment; however, future research would benefit from providing more specific trajectories for employment plans (e.g., 'employment in the first year after a child is born' rather than 'after a child is born'). Despite these limitations, these two studies make important contributions to our knowledge about how the next generation of potential worker-parents intends to balance work and family, and suggest that a traditionally gendered pattern will likely persist at least into the near future.

References

Ajzen, I. (1991). The theory of planned behavior. *Organizational Behavior and Human Decision Processes, 50,* 179–211.

Ajzen, I., & Fishbein, M. (1977). Attitude-behavior relations: A theoretical analysis and review of empirical research. *Psychological Bulletin, 84,* 888–918.

Alessandri, S. M. (1992). Effects of maternal work status in single-parent families on children's perception of self and family and school achievement. *Journal of Experimental Child Psychology, 54,* 417–433.

Arnett, J. J. (2004). *Emerging adulthood: The winding road from the late teens through the twenties*. Oxford: Oxford University Press.

Arnett, J. J. (2007). Emerging adulthood: What is it, and what is it good for? *Child Development Perspectives, 1,* 68–73.

Baber, K. M., & Monaghan, P. (1988). College women's career and motherhood expectations–New options, old dilemmas. *Sex Roles, 19,* 189–203.

Barker, K. (1993). Changing assumptions and contingent solutions: The costs and benefits of women working full- and part-time. *Sex Roles, 28,* 47–71.

Becker, G. (2010). The revolution in the economic empowerment of women. http://www.becker-posner-blog.com/2010/01/the-revolution-in-the-economic-empowerment-of-women-becker.html. Accessed 3 June 2012.

Bianchi, S. M., Milkie, M. A., Sayer, L. C., & Robinson, J. P. (2000). Is anyone doing the housework? Trends in the gender division of household labor. *Social Forces, 79,* 191–228.

Bianchi, S. M., Robinson, J. P., & Milkie, M. A. (2006). *Changing rhythms of American family life*. New York: Russell Sage.

Bolzendahl, C., & Myers, D. J. (2004). Feminist attitudes and support for gender equality: Opinion change in women and men, 1974–1998. *Social Forces, 83,* 759–790.

Boushey, H. (2008). "Opting out?" The effect of children on women' employment in the United States. *Feminist Economist, 14,* 1–36.

Brewster, K. L., & Padavic, I. (2000). Change in gender ideology, 1977–1996: The contributions of intracohort change and population turnover. *Journal of Marriage & the Family, 62,* 477–487.

Brines, J. (1994). Economic dependency, gender, and the division of labor at home. *American Journal of Sociology, 100,* 652–688.

Brooks, C., & Bolzendahl, C. (2004). The transformation of U.S. gender role attitudes: Cohort replacement, social-structural change, and ideological learning. *Social Science Research, 33,* 106–133.

Bureau of Labor Statistics, U.S. Department of Labor. (Dec 2010). Women in the labor force: A databook. http://www.bls.gov/cps/wlf-databook-2010.pdf. Accessed 2 June 2012.

Bureau of Labor Statistics, U.S. Department of Labor. (April 2012). Employment characteristics of families summary. http://www.bls.gov/news.release/famee.nr0.htm. Accessed 2 June 2012.

Coltrane, S. (1989). Household labor and the routine production of gender. *Social Problems, 36,* 473–490.

Corder, J., & Stephan, C. W. (1984). Females combination of work and family roles-adolescents aspirations. *Journal of Marriage and the Family, 46,* 391–402.

Correll, S. J. (2001). Gender and the career choice process: The role of biased self-assessments. *American Journal of Sociology 106*(6), 1691–1730.

Cotter, D., Hermsen, J. M., & Vanneman, R. (2011). The End of the Gender Revolution? Gender Role Attitudes From 1977 to 2008. *American Journal of Sociology,* 117, 259–289.

Davis, S. N., & Greenstein, T. (2009). Gender ideology: Components, predictors, and consequences. *Annual Review of Sociology, 35,* 87–105.
Davis, S. N., & Pearce, L. D. (2007). Adolescents' work–family gender ideologies and educational expectations. *Sociological Perspectives, 50,* 249–271.
de Valk, H. A. (2008). Parental influence on work and family plans of adolescents of different ethnic backgrounds in the Netherlands. *Sex Roles, 59,* 738–751.
Dennehy, K., & Mortimer, J. T. (1993). Work and family orientations of contemporary adolescent boys and girls. In J. C. Hood (Ed.), *Men, work, and family* (pp. 87–107). Newbury Park: Sage.
Dex, S. (2010). Can state policies produce equality in housework? In J. Treas & S. Drobnic (Eds.), *Dividing the domestic: Men, women, and housework in cross-national perspective.* Palo Alto: Stanford University.
Drobnic, S. (2010). Concluding thoughts on the societal context of housework. In J. Treas & S. Drobnic (Eds.), *Dividing the domestic: Men, women, and household work in cross-national perspective.* (pp. 241–251). Palo Alto: Stanford University.
Drobnic, S., & Witting, I. (1997). Part-time work in the United States of America. In H. P. Blossfield & C. Hakim (Eds.), *Between equalization and marginalization: Women working part-time in Europe and the United States of America* (pp. 289–314). New York: Oxford University.
Eagly, A. (1987). *Sex differences in social behavior: A social-role interpretation. John M. MacEachran memorial lecture series; 1985.* Hillsdale: Erlbaum.
Eagly, A. H., & Chaiken, S. (1993). *The psychology of attitudes.* Orlando: Harcourt Brace.
Eagly, A. H., Wood, W., & Diekman, A. B. (2000). Social role theory of sex differences and similarities: A current appraisal. In T. Eckes & H. M. Trautner (Eds.), *The developmental social psychology of gender* (pp. 123–174). Mahwah: Erlbaum.
Eccles, J. (1994). Understanding women's educational and occupational choices: Applying the Eccles et al. model of achievement-related choices. *Psychology of Women Quarterly, 18,* 485–609.
Eccles, J. S., & Hoffman, L. W. (1984). Sex roles, socialization, and occupational behavior. Child development research and social policy: Harold W. Stevenson & Alberta E. Siegel.
Fishbein, M., & Ajzen, I. (1975). *Belief, attitude, intention, and behavior: An introduction to theory and research.* Reading: Addison-Wesley.
Franco, J. L., Sabattini, L., & Crosby, F. J. (2004). Anticipating work and family: Exploring the associations among gender-related ideologies, values, and behaviors in Latino and White families in the United States. *Journal of Social Issues, 60,* 755–766.
Fuegen, K., Biernal, M., Haines, E., & Deaux, K. (2004). Mothers and fathers in the workplace: How gender and parental status influence judgements of job-related consequences. *Journal of Social Issues, 60,* 737–754.
Galambos, N. L. (2004). Gender and gender role development in adolescence. In R. M. Lerner & L. Steinberg (Eds.), *Handbook of Adolescent Psychology* (pp. 233–262). Hoboken: Wiley.
Goldberg, W. A. (2014). *Father time: The social clock and the timing of fatherhood.* London: Palgrave Macmillan.
Goldberg, W. A., & Lucas-Thompson, R. (2014). Stereotype accuracy: Do college women hit or miss the mark when estimating the "impact" of maternal employment on children's achievement and behavior? *Psychology of Women Quarterly, 38,* 1–13.
Goldberg, W. A., Kelly, E., Matthews, N. B., Kang, H., Li, W., & Sumaroka, M. (2012). The more things change, the more they stay the same: Gender, culture, and college students' views about work and family. *Journal of Social Issues, 68,* 814–837.
Goldberg, W. A., Michaels, G. Y., & Lamb, M. E. (1985). Husbands' and wives' adjustment to pregnancy and first parenthood. *Journal of Family Issues, 6,* 483–503.
Goldin, C., Katz, L. F., & Kuziemko, I. (2006). The homecoming of American college women: The reversal of the college gender gap. *Journal of Economic Perspectives, 20,* 133–156.
Goldin, C., Katz, L. F. (2008). Transitions: Career and Family Lifecycles of the Educational Elite. *American Economic Review: Papers and Proceedings 98,* (2), 363–369.
Greenberger, E., Goldberg, W. A., Crawford, T. J., & Granger, J. (1988). Beliefs about the consequences of maternal employment for children. *Psychology of Women Quarterly, 12,* 35–59.

Greenstein, T. N. (1996). Gender ideology and perceptions of the fairness of the division of household labor: Effects on marital quality. *Social Forces, 74,* 1029–1042.
Gupta, S. (2006). The consequences of maternal employment during men's childhood for their adult housework performance. *Gender & Society, 20,* 60–86.
Han, W. J., Ruhm, C. J., Waldfogel, J., & Washbrook, E. (2008). The timing of mothers' employment after childbirth. *Monthly Labor Review, 131,* 15–27.
Hardie, J. H., & Hayford, S. R. (2012). *Opting In: Adolescent girls' work and family plans. paper submitted at the inaugural work and family researchers network conference.* New York, USA.
Harris, K. M., Duncan, G. J., & Boisjoly, J. (2002). Evaluating the role of "nothing to lose" attitudes on risky behavior in adolescence. *Social Forces, 80,* 1005–1039.
Hegewisch, A., & Gornick, J. C. (2011). The impact of work–family policies on women's employment: A review of research from the OECD countries. *Community, Work, & Family, 14,* 119–138.
Hill, J. P., & Lynch, M. E. (1983). The intensification of gender-related role expectations during early adolescence. In J. Brooks-Gunn & J. Petersen (Eds.), *Girls at puberty: Biological and psychosocial perspectives* (pp. 201–228). New York: Plenum.
Himsel, A. J., & Goldberg, W. A. (2003). Social comparisons and satisfaction with the division of housework: Implications for men's and women's role strain. *Journal of Family Issues, 24,* 843–866.
Hochschild, A. R. (1989). *The second shift: Working parents and the revolution at home.* New York: Viking.
Hoffman, L. W. (1980). The effects of maternal employment on the academic attitudes and performance of school-age children. *School Psychology Review, 9,* 319–336.
Joint Economic Committee Majority Staff, U. S. C. (Dec 2010). Invest in women, invest in America: A comprehensive review of women in the U.S. Economy. http://jec.senate.gov/public/index.cfm?p=Reports1&ContentRecord_id=11dd6449-8d54-41ff-9bb2-87d98cbf66c2&ContentType_id=efc78dac-24b1-4196-a730-d48568b9a5d7&Group_id=c120e658-3d60-470b-a8a1-6d2d8fc30132. Accessed 2 June 2012.
Kaufman, G., & Uhlenberg, P. (2000). The influence of parenthood on the work effort of married men and women. *Social Forces, 78,* 931–947.
Kerpelman, J. L., & Schvaneveldt, P. L. (1999). Young adults' anticipated identity importance of career, marital, and parental roles: Comparisons of men and women with different role balance orientations. *Sex Roles, 41,* 189–217.
Kreider, R. M., & Elliott, D. R. (2009). *America's families and living arrangements 2007. Current Population Reports, P20-561.* Washington, DC: U.S. Census Bureau.
Kroska, A. (2007). Gender ideology and gender role ideology. In G. Ritzer (Ed.), *The Blackwell Encyclopedia of Sociology* (Vol. 4, pp. 1867–1868). Malden: Blackwell.
Laughlin, L. (2011). *Maternity leave and employment patterns of first-time mothers: 1961–2008. Current Population Report, P70-128.* Washington, DC: U.S. Census Bureau.
Machung, A. (1989). Talking career, thinking job-Gender differences in career and family expectations of Berkeley seniors. *Feminist Studies, 15,* 35–58.
McDonald, P., Pini, B., Bailey, J., & Price, R. (2011). Young people's aspirations for education, work, family and leisure. *Work, Employment and Society, 25,* 68–84.
Moen, P., & Yu, Y. (2000). Effective work/life strategies: Working couples, work conditions, gender, and life quality. *Social Problems, 47,* 291–326.
Nock, S. L. (1998). *Marriage in men's lives.* New York: Oxford University.
O'Connell, L., Betz, M., & Kurth, S. (1989). Plans for balancing work and family-life-Do women pursuing nontraditional and traditional occupations differ? *Sex Roles, 20,* 35–45.
Orbuch, T. L., & Eyster, S. L. (1997). Division of household labor among Black couples White couples. *Social Forces, 76,* 301–332.
Parker, K., & Wang, W. (2013). Modern parenthood: Roles of moms and dads converge as they balance work and family. Pew Research: Social & Demographic Trends. http://www.pewsocialtrends.org/2013/03/14/modern-parenthood-roles-of-moms-and-dads-converge-as-they-balance-work-and-family/. Accessed 5 Sep 2013.

Pew Research Center. (2010). *The decline of marriage and rise of new families*. Washington: Pew Research Center.
Pew Research Center. (2013). *On pay gap, millenial women near parity-For now*. Washington: Pew Research Center.
Ray, R. A. (2008). *A detailed look at parental leave policies in 21 OECD countries*. Washington: U.S. Center for Economic and Policy Research.
Ray, R. A., Gornick, J. C., & Schmitt, J. (2009). *Parental leave policies in 21 countries: Assessing generosity and gender equality*. Washington: U.S. Center for Economic and Policy Research.
Ridgeway, C. L., & Correll, S. J. (2004). Unpacking the gender system: A theoretical perspective on gender beliefs and social relations. *Gender & Society, 18,* 510–531.
Salmela-Aro, K., Aunola, K., & Nurmi, J. E. (2007). Personal goals during emerging adulthood: A 10-year follow up. *Journal of Adolescent Research, 22,* 690–715.
Sewell, W. H., & Hauser, R. M. (1980). The Wisconsin longitudinal study of social and psychological factors in aspirations and achievements. *Research in Sociology of Education and Socialization, 1,* 59–99.
Sjoberg, O. (2010). Ambivalent attitudes, contradictory institutions ambivalence in gender-role attitudes in comparative perspective. *International Journal of Comparative Sociology, 51,* 33–57.
Steil, J. M. (2000). Contemporary marriage: Still an unequal partnership. In C. Hendrick & S. Hendrick (Eds.), *Close relationships: A sourcebook* (pp. 125–152). Thousand Oaks: Sage.
Sylvester, K. (2001). Caring for our youngest: Public attitudes in the United States. (Review). *The Future of children/Center for the Future of Children, the David and Lucile Packard Foundation, 11,* 52–61.
Thornton, A., & Young-DeMarco, L. (2001). Four decades of trends in attitudes toward family issues in the United States: The 1960s through the 1990s. *Journal of Marriage and the Family, 63,* 1009–1037.
Townsend, N. W. (2002). *The package deal: Marriage, work, and fatherhood in men's lives*. Philadelphia: Temple University.
U.S. Census Bureau (2011). The 2011 statistical abstract. http://www.census.gov/compendia/statab/cats/labor_force_employment_earnings.html.
Weinshenker, M. N. (2006). Adolescents' expectations about mothers' employment: Life course patterns and parental influence. *Sex Roles, 54,* 845–857.
Wenzel, A. J., & Lucas-Thompson, R. G. (2012). Authenticity in college-aged males and females, how close others are perceived, and mental health outcomes. *Sex Roles, 67,* 334–350.
Wiese, B. S., & Freund, A. M. (2011). Parents as role models: Parental behavior affects adolescents' plans for work involvement. *International Journal of Behavioral Development, 35,* 218–224.

Chapter 2
Beyond the "Ideal" Worker: Including Men in Work–Family Discussions

Sunny L. Munn and Tomika W. Greer

2.1 Introduction

Traditional workplaces are based on the "ideal worker" (Williams 2000)—identifying a man as the earner of the primary paycheck within a family—and coincide with gender ideology that perpetuates the norm of the "ideal parent" (Sperling 2014), which names a woman as the primary caretaker of the family. The ideal worker's life is organized in a way that accommodates the demands of the employer, while the ideal parent's life accommodates the demands of family.

The ideal worker is the preferred employee in both white collar and blue collar contexts. This employee is willing to work swing shifts as a blue-collar worker and able to travel on short notice or work 80-hour weeks in white-collar positions. This employee is not distracted by the demands of children or commitments outside of work. The ideal worker is—nearly without exception—characterized as a male. Alternatively, the ideal parent provides unlimited support at home and handles all childcare responsibilities. The expectation is that the ideal parent is female and maintains this role regardless of whether or not she is working outside of the home. For employed women, their home responsibilities are frequently referred to as the "second shift" (Hochschild 1989).

Female employees are, therefore, thought to need work–family friendliness in their workplace more so than do male employees. Accordingly, organizations are more likely to offer work–family initiatives when the percentage of women employed in the organization is high (Konrad and Mangel 2000). Although alternative

S. L. Munn (✉)
Department of Leadership Studies, Dwight Schar College of Education, Ashland University, 128 Dwight Schar, 401 College Ave., Ashland, OH 44805, USA
e-mail: smunn2@ashland.edu

T. W. Greer
Department of Human Development and Consumer Sciences, College of Technology, University of Houston, 110 Cameron Building, Houston, TX 77204, USA
e-mail: twgreer@central.uh.edu

M. J. Mills (ed.), *Gender and the Work-Family Experience*,
DOI 10.1007/978-3-319-08891-4_2

work arrangements are becoming increasingly possible, men are less likely to take advantage of organizational work–family initiatives (Fried 1998; Kirby and Krone 2002). This is likely influenced by unspoken organizational norms and the attitudes of coworkers which perpetuate negative attitudes toward men who use work–family benefits. Furthermore, men's use of work–family initiatives challenges traditional perceptions of masculinity (Vandello et al. 2013). Employees who are most likely to use such initiatives are married, female, and/or have children (Thompson et al. 1999). As women are considered to be the ideal parents, there is little effort on behalf of organizations to offer work–family benefits to men, to accept that they might need to use such benefits, or to encourage a culturally responsive organization that allows men to do so.

In this chapter, we point to evidence that contemporary men do not always fit the ideal worker stereotype. Instead, men are taking on more responsibilities in the home and may struggle with the collision of work and family demands (Kaufman 2014)—a struggle that is stereotypically reserved for women. Even the gender neutral terms "work–family" and "working parent" are often interpreted as being primarily applicable to women (Levine and Pittinsky 1997), as well as excluding individuals without children.

Working men have real needs for work–family initiatives and balance just as working women might. According to data from the 1997 National Study of the Changing Workforce, collected by the Families and Work Institute, employed fathers with children under the age of 18 years reported 48.5 hours of work per week (Hill 2005). However, these working fathers also reported 24.7 hours in child care and 21.2 hours doing household chores each week (Hill 2005). Increased involvement with childcare and household responsibilities is one reason why "work–life research on men is necessary in order to challenge the norm of the 'ideal worker'" (Sav et al. 2013, p. 673) and the ideal parent. As a result, there is a need to consider men in work–family discussions and make workplace adjustments that consider the work–family interface for male employees.

2.2 From Ideal Worker to Contemporary Employee

Over the past four decades, the US workforce has experienced a general declining trend of men's prominence in the workforce as more women seek employment outside of the home (U.S. Bureau of Labor Statistics 2013). In the 1970s, men comprised about 61 % of the US workforce. Into the 1980s, that number dropped to about 56 % of the workforce. In the 1990s, men only made up 54 % of the workforce. This trend continued into the 2000s as men comprised 53 % of the workforce. Currently, women comprise about half of the workforce as the gap continues to close (U.S. Bureau of Labor Statistics 2013).

As women's presence in the workforce is equalizing with men's presence, there have been shifts in the traditional breadwinner status that men historically held in

American society. Since the late 1980s, the number of wives who earn more than their husbands in dual-earner families has steadily increased (U. S. Bureau of Labor Statistics 2013). In 1987, there were 29.7 million dual-earner couples and 17.8% of the wives earned more than their husbands. By 2011, there were 31.4 million dual-earner families. This number represents a relatively modest increase in dual-earner families over the preceding 24 years. However, 29.2% of the wives were earning more than their husbands in 2011, suggesting that nearly one-third of dual-earner couples no longer fit the male breadwinner family structure.

In conjunction with women taking on more participation and responsibilities in the paid labor force, men have increased their engagement in matters of the home and family. Although men's increased involvement in housework and childcare did not mirror women's entrance into the workforce during the 1960s and 1970s (Coverman and Sheley 1986), a marked increase in men's household involvement has been documented (Coltrane 2000).

Ultimately, as traditional male-role expectations are changing, more American men have started to transition from the breadwinner role to the involved family man. As a result, balancing work and family roles has become an important issue for working men just as it has been for women (Yonetani et al. 2007). In fact, in a recent study, Kaufman (2014) classified fathers into three types: old, new, and superdad. The "old" dads are the traditional breadwinners; "new" dads are a mixture between breadwinner and caregiver; and "superdads" are those whose priority is caregiving as opposed to work.

The changes in the contemporary definition of family also contribute to the need to consider work–family interactions for men. "While the definition of family can be interpreted widely (Powell et al. 2012) within the work–family literature, it is typically used to refer to married and dual-earner couples or those with children" (Munn 2013, p. 6). The work–family literature overwhelmingly fails to define the meaning of family, most frequently creating the assumption that the family structure is "traditional." The traditional family is comprised of an employed father and an unemployed mother (Schneer and Reitman 1993), thus perpetuating the notion of the ideal worker and the ideal parent. As evidenced by the rise in women's employment and the realization that 54% of married-couple families are dual-earner families (U.S. Bureau of Labor Statistics 2013), and 13.6 million families are separated or unmarried (U.S. Census Bureau 2012), the traditional family including the ideal worker and parent do not accurately reflect the lives of many Americans.

Instead, a "post-traditional" family can include dual-earner couples and children who require adult supervision and care. In this family, it may be the case that mothers pick up a "second-shift" by becoming active labor force participants and remaining primary caregivers at home (Bailyn et al. 2001; Damaske 2011; Hochschild 1989, 1997). Additionally, fathers may also share more household responsibilities and/or earn less income than mothers.

The post-traditional family can also be a single-parent family. The prevalence of single-parent families has been on the rise in the United States since the 1960s. In 1960, there were less than 300,000 households with minor children that were headed by a single father; in 2011, that number had risen above 2.6 million single father families (Livingston 2013). The number of single mother households has risen even more sharply in the same time period—from 1.9 million households in 1960 to 8.6 million households in 2011 (Livingston 2013). Therefore, the ability of single parents—including fathers—to balance work and family responsibilities is increasingly important.

In this post-traditional family era, the "new" father (Kaufman and Uhlenberg 2000) differs from the traditional breadwinner in that he spends more time with his children, although he may be torn between spending quality time and working more to provide better options for his family (Kaufman 2014; Roy 2005). Still, the work–family literature continues to perpetuate the ideal worker by differentially including women and men in work–family discussions according to stereotypical views of traditional gender roles. For example, in western societies, work–family research has focused on the experiences of married, white, educated women in professional/managerial job positions (Casper et al. 2007; Sav et al. 2013). Within this population, researchers have studied the relationships between working mothers and child outcomes, marital satisfaction, and issues of self-efficacy. This narrow focus is likely an outcome of the persistence of the ideals of the traditional family structure where women are thought to be plagued with higher demands to maintain equilibrium between work and the rest of the life (Guest 2002) due to the child- and home-care responsibilities not regularly expected of men. Researchers have also studied the effects of women in the workplace, organizational needs, and family needs to help shape work–family policies and practices for women and their children.

Alternately, compared to women, men are minimally studied in work–family research. When men are included, the research tends to be more concerned with work outcomes than family outcomes. However, we contend that a more thorough understanding of men's work–family issues is warranted to develop equitable work–family initiatives and make concessions for changing gender role expectations and the contemporary US workforce (Hill 2005). The myth of the ideal worker and ideal parent is now obsolete. Instead, we find men in the workforce who have demanding work and family responsibilities and a desire to perform well in both roles. Accordingly, the aim of this chapter is to portray a holistic view of men's work–family experiences and advocate for the value of consistently considering men in work–family discussions.

2.3 Theory of the Work–Family Interface: Conflict, Enrichment, and Balance

The work–family interface is often studied in terms of work–family conflict and work–family enrichment. Work–family conflict occurs when work or family demands hinder a person's performance in the alternate role. Work–family conflict follows when the responsibilities of work and family are incompatible (Greenhaus and Beutell 1985). Conversely, work–family enrichment ensues when work or family experiences enhance performance in the other domain. Enrichment occurs when resources are gained in one domain that can be used to improve performance or affect in the other domain (Carlson et al. 2006). Work–family conflict is more often studied than work–family enrichment. However, researchers advocate for studying both conflict and enrichment: The positive side of the work–family interface has been shown to predict work and nonwork outcomes over and above the effects of work–family conflict alone (van Steenbergen et al. 2007).

Work–family conflict and work–family enrichment have been theorized and empirically supported as bidirectional constructs (Carlson et al. 2006; Greenhaus and Powell 2006). The conflict can originate in either the work domain or the family domain. The conflict that originates in the work domain has been called work-interference-with-family (WIF). The conflict that originates in the family domain has been called family-interference-with-work (FIW). WIF is thought to be more prevalent than FIW among both men and women (Allard et al. 2011; Kinnunen and Mauno 1998). The work–family enrichment characterized by experiences in the work domain positively influencing the quality of life in the family domain has been called work-to-family enrichment (WFE). The enrichment characterized by experiences in the family domain that positively influence the quality of life in the work domain has been called family-to-work enrichment (FWE).

Previous studies have led researchers to believe that work–family conflict and work–family enrichment are independent constructs. Work–family conflict is not necessarily the opposite of work–family enrichment (Powell and Greenhaus 2006). For many, the elusive notion of "work–family balance" could exist in the case of minimized work–family conflict and maximized work–family enrichment. There is no single agreed-upon definition of work–family balance, but in general there is an agreement that work–family balance occurs when an employee is satisfied with the amount of time and effort spent in each life domain with as little conflict as possible (Clark 2000; Greenhaus et al. 2003; Grzywacz and Carlson 2007).

2.3.1 Differences Between Men's and Women's Work–Family Experiences

In 1992, Higgins and Duxbury published one of the earliest identified studies that looked specifically at men's work–family conflict amidst changing family structures. The primary premise of their study recognized that the woman's work–family conflict had been thoroughly studied as her role expectations were changing from homemaker to working mother while work–family conflict for men who found themselves in dual-earner families was drastically understudied. Higgins and Duxbury (1992) sought to compare the antecedents and consequences of work–family conflict for men in single-earner families compared to men in increasingly popular dual-earner families. Their results confirmed differences between the two groups of men in their model of work–family conflict.

The results of the Higgins and Duxbury (1992) study suggested that as men's roles in relation to work and family have evolved, so have their experiences with work–family conflict. A similar case can be made regarding work–family enrichment. The results of this study suggested that what has been discovered about work–family interactions based on women's experiences is not necessarily generalizable to contemporary men. It is, therefore, necessary to discuss men's work–family experiences separately from women's experiences because the expectations of men in their work and family roles differ from the expectations of women in similar roles. For instance, mothers spend more time in the presence of their children, dealing with daily hassles, and performing caregiving tasks as compared to fathers (Lee et al. 2003).

Although there is some evidence to support the idea that there are no significant differences between men and women in work–family conflict (Anafarta and Kuruüzüm 2012; Kinnunen and Mauno 1998), there is also research that suggests that men experience less work–family conflict and more work–family enrichment than women (e.g., Figueroa et al. 2012; Hill 2005; van Steenbergen et al. 2007). Such differences point to gender as an embedded factor in how employees negotiate their work and family role demands (Emslie and Hunt 2009). Indeed, working fathers have reported less individual stress, and greater family satisfaction, marital satisfaction, and life satisfaction than working mothers (Hill 2005). Even among self-employed men and women, women report more intrusions on their work from their family than do self-employed men (Loscocco 1997). Alternately, work intrudes more on family for self-employed men than for self-employed women (Loscocco 1997).

Much of the research around men's work–family experiences compared to women's experiences provides a foundation for continuing research in this area. There is clearly not enough research on men in this regard. However, there is also evidence that men's work–family experiences have different antecedents and consequences than women's work–family experiences. In the following sections, we explore the extant research on the antecedents and consequences of men's work–family conflict and work–family enrichment.

2.4 Understanding Men's Work–Family Conflict

2.4.1 Antecedents of FIW and WIF Conflict

For both men and women, FIW is best explained by family domain variables, such as the number of children living at home (Kinnunen and Mauno 1998). Other findings indicate that FIW is likely to increase when men have more advanced job tenure (Anafarta and Kuruüzüm 2012), and for those that are married or cohabiting and have eldercare responsibilities (Barrah et al. 2004). Furthermore, spousal support is negatively related to FIW (Aycan and Eskin 2005).

Compared to FIW, there is much more research on the WIF experiences of men. WIF is best explained by work domain variables (e.g., full-time job, poor leadership relations) among women, as well as by high education and number of children living at home (Kinnunen and Mauno 1998). For men, one study indicated that higher workloads and more work hours are associated with increased WIF (Sav et al. 2013). However, organizational support—including supervisory support, work–family policies, and time flexibility—is associated with less WIF for men (Aycan and Eskin 2005). Another study found that WIF is negatively correlated with men's education and job tenure (Anafarta and Kuruüzüm 2012). Additionally, for men, the frequency of family intrusions and total role involvement predict time-based WIF (Loerch et al. 1989). In another recent study, male senior leaders reported more WIF than female senior leaders (Mills and Grotto 2012). Although gender was not significant, this study also found that satisfaction with flexible work practices and organizational work–life support was important for reducing WIF.

Another important factor for men is relationship status. In general, men's marital status has been positively correlated with WIF (Anafarta and Kuruüzüm 2012). Employed fathers who are not partnered have reported greater work–family conflict and lower family-to-work enrichment than partnered fathers (Janzen and Kelly 2012). Men who are married with an employed spouse experience more work–family conflict than men in single earner families or who are partnered with a homemaker (Crowley 1998; Higgins and Duxbury 1992). Men who view themselves as adequate breadwinners reported a greater sense of work–family role overload than those who view themselves as inadequate breadwinners (Crowley 1998).

Gender role assignments remain prevalent within work and family situations. A recent *LA Times* (2013) article noted that women are more likely to break the gender divide by entering more male dominated fields such as medicine, business, or law while men are much less likely to take on traditional female-oriented employment opportunities like teaching, nursing, or administrative work. In fact, less than 1% of fathers were stay-at-home dads in 2013 while 24% of mothers were stay-at-home moms, according to U.S. Census data. Previous research findings suggest that while stereotypical gender-role attitudes tend to increase work–family conflict for women, they actually decrease work–family conflict for men (Izraeli 1993). Spending time with family on the weekends and being concerned about work performance contributes to more work–family conflict in men than in women (Izraeli 1993). For example, fathers who are also managers might have increased access to flexible work practices yet still tend to experience high levels of work–family conflict. However, for these same dads in more gender egalitarian families, access to flexible working practices creates less work–family conflict and also sets a positive example, encouraging other employees' use of such benefits (Allard et al. 2007).

2.4.2 Consequences of FIW and WIF Conflict

There is significant research demonstrating the impact of FIW and WIF conflict on women and children. However, much less is known about the impact on men and fathers. For instance, when fathers bring stress from work into the home, mothers are more likely to experience decreased work–family balance, thus increasing conflict for mothers (Fagan and Press 2008). Additionally, mothers tend to experience higher levels of work–family balance when fathers have more flexibility at work and are more involved at home with childcare (Fagan and Press 2008).

Higher levels of emotional exhaustion are common for both men and women experiencing work–family conflict. Work–family conflict was associated with poorer health among women and drinking problems among men (Leineweber et al. 2013). Another study found that work–family conflict was strongly related to problem drinking among both women and men (Roos et al. 2006). Aycan and Eskin (2005) found that work–family conflict had a negative relationship with psychological well-being, marital satisfaction, and parental role performance for men. Additionally, FIW was positively related to men's guilt (Livingston and Judge 2008).

2.5 Understanding Men's Work–Family Enrichment

Although work–family conflict is more prominently studied in the literature as compared to work–family enrichment, there is a small amount of research related to work–family enrichment for men, which is summarized here.

2.5.1 Antecedents of Men's Work–Family Enrichment

A qualitative study of Australian Muslim men revealed interesting experiences of work and family interactions (Sav et al. 2013). Results of the study suggest that these Muslim men experienced both conflict and enrichment, however enrichment appeared to dominate their experiences. The researchers in this study suggested that the high reports of work-to-family and family-to-work enrichment were likely due to the religious beliefs of the Muslim men, who view paid employment as a religious obligation and value the breadwinner role (Sav et al. 2013). The study concludes that religion can influence men's experience of work–family enrichment. Furthermore, these Muslim men also engaged in flexible work hours and perceived a supportive workplace, which is also likely to improve work–family enrichment (Sav et al. 2013).

Interestingly, in a representative sample of working fathers in the United States, work–family conflict was more prevalent among the employed fathers than work–family enrichment (Hill 2005). Moreover, as an additional contrast to the Australian Muslim men, supportive organizational culture was negatively related to family-to-work enrichment, suggesting that with a more supportive organization, American employed fathers are less likely to experience positive gains from the family to the work domain. In the same study, organizational commitment was also negatively associated with family-to-work enrichment (Hill 2005). So, when working fathers experienced family-to-work enrichment, they were less committed to remaining employed in their organizations. However, the more time these employed fathers spent on childcare, the less family-to-work enrichment they experienced (Hill 2005).

The findings from the studies of Australian Muslim men and the American working fathers highlight how context-specific experiences of work–family interactions can be. However, in both cases, the men appear to value their work and their family roles, which is consistent with the idea of contemporary men who are not conforming to the ideal worker stereotype.

2.5.2 Consequences of Men's Work–Family Enrichment

Work-to-family enrichment has been positively related to job satisfaction and life satisfaction, and negatively related to individual stress (Hill 2005). Family-to-work enrichment has been positively related to marital satisfaction, family satisfaction, and life satisfaction, and negatively related to organizational commitment (Hill 2005).

Others took a more granular approach to looking at the consequences of men's work–family enrichment by measuring its distinct facets (van Steenbergen et al. 2007). Specifically, they looked at enrichment as being energy-based, time-based, behavioral, and psychological in addition to being bidirectional. For men, energy-based work-to-family enrichment was a significant predictor of life satisfaction and job satisfaction (van Steenbergen et al. 2007). This finding suggests that when men perceive that their work gives them additional energy to perform at home, they are more satisfied with both their work and nonwork roles. Higher psychological work-to-family enrichment predicted better job performance and lower job search behavior, suggesting that these men were performing well and less likely to be looking for a job change. Furthermore, energy-based work-to-family enrichment predicted higher affective commitment for men. It is important to note that many of these significant findings are different between men and women, reinforcing the notions that the outcomes of men's and women's work–family interactions are experienced differently.

2.6 Practical Implications

"The way work itself is organized—around stereotypical [heterosexual white] male employees with no substantial responsibilities outside of the workplace—is often a major obstacle for people trying to combine work and family" (Rapoport et al. 2002,

p. 183). Yet, there is often an unconscious disconnect between the existence and the use of work–family benefits because the "ideal worker" (Bailyn et al. 2001; Williams 2010) (also called a "zero-drag" worker; Hochschild 1997) is most accurately depicted as the traditional male worker, while work–family benefits were created to assist female employees with children (Lewis 2001). The "ideal worker" is traditionally male and works full-time. He is able to keep the spheres of work and family separate thus not "needing" to use work–family policies (Allen 2001; Bailyn et al. 2001; Campbell 2001; Thompson et al. 1999; Williams 2010; Williams et al. 2006). However, while work may still be organized this way, the way individuals work and interact with family have changed over time—especially for fathers. Unfortunately, organizational expectations and the actions of male employees who are also fathers have not caught up with one another. "Opportunities and [organizational] rewards go to those who most closely conform to the "ideal worker" by compartmentalizing work and family caregiving so that these are separate spatially, temporally, and psychologically" (Winfield and Rushing 2005, p. 58). The desire to fulfill this ideal worker norm causes many employees to fear and, therefore, avoid using any policies that may provide "family-friendly" benefits (Bailyn et al. 2001; Blair-Loy 2001; Kirby and Krone 2002; Williams et al. 2006; Winfield and Rushing 2005). Similarly, Berdahl and Moon (2013) found that men who take on childcare responsibilities, thus acting outside of the role of an ideal worker and traditional father, are typically mistreated at work via criticisms of their masculinity. This suggests that adjustments need to be made regarding how we conceptualize work and fatherhood—adjustments which allow for a new definition of fatherhood that goes beyond the provider role to also include the caretaker role. In other words, the "new dad" and "superdad" conceptualizations should also be perceived as strengths of a man's masculinity.

While research has shown that men also value flexibility and work–family balance, they tend to seek out opportunities for improving such balance less frequently than do women (Vandello et al. 2013), perhaps because of the fear of stigmatization and ridicule (Berdahl and Moon 2013). Fathers are more dependent on spousal support than organizational support (Hill 2005), sustaining research demonstrating men's underuse of work–family benefits (Kirby and Krone 2002; Lewis 1997). With the presence of a more supportive organizational culture, supervisor-supported flexibility, and greater use of family-oriented benefits, mothers experience less work–family role strain (Warren and Johnson 1995). Winfield and Rushing (2005) found, for both men and women, that in organizations with "family-friendly" policies and jobs that provide autonomy "employees are more likely to perceive their supervisors as supportive of interactions in the workplace that bridge the borders between work and family life" (p. 56).

Frequently, companies have cultural norms that keep work and family separate from one another. When a family-supportive organizational culture is not well developed, fathers tend to experience more work–family conflict. However, when a family-supportive culture exists within the organization, work and family are more easily combined (Allard et al. 2011, Galinsky et al. 2013). A common perception applied to working mothers is the "mommy track", which includes lower earnings and less challenging work for women with children who seek more flexible work schedules. Recently, it was found that fathers who choose the "daddy track"—opting for more flexibility for family purposes—also incur decreased earnings over the course of their careers because they are seen as less focused (Coltrane et al. 2013). Similarly, managers are more likely to accommodate men who request flexible work practices for career advancement rather than family (Brescoll et al. 2013).

Employees who believe their managers support the use of family-friendly policies and programs are more likely to use available options (Allen 2001). When employees do not perceive informal support from their managers and peers, they are less likely to take advantage of family-friendly interventions. Although Hill et al. (2003) found that fathers were less likely than mothers to have used corporate programs to help find harmony between work and family life, fathers frequently chose options that provided flexibility as to when and where work was done. Overall, use of work–family programs such as flexible work practices by fathers were found to be work–family adaptive strategies that predicted greater work–family fit (Hill et al. 2003).

A very basic work–family policy offered in many countries is some type of national parental leave policy (Block et al. 2013). The United States has no national paid maternity or paternity leave policies, thereby leaving this decision to each individual employer. Even without the existence of a national paternity leave policy, which would provide fathers with the ability to take paid time off work after the birth or adoption of a child, many fathers still find a way to take leave for varied amounts of time. This might be through the use of sick days, vacation time, flexible work practices, or even unpaid time off such as the Family and Medical Leave Act. Use of leave, regardless of type, is influenced by fathers' employment characteristics, such as type of employer, tenure of position, level of earnings, etc. The fact that fathers are taking leave regardless of policies or payment indicates that they want and need to spend time with their children and partners after this significant life event. If leave after the birth of a child can increase a father's work–family balance, then it is likely that work commitment and productivity will also be greater due to reduced stress and conflict levels at home. Similar situations exist in the UK and Australia, where paternity leave is either not available or is difficult to use due to cultural barriers and stigmatization of appropriate family roles (Fox et al. 2009; Whitehouse et al. 2007).

Overall, we know that work–family balance programs in the workplace have received great attention, but typically focus on assisting mothers with work–family issues, thus excluding fathers and individuals without children (Hill 2005). Yet, we know that taking leave and working shorter hours are related to fathers being more involved with their infants (Nepomnyaschy and Waldfogel 2007; O'Brien et al. 2007). Employee autonomy at work has also been shown to impact the relationship between work hours and time spent with children (MacDonald and Almeida 2004), as well as decrease work–family conflict (Galinsky 2013). Available work–family policies have the ability to impact fathers' behavior both at home and on the job. Therefore, policies that provide parental leave, shortened work hours, or flexible work practices are likely to increase father involvement (Tanako and

Waldfogel 2007). For the employer, the goal is to create and successfully implement programs which not only assist the worker but also maintain or increase productivity of their employees on the job.

Similarly, developing work–family initiatives that specifically aim to benefit fathers and those without children has the potential to increase productivity, retention, and company loyalty. For example, through the existence of maternity leave but not paternity leave, the policies imply that a mother's responsibility is to childcare and a father's responsibility is financial support, thereby reinforcing the gendered ideal parent and worker stereotypes. "Social policies supporting men's care—particularly parental leave dedicated to fathers—are needed to enhance gender equality and work–family reconciliation for men and for women" (Fox et al. 2009, p. 313).

2.7 Opportunities for Future Research

Future research regarding men and their work–family experiences is very necessary, and there are ample research streams to pursue (Hill 2005). For instance, there are relatively few published research studies that analyze men separately from women. As demonstrated earlier in this chapter, there are some differences in the ways that men and women experience work–family conflict and enrichment. By not considering men separately from women in work–family research, researchers send the message that they do not recognize the need to understand men's work–family interactions distinctly from women's. Omitting such research diminishes our understanding of the work–family interface and disenfranchises men, especially fathers.

In addition to analyzing men's experiences separately from women's experiences, future work–family research should also consider more cross-cultural studies of men. This should include fathers and men without children, sexual minorities, and others with responsibilities outside of the family, such as community. Other countries appear to be ahead of the USA in terms of understanding men's work–family experiences. For instance, Canada (Doucet 2004; Konrad and Yang 2012), Belgium (Doucet and Merla 2007), Sweden (Allard et al. 2011), and Australia (Sav et al. 2013; Whitehouse et al. 2007) have been represented in men's work–family research. However, this research is not necessarily generalizable to American men, given the differences in work–family accommodations at national levels among the various countries and the role that culture can play in perceptions of work–family experiences (Sav et al. 2013).

Additionally, cultural differences based on race, ethnicity, and country of origin are likely to provide further insight into men's work–family experiences, especially in the USA, where cultural diversity is prevalent. For example, one study found differences in the work–family experiences of Hispanics versus Blacks and Whites. Hispanics are more likely to demonstrate an increased difference between men and women, likely because of differences in culture and work experiences (Roehling et al. 2005). Future research is needed to continue to build understanding of different cultures and perceptions of gender in terms of work–family research.

While we agree that paternity leave allowance is an important starting point for accommodating the evolution of men's work and family involvement, there is a need for future research to be devoted to further understanding the determinants and consequences of paternal leave-taking (Nepomnyaschy and Waldfogel 2007). Researchers have reported that taking advantage of parental leave policies may have a negative stigma within an organization that generally discourages employees from taking advantage of such policies. When women take maternity leave, they may find themselves perceived as less devoted to their work than either before having children and/or in comparison to their male coworkers. For many women, their maternity leave initiates their entrance onto the "mommy-track" where they have fewer upward mobility options within their organization, regardless of whether or not they are on the mommy-track by choice. Future research should be devoted to determining whether such consequences also await men who take advantage of paternity leave options. We surmise that because the length of maternity leave is generally longer than a paternity leave, men may not necessarily face the same consequences as women, but understanding what consequences men will face is critical to fully exploring paternity leave policies as a consideration for men's changing roles in both the work and family domains.

Similarly, women usually take the maternity leave that is offered to them because of the physical complications associated with giving birth, in addition to the desire to bond with their new child (which would also apply to adoption). However, men's motivations for engaging in paternity leave are somewhat less obvious than women's reasons for taking maternity leave. Future research into the determinants of men's use of paternity leave will be important for determining how best to devise paternity leave policies that actually meet the needs of employed fathers.

Finally, future research should also consider the roles of occupational status and/or differences in place of employment as potential explanatory variables for differential work–family experiences between men and women (Izraeli 1993). Since the work–family literature is primarily applicable to professional/managerial employees, little is known about the work–family experiences of employees who are employed in blue-collar positions, earn hourly wages, and/or are not eligible for benefits such as the paternity leave policies for which we advocate. For this segment of the population, there may be fewer differences between men and women with regard to work–family experiences. This speculation is based on the assumption that lower wage workers have fewer occupational options than their counterparts in higher status positions. So, both women and men in the lower status demographic may feel like they need their jobs to support their families, whereas managerial/professional employees may have the option of reducing work hours, working a flexible schedule, working from home, or utilizing benefits to help them manage work and family demands with less fear of losing their livelihood. Such options, of course, will vary from one organization to the next, based on the organizational culture and "work–family friendliness".

2.8 Conclusion

While we are moving away from the notions of the "ideal worker" and the "ideal parent" in contemporary society, they have not gone without penalizing men who desire more flexibility in the workplace or more time with family. Two recent studies found that men who sought to use workplace flexibility practices were deemed poor "organizational citizens," seen as uncommitted to their workplace, and were characterized as portraying more "undesirable" feminine traits (Rudman and Mescher 2013; Vandello et al. 2013). Such a reaction is unfortunate, as men—especially fathers—are increasingly committed to family at emotional and caretaking levels. As Kaufman (2014) demonstrates, an increasing number of fathers are filling the roles of "new" or "super" dads, as described earlier, in an effort to contribute more equally with their female partners. One step to including men in the work–family discussion is first to recognize that they—like women—have work–family needs. We can begin to be inclusive of men by more actively pursuing research which investigates men's work–family issues independently from those of women. It is time to recognize that everyone, not just mothers, have work–family needs. As such, we start by including men, specifically fathers, in the conversation.

References

Allard, K., Hass, L., & Hwang, C. P. (2007). Exploring the paradox: Experiences of flexible working arrangements and work–family conflict among managerial fathers in Sweden. *Community, Work, and Family, 10,* 475–493.

Allard, K., Haas, L., & Hwang, C. P. (2011). Family-supportive organizational culture and fathers' experiences of work–family conflict in Sweden. *Gender, Work, and Organization, 18,* 141–157.

Allen, T. D. (2001). Family-supportive work environments: The role of organizational perceptions. *Journal of Vocational Behavior, 58,* 414–435.

Anafarta, N., & Kuruüzüm, A. (2012). Demographic predictors of work–family conflict for men and women: Turkish case. *International Journal of Business and Management, 7,* 145–158.

Aycan, Z., & Eskin, M. (2005). Relative contributions of childcare, spousal support, and organizational support in reducing work–family conflict for men and women: The case of Turkey. *Sex Roles, 53,* 453–471.

Bailyn, L., Drago, R., & Kochan, T. A. (2001). *Integrating work and family life: A holistic approach.* A report of the Sloan work–family policy network. MIT: Sloan School of Management.

Barrah, J. L., Shultz, K. S., Baltes, B., & Stolz, H. E. (2004). Men's and women's eldercare-based work–family conflict: Antecedents and work-related outcomes. *Fathering, 2,* 305–330.

Berdahl, J. L., & Moon, S. H. (2013). Workplace mistreatment of middle class workers based on sex, parenthood, and caregiving. *Journal of Social Issues, 69,* 341–366.

Blair-Loy, M. (2001). Cultural constructions of family schema: The case of women finance executives. *Gender and Society, 15,* 687–709.

Block, R. N., Park, J. Y., & Kang, Y. H. (2013). Statutory leave entitlements across developed countries: Why US workers lose out on work–family balance. *International Labour Review, 152,* 125–143.

Brescoll, V. L., Glass, J., & Sedlovskaya, A. (2013). Ask and Ye shall receive? The dynamics of employer-provided flexible work options and the need for public policy. *Journal of Social Issues, 69,* 367–388.

Campbell, C. S. (2001). Work cultures and work/family balance. *Journal of Vocational Behavior, 58,* 348–365.

Carlson, D. S., Kacmar, K. M., Wayne, J. H., & Grzywacz, J. G. (2006). Measuring the positive side of the work–family interface: Development and validation of a work–family enrichment scale. *Journal of Vocational Behavior, 68,* 131–164.

Casper, W. J., Eby, L. T., Bordeaux, C., Lockwood, A., & Lambert, D. (2007). A review of research methods in IO/OB work–family research. *Journal of Applied Psychology, 92,* 28–43.

Clark, S. C. (2000). Work/family border theory: A new theory of work/family balance. *Human Relations, 53,* 747–770.

Coltrane, S. (2000). Research on household labor: Modeling and measuring the social embeddedness of routine family work. *Journal of Marriage and family, 62,* 1208–1233.

Coltrane, S., Miller, E. C., DeHaan, T., & Stewart, L. (2013). Fathers and the flexibility stigma. *Journal of Social Issues, 69,* 279–302.

Coverman, S., & Sheley, J. F. (1986). Change in men's housework and child-care time, 1965-1975. *Journal of Marriage and Family, 48,* 413–422.

Crowley, M. S. (1998). Men self-perceived adequacy as the family breadwinner: Implications for their psychological, marital and work–family well-being. *Journal of Family and Economic Issues, 19,* 7–23.

Damaske, S. (2011). *For the family? How class and gender shape women's work.* Oxford: Oxford University Press.

Doucet, A. (2004). "It's almost like I have a job, but I don't get paid": Fathers at home reconfiguring work, care, and masculinity. *Fathering, 2,* 277–303.

Doucet, A., & Merla, L. (2007). Stay-at-home fathering: A strategy for balancing work and home in Canadian and Belgian families. *Community, Work, and Family, 10,* 455–473.

Emslie, C., & Hunt, K. (2009). 'Live to work' or 'work to live'? A qualitative study of gender and work-life balance among men and women in mid-life. *Gender, Work, and Organization, 16,* 151–172.

Fagan, J., & Press, J. (2008). Father influences on employed mothers' work–family balance. *Journal of Family Issues, 29,* 1136–1160.

Figueroa, A. J., Aburto, M. A. C., & Acevedo, R. Z. (2012). Work-family conflict, parental efficacy and perceived parenting styles in fathers and mothers from the city of Talca, Chile. *Acta Colombiana de Psicología, 15,* 57–65.

Fried, M. (1998). *Taking time: Parental leave policy and corporate culture.* Philadelphia: Temple University Press.

Fox, E., Pascall, G., & Warren, T. (2009). Work-family policies, participation, and practices: Fathers and childcare in. *Europe. Community, Work, and Family, 12,* 313–326.

Galinsky, E., Aumann, K., & Bond, J. T. (2013). Times are changing: Gender and generation at work and at home in the USA. In S. Poelmans, J. Greenhaus, & M. Las Heras Maestro (Eds.), *Expanding the boundaries of work–family research: A vision for the future* (p. 279). London: Palgrave Macmillan.

Greenhaus, J. H., & Beutell, N. J. (1985). Sources of conflict between work and family roles. *Academy of Management Review, 10,* 76–88.

Greenhaus, J. H., & Powell, G. N. (2006). When work and family are allies: A theory of work–family enrichment. *Academy of Management Review, 31,* 72–92.

Greenhaus, J. H., Collins, K. M., & Shaw, J. D. (2003). The relation between work–family balance and quality of life. *Journal of Vocational Behavior, 63,* 510–531.

Guest, D. E. (2002). Perspectives on the study of work-life balance. *Social Science Information, 41,* 255–279.

Grzywacz, J. G., & Carlson, D. S. (2007). Conceptualizing work–family balance: Implications for practice and research. *Advances in Developing Human Resources, 9,* 455–471.

Higgins, C. A., & Duxbury, L. E. (1992). Work-family conflict: A comparison of dual-career and traditional-career men. *Journal of Organizational Behavior, 13,* 389–411.

Hill, E. J. (2005). Work-family facilitation and conflict, working fathers, and mothers, work–family stressors and support. *Journal of Family Issues, 26,* 793–819.

Hill, E. J., Hawkins, A. J., Märtinson, V., & Ferris, M. (2003). Studying 'working fathers': Comparing fathers' and mothers' work–family conflict, fit, and adaptive strategies in a global high-tech company. *Fathering, 1,* 239–261.

Hochschild, A. R. (1989). *The second shift*. New York: Avon Books.

Hochschild, A. R. (1997). *The time bind: When work becomes home and home becomes work*. New York: Holt.

Izraeli, D. N. (1993). Work/family conflict among women and men manager in dual-career couples in Israel. *Journal of Social Behavior & Personality, 8,* 371–385.

Janzen, B. L., & Kelly, I. W. (2012). Psychological distress among employed fathers: Associations with family structure, work quality, and the work–family interface. *American Journal of Men's Health, 6,* 294–302.

Kaufman, G. (2014). *Superdads: How fathers balance work and family in the 21st century*. New York: New York University Press.

Kaufman, G., & Uhlenberg, P. (2000). The influence of parenthood on the work effort of married men and women. *Social Forces, 78,* 931–947.

Kinnunen, U., & Mauno, S. (1998). Antecedents and outcomes of work–family conflict among employed women and men in Finland. *Human Relations, 51,* 157–177.

Kirby, E. L., & Krone, K. J. (2002). "The policy exists but you can't really use it": Communication and the structuration of work–family policies. *Journal of Applied Communication Research, 30,* 50–77.

Konrad, A. M., & Mangel, R. (2000). The impact of work-life programs on firm productivity. *Strategic Management Journal, 21,* 1225–1237.

Konrad, A. M., & Yang, Y. (2012). Is using work-life interface benefits a career-limiting move? An examination of women, men, lone parents, and parents with partners. *Journal of Organizational Behavior, 33,* 1095–1119.

Lee, M., Vernon-Feagans, L., Vazquez, A., & Kolak, A. (2003). The influence of family environment and child temperament on work–family role strain for mothers and fathers. *Infant and Child Development, 12,* 421–439.

Leineweber, C., Baltzer, M., Hanson, L. L. M., & Westerlund, H. (2013). Work-family conflict and health in Swedish working women and men: A 2-year prospective analysis (the SLOSH study). European Journal of Public Health. http://eurpub.oxfordjournals.org/content/early/2012/06/08/eurpub.cks064.full.pdf+html. Accessed 15 Jan 2014.

Levine, J. A., & Pittinsky, T. L. (1997). *Working fathers: New strategies for balancing work and family*. Reading: Addison-Wesley.

Lewis, S. (1997). 'Family friendly' employment policies: A route to changing organizational culture or playing about at the margins? *Gender, Work and Organization, 4* (1), 13–23.

Lewis, S. (2001). Restructuring workplace cultures: The ultimate work–family challenge? *Women in Management Review, 16,* 21–29.

Livingston, B. A., & Judge, T. A. (2008). Emotional responses to work–family conflict: An examination of gender role orientation among working men and women. *Journal of Applied Psychology, 93,* 207–216.

Livingston, G. (2013). *The rise of single fathers: A ninefold increase since 1960*. Pew Research Center: Washington, D.C. (http://www.pewsocialtrends.org/files/2013/07/single-fathers-07-2013.pdf).

Loerch, K. J., Russell, J. E., & Rush, M. C. (1989). The relationships among family variables and work–family conflict for men and women. *Journal of Vocational Behavior, 35,* 288–308.

Loscocco, K. A. (1997). Work-family linkages among self-employed women and men. *Journal of Vocational Behavior, 50,* 204–226.

MacDonald, D. A., & Almeida, D. M. (2004). The interweave of fathers' daily work experiences and fathering behaviors. *Fathering, 2,* 235–251.

Mills, M. J., & Grotto, A. R. (2012). Work-life and the upper echelon: Perceptions, outcomes, and gender differences in senior leadership. Paper presented at the Academy of Management Conference. Boston, Massachusetts, USA.

Munn, S. L. (2013). Unveiling the work-life system: The influence of work-life balance on meaningful work. *Advances in Developing Human Resources, 15,* 401–417.

Nepomnyaschy, L., & Waldfogel, J. (2007). Paternity leave and fathers' involvement with their young children. *Community, Work, and Family, 10,* 427–453.

O'Brien, M., Brandth, B., & Kvande, E. (2007). Fathers, work, and family life. *Community, Work, and Family, 10,* 375–386.

Powell, B., Bolzendahl, C., Geist, C., & Steelman, L. C. (2012). *Counted out: Same-sex relations and Americans' definitions of family.* New York: Russell Sage.

Powell, G. N., & Greenhaus, J. H. (2006). Managing incidents of work–family conflict: A decision-making perspective. *Human Relations, 59,* 1179–1212.

Rapoport, R., Lotte, B., Fletcher, J. K., & Pruitt, B. H. (2002). *Beyond work–family balance: Advancing gender equity and workplace performance.* San Francisco: Jossey-Bass.

Roehling, P. V., Jarvis, L. H., & Swope, H. E. (2005). Variations in negative work–family spillover among White, Black, and Hispanic American men and women: Does ethnicity matter? *Journal of Family Issues, 26,* 840–865.

Roos, E., Lehelma, E., & Rahkonen, O. (2006). Work-family conflict and drinking behaviours among employed women and men. *Drug and Alcohol Dependence, 83,* 49–56.

Roy, K. M. (2005). Transitions on the margins of work and family life for low-income African-American fathers. *Journal of Family and Economic issues, 26,* 77–100.

Rudman, L. A., & Mescher, K. (2013). Penalizing men who request a family leave: Is flexibility stigma a femininity stigma? *Journal of Social Issues, 69,* 322–340.

Sav, A., Harris, N., & Sebar, B. (2013). Work-life conflict and facilitation among Australian Muslim men. *Equality, Diversity, & Inclusion, 32,* 671–687.

Schneer, J. A., & Reitman, F. (1993). Effects of alternate family structures on managerial career paths. *Academy of Management Journal, 36,* 830–843.

Sperling, J. H. (2014). Reframing the work–family conflict debate by rejecting the ideal parent norm. *American University Journal of Gender, Social Policy & the Law, 22,* 47–90.

Tanako, S., & Waldfogel, J. (2007). Effects of parental leave and work hours on fathers' involvement with their babies. *Community, Work, and Family, 10,* 409–426.

Thompson, C. A., Beauvais, L. L., & Lyness, K. S. (1999). When work–family benefits are not enough: The influence of work–family culture on benefit utilization, organizational attachment, and work–family conflict. *Journal of Vocational Behavior, 54,* 392–415.

U.S. Bureau of Labor Statistics. (2013). Women in the labor force: A databook. http://www.bls.gov/cps/wlf-databook-2012.pdf. Accessed 29 March 2014.

U. S. Census Bureau. (2012). Profile America factors for features: Unmarried and single Americans week Sept. 16–22, 2012. http://www.census.gov/newsroom/releases/pdf/cb12ff-18_unmarried.pdf.

Vandello, J. A., Hettinger, V. E., Bosson, J. K., & Siddiqi, J. (2013). When equal isn't really equal: The masculine dilemma of seeking work flexibility. *Journal of Social Issues, 69,* 303–321.

van Steenbergen, E. F., Ellemers, N., & Mooijaart, A. (2007). How work and family can facilitate each other: Distinct types of work–family facilitation and outcomes for women and men. *Journal of Occupational Health Psychology, 12,* 279–300.

Warren, J. A., & Johnson, P. J. (1995). The impact of workplace support on work–family role strain. *Family Relations: An Interdisciplinary Journal of Applied Family Studies, 144,* 63–169.

Winfield, I., & Rushing, B. (2005). Bridging the border between work and family: The effects of supervisor-employee similarity. *Sociological Inquiry, 75,* 55–80.

Whitehouse, G., Diamond, C., & Baird, M. (2007). Fathers' use of leave in Australia. *Community, Work, & Family, 10,* 387–407.

Williams, J. C. (2000). *Unbending gender: Why work and family conflict and what to do about it.* Oxford: Oxford University Press.

Williams, J. C. (2010). *Reshaping the work–family debate: Why men and class matter. Cambridge.* Massachusetts: Harvard University Press.

Williams, J. C., Manvell, J., & Bornstein, S. (2006). *How the press covers work/family conflict: The untold story of why women leave the workforce*. The Center for Worklife Law, University of California, Hastings College of the Law.

Yonetani, Y., Watanabe, S., & Kanazawa, Y. (2007). On the relationships among organizational family supportiveness, work–family conflict, and turnover intention: Evidence on Japanese men. *International Journal of Human Resources Development and Management, 7,* 319–334.

Chapter 3
Gender, Poverty, and the Work–Family Interface

Heather Odle-Dusseau, Anna C. McFadden, and Thomas W. Britt

3.1 Introduction

The work–family interface cannot be discussed without taking into consideration the role that gender plays in work and family systems. Yet much of our understanding of gender and the work–family interface has been through the lens of middle- and upper-class, as well as professional-level, employees' experiences. As such, the work–family experiences of low-income individuals and those living at or below the poverty line are less understood. Given that women are more likely to be in poverty than men, leading to the coined phrase "feminization of poverty" (Pearce 1978), it is important to consider gender and work–family interactions within the context of poverty. Drawing from multiple disciplines (e.g., psychology, sociology, gender studies, and economics), this chapter examines how gender and the work–family interface interact for individuals who are working in low-wage jobs, and are often found to be living at or below the poverty line. Combining the theoretical frameworks of segmented labor markets and the Job Demands-Resources (JD-R) model (Demerouti et al. 2001), our goal is to integrate the themes of gender, poverty, and work–family experiences, and to develop avenues for future research.

In order to guide our discussion of these issues, in Fig. 3.1 we provide a descriptive model for how gender interacts with employment in low-wage jobs to affect work–family dynamics, which then affect the health and well-being of women. We begin this chapter by first addressing descriptions and explanations of the sex seg-

H. Odle-Dusseau (✉)
Department of Management, Gettysburg College, 300 North Washington Street, Box 395, Gettysburg, PA 17325, USA
e-mail: hodle@gettysburg.edu

A. C. McFadden
Department of Psychology, Clemson University, 418 Brackett Hall, Clemson, SC 29634, USA
e-mail: amcfadd@clemson.edu

T. W. Britt
Department of Psychology, Clemson University, 418 Brackett Hall, Clemson, SC 29634, USA
e-mail: twbritt@clemson.edu

M. J. Mills (ed.), *Gender and the Work-Family Experience*,
DOI 10.1007/978-3-319-08891-4_3

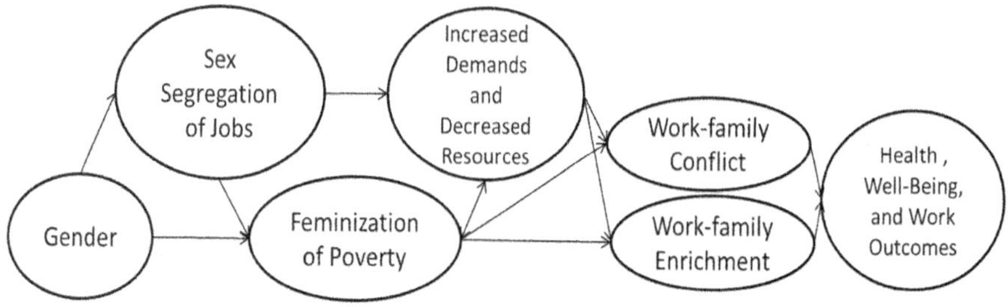

Fig. 3.1 Model of the integration of gender, poverty, and the work–family interface

regation of jobs, or the trend that certain jobs are more likely to be filled by men (e.g., construction workers) while other jobs are more likely to be filled by women (e.g., child care providers). This leads into a discussion of the phenomenon of the "feminization of poverty," examining the organizational, economic, and labor structures that contribute to the fact that women are more likely to live in poverty than men, which can be directly linked to the sex segregation of jobs.

We then apply the framework of the Job Demands-Resources (JD-R) model (Demerouti et al. 2001) to help describe how different types of jobs are also associated with different demands, resources, and subsequent outcomes for males and females. Specifically, we describe how low-wage jobs, which are more likely to be filled by women, often have higher demands and fewer resources (e.g., wages, flexibility, autonomy) for managing family responsibilities. The lack of resources then contributes to a higher potential for work–family conflict, a lower potential for work–family enrichment, and subsequently compromised levels of health and well-being. We also discuss public programs aimed at curbing poverty and its correlates, relative to the interaction of gender, poverty, and the work–family interface. Our overall model addresses how the sex segregation of jobs contributes toward a context of poverty that is experienced at different rates for men and women, subsequently creating situations in which men and women differentially experience job demands and resources. These differential demands and resources then influence work–family experiences and subsequent work and well-being outcomes.

3.2 Sex Segregation of Occupations and the Feminization of Poverty

The number of low-income working families in the United States reached 10.4 million in 2011 (an increase from 10.2 million in 2010), according to the Working Poor Families Project (Roberts et al. 2012). Across the globe, and especially in the United States, women are more likely to live in poverty than men; in 2011, the poverty rate for women was 14.6 %, while the poverty rate for men was 10.9 % (National Women's Law Center 2012). Given that this difference can be largely attributed to the fact that there are higher proportions of women found in low-wage jobs (Litchenwalter 2005), we attempt to further explore the work–family interface within these contexts.

Single mothers and their children are particularly vulnerable to poverty, often due to limited access to employment and the cost associated with raising children (Misra et al. 2012). When looking at poverty rates of female-headed households with children, the proportion of those women living in poverty jumps (from 14.6% overall) to 40.0% (National Women's Law Center 2012). Because women are often the main caregivers for children, and because of the risk of poverty associated with women and children, it is imperative to examine how this systemic, dynamic interaction of work, family, gender, and poverty influences the work–family interface.

Occupations can be sex segregated, meaning that some occupations are held by a higher proportion of men, while others are held by higher proportions of women. Powell (2011) used the terms "female-intensive" and "male-intensive" to describe those jobs that have two-thirds or more of the workforce made up by males or females, such that those jobs where women make up at least 66.7% of the workforce are considered "female-intensive." Scholars have described various mechanisms to explain why this differentiation exists, with many explanations being traced back to societal categorizations of sex and the prescribed gender roles that form the expectations of male and female roles in society. One set of these expectations is the division of labor, which outlines the paid work domain as mainly the responsibility of men, while the nonwork, home, and caregiver domains are the obligation of women. Although women have increased their labor force participation to approximately 47% (Powell 2011), there still persists a division of labor in the form of sex segregation of occupations.

There are a myriad of inter- and intraorganizational reasons that help explain why sex segregation takes place, such as the sex composition of the applicant pool, job search techniques of applicants, job assignment, and promotion practices (Reskin and Bielby 2005). While some of these reasons lie with individuals' choices, there are organizational structures and practices that also contribute to the segregation. Kmec (1995) proposed that sex segregation can arise from both the job applicants' techniques for attaining jobs, as well as the employer's organizational practices and policies and their subsequent discretion in hiring decisions. Similarly, Reskin and Bielby (2005) suggested that there are two specific ways that organizations create sex segregation. First, contributing to trends at the societal level, by not hiring a woman for a particular organization, the chance that she will go to another firm that is more likely to hire women increases. Stemming from psychological biases, although some organizational decision-makers may not consider sex when making the initial hiring decision, sex can be a consideration when making job assignments (Reskin and Bielby 2005). For example, in a factory, males may be more likely to be assigned a job that requires heavy lifting, while females are more likely to be assigned to support staff jobs that do not require heavy lifting. So while sex segregation across organizations may be lowered by hiring practices that explicitly, and legally, disregard biological sex, segregation within an organization could still exist and be reinforced through organizational structures, polices, and practices (Reskin and Bielby 2005).

Noting the shifts in our country's economic structure over the past 40 years, Reid and Rubin (2003) recommended Dual Labor Market Segmentation Theory to help describe potential explanations of the wage inequality among men and women. This framework of segmented labor markets, which became popular in the 1960s and 1970s, is often used to describe two types of labor markets: (1) the primary sector that consists of jobs requiring high levels of skills, education, and training, and rewards employees with high wages and benefits, (2) the secondary sector consisting of low-wage jobs that require little training and education, low levels of skills, and pay low wages with little opportunity for promotion (Reid and Rubin 2003). There is an obvious parallel between these two sectors and the differences seen between the jobs that are male-intensive and female-intensive. Not surprisingly, jobs in the secondary sector tend to be female-intensive. Thus, segmented labor theories provide us with a framework for describing the sex segregation of occupations and jobs.

Although not without its critiques (see Reid and Rubin 2003), segmented labor market theories can aid in describing sex segregation of occupations for several reasons. As outlined by Reid and Rubin (2003), wage inequality, and the place of human capital in work outcomes, is of interest to scholars. Additionally, women and minorities continue to disproportionately make up low-wage occupations and do not as often occupy jobs where there are opportunities to develop new skills and "move up" in the organization. Reid and Rubin (2003) note that although intraorganizational processes do influence wage inequality for gender and race, labor market and industrial sectors are also important influences.

3.2.1 The Feminization of Poverty

As seen in Fig. 3.1, the sex segregation of jobs contributes to the feminization of poverty, a term coined in 1978 by Diana Pearce in reference to the concentration of poverty among women as compared to men. When describing this trend, it is important to understand that it is too simplistic to designate the feminization of poverty as that which describes poor women in need of financial assistance. Rather, beyond the struggle to obtain basic living wages for food and housing, the feminization of poverty also refers to the lack of opportunity to move out of poverty and obtain a quality of life that considers more than basic needs. These effects on quality of life then permeate to the family structures in which these women live.

The disproportionate number of women in poverty is seen despite increased workforce participation by women and increased education levels. Litchenwalter (2005) analyzed data from the 2000 census in order to examine the contributors to the gender-poverty disparity in the 70 largest cities in the United States. Noting the long-standing sex differences in paid and unpaid labor (i.e., women are usually more responsible for unpaid labor like childrearing and domestic work), the shift toward more single female-headed families, and organizational structures that are themselves hindrances to working women and mothers, Litchenwalter (2005) found that women were more likely than men to be in poverty when in cities where women work more low-wage jobs and where there were a high proportion of women heading single parent homes. In addition, there was no significant correlation of poverty with education. When using regression analysis, which included the predictors of overall earnings, female representation in low- and high-wage jobs, labor force participation, and proportion of female-headed households, only the proportion of females in low-wage jobs remained a significant predictor of poverty disparity between men and women. What is more, it explained a substantial 41 % of the variance in that disparity (Litchenwalter 2005).

The feminization of poverty is not unique to the United States, although it is more prominent in the United States. For example, the risk of poverty for single mothers is below 2 % in Sweden, but is 35 % in the US (Misra et al. 2012). Casper et al. (1994) compared the correlates of the gender-poverty gap in the US to those of other Western industrialized countries. The results revealed that the US has the largest gender–poverty gap, with women being 41 % more likely to be living in poverty than men. In a more recent analysis, Brady and Kall (2007) examined the pattern of men and women's poverty in 18 countries across 31 years. They found that important correlates of poverty for both men and women were economic growth, manufacturing employment, social security transfers (e.g., social security pensions, family allowances, unemployment), public health spending, and labor force participation. However, the feminization of poverty was most related to social security transfers, single motherhood, and labor force participation. In other words, the experiences of work and family are different for women in poverty. We consider these factors when discussing the implications of the feminization of poverty for the work–family interface.

A related issue when discussing the feminization of poverty is that of the motherhood wage penalty, or the occurrence of overall loss in wages and benefits that mothers experience as compared to fathers and to women in the labor force who do not have children. Budig and Hodges (2010) examined whether the motherhood penalty affected women across income levels similarly. They compared low-wage, middle-wage, and high-wage white[1] female workers. High-waged women were more likely to have access to resources that assist in work–family management than their lower-waged counterparts, as well as hold more family-friendly jobs (e.g., have workplace policies that assist in managing family responsibilities).

There are various contexts the authors analyzed to better understand how the motherhood penalty may impact those differently across wage levels, such as spouse's earnings, welfare receipt, age of children at home, and timing of motherhood. Although human capital (e.g., education and experience) plays a part, it is small in that the motherhood penalty decreases (but does not go away) as education increases, yet the motherhood penalty increases with skill levels. What is

[1] Of course, left out of this discussion is the important issue of race and ethnicity that intersects with gender and class in terms of income inequality. See Frevert, Culbertson, and Huffman (Chap. 4 in this book), and Elmelech and Lu (2004) for an insightful analysis of gender, race, ethnicity, and poverty.

more, the authors found that low-wage workers experienced the largest motherhood wage penalty, and that the penalty for low-wage women with young children is five times higher than that of high-wage women with young children. Budig and Hodges (2010) concluded that mothers who are most in need of stable wages (low-income mothers) are the ones most likely to experience the motherhood penalty.

In addition, Glauber (2012) examined if the wage penalty is larger for women in female-intensive jobs or for those in male-intensive jobs. She pointed out that both men and women pay a wage penalty when working in female-intensive jobs, but the penalty is greater for women. Glauber outlined some of the arguments for the production of sex segregation, such as differences in human capital (i.e., women lose job experience and skills after a child is born while they take time off), and discrimination against hiring and promoting mothers. Yet even when controlling for job characteristics, part-time work, education, and experience, the motherhood wage penalty still exists. Based on data collected longitudinally from a national sample, Glauber (2012) found that women in female-intensive jobs were paid less, were more likely to be married and to have children, and were also more likely to work part-time than were women working in male-intensive or sex-neutral jobs. In addition, the wage penalty for women working in female-intensive jobs increased with the number of children a mother had (7 % for one or two children, and 15 % for three or more), while those women in neutral or male-intensive jobs only paid a penalty when the number of children reached three or more (10 %). Overall, women in female-intensive jobs "start out with lower wages and pay a large wage penalty for each child they have" (p. 126). What is more, this penalty does not appear to be offset or compensated for by benefits in female-intensive jobs, such as job satisfaction, access to health insurance, vacation time, flexible scheduling, or maternity leave.

3.2.2 *Feminization of Poverty and the Work–Family Interface*

Research has provided evidence that low-wage workers experience work and family responsibilities differently, and when we consider gender, these negative effects become even more robust. Low-income families have different experiences when managing work and family domains compared to the more commonly studied middle- to upper-class families. Perry-Jenkins (2005) interviewed 153 dual-earner, working-class couples during their transition to parenthood. The parents were working in occupations that would be classified in the "secondary sector" based on the level of education and experience required, as well as the wages paid. Participants described experiencing unstable work hours, the need to "piece together" sick and personal time for maternity leave (thereby leaving limited or no time to take off from work when a child was sick or had a doctor's appointment), limited health insurance coverage, and rarely any child care assistance or benefits. Relatedly, Offer (2012a) points out that recent research undermines prior thinking that low-income individuals rely more on social support networks for childcare than high-income individuals, finding that in terms of total financial, instrumental, and emotional support, low-income families tend to have fewer support networks when compared to middle and upper-class families.

When limiting analyses to female-headed households in low-wage families, the picture becomes even bleaker. Offer (2012b) examined how low-income mothers, who often rely on social support for childcare, also face barriers to achieving that support. These barriers include poor health, which is experienced at higher rates among low-income individuals than middle- and upper-class individuals (Burton et al. 2005), as well as "adverse life events" such as domestic violence incidents and illegal activities. Offer (2012b) provided data suggesting that both poor physical and psychological health serve as barriers to social support, including child care support, emotional support, instrumental support, and financial support. Specifically, participants who reported low health at Time 1 reported low perceived support at Time 2. This pattern was also observed for women who experienced domestic violence. Moreover, there appeared to be a mediating effect of poor health on the relationship between domestic violence and low support, in that the experiences of domestic violence lead to poor health, which in turn leads to low levels of perceived support.

In summary, sex segregated occupations have been demonstrated to contribute to the higher proportion of females in poverty as compared to males. This propensity to live in poverty is even higher when considering the presence of children in a household. What is more, individuals in low-wage jobs have very different experiences when managing work and family domains. In the next section, we utilize the Job Demands-Resources (JD-R) model to provide a framework for explaining the effects that the sex segregation of jobs and poverty may have on the work–family experiences of women in low-wage jobs. Components of this model are highlighted in Fig. 3.1.

3.3 Applying the JD–R Theory to Gender, Poverty, and the Work–Family Interface

The JD-R model (Demerouti et al. 2001) contends that job demands deplete energy, and therefore have negative effects on employees, leading to burnout. Alternatively, job resources can activate motivational processes, thereby having positive effects that lead to job engagement. This theory has been successfully applied to the work–family interface, in that resources have also been associated with positive outcomes in the context of work–family experiences. For example, perceptions of family-supportive work environments have been associated with employee well-being (e.g., Odle-Dusseau et al. 2013; Thompson and Prottas 2006).

In considering how demands and resources differ for low-wage individuals, and how these differences might contribute to problems managing the work–family interface, we turn to an analysis of how poverty affects individuals, as provided by Leana et al. (2012). Specifically, these authors view the effect poverty may have on low-income individuals as developing for three potential reasons: categorical explanations, whereby individual-level factors are seen as the source (e.g., less training can mean fewer skills to take with them to the next job or to deal with specific work stressors, causing an increase in negative personal and work-related outcomes); compositional explanations, whereby the structure of the environment (such as the organization) is the focus (e.g., low-wage workers may not be well integrated into the organization with those who earn higher wages, which can limit opportunities for advancement); and relational explanations, whereby individual relationships and social connections are the focus (e.g., low-wage workers may have a more difficult time engaging in social or networking relationships with higher wage earners within the organization). Each facet may exert a negative influence when explaining how lower income individuals may lack the resources necessary to appropriately combat demands at work, resulting in negative work–family experiences.

Understanding why women in single-parent households are more likely to experience poverty and other negative consequences of low-wage work can be considered within the JD-R framework. Specifically, children tend to create more demands on a household, and are not able to provide equivalent resources to offset these demands (Brady and Kall 2007). In the same vein, childcare (a potential resource) is not available in poor communities at the same rate that it is in more affluent communities, making childcare for low-wage mothers even more difficult to obtain (Budig and Hodges 2010). Thus the demands of having children in single-parent households, in combination with a lack of resources to manage these responsibilities, can contribute to the poverty of single mothers and their children.

The JD-R model can also assist us in understanding how sex segregation of occupations influences different work and family experiences. Reskin and Bielby (2005) point out that segregation, whether at the organizational level or the job level, can result in unequal rewards for men and women. Therefore, inequalities between men and women can be traced to sex compositions of organizations and jobs, not actual differences between men and women (i.e., their biological sex). Some researchers suggest that this can be partly attributed to the devaluation of jobs that are female-intensive (e.g., Rapoport et al. 2002). Importantly, the inequalities are not due to the amount of effort put into work by men and women. Past research has contradicted this suggestion, finding women to report just as much or more effort compared to men with similar household responsibilities (Bielby and Bielby 1988). As this chapter highlights, there are more valid explanations of these inequalities.

When considering why resources may differ for jobs that are lower wage and are more likely to be filled by women, Glauber (2011) compared the opportunities for flexibility in male-intensive, female-intensive, and integrated/neutral (i.e., neither male- nor female-intensive) jobs. Based on the theory of compensating wage differentials, female-intensive jobs should provide employees more access to flexibility as a trade-off for the lower wages. However, Glauber's (2011) results did not support this—individuals in integrated occupations reported more flexibility access than individuals in female-intensive jobs. These results suggest that dual labor market theory is a more appropriate framework for understanding how resources differ among male- and female-intensive jobs, in that female-intensive jobs tends to be those in the secondary sector, thus having fewer benefits like flexibility.

As seen in Fig. 3.1, the sex-segregation of jobs has the effect of increasing the number of demands for female employees, while decreasing the resources available for offsetting those demands. The differential experience of demands and resources has implications for the work–family interface of employees in low-wage, female-intensive occupations. Yet, while there has been some research on the work–family experiences of low-wage individuals, as well as research on how work–family experiences can differ for men and women, the research incorporating all three components is sparse. As such, we turn first to research that assessed how work–family experiences differ for low-wage workers, followed by research showing how males and females can differentially experience work and family interactions. We then discuss how to integrate these findings to fit within the larger context of our proposed model.

Recently, Sinclair et al. (2013) suggested that income or economic status may have an important relationship with work–family conflict. Relatedly, Leana et al. (2012) suggested that poverty is a "strong situation" that affects how individuals process information and respond to their environment. Thus differences in economic standing have the potential to affect how low-income individuals differ on perceptions of various work and family experiences, as well as work-related outcomes. The negative impact of work–family conflict on work, health, and well-being outcomes may be reduced for those individuals in high-earning jobs because of the increased resources and control over work. Looking specifically at the part one's income plays on the relationships among work demands and work–family experiences, Ford (2011) tested models of the cross-domain effect of work-to-family conflict and family-to-work conflict, hypothesizing that work-to-family conflict would mediate the relationship between work demands and family strain, while incorporating income as a moderator into the models. Finding income to have an important moderating role, Ford (2011) concluded that while high levels of income did not appear to lower the rates of work–family conflict, higher income did seem to provide resources to lower the influence of work–family conflict onto family strain. If gender is taken into account, this effect perhaps could be exacerbated for women, given the evidence that women are more likely to live in poverty.

Other empirical research has shown a direct impact of perceived economic hardship on work and family outcomes. Schieman and Young (2011) hypothesized that the stress from difficulty in obtaining basic necessities due to economic hardship would spill-over into other domains (namely the work domain) and might result in family-to-work conflict. Relying on the premises of the JD-R framework, Schieman and Young (2011) expected that more demanding work conditions would intensify the relationship between economic hardship and family-to-work conflict, but conditions which acted as resources would buffer the negative association between the two. The study found that economic hardship was predictive of family-to-work conflict, and that work conditions also acted as a moderator. For example, those individuals in jobs with less job authority and more job demands experienced a stronger relationship between economic hardship and family-to-work conflict. Although not including gender in their analyses, these findings become relevant as women may be more likely to work in demanding situations with low autonomy, based on the segmented labor theories (Reid and Rubin 2003), therein perhaps increasing their experiences of family-to-work conflict.

Turning to the part that gender plays in the links among poverty and work–family experiences, it is difficult to find research that specifically addresses these relationships simultaneously. The experience of women in professional and managerial-levels jobs has been studied to a much larger extent. For example, in a study of white collar, dual-earner workers, Batt and Valcour (2003) found that women reported marginally higher levels of work–family conflict than did men, but significantly less control over managing work and family conflict. So how do these experiences translate for low-wage women? Unfortunately, the influence that income may have on these relationships is not well understood. As seen in Fig. 3.1, we would hypothesize that the higher levels of work–family conflict experienced by employees in low-wage jobs (that are more likely to be occupied by a greater percentage of women) have the potential to more negatively affect the work, health, and well-being of the employees.

The negative work outcomes brought on by lack of resources when facing a stressor can be numerous, and in the work–family literature, the outcomes experienced by those facing work-to-family conflict have been shown to include lower performance, job satisfaction (Bruck et al. 2002), and organizational commitment (Aryee et al. 2005), as well as higher turnover intentions and actual turnover (Shaffer et al. 2001), and absenteeism (Kirchmeyer and Cohen 1999). Work–family conflict has also been linked with job performance, with meta-analyses finding that such conflict is related to decreased employee performance. In a review of work-to-family conflict and performance outcomes, Kossek and Ozeki (1999) found that, on average, increases in both work-to-family conflict and family-to-work conflict were associated with decreased performance metrics. This finding was echoed by Hoobler et al. (2010), who reported both work-to-family conflict and family-to-work conflict were negatively related to manager-rated performance ($r = -0.19$ for work-to-family conflict; $r = -0.16$ for family-to-work conflict), and self-rated performance ($r = -0.03$ for work-to-family conflict; $r = -0.22$ for family-to-work conflict). In addition, the perception of family support from one's supervisor (a potential resource) has been linked across time with increased perceptions of work–family enrichment, and to subsequent supervisor ratings of performance (Odle-Dusseau et al. 2012). If, as outlined by our model, we expect resources to be fewer for those working in low-wage jobs, we would then expect less likelihood of increases in work–family enrichment and any consequent effects on job performance.

Advancement in one's career is another work-related outcome that stands to be differentially influenced by income, demands, and resources for women. The "glass ceiling effect," or the seemingly invisible barriers women face in advancing their careers, was the focus of Hoobler et al.'s (2009) research. When asked to rate their subordinates' family-to-work conflict and performance, managers tended to rate females lower in performance. These results were obtained even while controlling for a number of variables that can be related to family-to-work conflict (i.e., caring for a dependent, number of children, and marital status). Additionally, managers also perceived those subordinates high in family-to-work conflict as having less fit with the organization, a variable that was also shown to have a significant impact on subordinate promotability. These results show that women in particular are perceived as experiencing more family-to-work conflict, regardless of how much conflict they may actually experience. In turn, these perceptions predicted how employees were rated for performance and fit with the organization, ultimately affecting the promotions an employee may receive.

Health and well-being outcomes are also important factors to consider when examining the outcomes of work–family conflict. The JD-R model (Demerouti et al. 2001) provides an explanation as to why individuals experiencing work–family conflict may subsequently experience other negative outcomes, such as depression (Kossek et al. 2006), hypertension, poor physical health, and heavy alcohol use (Frone et al. 1997), decreased well-being (Karimi et al. 2011), and decreased life satisfaction (Greenhaus et al. 2003). Individuals experiencing the demand of work–family conflict may use up their resources attempting to deal with the demand, leading to negative personal outcomes. Additionally, individuals in low-wage jobs may be at a further disadvantage in that they also likely have fewer resources to buffer the negative consequences of work–family conflict, again leading to negative personal and work-related outcomes. For certain, the research examining the intersection of work–family outcomes, gender, and poverty is limited. Additional research is clearly needed in this area in order to understand more fully how contextual variables such as poverty and gender can help to explain differences in work–family experiences.

3.4 The Effects of Public Programs on Managing the Work–family Interface

We have established that low-income workers, who are more likely to be female, are more likely to experience negative work and family interactions. Public policy has been developed to address some of the correlates of these patterns, in the spirit of decreasing the negative outcomes on one's health and well-being. One important assumption of work–family policies on a societal level is that people should not be at risk of falling into poverty because of family care demands (Misra et al. 2007). Although there are public policies in place in the United States that are aimed to assist low-income individuals, Casper et al. (1994) noted that some feminist analyses have demonstrated that welfare programs are often unsuccessful at increasing gender equality, but rather reward households comprised of heterosexual, married couples. In other words, single mothers are often unable to become financially independent with current welfare programs.

It is important to understand how public policy influences all types of families so that the effectiveness of such policies can be evaluated holistically. Hennessy (2009) proposed that societal expectations of the roles held by men and women are exacerbated by the current policies that are created to assist low-income women, creating a moral dilemma for these women who need to provide financially for their families, but are also expected to be the primary caregiver to their children. Hennessy (2009) described how low-income women are expected to fulfill work responsibilities because they should be responsible for pulling themselves out of the need for welfare. At the same time, a mother's commitment to her family, rooted in societal expectations, is one associated with intense mothering, and is based on the experiences of white, middle-class women. Specifically, work and family conflict arises not only from the need to provide for families, but also from "cultural and moral contradictions that arise out of constraints on poor mothers' ability to do so" (p. 560). The part that public policy plays to reinforce societal expectations that perpetuate scenarios for women to remain in poverty is an important component of this discussion.

Looking directly at how work–family policies (i.e., parental leave and child care policies) influence poverty outcomes via support for employment, Misra et al. (2012) noted that we need to be aware of how individual and societal factors intersect to influence the risk of poverty. Misra et al. (2012) examined two types of policies across countries: those that provide state support (such as financial allowances), and those that provide employment opportunities (such as parental leave policies). Based on a sample of women with children, across countries in 11 developed welfare states (i.e., wealthy Western Europe and North American countries, as well as Australia, Israel, and former socialist nations in Eastern Europe), Misra et al. (2012) found that single mothers were at a higher risk of poverty than mothers with partners, and that this probability of poverty was increased when there were fewer family allowances, less generous parental leave policies, and fewer child care provisions. For example in Sweden, where mothers have a low probability of falling into poverty, there are moderate levels of government financial allowance along with generous child care provisions, and high levels of women working full-time. In the United States, where women have a high risk of falling into poverty, there are high levels of women working full-time, but no government allowance for paid leave and low amounts of childcare provisions. Thus, policies that support single mothers outside the home are just as important as supporting them inside the home when it comes to reducing the risk of poverty.

Relatedly, Ray et al. (2009) noted the need to consider the effect that generosity (of time) of family leave has on gender equality. These authors looked at the degree to which family leave policies, across 21 countries, promote an even distribution of time devoted to child care by a mother and father. Interestingly, policies that were more generous to the mother actually created less gender equality, in that the women receive more incentive to take time off of work, therein decreasing the ease with which they could re-enter the workforce after giving birth because of the amount of time she is away from the workplace. With more generous family leave time, mothers end up working even less compared to fathers. What's more, there is also evidence that policies requiring fathers to take parental leave or "lose it" (i.e., not transfer it to the mother) increases gender equality.

Yet, a lack of family paid leave is also harmful. The United States is the only industrialized country to not offer paid leave when a child is born or adopted into a family. Although the United States does not currently provide paid leave, there is some protection of one's job if time is taken off work when a child is born or adopted, as well as due to the illness of an individual (or one of their family members). The Family and Medical Leave Act (FMLA) protects jobs up to 12 weeks for those employees who have been working for at least 1250 hours over the past year at an organization that has 50 or more employees. However, there are several limitations of the FMLA. For one, there is a large number of workers not covered—only 11 % of work establishments are eligible (Kelly 2008). In addition, those who are eligible also tend to have higher levels of education and income. Put another way, the poorest individuals and families have the least eligibility (Ray et al. 2009), yet these are the ones who need it the most. Finally, the lack of pay makes it hard to take time off. As a result, men are less likely to use FMLA, because they tend to be paid higher amounts than women, and people tend to take shorter leaves so as not to lose out on pay (Kelly 2008). Given that those who fall into low-income categories are in greater need of such a resource, it becomes clear that improvements are necessary. By comparison, Sweden provides 47 weeks of paid leave, the United Kingdom provides 31 weeks, Canada provides 28 weeks, Japan provides 26 weeks, and Italy provides 25 weeks of paid leave (Ray et al. 2009).

As of January 2014, there is a proposal in the United States Senate that would pass the Family and Medical Insurance Leave Act, otherwise known as the FAMILY Act. The FAMILY Act would allow both full-time and part-time employees, regardless of the size of their employer or tenure with their current employer, the opportunity to take partially paid leave in the event of pregnancy or childbirth, a personal serious health condition, or a serious health condition of a child, parent, spouse, or domestic partner, or for specific military leave purposes. Paid leave would be available for 12 weeks at 66 % of the average monthly income, with a cap of $ 1000 per week (Center for American Progress 2013). The ability to take paid leave from work would assist low-wage workers in managing health issues and would be particularly important for women, to whom the majority of caregiving responsibilities (not to mention childbirth medical needs) fall.

Policy makers, therefore, need to consider the information gained through research on the influence of work–family policies on those families they are intended to help. It would be advantageous for policy researchers and work–family researchers to work together to assess the intricate interactions that influence the success of such policies for individuals, organizations, and society, so that policy makers have the information that is necessary to help those who are most in need.

3.5 Conclusion

In sum, it becomes apparent that sex (the biological characteristics that make an individual male or female) and gender (the societal expectations of how women and men are to behave/stereotypes) are critical considerations when having conversations surrounding the experiences of low-income individuals and the work–family interface. Based on this review and integration of information on poverty, gender, and work–family experiences, we make several conclusions:

1. Women are more likely to fill lower-wage jobs, a result of sex segregation of jobs. One of the correlates of this sex segmentation of jobs is the fact that women are more likely to live at or below the poverty line.
2. These low-wage, secondary market sector jobs have more demands and fewer resources, including the ability to move into higher levels of the organizational hierarchy (that are also paid higher incomes), as well as resources that allow for the successful managing of family demands in conjunction with work demands.
3. The high level of demands and low amount of resources can create a higher probability of work–family conflict and lower levels of work–family enrichment.
4. This interaction of gender, poverty, and work–family interactions therein produce a greater likelihood of lower well-being and greater numbers of health symptoms for women compared to men when balancing work and family responsibilities in the context of poverty.

We see these interactions as a cycle wherein women and others in low-paying jobs have difficulties in managing the work–family interface that place them at greater risk for well-being and health-related problems, which hurts the quality of life for themselves and their families. As such, there is a systematic nature of poverty that includes feedback loops, with a myriad of predictors and outcomes. Work–family researchers have recently begun to incorporate a systems approach to understanding the work–family interface (e.g., Hammer and Zimmerman 2011), allowing for a more holistic evaluation of work and family systems. This approach incorporates the importance of reciprocal relationships, which clearly become important when poverty and gender are incorporated into the overall systemic nature of work and family domains.

To add to the understanding of the interactions among these systems, we encourage future research that examines how workplace demands and resources differentially impact work–family conflict, work–family enrichment, and subsequent work, family, health, and well-being outcomes for low-wage workers compared to the more traditionally-studied professional and managerial employees. In addition, a better picture of how policy change could improve the ability of low-wage employees, especially women and single mothers, to move out of poverty and into positions where their overall life quality can improve is warranted. We also recommend using a systems-based approach for modeling these variables and their dynamic, interrelated contexts and processes.

We have proposed a descriptive model (Fig. 3.1) to understand the part that poverty plays on the relationship between gender and work–family experiences. We see poverty as a moderator of this relationship, in that poverty differentially impacts women's work–family experiences compared to men's work–family experiences. This is especially important to consider given the societal role expectations that women are assumed responsible to fill. The restrictions poverty imposes on resources available to manage the work–family interface is pronounced among women in comparison to men. However, we also see poverty as part of the process that explains *how* sex impacts work–family experiences. Specifically, we see sex as a predictor of poverty, which in turn predicts work–family experiences. As such, we also view poverty as a mediating mechanism explaining how sex can predict work–family experiences. In sum, poverty creates a context for understanding these differences between men and women in work and family domains, and as a result, should be included in discussions of gender and work–family experiences.

References

Aryee, S., Srinivas, E. S., & Tan, H. H. (2005). Rhythms of life: Antecedents and outcomes of work–family balance in employed parents. *Journal of Applied Psychology, 90,* 132–146.

Batt, R., & Valcour, P. M. (2003). Human resources practices as predictors of work–family outcomes and employee turnover. *Industrial Relations: A Journal of Economy and Society, 42,* 189–220.

Bielby, D. D., & Bielby, W. T. (1988). She works hard for the money: Household responsibilities and the allocation of work effort. *American Journal of Sociology, 93,* 1031–1059.

Brady, D., & Kall, D. (2007). Nearly universal, but somewhat distinct: The feminization of poverty in affluent Western democracies, 1969–2000. *Social Science Research, 37,* 976–1007.

Bruck, C. S., Allen, T. D., & Spector, P. E. (2002). The relation between work–family conflict and job satisfaction: A finer-grained analysis. *Journal of Vocational Behavior, 60,* 336–353.

Budig, M. J., & Hodges, M. J. (2010). Differences in disadvantage: Variation in the motherhood penalty across white women's earnings distribution. *American Sociological Review, 75,* 705–728.

Burton, L. M., Lein, L., & Kolak, A. (2005). Health and mothers' employment in low-income families. In S. M. Bianchi, L. M. Casper, & R. B. King (Eds.), *Work, family, health, and well-being* (pp. 493–509). Mahwah: Lawrence Erlbaum.

Casper, L. M., McLanahan, S. S., & Garfinkel, I. (1994). The gender-poverty gap: What we can learn from other countries. *American Sociological Review, 59,* 5949–5605.

Center for American Progress. (2013). The FAMILY Act: Facts and frequently asked questions. http://www.americanprogress.org/wpcontent/uploads/2013/12/FamilyActFactsheet-FAQs1.pdf. Accessed Jan 2014.

Demerouti, E., Bakker, A. B., Nachreiner, F., & Schaufeli, W. B. (2001). The job demands-resources model of burnout. *Journal of Applied Psychology, 86,* 499–512.

Elmelech, Y., & Lu, H. (2004). Race, ethnicity, and the gender-poverty gap. *Social Science Research, 31,* 158–182.

Ford, M. T. (2011). Linking household income and work–family conflict: A moderated mediation study. *Stress and Health, 27,* 144–162.

Frone, M. R., Russell, M., & Cooper, M. L. (1997). Relation of work–family conflict to health outcomes: A four-year longitudinal study of employed parents. *Journal of Occupational and Organizational Psychology, 70,* 325–335.

Glauber, R. (2011). Limited access: Gender, occupational composition, and flexible work scheduling. *The Sociological Quarterly, 52,* 472–494.

Glauber, R. (2012). Women's work and working conditions: Are mother's compensated for lost wages? *Work and Occupations, 39,* 115–138.

Greenhaus, J. H., Collins, K. M., & Shaw, J. D. (2003). The relation between work–family balance and quality of life. *Journal of Vocational Behavior, 63,* 510–531.

Hammer, L. B., & Zimmerman, K. L. (2011). Quality of work life. In S. Zedeck (Ed.), *APA handbook of industrial and organizational psychology, Vol 3: Maintaining, expanding, and contracting the organization* (pp. 399–431). Washington, DC: American Psychological Association.

Hennessy, J. (2009). Morality and work–family conflict in the lives of poor and low-income women. *The Sociological Quarterly, 50,* 557–580.

Hoobler, J. M., Wayne, S. J., & Lemmon, G. (2009). Bosses' perceptions of family-work conflict and women's promotability: Glass ceiling effects. *Academy of Management Journal, 52,* 939–957.
Hoobler, J. M., Hu, J., & Wilson, M. (2010). Do workers who experience conflict between the work and family domains hit a "glass ceiling?": A meta-analytic examination. *Journal of Vocational Behavior, 77,* 481–494.
Karimi, L., Karimi, H., & Nouri, A. (2011). Predicting employees' well-being using work–family conflict and job strain models. *Stress and Health, 27,* 111–122.
Kelly, E. L. (2008). Work-family policies: The United States in international perspective. In M. Pitt-Catsouphes, E. E. Kossek, & S. Sweet (Eds.), *The work and family handbook: Multi-disciplinary perspectives and approaches* (pp. 99–123). Mahwah: Lawrence Erlbaum.
Kirchmeyer, C., & Cohen, A. (1999). Different strategies for managing the work non-work interface: A test for unique pathways to work outcomes. *Work & Stress, 13,* 59–73.
Kmec, J. A. (1995). Setting occupational sex segregation in motion: Demand-side explanations of sex traditional employment. *Work and Occupations, 32,* 322–354.
Kossek, E. E., & Ozeki, C. (1999). Bridging the work–family policy and productivity gap: A literature review. *Community, Work & Family, 2,* 7–32.
Kossek, E. E., Lautsch, B. A., & Eaton, S. C. (2006). Telecommuting, control, and boundary management: Correlates of policy use and practice, job control, and work–family effectiveness. *Journal of Vocational Behavior, 68,* 347–367.
Leana, C. R., Mittal, V., & Stiehl, E. (2012). Organizational behavior and the working poor. *Organization Science, 23,* 888–906.
Litchenwalter, S. (2005). Gender poverty disparity in US cities: Evidence exonerating female-headed families. *Journal of Sociology and Social Welfare, 32,* 75–96.
Misra, J., Moller, S., & Budig, M. J. (2007). Work-family policies and poverty for partnered and single women in Europe and North America. *Gender and Society, 21,* 804–143.
Misra, J., Moller, S., Strader, E., & Wemlinger, E. (2012). Family policies, employment and poverty among partnered and single mothers. *Research in Social Stratification and Mobility, 30,* 113–128.
National Women's Law Center (2012). *Poverty rates among women, men, and children, 2011, 2010, 2000.* http://www.nwlc.org/resource/summary-table-poverty-rates-among-women-men-and-children-2011-2010-2000. Accessed Dec 2013.
Odle-Dusseau, H. N., Britt, T. W., & Greene-Shortridge, T. M. (2012). Work resources as predictors of job attitudes and performance: The process of work–family enrichment. *Journal of Occupational Health Psychology, 17,* 28–40.
Odle-Dusseau, H. N., Herleman, H. A., Britt, T. W., Moore, D. D., Castro, C. A., & McGurk, D. (2013). Family-supportive work environments and psychological strain: A longitudinal test of two theories. *Journal of Occupational Health Psychology, 18,* 27–36.
Offer, S. (2012a). Barriers to social support among low-income mothers. *The International Journal of Sociology and Social Policy, 32,* 120–133.
Offer, S. (2012b). The burden of reciprocity: Processes of exclusion and withdrawal from personal networks among low-income families. *Current Sociology, 60,* 788–805.
Pearce, D. (1978). The feminization of poverty: Women, work, and welfare. *Urban and Social Change Review, 11,* 28–36.
Perry-Jenkins, M. (2005). Work in the working class: Challenges facing families. In S. M. Bianchi, L. M. Casper, & R. B. King (Eds.), *Work, family, health, and well-being* (pp. 453–472). Mahwah: Lawrence Erlbaum.
Powell, G. N. (2011). *Women and men in management* (4th ed.). Thousand Oaks: Sage.
Rapoport, R., Bailyn, L., Fletcher, J. K., & Pruitt, B. H. (2002). *Beyond work–family balance: Advancing gender equity and workplace performance.* San Francisco: Jossey-Bass.
Ray, R., Gornick, J. C., & Schmnitt, J. (2009). Parental leave policies in 21 countries: Assessing generosity and gender equality. *The Sloan Work and Family Research Network News, 11.*

Reid, L. W., & Rubin, B. A. (2003). Integrating economic dualism and labor maker segmentation: The effects of race, gender, and structural location on earnings, 1974–2000. *The Sociological Quarterly, 44,* 405–432.
Reskin, B. F., & Bielby, D. D. (2005). A sociological perspective on gender and career outcomes. *Journal of Economic Perspectives, 19,* 71–86.
Roberts, B., Povich, D., & Mather, M. (2012). The working poor families project: Policy Brief Winter 2012–2013. The Working Poor Families Project. www.workingpoorfamilies.org. http://www.workingpoorfamilies.org/wp-content/uploads/2013/01/Winter-2012_2013-WPFP-Data-Brief.pdf. Accessed Sept 2013.
Schieman, S., & Young, M. (2011). Economic hardship and family-to-work conflict: The importance of gender and work conditions. *Journal of Family and Economic Issues, 32,* 46–61.
Shaffer, M. A., Harrison, D. A., Gilley, K. M., & Luk, D. M. (2001). Struggling for balance amid turbulence on international assignments: Work-family conflict, support and commitment. *Journal of Management, 27,* 99–121.
Sinclair, R. R., Probst, T., Hammer, L. B., & Schaffer, M. M. (2013). Low income families and occupational health: Implications of economic stress for work–family conflict research and practice. In A. Antoniou & C. Cooper (Eds.), *The psychology of the recession on the workplace* (pp. 308–323). Cheltenham: Edward Elgar.
Thompson, C. Q., & Prottas, D. J. (2006). Relationships among organizational family support, job autonomy, perceived control, and employee well-being. *Journal of Occupational Health Psychology, 10,* 100–118.

Chapter 4
Exploring the Double Jeopardy Effect: The Importance of Gender *and* Race in Work–Family Research

Tonya K. Frevert, Satoris S. Culbertson, and Ann H. Huffman

4.1 Historical Background

The passage of the Civil Rights Act in 1964 created significant economic, political, and social changes within the USA. Title VII of this historic legislation changed the structure of the labor market in the United States by outlawing some forms of discrimination in the workplace, most notably (at least for discussion of work–life issues) in terms of gender and race. For example, the ratio of women to men in the workforce has moved to near equal numbers (Domenico and Jones 2006). As the USA has slowly implemented and adapted to these changes in workforce demographics, researchers have responded in kind, by examining how these changes differentially impact women versus men (e.g., England 2010; Kmec 2005; Padavic and Reskin 2002) and, in a separate but related research stream, how these changes differentially impact individuals from different racial/ethnic groups, such as blacks versus whites (e.g., Collins 1997; Pager et al. 2009) or blacks versus Latinos (e.g., Zamudio and Lichter 2008). While these separate streams of research certainly inform us, there is a pressing need to reframe research such that we categorize individuals according to their multiple identities (e.g., black women, Asian men, upperclass Hispanics) to allow for a better understanding of how experiences differ not only between groups (e.g., women vs. men) but also within groups (e.g., black

T. K. Frevert (✉)
Organizational Science PhD Program, University of North Carolina at Charlotte,
9201 University City Boulevard, Charlotte, NC 28223, USA
e-mail: tfrevert@uncc.edu

S. S. Culbertson
Department of Management, Kansas State University,
110 Calvin Hall, Manhattan, KS 66506, USA
e-mail: satoris@ksu.edu

A. H. Huffman
Departments of Psychology and Management, Northern Arizona University,
P.O. Box 15106, Flagstaff, AZ 86011, USA
e-mail: ann.huffman@nau.edu

M. J. Mills (ed.), *Gender and the Work-Family Experience*,
DOI 10.1007/978-3-319-08891-4_4

women vs. white women).[1] For example, whereby some have suggested that all women are already disadvantaged in the workplace (e.g., Hakim 2004), women of color are considered to be in "double jeopardy" for belonging to two disadvantaged status categories—gender and race (King 1988). As such, given their status, it is reasonable to suspect that the work–family needs, resources, and experiences of women of color may be significantly different from the professional white women who have been the primary source of data for work–family researchers. Thus, our goal in this chapter is to demonstrate why using a multiple identities approach is crucial to future work–family research.

4.2 Multiple Identities in Work–Family Research: The Intersection of Gender *and* Race

There appears to be a paucity of work–family research that examines the experiences of people of color, as the majority of research has been conducted on white employees who live in the USA (Casper et al. 2007). Furthermore, in studies directed at women, the emphasis has been on professional white women to the exclusion of women of color. Given the extant research combined with the beliefs espoused in the popular press that women are getting the short end of the work–family stick (so to speak), researchers have attempted to examine the needs of women in particular as they attempt to fit into a work structure that remains best suited for men (Sandler and Rao 2012). One emergent criticism of this research stream, however, is that the existing research has tended to emphasize work–family experiences of professional white women (typically in management positions; Bianchi and Milkie 2010; Blair-Loy 2003), while work–family experiences of women of color have been largely overlooked (for exceptions, see Glauber 2008; Glauber and Gozjolko 2011; Grzywacz et al. 2007; Han et al. 2008). The advancement of theoretical and empirical work–family research rests on developing a meaningful understanding of women of color's work–family experiences that are situated within the complex power relations affecting their daily lives. In the following section, we discuss the possible reasons for this oversight, both in the academic research and in the popular press.

Although all women are linked by their gender (or more specifically, their biological sex), race separates women of color from white women and thus their access to power, such that black women largely remain in the lowest-paid and lowest-status occupations (Branch 2011). Their position at the bottom of the labor market is one potential reason why women of color have been overlooked in work–family research. Holvino (2010) put forth that "women of color have always worked and been seen as workers" (i.e., throughout history as slaves, indentured servants, and domestic service workers) and "have been generally confined to secondary labor

[1] For a scholarly debate about why and how organizational scientists and practitioners should study workers' multiple identities, see Ruggs et al. (2013) and its twelve associated commentaries in *Industrial and Organizational Psychology: Perspectives on Science and Practice.*

markets and to positions at the bottom of the organizational hierarchy" (p. 252). Holvino further posits that during the early stages of the women's movement, the contentious division between the private and the public spheres primarily reflected the reality of white women. While white women desired for both the role of housewife or mother to be recognized as work and also for access to the paid workplace, women of color considered "being able to stay at home and being supported by a husband's paycheck…a luxury that only affluent white women have" (p. 252). In contrast to their white peers, women of color—traditionally confined to secondary labor markets and jobs at the bottom—desired better working conditions and more job opportunities. Arguably, all women continue to encounter the effects of sexism. The differences in the daily realities between black women and white women, however, reflect the privileges and deficits that stem not only from sexism but also from the simultaneous intersection with racism.

The omission of women of color has been reflected not only in scholarly research, but also within the contemporary popular press, where the ongoing debate of whether women can "have it all" still assumes that the question is most germane to professional white women. For example, while the 2013 bestselling book *Lean In* by Sheryl Sandberg (2013) was widely lauded as helpful career advice for women, dissenters criticized it for being applicable to only a very small percentage of the female workforce (Rottenberg 2013). Sandberg is a Harvard graduate who once worked as Chief of Staff to the US Secretary of the Treasury and has been Facebook's Chief Operating Officer since 2008 (CNBC.com 2012). Critics argue that, while she is certainly credentialed, Sandberg sits in an extremely high position of privilege that precludes her from grasping the day-to-day hurdles that the majority of women face in simply trying to survive in a rough economy (Dowd 2013) where choices and access are often limited. Books such as *Lean In* may help women who have fought their way into the C-suite (i.e., corporate officers and directors), but they do not address the needs and realities of women (regardless of race) working in retail/service/low-wage jobs that typically have low autonomy, low power, and few career ladders. Further, it assumes that all women have the freedom and resources to make choices as women in Sandberg's position do, when the reality for many women is a job that is not due to choice, but merely due to survival. That is not to say that the work–family experiences among all women (and for that matter men) do not share commonalities (e.g., needing time off from work to handle family matters), but the resources available to manage both are far from universal (e.g., actual time-off policies), and thus it behooves work–family researchers to investigate how and when these differences and similarities occur. Ultimately, such research should thus help inform organizations' work–family policies to fit the needs and realities of their workforces, at all levels of the hierarchy.

4.2.1 Gender in Work–Family Research

The role of gender in work–family research has dramatically changed over the years. Historically, within family settings, men were seen as the breadwinners whereas women were seen as the caretakers, responsible for fulfilling domestic duties (Diekman and Goodfriend 2006; Eagly et al. 2000). These beliefs about where men and women belong—men at work and women at home—persisted long after women joined the paid workforce en masse and began performing alongside their male counterparts. Indeed, whether it is a case of art imitating life or life imitating art, the 1983 comedy-drama film *Mr. Mom* was arguably successful because it depicted what was seen as a seemingly absurd situation at the time: A married man (portrayed by Michael Keaton) takes on the role of a stay-at-home dad while his wife (portrayed by Teri Garr) becomes the primary breadwinner.[2] Thirty years later, the demarcation line persists as men's and women's work and family roles remain relatively divided, particularly at home. Advertisements for cleaning products typically feature women (Lindner 2004) and qualitative research suggests that men who act as primary caregivers to their children are often viewed as an anomaly, despite the practice becoming increasingly common (Rochlen et al. 2008). However, there has been a slow shift away from this traditional framework in which men work outside the home while women work within it, toward a more contemporary one, in which men and women work outside of the home in approximately equal numbers (Friedman and Greenhaus 2000).

Despite the proportion of men and women in the workforce being relatively even in 2013, gender differences persist in terms of family responsibilities as well as perceptions of women who work. The playing field remains far from even, with research demonstrating that women, unlike their male counterparts, face several penalties in both domains. For example, within the workplace, women suffer lower wages compared to men, and remain underrepresented in managerial positions and, in particular, the C-suite (O'Neil et al. 2008). Women also appear to be penalized within the workplace for choices they make outside of the work domain, such as having children. Women with children often suffer a "motherhood penalty"[3] in the workplace whereby their careers stagnate, they are seen as less serious workers, and they are not promoted because people assume they prioritize family over the job, career, or firm (Budig and England 2001). Along with penalties in the workplace, women also face penalties at home. Although men have become more involved as caregivers, women are by and large still the ones that are primarily responsible for childcare (Bianchi et al. 2012), even when they are working outside of the home just as much as or more than their partners. As Duxbury

[2] Arguably, the plot device in this film was not only a man being a stay-at-home father or a woman being the primary breadwinner, but also from the difficulties that each faced in his/her new role, which speaks even more to prevailing social norms that these were not "typical" or "natural" roles for these individuals because of their gender. Further, the film presents the switch as forced: the husband is laid off and unable to find a new job, thus the wife dusts off her college degree and gets a job in advertising. At the film's end, he is called back to work and she happily quits her job, insinuating the role reversal was an anomaly and life has returned to "normal."

[3] The persistence of traditional gender norms is further demonstrated by the sharp contrast between the expectations of mothers at work and the expectations of fathers at work, as men appear to be a given a wage premium for fatherhood (Lundberg and Rose 2000, 2002). The "fatherhood premium," however, seems to advantage white and Latino males, but not necessarily black males (Glauber 2008).

and Higgins (1991) aptly noted over two decades ago, and which seems to hold true today, "…there have been very few changes in society's perception of gender-specific work- and family-role responsibilities over the past few decades," and that "…women have fewer options than men for achieving control over competing role demands" (p. 71).

The "gender perspective posits that caregiving responsibilities reflect cultural prescriptions about who *should* perform these tasks" (Maume 2011, p. 414; emphasis in original). For example, when a woman has a child, she is often expected by both her coworkers and her family and friends to reduce her work hours or quit her job, although this assumption is not made about men (Nsiah et al. 2013). In fact, even when women earn more than their husbands, they will often leave their job to care for their children (e.g., Blair-Loy 2003). Moreover, once a woman does leave the workplace for family reasons, research suggests that it is very difficult for her to regain her footing and pick up where she left off in her career (Budig and England 2001).

Of course, it is not just the academics who have noticed these gender discrepancies. In the popular press, a 2012 article in *The Atlantic* generated much controversy when its female author argued that women "cannot have it all"—career and family—given today's economic and social structures (see Slaughter 2012)[4] and must often choose one or the other (Hewlett 2002). Yet men do not face the dilemma of choosing between career or family—it is assumed they will have both. A 2001 survey of ultra-achieving career professionals (i.e., those earning more than $ 100,000) by economist Hewlett (2002) found that 49 % of the women were childless, contrasted with 19 % of the men. Although ambitious careers make high demands of all individuals pursuing them, men often do not have to make tradeoffs, as their likelihood of finding a spouse and having children increases as they become increasingly successful. The opposite is true for women and thus those pursuing careers often put off childbearing until later in life or drop out of the career track if they do have children[5]. It is clear that differences persist between men and women in terms of the work and family expectations that they encounter both in the labor market and in society-at-large.

4.2.2 Race in Work–Family Research

The role of race in work–family research has also been examined, but to a much lesser extent than gender. In 2000, Perry-Jenkins et al. (2000) compiled a review of work–family research conducted in the 1990s, noting that the focus was almost

[4] As of 2013, Slaughter's article is the most widely read piece in *The Atlantic's* history (Rottenberg 2013).

[5] Indeed, Hewlett once suggested that women should start having babies in their twenties or risk ending up being childless and sad (see *Creating a Life* 2003). Her controversial message was trumpeted by news media outlets as a dire warning to women to mind their biological clocks (St. John 2002), yet was criticized by the feminist community (Gilbert 2008), attributed to the "baby panic" narrative (Faludi 2007), and lampooned on *Saturday Night Live* (Hewlett 2009).

entirely placed on white families who were typically middle-class professionals. An updated review of work–family research conducted from 2000 to 2010 by Bianchi and Milkie (2010) noted that national changes in the economy and the demographic composition of the US population has driven an expansion in the scope of work–family research. For example, increased immigration from Latin America and Asia has led to increased research on families of color (e.g., Goldberg et al. 2012; Grzywacz et al. 2007; Olson et al. 2013; Roehling et al. 2005). While this expansion is most welcome, it still largely fails to address the experiences of the United States' historically oppressed and largest racial/ethnic minority: black Americans.

It is worth noting at this point that although we are attempting within this chapter to remedy some of the oversight in the work–family literature for not substantially addressing the needs of people of color, the scant research that does exist makes it difficult to paint a precise picture across all racial or ethnic groups (i.e., combining all people of color into a "nonwhite" category), let alone between them (i.e., comparing blacks to Asians to Hispanics/Latinos). Although we do highlight some work–family research studies representing both approaches, our primary frame is comparing and contrasting the experiences of black women to white women. We take this approach for two reasons: (1) although the work–family literature is lacking in its inclusion of all women of color, the parallel inequality literature from sociology does inform our understanding of the experiences of black women (but to the large exclusion of Hispanic/Latina women and Asian women) and (2) it has been hypothesized that *colonized* groups (i.e., in the US, blacks) experience greater prejudice and discrimination than *immigrant* groups (i.e., in the US, Asians and Hispanics/Latinos; Healey 2012). For example, Asian Americans who were schooled in the United States have recently shown an approximate parity in the labor market with whites (Sakamoto et al. 2009). However, while much more empirical research is needed to truly understand these differences, methodological considerations when employing a multiple identities approach pose some hurdles, given the variability that occurs within racial/ethnic groups (as we discuss later). Further, the United States' tumultuous history regarding race relations suggests that the "answers" are embedded within a network of complex relationships at the individual, familial, organizational, and larger social, political, or economic levels that will take some effort to unravel.

Structural inequalities in terms of race and gender stem from centuries ago, when white males colonized the New World and people of color and women had little to no rights. While there certainly have been some significant moves toward equality following the US Civil War and in the 150 years that subsequently followed, these old threads of race and gender inequality unfortunately persist, despite legislation and efforts otherwise. As history marches on, old patterns of discrimination are reinforced—often without our awareness—as they are so deeply embedded in our social, political, and economic structures. Complex power relations shape the experiences of people of color (Wight et al. 2013), as argued by contemporary scholars such as Patricia Hill Collins, Kimberlé Crenshaw, bell hooks, and Charles W. Mills. Because sexism and racism remain embedded in our social structures, those individuals who belong to a dominant social group (i.e., whites) have different experiences than those individuals who do not belong to a dominant social group (i.e., people of color). To a vast extent, work–family research has acknowledged the complex power relations of sexism by exploring how women manage the work–family interface[6], but at the same time has failed to acknowledge the complex power relations of racism.

Over the course of the last several decades since the passage of the Civil Rights Act, research has consistently demonstrated that women have faced penalties in both the work and home domains. In parallel to women's penalties, individuals in minority racial/ethnic groups have also been penalized in both the work and home domains. For example, upon comparing whites and blacks (without consideration of other racial minority groups for the sake of simplicity and brevity), black individuals have been, and continue to be, at a disadvantage within the workplace. An experimental study found that—all else being equal in terms of education and experience on job applicants' resumes—white applicants were twice as likely than black applicants to get a callback or job offer (Pager et al. 2009). This finding suggests that employers still discriminate against black workers in favor of white workers. Although many blacks have moved into management positions, they remain underrepresented at executive management levels (Collins 1997). Further, despite years of legislation and organizations' well-intentioned attempts to diversify their workforces, affirmative action policies and diversity training programs have been shown to be largely ineffective due to larger structural forces that reinforce discriminatory beliefs and attitudes (Kalev et al. 2006). For example, an individual manager or supervisor may want to promote a black employee, but unspoken barriers within some organizations (e.g., a black person has never been in a position of authority in that organization) prevent career advancement from occurring.

Along with workplace changes following the Civil Rights Act, the subsequent decades also saw shifts in family structures, such as the increased prevalence of single parents (McLanahan and Percheski 2008). Indeed, over half of today's children are projected to spend some time living with a single-parent family before the age of 18. What effect this will have on shaping their life chances is beginning to be explored by researchers, as family structure is argued to be a key link between inequality and intergenerational mobility. Although some previous research found that married black couples divide housework and paid work more equally than do married white and Latino couples (Glauber 2008), recent trends indicate that more black households are headed by women and that blacks have also seen a decline in marriage rates (Branch 2011). As such, increases in single motherhood are more prevalent among black women as compared to white women (McLanahan and Percheski 2008). Additionally, black women have lower education levels relative to white women and black women are overrepresented in low-wage occupations such as service work (e.g., home health aides)—in 2008, 25 % of black women held such jobs (Branch 2011). This overrepresentation is problematic, because individuals in service work (regardless of race and gender) face higher poverty levels. We must make clear, however, that we are not reporting these recent trends to deem single parenthood as "immoral"—rather, we report these recent trends to demonstrate that

[6] For a review on men and work–family research, see Chap. 2.

single parents are often penalized economically, particularly if the single parent is a woman of color. With fewer economic resources available, it stands to reason that single parents will face high levels of work–family conflict. Furthermore, for all individuals who live in precarious economic conditions, the stress of such daily living conditions (often correlated with poverty, crime, and substandard housing) translates into greater disparities in physical and mental health outcomes for those individuals (Jackson et al. 2010). Again, this suggests the potential for work–family conflict to be higher among single parents, especially for women of color.

As empirical research on the work–family experiences of blacks is scant, however, such conclusions are merely speculative and may not be empirically supported. For example, blacks may tap into noneconomic resources to buffer against these stressors, such as social support from extended-kin networks and the larger community (McLanahan and Percheski 2008). Until work–family research is extended beyond the experiences of professional white women, however, nuanced differences will remain unknown. As we have outlined above, gender inequality and racial inequality have been traditionally examined as *separate* complex power relations. In the past few decades, however, the recognition that individuals exist in the social structure in multiple categories that differentially affect their individual experiences (e.g., not just as women, but as white women or black women) has spurred researchers to study multiple identities through the *intersection* of gender and race.

4.3 The Consequences of Multiple Identities: The Double Jeopardy Effect

One particularly salient concept for work–family research is *the double jeopardy effect*, which occurs when race and gender intersect in ways that disadvantage individuals in the social structure (King 1988). For example, white men have historically held the most advantages in US society, seconded by black men and white women (often on parallel trajectories), with black women suffering the most disadvantages at the bottom (Stainback and Tomaskovic-Devey 2012). Since 1964, when institutionalized white male privilege began to be officially dismantled, gains in equal opportunity have spread to black men, white women, and black women. However, these gains have been uneven and inconsistent, tempered by varying trends and varying enforcement during each subsequent decade. For example, the strength of the civil rights movement in the 1960s yielded gains primarily for black men. When legal enforcement of Title VII began in earnest in the 1970s, both white women and black women made progress into better jobs. Indeed, as a negative response to affirmative action by some groups, black women were falsely accused of getting a "double advantage" at work, as they fulfilled both race and gender requirements for employers seeking to be compliant with the new laws (Sokoloff 1992). This advantage, however, was a myth. As the civil rights movement declined in the 1980s and corporate human resource practices grew in response to legal oversight, pressures on employers began to wane (Stainback and Tomaskovic-Devey 2012).

The women's movement was able to maintain pressure on employers until the 1990s, although white women were the primary beneficiaries. For example, although wage inequality between black women and white women had decreased in the 1970s, black women's wages lagged behind white women's wages by 14% by 1991 (Branch 2011). Additionally, by 1999, the unemployment rate for black women was double that of white women.

Stainback and Tomaskovic-Devey (2012) argue that without pressures from both the government and affected constituencies today, many organizations are slipping back toward resegregation in terms of race and gender (see also Sokoloff 1992). If this regressive trend persists, black women, holding minority status for both race and gender—*double jeopardy*—are thus most at risk for deleterious treatment within the workforce. For example, black women experience more overall harassment in the workplace than white women (Berdahl and Moore 2006). Overall, research supports the hypothesis that black women are most disadvantaged in the workplace, but how that plays out between the work–family domains remains unclear. As we discuss below, the scant work–family research including women of color has yielded inconsistent findings.

4.4 Work–Family Research Including Gender and Race

Studies considering both gender and race are infrequent in work–family research, although the few studies that have done so categorized participants differently such that patterns are hard to discern. For example, in a study using employed women (those working at least 30 hours per week) from a variety of occupations and income ranges, Bernas and Major (2000) found that women of color (defined as nonwhite) experienced significantly less work-to-family conflict and less job stress compared to the women in their sample who were white. Such findings are contradictory to the expectations posited by the double jeopardy effect, but may be due to grouping all women of color into a nonwhite group, as findings may be different when people of color are distinguished between racial/ethnic groups. Further, Bernas and Major make a point of mentioning that they "found recruiting a sufficient number of working women with families to be quite challenging and, as a result, relied on several convenient sources" (pp. 175–176). We further address methodological considerations and limitations below.

Other studies, however, have distinguished between racial/ethnic groups. For example, Glauber (2008) posits that black women face a second penalty at work beyond the motherhood penalty that all women face. Citing an earlier study by Kennelly (1999)—which found that while employers view *all* women workers as mothers and less capable in their jobs, they also view *all* black women as single mothers—Glauber argues that black women are thus perceived as having children out of wedlock, which exacerbates the motherhood penalty. Yes, recent data indicate that more black women are single mothers than white women (Branch 2011; McLanahan and Percheski 2008), but anti-discrimination laws prohibit employers from making decisions rooted in both sex-based and race-based stereotyping (Equal Employment Opportunity Commission 2011). As men often get a double bonus for both marriage and fatherhood in the workplace, this benefit stands in stark contrast to black women who are often penalized in the workplace not only for motherhood, but also for a perceived lack of marriage. This unequal treatment provides further evidence of the double jeopardy effect for black women.

Compared to their white counterparts, however, African American women who are married and have children are more likely to be employed (Han et al. 2008). Recent research conducted by Glauber and Gozjolko (2011) suggests that wives of white men who hold traditional views (e.g., "a woman's place is in the home") are less likely to work outside of the home compared to wives of white men who hold egalitarian views. In contrast, wives of African American men are equally likely to work outside of the home, regardless of their husbands' beliefs about whether this is acceptable or not. One would imagine that tension would arise for women who are employed and whose husbands are against this. If this is indeed the case, it would not be surprising to discover that African American women experience greater levels of work–family conflict than do white women.

Reflecting Bianchi and Milkie's (2010) earlier finding that since 2000, work–family research has responded to rising immigration rates from Asia and Latin America, studies have started to reflect this growth among their samples. For example, Grzywacz et al. (2007) quantitatively and qualitatively examined work–family conflict and health experiences of immigrant Latino men and Latina women, and found that work–family conflict was greater for the women than it was for the men. As the authors noted, "women described clear examples of work-to-family conflict in their daily life, whereas men saw little connection between their work and their family" (p. 1125). Grzywacz et al., however, did not examine any non-Latino/a individuals in their study. In a study that did contrast work–family conflict between Hispanic Americans and whites, Hispanic individuals reported more strain-based family interference with work (Olson et al. 2013). In another study that included whites, blacks, and Hispanics, larger gender differences in family-to-work and work-to-family spillover were found among Hispanics than among whites or blacks (Roehling et al. 2005).

Due to the limited research on the intersection of gender and race in work–family research, we now turn to recent labor force data to highlight larger trends in the differences between white women and black women that may inform future work–family research.

4.4.1 Labor Force Characteristics of White and Black Women

Progress toward race and gender equality in the workplace is best advanced by increasing the number of women and people of color in management and professional occupations (Stainback and Tomaskovic-Devey 2012). When management and professional positions become increasingly diverse, the odds increase that women and people of color in these positions will help "pull-up" other women and people of color into these positions. If women and people of color remain underrepresented in these positions, however, opportunities for advancement stall and patterns of work inequality perpetuate; gains are made, but at a very slow pace. Furthermore, these gains are made disproportionately in terms of race. While women are advancing into management and executive positions, white women are gaining over black women. While women's wages are getting closer to those of men, white women are gaining over black women. While women are participating in the labor force at an increasing rate, white women are gaining over black women.

Recent labor force data from the US Bureau of Labor Statistics (BLS 2011) supports this state of affairs. Among white women, 42 % were employed in management, professional, and related occupations—the highest paying major job category—compared to 34 % of black women. This difference is very important to work–family research, as the emphasis on management/professional participants leads to more white women participating in said research, thus reflecting their experiences more than others. Ideally, work–family research should reflect the experiences of all workers at all levels of the labor market, which would certainly include those in management/professional occupations. If the default remains set to management/professionals occupations, however, we are missing the needs of workers in other jobs and occupations who have work–family issues to tackle too. For example, as black women are more likely than white women to work in service occupations (28.3% vs. 20.1 %), it is crucial that we do not leave service workers out of work–family research. We recognize, however, that this limitation is partly due to access to and representation of people of color across the labor force, as discussed above. However, researchers can overcome this limitation by examining more occupational and industrial sectors so as to include those on the fringes and lower tiers of the labor market.

The need for work–family research to incorporate racial diversity is also reflected in labor force data about families and mothers (BLS 2011), as previously discussed. "In 2010, nearly one-half (45 %) of black families were maintained by women without a spouse present" (p. 2), compared to about 15 % of white women. Black women are three times as likely as white women to be "going it alone." If we consider Hobfoll's conservation of resources theory (1989) as it pertains to work–family research in terms of resource allocation, black women are thus at a greater disadvantage than white women in terms of resources and support, often lacking a second income and emotional support from a partner.

Although women as a group overall earn less than men, full-time black female employees typically earn about 85 % of what their full-time white female counterparts earn (BLS 2011). The 2008 recession also hit black women harder than white women, as labor force participation for white women fell 2.3 % from 2008 to 2010 (56.3%–54.0%), but fell 4.1 % for black women (55.8%–51.7%) during the same time period. Further, "among mothers with children under 18, black mothers are more likely to be in the labor force than white mothers" (75 % vs. 71 %; p. 2). For households with children under six years old—arguably when demands for flexible work–family policies are at their highest—black mothers are more likely to be in the labor force than white mothers (70 % vs. 63 %). In today's global 24/7 economy where the boundary between work and home is diminishing, all employees need tools, skills, and resources to successfully manage their work and personal lives. Since work–family research helps inform the policies that organizations implement for their employees' benefit, knowing the needs of the factory worker on the line are just as important as knowing the call center manager's needs. If we do not know how those needs differ—not only within the organization but also across occupations/industries/locations—and how those needs are compounded by multiple identities that differentially locate individuals within the overarching social structure, then we are only serving a limited subset of the population. Some might argue that policies implemented in one sector will trickle down to another, but only empirical research can answer our questions and tell us if those needs have been met or are yet to be met.

Thus far, we have contrasted the similarities and differences between white women and women of color in terms of their work and family experiences. Next, we address some of the methodological considerations and limitations that arise with intersectional models.

4.5 Methodological Considerations

Because the racial divide in the United States has historically fallen along a black-white dichotomy, there is scant social science research that explicitly includes other racial/ethnic groups, such as Hispanics/Latinos, Asians, or Native Americans. These groups are frequently lumped together with blacks into a "nonwhite" category and findings generalized to minorities as a whole (Ruggs et al. 2013). While this approach is an attempt to include other racial/ethnic groups in research, it fails to not only consider the differences between these racial/ethnic groups (e.g., social class, education, family norms), but also the differences within the various racial/ethnic groups (e.g., outcomes for light-skinned blacks vs. dark-skinned blacks; Marira and Mitra 2013). That said, it is important to remember that researchers rarely have free, easy, and open access to whatever data they desire. As Thompson et al. (2013) point out, researchers are often limited by (1) numerical representation of minority groups, such as Native Americans comprising 1.7 % of the general population and (2) methodological issues that may violate assumptions of sampling, power, and generalizability in such targeted approaches. Nevertheless, given that the overall population of people of color in the United States is projected to become the numerical majority of the total US population by 2043 (Ortman 2013), these limitations should start to ease. Further, as scholarly research usually reflects the larger culture, a greater number of studies will likely give way to more diverse participants in time. If work–family researchers want to be ahead of the curve and not stuck in the past or scrambling to catch up, however, it is incumbent upon us to remedy this oversight sooner rather than later.

A second methodological consideration for intersectional research is that it should be employed as a multiplicative model, not an additive one. One of the frequent assumptions of measurement in data analyses is that social identities are additive (e.g., black + woman) versus intersectional (e.g., black woman; Bowleg 2008). An additive approach, however, contradicts the central tenet of intersectionality: Social identities and inequality are interdependent for groups such as black women, not mutually exclusive. They do not act independently (i.e., one is never just a person of color without also being of one sex or the other). Intersectionality theory requires that we conceptualize social categories in terms of the stratification that arises through the practices of individuals, institutions, and cultures rather than merely as individual characteristics (Cole 2008). For example, the life experiences of a black woman are a product of the intersection of sexism with racism such that her simultaneous social identity both as a woman and as a person of color marginalizes her in both socially structured categories (Crenshaw 1991).

Moreover, as "psychologists aim to simplify models for parsimony, either by omitting variables or by statistically controlling for membership in categories other than the one of interest" (Cole 2009, p. 170), work–family researchers should move forward by considering "the meaning and consequences of social categories" (p. 176). Cole (2009) urges researchers to ask three pertinent questions during the research process (*Who is included within this category?*, *What role does inequality play?*, and *Where are the similarities?*), so that we move away from empirical models in which self-evident demographic variables shape how participants are categorized and thus move toward empirical models that employ intersectional frameworks. Intersectional frameworks may increase our understanding of the complex, intertwined relationships that differentially locate individuals within the overarching social structure. That is not to say that work–family researchers must do away with all methodological practices and turn all of their focus onto underrepresented groups. Rather, work–family researchers can use an intersectional framework

> to look for causes of human behavior both upstream and downstream, to notice and hypothesize about the multiple paths that may lead individuals to the same or similar outcomes, and to understand the ways that different social categories depend on each other for meaning and, thus, mutually construct one another and work together to shape outcomes. (Cole 2009, p. 179)

4.6 Broader Impacts and Future Research

Although overt prejudice and discrimination have been substantially tempered over the past 50 years, covert prejudice and discrimination persist. For example, women and people of color still face significant barriers to getting a seat at the boardroom table, and those barriers are fortified by inequalities of place, education, and opportunity. As these inequalities come to a head, however, they are on a collision course with changing definitions of family as well as changing roles and role expectations that men and women have traditionally held. The en masse entry of women into the workforce in the 1960s and 1970s coincided with major shifts in work arrangements in the post-Fordist era (e.g., the disappearance of career ladders; Rubin 1995). As men and women negotiated new institutional arrangements in both the work domain and the family domain, their race/ethnicity rode along with their gender. The long crusade toward workplace equality cannot be achieved with a sole gender lens or a sole racial/ethnic lens—a proper set of glasses includes both lenses.

To that end, it behooves researchers to expand their populations of study so that the larger conversation taking place among the popular press, public policy makers, and business leaders is not exclusionary. As such, another factor for consideration is differences by occupational and industrial sector. Not only do different occupations have their own unique stressors, but they are also gendered and/or racialized. For example, women of color account for an above-average percentage of representation in the field of nursing aides (Alonso-Villar and del Rio 2013). Research has shown that the job of nursing aide—a job that does not require a college degree—has many characteristics that can lead to high stress. Nursing aides primarily focus on caregiving, are more likely to have shift work, and have lower than average pay. But this pattern also exists for jobs that require college degrees. The field of social work, for example, also has a disproportionate number of employees who are women of color. Similar to nursing aides, social work is also considered a high stress job (Wooten et al. 2011). Work–family research has consistently shown that high demand and low resource jobs are especially susceptible to work–family stress, and thus simply examining different occupations may be one way to diversify work–family research.

Differences in family characteristics should also be considered. The age of becoming a mother for women of color is younger than other women. A report by the Centers for Disease Control and Prevention (2013) showed that women of color have their first child, on average, at the age of 22.7, compared to white women at the age of 26.0. Research has suggested that this age difference could have several implications. Starting a family at a younger age could introduce some additional stressors for women of color. For example, younger parents are likely to be less financially secure and less mature to handle this responsibility. On the other hand, research has shown that the work–family interface can vary over the life course (Huffman et al. 2013), with the least work–family stressors occurring early in life and then again late in life. This inverted u-shaped curve could mean that individuals who have children early might have fewer stressors since they are not also burdened with extensive job demands. Whatever the case, future research should examine the implications of younger parenting for women of color and their associated work–family stressors.

We suggested earlier that the numerical representation of people of color makes it methodologically more challenging to assess work–family issues based on both gender and race/ethnicity. To overcome these challenges, the work–family community needs to find strategies that will allow these groups to be included in work–family research. For example, qualitative methodologies allow us "to generate new conceptualizations and interpretations of culture that will enable us to make sense of increasingly complex cultural phenomena" (Birkinshaw et al. 2011, p. 574), an approach that seems particularly suited to the complexity of intersectional research. Additionally, archival data sets exist (e.g., *General Social Survey, National Study of the Changing Workforce, Midlife Development in the United States, Panel Study of*

Income Dynamics) that tap into work–family issues and provide demographic information that would allow researchers to answer questions related to the intersection of gender and race. These extensive data sets may provide work–family researchers with the necessary respondents and variables to answer research questions specific to women of color.

Work–family researchers have used different theories to describe race and/or gender differences in work–family experiences (e.g., stress resource perspective, organizational leadership theory; Bernas and Major 2000). Work–family researchers need to continue to build on these different theories to develop a comprehensive model of how the characteristics associated with being a woman of color affect the work–life interface. For example, the demands-resource paradigm has become very relevant in trying to explain work and family experiences. The job demands–resources model (Bakker and Demerouti 2007) suggests that every occupation has its own specific risk factors and resources that are associated with the job, and when the worker experiences high risks/demands and low resources, the individual is likely to experience negative outcomes. Bakker and Demerouti (2007) suggest that this comprehensive model could be applied to various occupational settings. We extend this idea and suggest that this could also be applied to individuals with different personal characteristics. For example, women of color might experience additional demands due to discrimination they endure at work compared to white males (Sokoloff 1992), and these demands that women of color experience may result in increased distress. Although this is just one example of using one theory, we propose that there are others across the social sciences that can provide researchers with a more comprehensive understanding of the workplace experiences of women of color.

Although our chapter focuses on the two minority characteristics of gender and race/ethnicity (specifically women of color), we should also note that there are many other minority characteristics that could further affect women of color. For example, women of color who are lesbian, gay, bisexual, or transgender (LGBT) experience additional stressors. Potentially, a lesbian woman of color who has children could face "quadruple jeopardy" since she is dealing with four minority status characteristics (i.e., gender, race/ethnicity, sexual orientation, and lesbian parent) that not only carry each of their own disadvantages, but also intersect to compound those disadvantages (Huffman et al. 2012).

4.7 Conclusion

The negotiation between work and family is not a woman's problem; it is a problem that belongs to all of us, as we all interact in the larger social structure that encompasses our work days, our home lives, and the interface between the two. An individual's success in negotiating the increasingly fuzzy work–family boundary depends upon not only her gender, but also upon her race/ethnicity. Work–family researchers have done a commendable job helping organizations understand why it is in their best interest to offer policies that help workers manage their work and home lives. However, because of structural inequalities that keep women of color out of management/professional positions, not everyone has benefitted from these efforts. As such, if work–family researchers can inform the leaders of work organizations as well as public policy makers about what needs to be done to eradicate these inequalities, then we must ensure that work–family research reflects the experiences of everyone.

References

Alonso-Villar, O., & del Rio, C. (2013). *The occupational segregation of black women in the United States: A look at its evolution from 1940 to 2010*. Number 304, Working Papers, ECINEQ, Society for the Study of Economic Inequality.

Bakker, A., B., & Demerouti, E. (2007). The job demands-resources model: State of the art. *Journal of Managerial Psychology, 22,* 309–328.

Berdahl, J. L., & Moore, C. (2006). Workplace harassment: Double jeopardy for minority women. *Journal of Applied Psychology, 91,* 426–436.

Bernas, K. H., & Major, D. A. (2000). Contributors to stress resistance: Testing a model of women's work–family conflict. *Psychology of Women Quarterly, 24,* 170–178.

Bianchi, S. M., & Milkie, M. A. (2010). Work and family research in the first decade of the twentyfirst century. *Journal of Marriage and Family, 72,* 705–725.

Bianchi, S. M., Sayer, L. C., Milkie, M. A., & Robinson, J. P. (2012). Housework: Who did, does or will do it, and how much does it matter? *Social Forces, 91,* 55–63.

Birkinshaw, J., Brannen, M. Y., & Tung, R. L. (2011). From a distance and generalizable to up close and grounded: Reclaiming a place for qualitative methods in international business research. *Journal of International Business Studies, 42,* 573–581.

Blair-Loy, M. (2003). *Competing devotions: Career and family among women executives*. Cambridge: Harvard University Press.

Bowleg, L. (2008). When black + lesbian + woman ≠ black lesbian women: The methodological challenges of qualitative and quantitative intersectionality research. *Sex Roles, 59,* 312–325.

Branch, E. H. (2011). *Opportunity denied: Limiting black women to devalued work*. New Brunswick: Rutgers University Press.

Budig, M. J., & England, P. (2001). The wage penalty for motherhood. *American Sociological Review, 66,* 204–225.

Bureau of Labor Statistics. (Aug 2011). *Labor force characteristics by race and ethnicity, 2010*. Report 1032. http://www.bls.gov/cps/cpsrace2010.pdf. Accessed 25 Sep 2013.

Casper, W. J., Eby, L. T., Bordeaux, C., Lockwood, A., & Lambert, D. (2007). A review of research methods in IO/OB work–family research. *Journal of Applied Psychology, 92,* 28–45.

Centers for Disease Control and Prevention. (21 Nov 2013). *Births and natality*. http://www.cdc.gov/nchs/fastats/births.htm. Accessed 18 Jan 2014.

CNBC.com. (22 May 2012). *Sheryl Sandberg: Facebook IPO*. http://www.cnbc.com/id/47386998.

Cole, E. R. (2008). Coalitions as a model for intersectionality: From practice to theory. *Sex Roles, 59,* 443–453. Accessed 9 Jan 2014.

Cole, E. R. (2009). Intersectionality and research in psychology. *American Psychologist, 64,* 170–180.

Collins, S. M. (1997). Black mobility in white corporations: Up the corporate ladder but out on a limb. *Social Problems, 44,* 55–67.

Crenshaw, K. W. (1991). Mapping the margins: Intersectionality, identity politics, and violence against women of color. *Stanford Law Review, 43,* 1241–1299.

Diekman, A. B., & Goodfriend, W. (2006). Rolling with the changes: A role congruity perspective on gender norms. *Psychology of Women Quarterly, 30,* 369–383.
Domenico, D. M., & Jones, K. H. (2006). Career aspirations of women in the twentieth century. *Journal of Career and Technical Education, 22,* 1–7.
Dowd, M. (23 Feb 2013). Pompom girl for feminism. *The New York Times*. http://www.nytimes.com/2013/02/24/opinion/sunday/dowd-pompom-girl-for-feminism.html?_r=2&.
Duxbury, L. E., & Higgins, C. A. (1991). Gender differences in work–family conflict. *Journal of Applied Psychology, 76,* 60–74.
Eagly, A. H., Wood, W., & Diekman, A. (2000). Social role theory of sex differences and similarities: A current appraisal. In T. Eckes & H. M. Trautner (Eds.), *The developmental social psychology of gender* (pp. 123–174). Mahwah: Erlbaum.
England, P. (2010). The gender revolution: Uneven and stalled. *Gender & Society, 24,* 149–166.
Equal Employment Opportunity Commission. (8 Feb 2011). Enforcement guidance: Unlawful disparate treatment of workers with caregiving responsibilities. http://www.eeoc.gov/policy/docs/caregiving.html.
Faludi, S. (2007). *The terror dream: Fear and fantasy in post-9/11 America*. New York: Metropolitan Books.
Friedman, S. D., & Greenhaus, J. H. (2000). *Work and family-allies or enemies?* New York: Oxford University Press.
Gilbert, N. (2008). *A mother's work: How feminism, the market, and policy shape family life*. New Haven: Yale University Press.
Glauber, R. (2008). Race and gender in families and at work: The fatherhood wage premium. *Gender and Society, 22,* 8–30.
Glauber, R., & Gozjolko, K. L. (2011). Do traditional fathers always work more? Gender ideology, race, and parenthood. *Journal of Marriage and Family, 73,* 1133–1148.
Goldberg, W. A., Kelly, E., Matthews, N. L., Kang, H., Li, W., & Sumaroka, M. (2012). The more things change, the more they stay the same: Gender, culture, and college students' views about work and family. *Journal of Social Issues, 68,* 814–837.
Grzywacz, J. G., Arcury, T. A., Marín, A., Carrillo, L., Burke, B., Coates, M. L., et al. (2007). Work-family conflict: Experiences and health implications among immigrant Latinos. *Journal of Applied Psychology, 92,* 1119–1130.
Hakim, C. (2004). *Key issues in women's work: Female diversity and the polarisation of women's employment*. London: The Glass House.
Han, W. J., Ruhm, C. J., Waldfogel, J., & Washbrook, E. (2008). The timing of mother's employment after childbirth. *Monthly Labor Review, 131,* 15–27.
Healey, J. F. (2012). *Race, ethnicity, gender, and class: The sociology of group conflict and change*. Thousand Oaks: Sage.
Hewlett, S. A. (April 2002). Executive women and the myth of having it all. *Harvard Business Review*, Reprint R0204E, 1–11.
Hewlett, S. A. (2003). *Creating a life*. New York: Hyperion.
Hewlett, S. A. (2009). *Top talent: Keeping performance up when business is down*. Cambridge: Harvard Business Press.
Hobfoll, S. E. (1989). Conservation of resources. *American Psychologist, 44,* 513–524.
Holvino, E. (2010). Intersections: The simultaneity of race, gender and class in organization studies. *Gender, Work & Organization, 17,* 248–277.
Huffman, A. H., Culbertson, S. S., Henning, J., & Goh, A. (2013). Work-family conflict across the lifespan. *Journal of Managerial Psychology, 28, 761–780.*
Huffman, A. H., King, E., & Goldberg, A. E. (2012). Valuing lesbian and gay parenting in the workplace. In M. Paludi (Ed.), *Managing diversity in today's workplace* (pp. 163–185). Westport: Praeger.
Jackson, J. S., Knight, K. M., & Rafferty, J. A. (2010). Race and unhealthy behaviors: Chronic stress, the HPA axis, and physical and mental health disparities over the life course. *American Journal of Public Health, 100,* 933–939.

Kalev, A., Dobbin, F., & Kelly, E. (2006). Best practices or best guesses? Assessing the efficacy of corporate affirmative action and diversity policies. *American Sociological Review, 71,* 589–617.
Kennelly, I. (1999). "That single-mother element": How employers typify Black women. *Gender & Society, 13,* 168–192.
King, D. K. (1988). Multiple jeopardy, multiple consciousness: The context of black feminist ideology. *Signs, 14,* 42–72.
Kmec, J. (2005). Setting occupational sex segregation in motion. *Work and Occupations, 32,* 322–354.
Lindner, K. (2004). Images of women in general interest and fashion magazine advertisements from 1955 to 2002. *Sex Roles, 51,* 409–421.
Lundberg, S., & Rose, E. (2000). Parenthood and the earnings of married men and women. *Labour Economics, 7,* 689–710.
Lundberg, S., & Rose, E. (2002). The effects of sons and daughters on men's labor supply and wages. *Review of Economics and Statistics, 84,* 251–268.
Marira, T. D., & Mitra, P. (2013). Colorism: Ubiquitous yet understudied. *Industrial and Organizational Psychology: Perspectives on Science and Practice, 6,* 103–107.
Maume, D. J. (2011). Reconsidering the temporal increase in fathers' time with children. *Journal of Family and Economic Issues, 32,* 411–423.
McLanahan, S., & Percheski, C. (2008). Family structure and the reproduction of inequalities. *Annual Review of Sociology, 34,* 257–276.
Nsiah, C., DeBeaumont, R., & Ryerson, A. (2013). Motherhood and earnings: Wage variability by major occupational category and earnings level. *Journal of Family and Economic Issues, 34,* 224–234.
Olson, K. J., Huffman, A. H., Leiva, P. I., & Culbertson, S. S. (2013). Acculturation and individualism as predictors of work–family conflict in a diverse workforce. *Human Resource Management, 52,* 741–769.
O'Neil, D. A., Hopkins, M. M., & Bilimoria, D. (2008). Women's careers at the start of the twentyfirst century: Patterns and paradoxes. *Journal of Business Ethics, 80,* 727–743.
Ortman, J. M. (7 Feb 2013). *U.S. population projections: 2012 to 2060.* U.S. Census Bureau presentation for the Federal Forecasters Consortium Brown Bag Seminar Series on Forecasting at George Washington University, Washington, D.C.
Padavic, I., & Reskin, B. (2002). *Women and men at work.* Thousand Oaks: Pine Forge.
Pager, D., Western, B., & Bonikowski, B. (2009). Discrimination in a low-wage labor market: A field experiment. *American Sociological Review, 74,* 777–799.
Perry-Jenkins, Repetti, R. L., & Crouter, A. C. (2000). Work and family in the 1990s. *Journal of Marriage and the Family, 62,* 981–998.
Rochlen, A. B., Suizzo, M., McKelley, R. A., & Scaringi, V. (2008). "I'm just providing for my family": A qualitative study of stay-at-home fathers. *Psychology of Men & Masculinity, 9,* 193–206.
Roehling, P. V., Jarvis, L. H., & Swope, H. E. (2005). Variations in negative work–family spillover among White, Black, and Hispanic American men and women: Does ethnicity matter? *Journal of Family Issues, 26,* 840–865.
Rottenberg, C. (2013). The rise of neoliberal feminism. *Cultural Studies, 28,* 418–437.
Rubin, B. A. (1995). *Shifts in the social contract.* Thousand Oaks: Pine Forge.
Ruggs, E. N., Hebl, M. R., Law, C., Cox, C. B., Roehling, M. V., Wiener, R. L., et al. (2013). Gone fishing: I-O psychologists' missed opportunities to understand marginalized employees' experiences with discrimination. *Industrial and Organizational Psychology: Perspectives on Science and Practice, 6,* 39–60.
Sakamoto, A., Goyette, K. A., & Kim, C. H. (2009). Socioeconomic attainments of Asian Americans. *Annual Review of Sociology, 35,* 255–276.
Sandberg, S. (2013). *Lean in: Women, work, and the will to lead.* New York: Knopf.
Sandler, J., & Rao, A. (2012). The elephant in the room and the dragons at the gate: Strategising for gender equality in the twentyfirst century. *Gender & Development, 20,* 547–562.

Slaughter, A. (July/Aug 2012). Why women still can't have it all. *The Atlantic*. http://www.theatlantic.com/magazine/archive/2012/07/why-women-still-cant-have-it-all/309020/. Accessed 25 Sep 2013.
Sokoloff, N. J. (1992). *Black women and white women in the professions*. New York: Routledge.
John, S. W. (20 May 2002). The talk of the book world still can't sell. *The New York Times*. http://www.nytimes.com/2002/05/20/us/the-talk-of-the-book-world-still-can-t-sell.html?pagewanted=all&src=pm.
Stainback, K., & Tomaskovic-Devey, D. (2012). *Documenting desegregation: Racial and gender segregation in private-sector employment since the Civil Rights Act*. New York: Sage.
Thompson, R., Bergman, M., Culbertson, S. S., & Huffman, A. H. (2013). Yes, we're fishing-in rough waters for hard-to-find fish. *Industrial and Organizational Psychology: Perspectives on Science and Practice, 6,* 61–65.
Wight, V. R., Bianchi, S. M., & Hunt, B. R. (2013). Explaining racial/ethnic variation in partnered women's and men's housework: Does one size fit all? *Journal of Family Issues, 34,* 394–427.
Wooten, N. R., Kim, H., & Fakunmoju, S. B. (2011). Occupational stress in social work practice. In J. Langan-Fox & C. L. Cooper (Eds.), *New horizons in management. Handbook of stress in the occupations* (pp. 71–87). Northampton: Edward Elgar.
Zamudio, M. M., & Lichter, M. I. (2008). Bad attitudes and good soldiers: Soft skills as a code for tractability in the hiring of immigrant Latina/os over native Blacks in the hotel industry. *Social Problems, 55,* 573–589.

Chapter 5
Challenging Heteronormative and Gendered Assumptions in Work–Family Research: An Examination of LGB Identity-Based Work–Family Conflict

Katina B. Sawyer, Christian N. Thoroughgood, and Jeanette N. Cleveland

5.1 Introduction

A vast body of research on work–family conflict (WFC) exists across a variety of disciplines, with studies accumulating rapidly since the formalized inception of the term in 1985. WFC refers to a form of interrole conflict in which role-related pressures from the work and family domains are incompatible in some respect - that is, participation in the work role is made more difficult by virtue of participation in the family role and vice versa (Greenhaus and Beutell 1985). However, despite many important contributions made by scholars over time, studies of WFC continue to suffer from certain heteronormative assumptions that organize, make coherent, and privilege heterosexuality by building it into the fabric of organizational cultures and structures (Berlant and Warner 1998). This chapter seeks to highlight how these assumptions may inform our conceptualization of the family as a unit of study, which constrains the extent to which we capture the experiences of WFC for lesbian, gay, and bisexual (LGB) individuals. Specifically, we suggest that WFC may be experienced differently for LGB employees due to the exclusion of LGB families within traditional conceptualizations of the family structure.

By expanding our definition of the family, and by implication, WFC, more inclusive measures that are less susceptible to heterosexual bias are made possible. In

K. B. Sawyer (✉)
Department of Psychology, Villanova University, St. Mary's Hall, Suite 119, 800 Lancaster Avenue, Villanova, PA 19085, USA
e-mail: katina.sawyer@villanova.edu

C. N. Thoroughgood
Department of Management and Organizational Development, Northeastern University, 360 Huntingdon Avenue, 112 Hayden Hall, Boston, MA 02115, USA
e-mail: c.thoroughgood@neu.edu

J. N. Cleveland
Department of Psychology, Colorado State University, 228 Behavioral Sciences Building, 1876 Campus Delivery, Fort Collins, CO 80523, USA
e-mail: jeanette.cleveland@colostate.edu

M. J. Mills (ed.), *Gender and the Work-Family Experience*,
DOI 10.1007/978-3-319-08891-4_5

turn, such work promises to provide an understanding of the underlying biases that may exist within the current WFC framework, as well as a greater awareness of the ways in which WFC operates across certain nontraditional family structures. In contrast, by ignoring heterosexual bias in our conceptualizations of WFC, we run the risk of perpetuating potential construct contamination and deficiency in our measures and limiting the construct validity of the WFC construct more broadly. Even more importantly, we may risk limiting the explanatory power of our theories, as well as silencing and rendering invisible members of LGB families in future WFC studies. Finally, because LGB individuals make up an increasingly greater proportion of the workforce (Day and Schoenrade 2000), with estimates of anywhere between 4 and 17% (Ragins et al. 2007), employers stand to gain from work–family policies that effectively attract and retain top LGB talent.

In order to highlight previously unexamined heterosexual biases within the WFC literature, we discuss how conceptualizing WFC as an issue of time, strain, or behaviors *only*, without considering issues related to identity, may restrict our definition of what a family can be and how families are envisioned in the workplace. Specifically, we examine how the current framing of WFC creates a heteronormative view of the family by overlooking the potentially unique identity-related experiences of LGB individuals (e.g., conflicting pressures between partners and coworkers to come out at work, reluctance to ask for family insurance and other benefits) that may contribute to tensions between their work and family lives.

LGB experiences of WFC may differ dramatically from those of heterosexuals, and thus have implications for the effectiveness of potential work–family policies. Given that LGB individuals may not be accepted at work (Croteau 1996; Foldy and Creed 2003; Ragins 2004; Ragins et al. 2007; Ragins and Cornwell 2001), WFC may occur when individuals have families who fall within the LGB domain (i.e., when they are members of same sex couples/families). Examining WFC for members of same sex couples allows for the examination of unique WFC issues which have not previously been considered, and calls for more inclusive WFC policies within organizations.

To provide a theoretical foundation for our propositions, we take an interdisciplinary perspective by drawing on the field of women's studies and, in particular, Intersectionality Theory (Crenshaw 1989). Intersectionality refers to the ways in which multiple aspects of identity, including race, gender, class, and sexual orientation, combine and interact with one another to form qualitatively different meanings and social experiences (Warner 2008). Intersectionality allows us to examine experiences and outcomes for members of more specific identity groups (e.g., black women instead of women more broadly, or with an additional layer, black gay women instead of all black women). Given that previous work has not considered LGB identity as an additional layer that might affect the work–family interface, intersectionality offers a useful tool for examining how LGB identities might impact relationships between work and family. Thus, the current work extends our understanding of WFC beyond a singular focus on traditional gendered and sexuality-based experiences and toward the inclusion of more diverse populations. This added layer may alter some of the prevailing assumptions within the WFC literature and expand our conceptualization of WFC moving forward.

To organize our discussion, we first briefly discuss how WFC has been traditionally conceptualized and assessed in the literature. Second, we discuss the origins and prevalence of LGB discrimination in the workplace, and the implications of prejudice on LGB employees' decisions to "come out" at work, in order to provide a basis for understanding how LGB workers may experience WFC differently from their heterosexual peers. Third, based on our discussion, we suggest that current measures of WFC may suffer from heterosexual bias in that such scales consist of items that may be uniquely interpreted by LGB individuals. Furthermore, we argue that an additional dimension (identity-based conflict) may be necessary to better capture the WFC experiences of LGB employees. Fourth, we suggest how to proceed with developing a more inclusive measure of WFC, highlight the potentially unique antecedents of LGB identity-based WFC, and describe several other important avenues for future research. Finally, we conclude with practical implications.

5.2 Defining Work–Family Conflict

As noted earlier, WFC broadly refers to the ways in which aspects of one's work life interfere with one's family life and vice versa. A number of researchers have called attention to the need to distinguish between two separate constructs—one that focuses on the ways in which work demands impede on the family (WFC) and the other examining the ways in which family interferes with work (family-work conflict, FWC) (Frone et al. 1992, 1997; MacEwen and Barling 1994; O'Driscoll et al. 1992; Williams and Alliger 1994). Both WFC and FWC have been traditionally conceptualized and measured using time, strain, and behavior-based dimensions (Carlson et al. 2000; Greenhaus and Beutell 1985; Greenhaus et al. 2006).

Time-based conflict occurs when time devoted to one role makes it difficult to devote time to another role, reducing one's performance in the latter role. For example, time-based conflict may arise when a family member's birthday dinner falls on an evening when an employee is required to stay late at work. *Strain-based conflict* exists when stress experienced in one role spills over into another role, causing strain symptoms (e.g., anxiety, irritability) and reducing one's ability to perform in the second role. People may experience strain-based conflict, for instance, when work-related stress leads to a conflict with a family member or members. Finally, *behavior-based conflict* occurs when behaviors required to be effective in one role are incompatible with those required to be effective in another role. For example, behavior-based conflict might occur when an individual is lacking authority at work, but is then required to act as an authoritative figure at home.

It is important to note that we use the term "family" to refer more specifically to "families of choice", a distinction that captures the experiences of individuals with LGB family structures (Cherlin 2004). Families of choice do not necessarily include biological or legal relationships, but nonetheless encompass relationships that are considered as close as those in which blood or legal ties are present (Weeks et al.

2001). As such, we define "family" as those individuals that one identifies as family members, without the necessity of blood or legal ties, allowing us to categorize those in same-sex relationships as families.

5.3 Gender and Sexuality: Intersecting Identities and the Roots of Heterosexism

In order to better understand why LGB individuals might experience WFC differently than their heterosexual counterparts, it is important to first consider the influence of gender and gender norms in creating heterosexist attitudes within society. While sex is determined by one's biology, gender refers to a more general term that encompasses "all social relations that separate people into different gendered statuses" (Lorber 1994, p. 3). As such, gender is not solely a reflection of biology, but rather is a product of a complex and interwoven pattern of social interactions, which constitutes and reconstitutes what it means to be "male" and "female" at a societal level.

Butler (2004) further focused on the link between gender and sexuality by questioning the extent to which both categories are purely performative. Specifically, she argued that gender, as well as sexuality, should not be thought of categorically, but rather as a continuous state of being that can fluctuate over time. Butler (2004) also suggested that our construction of gender assumes that part of being male and part of being female is implicated in who we choose as a sexual partner (i.e., someone of the opposite sex). That is, once one is labeled as male or female in terms of their gender, the individual is assumed a priori to have a partner of the opposite sex. In this way, gender and sexuality are inextricably linked within our current heteronormative societal framework.

Similarly, our performance of sexuality assumes that there exists a "natural" sexual orientation (heterosexual) and that any other orientation reflects merely a poor imitation (Butler 2004). In turn, binaries between heterosexuality and all other forms of sexuality are created, along with a false sense of naturalness for heterosexuality and an assumption of abnormality for any other form of sexuality. Given that gender norms lay the framework for the assumption that people should prefer romantic associations with those of the opposite sex, the link between the false naturalization of gendered performance and heterosexuality is made (Butler 2004). Consequently, LGB individuals may be perceived negatively at a societal or individual level because they simultaneously break with deeply rooted gender norms *and* demonstrate assumedly "unnatural" sexual behavior. In the current work, we call for work–family research that begins to challenge these heteronormative assumptions and examines the intersections of gender and sexuality in a less biased way, by placing a greater emphasis on LGB identities in experiences of WFC.

5.4 LGB Discrimination in the Workplace

Making clear the discrimination that LGB employees experience at work contributes to a better understanding of why they may view the workplace as particularly insensitive, or even hostile, toward their LGB identity and family status, in turn contributing, as we argue below, to differential experiences of WFC compared to their heterosexual peers. It has been estimated that between 25 and 66 % of LGB employees have been discriminated against in the workplace, based upon their sexual orientation (Croteau 1996). Further, Ragins and Cornwell (2001) found that one-third of gay and lesbian professionals had been verbally or physically harassed at work and a little over a third had been harassed just because they were assumed to be gay or lesbian. Nearly 12 % found the harassment to be so severe that they decided to leave their jobs entirely. Because sexual orientation is not yet a legally protected class, organizations are not required to include sexual minority status in nondiscrimination statements or to be LGB-friendly. Thus, LGB workers can be fired without any legal protection (Van Den Bergh 2004). Employees are particularly vulnerable to discrimination if they are not living in one of the 21 US states (or the District of Columbia) which have made LGB discrimination illegal at the state level. Even these state laws, however, can be overturned at the federal level, demonstrating a lack of real legal protection for LGB individuals at work.

In addition to interpersonal prejudice, certain structural features of organizations, including policies and practices related to work–family issues, play a major role in the level of discrimination that LGB employees experience (Ragins and Cornwell 2001; Button 2001). Many organizations do not provide domestic partner benefits and will not extend the Family and Medical Leave Act (FMLA) to domestic partners (Van Den Bergh 2004). The lack of policies that are sensitive to the experiences of LGB individuals and their families is problematic given that their absence has been previously shown to be the best predictor of frequency and severity of discrimination at work (Button 2001; Ragins and Cornwell 2001). Because LGB employees are frequently not able to benefit from inclusive antidiscrimination policies, inconsistent and potentially harmful experiences for LGB employees are more likely to occur across their careers. Further, organizations that do not endorse a friendly climate toward LGB employees create spaces in which it is both frightening and detrimental for individuals to reveal their "family of choice" (Van Den Bergh 2004). Although it has been demonstrated that participation in diversity training, which includes information about sexuality, may produce more positive attitudes toward LGB individuals (Probst 2003), diversity training sessions, especially those including sexuality, may not be offered within organizations (Day and Schoenrade 2000).

Thus, as a result of prejudice toward LGB employees and their families, LGB individuals may experience unique WFC when compared to heterosexual employees and their families. The pathologizing of homosexuality and the belief that LGB individuals suffer from mental illness or that they make the choice to be LGB (Sedgwick 1988) allows individuals to feel as if discrimination against LGB individuals is warranted. If the general population believes that LGB individuals are inherently "sick", then fully incorporating LGB individuals into the workplace is not seen as a given, but rather as a choice that should be made on an individualized basis. Thus, LGB individuals are not granted the same rights as other minority groups, who have identities which are viewed as immutable and psychologically "normal".

Indeed, Colgan et al. (2000) found evidence for many people's restricted definitions of "family" with regard to LGB families versus heterosexual families. The authors highlighted the extent to which stereotypical markers of a heterosexual family (in this instance, children), may lead to confusion when an employee reveals an LGB identity. Thus, based on stereotypically heterosexual family indicators, coworkers may make assumptions that fellow employees must also be heterosexual. In the same vein, Williams et al. (2009) highlighted the ways in which organizations privilege heterosexual families through policy, reinforcing heterosexual relationship norms, and by implicitly encouraging employees and clients to normalize heterosexuality in their interactions with one another. Overall, it appears that (in many instances) LGB families are rendered invisible and impossible (Foucault 1992) within organizations. However, because LGB individuals are able to choose whether or not to reveal their LGB identity, these individuals have the option to either remain silent or to become visible within their organization with regard to their LGB identity. Thus, LGB individuals have a unique WFC vantage point—their partner or family identity must be actively revealed in order for individuals at work to be aware of its existence.

5.5 Implications of LGB Discrimination on "Coming Out" at Work

Because LGB employees may be well aware of the risks inherent in being LGB at work, they may choose not to reveal their LGB identity in the workplace. Ragins et al. (2007) found that fear of disclosure predicted a variety of important workplace outcomes in addition to employee strain, over and above actual disclosure. Thus, fear of disclosure is an important consideration when estimating the effects of acceptance (or lack thereof) for LGB employees in the workplace. Further, Croteau (1996) found that, across nine studies, fear of disclosure is a major concern for LGB employees. Results also demonstrated that LGB employees were more likely to be discriminated against when they were "out" at work. This is pertinent to WFC because LGB individuals may be unlikely to disclose their LGB identity and, at the same time, their family identity in order to avoid this discrimination. In this way, the fear of being LGB at work causes LGB individuals to monitor their behavior at all times, self-policing and managing their identity constantly, similarly to the way in which Foucault (1992) described the watchtower mentality. Even when an authoritative figure is not physically present, individuals continue to monitor their identity, fearing the repercussions that might befall them if they are "discovered" as their true selves. This constant experience of invisibility and the impossibility of truly "being" at work may be both mentally and physically exhausting for LGB employees (Colgan et al. 2008; Ellis and Riggle 1996; McDermott 2006). Thus, if individuals actively wish to be out of the closet and are unable to do so because of a hostile work environment (c.f., Croteau 1996; Ragins et al. 2007; Ellis and Riggle 1996), the experienced push and pull between identity preferences and situational reality may lead to increased conflicts between work life and home life. We focus here on the relationships between being closeted and WFC stressors that may arise as a result.

5.6 Disclosure Disconnects and LGB Work Family Conflict

Given the impact of actual and perceived discrimination on LGB employees' decisions to "come out" at work, it is easy to imagine the various pushes and pulls between the work and family domains on such individuals. Ragins (2004) noted that LGB individuals may be "out" to varying degrees in both their work and personal lives. Indeed, research suggests that LGB employees disclose at different rates to parents, spouses, friends, schoolmates, and coworkers (Schope 2002). This variation in "outness" across groups produces a "disclosure disconnect" (Ragins 2008), which creates stress for LGB employees. Hill (2009), for instance, noted that LGB employees are often expected to leave their family lives at home, while heterosexual employees may not have to worry about creating separation between work and family life.

This creates an important difference in the WFC experienced by heterosexual employees versus LGB employees. It may be the case that for heterosexual individuals the separation between work and family leads to lower WFC, given that heterosexual employees are able to freely choose the extent to which they disclose various aspects of their family lives at work. It may also be the case that, when convenient, heterosexual employees are also able to effectively fuse, or reduce the space between, their work and family lives through various work–family policies (e.g., on-site childcare, bringing family to work events). Thus, the impetus to separate work and family domains by choice or increase the ways in which work and family life can be combined may benefit heterosexual employees who can freely select between a number of viable WFC solutions. In contrast, the option to mix work and family may not be available for LGB employees, resulting in the forced construction of barriers between the work and family realms.

Thus, within organizations that do not accept LGB families as legitimate, the active separation between the work and family domains is not done by choice, such that even speaking about one's LGB relationship/family at work is considered taboo. Consequently, it may be that the separation of the work and family domains is an issue of having options—an employee (no matter their sexual identity) benefits from the personal choice to leave work at the office and family at home when it is convenient. However, for LGB employees this decision is made a priori—the family domain is deemed unacceptable within the work domain. The conclusion is that, while attempting to extricate the work and family domains from one another may reflect a plausible solution for WFC among heterosexual employees, this very act may produce WFC for LGB employees. The implicit message sent when organizations allow for selective separation of work and family time is that the organization is cognizant of the heterosexual family *only*, and thus creates policies that make it possible for *certain* employees to keep family time "sacred."

However, when LGB relationships/families are invisible at work (thereby forcibly separating the work and family spheres), it fosters a belief that the organization views LGB families as nonexistent. This belief is propagated by the lack of fair and inclusive workplace policies and practices for LGB employees. In effect, the experience of being "allowed" to keep work and family life separate or integrated is quite different from the experience of forcible separation of work and family realms through fear and a lack of acceptance, especially when this separation is not favorable or preferred. Consistent with this assertion, Day and Schoenrade (2000) found that higher levels of disclosure were related to less perceived WFC.

Overall, the persistence of LGB discrimination seems to reflect a continued social stigma related to being gay, thereby leading to fear, ostracism, disregard, or even disgust toward LGB employees in the workplace (Embrick et al. 2007). Given that WFC is a major issue at work, and given that members of LGB families may be discriminated against with respect to work–family policies, it is vital that we study the ways in which our assessments of and preventative measures regarding WFC may be biased toward heterosexism. A necessary first step is to examine how current conceptualizations and measures of WFC may be contaminated or deficient, potentially leading to more inclusive work–family studies and policies.

5.7 Heterosexual Bias in Measures of Work–Family Conflict

While measurement bias and unfair testing practices remain a consistent issue of concern to psychologists, the impact of heterosexual bias on many popular survey measures is still understudied. Heterosexual bias is a belief system that places more value on heterosexuality and views heterosexuality as a more "natural" form of sexuality than homosexuality (Morin 1977). Heterosexual bias is reinforced by systems and methodologies, which assume heterosexuality as a given (heteronormativity), privileging heterosexual views and rendering others unnecessary or invisible (Morin 1977). Indeed, most surveys are constructed and tested within populations that are assumed a priori to be heterosexual. As a result, heterosexuality tends to be the normative lens through which researchers study "natural" phenomena. However, given that LGB individuals make up between 4 and 17 % of the workforce (Gonsiorek and Weinrich 1991), questions remain regarding the extent to which various surveys used in studies of organizational phenomena function equally across participants and capture certain populations' unique experiences.

Given our discussion in the preceding sections, we suggest that it is important to consider the possibility that LGB workers may experience WFC differently given real and perceived prejudicial barriers that prevent them from discussing their LGB identities and families at work. More specifically, we argue that current WFC measures contain items that may be differentially interpreted across heterosexual and LGB groups, introducing construct contamination and inaccuracy into studies of WFC. We also suggest the possibility that the WFC construct may be deficient in that it may not fully capture the ways in which work and family can conflict with one another, particularly for LGB individuals. In the following section, we examine the ways in which LGB members may uniquely interpret WFC items from existing scales.

5.7.1 Differential Item Interpretation Among LGB Members

For the purposes of the present effort, we discuss Carlson et al.'s (2000) measure as a potential example of heterosexual bias in measures of WFC. Carlson et al.'s measure is comprised of six dimensions: time (WFC and FWC), strain (WFC and FWC), and behavior-based (WFC and FWC) conflict. As such, it conforms to the popular three-dimensional framework introduced by Greenhaus and Beutell (1985), while also acknowledging more recent distinctions made between WFC and FWC. Carlson et al. (2000) selected nonredundant items across 25 previously existing scales in the work–family literature, resulting in their inclusion of 31 items from 8 scales. This initial pool of items was then factor-analyzed and narrowed down to a final set of 18 items, which were then validated against various work–family criteria. Because the measure represents a synthesis of 25 existing measures, it is the most comprehensive to date, and therefore provides a useful starting point for identifying potential heterosexual bias inherent in various WFC scales. (See Carlson et al. 2000 for the full measure, although sample items are discussed below.)

5.7.1.1 Time-Based WFC and FWC

Beginning with time-based work interference with family, from a heterosexual viewpoint, items such as "My work keeps me from my family activities more than I would like" clearly relate to time. However, from an LGB perspective, this item may be differently interpreted. Being kept from family activities because of work could be due to a variety of circumstances, which may have little to do with time. For example, if one works in a small town and does not feel inclined to reveal his/her LGB identity to an employer, then work may serve to keep LGB employees away from taking part in family activities where it is possible they will be observed by a coworker (e.g., going to a local park with one's LGB family, grocery shopping with one's LGB partner), even if there is ample time to perform such activities. Further, being able to bring a spouse or significant other to work events has been noted as a major determinant of satisfaction at work for LGB individuals (Ragins and Cornwell 2001). Those who are unable to bring partners or other family members to work events may feel that they are missing family time given that they are unable to combine work and family time, even when they are "off the clock."

Authors have noted that those who hide their sexual orientation at work may find it stressful merely discussing summer vacations, weekend activities, or other occurrences outside of work (Preston et al. 2006; Gedro 2007). As such, the fear of revealing one's sexual identity may keep employees from participating in family activities through which they may be "outed." This is likely to vary according to one's level of outness, however. Those who are "out" at work are unlikely to feel that they need to shield themselves from being seen at events outside of the workplace. However, for those who are "out" to only a few or to none, the consequences of being seen with one's partner or family outside of work are much greater. The other two items within time-based WFC are more clearly worded to be about time specifically and, as such, are unlikely to pose a problem with respect to heterosexual bias. As such, we believe that current measures of time-based WFC may suffer from heterosexual bias such that LGB individuals will interpret certain scale items differently than heterosexual individuals.

Moving from WFC to FWC, time-based family interference with work also contains another potentially problematic item—"The time I spend with my family often causes me not to spend time in activities at work that could be helpful to my career." When read in the context of a heterosexual family, the item reflects an issue of time—if you spend a lot of time with your family, there may not be enough time to complete work tasks. Yet those in LGB families may interpret spending time with their family as inextricably linked with being a part of a family structure which is not well accepted at work. As such, for those who are "out" at work, this item might read very differently, such that the interpretation may be, "Because I am a part of an LGB family, I am passed over when opportunities arise at work." Further, if a closeted LGB employee is unable to engage in social gatherings where employees are expected to bring their partners, or becomes involved in conversations surrounding weekend plans, vacations, etc., he/she may feel disconnected from coworkers and less likely to receive job rewards. Thus, deciding whether to engage in work activities that could result in rewards may have nothing to do with whether one has time to complete such activities and more to do with whether one feels comfortable engaging in them.

It is important to mention that one of the most popular interventions to WFC stems from the time-based dimension: flexible working arrangements (FWAs). FWAs provide the ability to vary working hours and scheduling around personal obligations and family needs (Rau and Hyland 2006). For example, Shockley and Allen (2007) found that FWAs were negatively related to WFC for women with high levels of family responsibility. FWAs are becoming increasingly popular in organizations as effective interventions for WFC. However, FWAs have only been demonstrated to have beneficial outcomes for those who experience high levels of WFC as it is *traditionally* measured (Rau and Hyland 2006). Therefore, time reflects only one cause of work–family constraints and while a lack of time may be a primary facet of WFC for LGB employees, similar to their heterosexual counterparts, there may be additional layers of WFC that LGB individuals experience. Following this logic, it is possible that current measures of time-based FWC may suffer from heterosexual bias such that LGB individuals will interpret certain scale items differently than heterosexual individuals.

5.7.1.2 Strain-Based WFC and FWC

Strain-based items focus in on a different facet of WFC, such that their interpretation may be similar across heterosexual and LGB participants, yet their antecedents may differ. For example, the strain-based WFC scale includes the items, "When I get home from work, I am often too frazzled to take part in family activities/responsibilities," "I am often so emotionally drained when I get home from work that it prevents me from contributing to my family", and "Due to pressures at work, sometimes when I come home I am too stressed to do the things I enjoy." Here, the root cause for being "frazzled", "emotionally drained", or "stressed" may vary for LGB employees. Higher levels of stress and strain at home may reflect not only job-related demands but also a need to conceal one's LGB identity/family at work. Thus, LGB employees may score higher on these items than their heterosexual peers for reasons that reflect their LGB identities and family situations, rather than simply job demands. Thus, current measures of strain-based WFC may suffer from heterosexual bias such that LGB individuals may interpret certain scale items differently than heterosexual individuals.

Similarly, items within the strain-based FWC scale that read, "Due to stress at home, I am often preoccupied with family matters at work", "Because I am often stressed from family responsibilities, I often have a hard time concentrating on my work", and "Tension and anxiety from my family life often weakens my ability to do my job", may elicit higher endorsement from LGB workers. Stress, tension, and anxiety at work arising directly from one's family life may stem from the stress and strain of daily living (e.g., conflicts with a spouse, caring for a disabled child), but can also be exacerbated by the inability to reveal one's LGB family structure at work. Such items may be assessing a different kind of strain from an LGB standpoint, given that stress and anxiety can arise when employees are discriminated against for coming out at work or are "closeted" and find themselves in heterosexist work environments. Further, some individuals may experience conflict at home about whether or not to come out at work. For example, it may be the case that one's partner is out at work, while they are not. The partner who is out might put pressure on the closeted partner to reveal his/her identity. In this way, being a part of an LGB family may add to tension and stress at work given there may be more complicated boundaries to navigate between partners when only one person in a couple is willing or able to reveal the existence of the other. Thus, we may find a higher level of endorsement (reflecting contamination) and a different set of antecedents for such items. As discussed earlier, all of this may be due to overflow from other unmeasured domains of WFC (i.e., identity-based) for LGB relationships and families, potentially leading to criterion deficiency.

For example, Button (2001) found that LGB individuals who experienced greater workplace discrimination were more likely to use strategies such as counterfeiting (pretending to be heterosexual) or avoiding (acting as if one has no sexuality at all) at work. The use of such strategies may be stressful for LGB employees, especially if they are used in order to avoid discrimination. While there are various reasons that one may wish to remain closeted (and power may often reside in the closet) (Brown 2000; Ferfolja 2009), for those who do not wish to be closeted, yet feel they have no other choice, choosing strategies of silence may create anxiety. Indeed, there is evidence to suggest that LGB individuals who work in gay-friendly environments and who are out in the workplace experience higher job satisfaction and lower stress and anxiety (Day and Schoenrade 2000; Driscoll et al. 1996; Griffith and Hebl 2002). Therefore, current measures of strain-based FWC may suffer from heterosexual bias such that LGB individuals will interpret certain scale items differently than heterosexual individuals.

5.7.1.3 Behavior-Based WFC and FWC

Heterosexist bias may also exist in the behavior-based WFC items: "The problem solving behaviors I use in my job are not effective in solving problems at home", "Behavior that is effective and necessary for me at work would be counterproductive at home", and "The behaviors I perform that make me effective at work do not make me a better parent and spouse." For example, the behaviors that may make an LGB individual more "effective" at work (e.g., concealing one's family status, pretending to be heterosexual) would not contribute to being an effective member of an LGB family. While these behaviors are obviously not the only behaviors that contribute to on-the-job performance, they reflect a subset of activities that are not required of heterosexual employees and thus expand the requirements for what it takes to be "successful" at work as an LGB employee. Further, while faking or passing behaviors are not equivalent to actual job-related tasks (typing, answering calls), they must be constantly monitored, and thus may infringe upon or affect behaviors that are directly job-related. As such, it is possible that LGB individuals may be aware of the necessity of these behaviors in the workplace and interpret items in light of this range of seemingly "required" on-the-job behaviors. This suggests that current measures of behavior-based WFC may suffer from heterosexual bias such that LGB individuals will interpret certain scale items differently than heterosexual individuals.

Similarly, the behavior-based FWC items highlight similar themes: "The behaviors that work for me at home do not seem to be effective at work", "Behavior that is effective and necessary for me at home would be counterproductive at work", and "The problem solving behavior that works for me at home does not seem to be as useful at work." Such items may be differently interpreted given that behaviors that are necessary at work and behaviors that "work" at home may not coincide for individuals with LGB families. In a heterosexist workplace, behaviors that LGB individuals enact at home (displaying affection toward one's partner [while at a company party, for example], talking freely about one's LGB family structure and other LGB-related issues or concerns in the presence of coworkers) may be damaging when performed

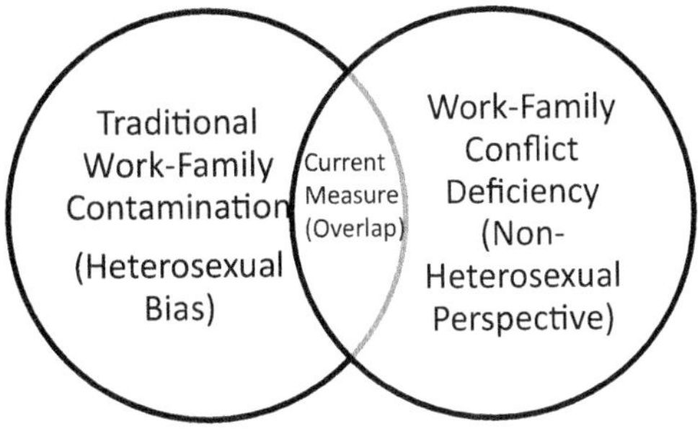

Fig. 5.1 Conceptual model of current work–family measures

at work and are most likely limited in coworker discussions on the job. Finally, in line with the previously discussed dimensions, it may be the case that current measures of behavior-based FWC suffer from heterosexual bias such that LGB individuals will interpret certain scale items differently than heterosexual individuals.

Figure 5.1 illustrates the hypothesized overlap between WFC as it is currently assessed and a more inclusive measure of the construct. The figure suggests that preexisting scales may suffice for LGB and heterosexual individuals with respect to certain items (e.g., "The time that I spend at work keeps me from family responsibilities more than I would like"). Other items, however, may be contaminated (e.g., "The behaviors that work for me at home don't seem to be as effective at work" may be interpreted quite differently for LGB individuals) and deficient, such that individuals cannot talk about their family at work but do not have a place within present measures to report that experience. Current measures may contain possible contamination and construct overlap, but we have not yet explored their deficiencies.

5.8 LGB Identity-Based Work-Family Conflict: A New Dimension of WFC

Based on our discussion above, it is also possible that we are omitting an entire dimension of WFC for LGB individuals, which stems directly from their LGB family identity. Given that LGB individuals may face discrimination that leads to a lack of "outness" at work (Ragins and Cornwell 2001; Waldo 1999), it may be the case that WFC stems directly from one's LGB family identity. For example, if employees are not out at work, or are out only to some individuals, they may experience difficulty asking about LGB family-friendly benefits or taking advantage of other work–family policies within the organization that might be useful to them. Moreover, given that LGB individuals may feel uncomfortable coming out at work, they may be less likely to bring their partner to company events or display pictures of their partner on their desks at work. These conflicts stem more from one's LGB family status and are not currently being captured in the work–family domain. While some of these items have been captured in other measures (e.g., Griffin 1992; Ragins 2004), it seems that these issues are more clearly tied to work and family domain conflicts than to other constructs within the psychological domain. As such, we suggest that an additional dimension of WFC, identity-based conflict, may be necessary in order to more fully capture the WFC experiences of LGB populations. Here, we define identity-based conflict as occurring when *one's relationship/family identity is in conflict with the range of acceptable/recognized relationship/family identities at work.* Thus, we propose that an additional dimension of WFC, identity-based conflict, is necessary in order to more fully capture the unique WFC experiences of LGB individuals.

5.8.1 *Potential Antecedents of LGB Identity-Based Work–Family Conflict*

In order to properly evaluate the conditions under which LGB individuals may experience WFC to a greater or lesser degree, it is also important to consider potential antecedents of LGB identity-based WFC. That is, while the larger WFC literature has explored various predictors of WFC in the general population, we still know relatively little regarding the potentially unique antecedents of WFC within LGB samples. Greater insight into the links between LGB-specific antecedents and LGB identity-based WFC is further necessary given that different predictive models of WFC may exist for LGB individuals as compared to their heterosexual counterparts.

5.8.1.1 Level of "Outness" at Work

As noted earlier, while some LGB employees may derive a certain degree of power from remaining closeted and freely choose to conceal their LGB identities for strategic purposes (Brown 2000), others may wish to come out but do not believe that they have the choice if the workplace is believed to be discriminatory toward them and their LGB families. As noted by Ragins (2004), one's level of "outness" across different life domains, such as work and family, tends to produce disclosure disconnects that are stressful for LGB individuals. We argue that lower levels of "outness" in the workplace lead to higher levels of identity-based WFC for LGB employees, given that disclosure disconnects are likely to be associated with perceptions that the organization is imposing barriers between the work and family domains and restricting the choice to freely intermix elements of work and family when convenient. It may be the case, then, that lower levels of "outness" at work among LGB individuals may be associated with higher levels of LGB identity-based WFC.

5.8.1.2 Fear of Disclosure

Although one's fear of disclosure is likely to be negatively related to his/her level of "outness" in the workplace (Ragins et al. 2007), the two constructs may nonetheless be unique predictors of LGB identity-based WFC given that decisions to remain closeted may reflect other factors outside of such fear (e.g., self-esteem, introversion, locus of control). Fear of disclosure may stem from real and perceived discrimination at work, which causes LGB employees, in most cases, to hide their sexual orientation and family status from supervisors and colleagues. In turn, they are likely to experience a clash between the work and family realms, given that they are unable to freely select among the range of work–family solutions that are more accessible to heterosexual employees. As a result, we predict that fear of disclosure may be positively related to higher levels of identity-based WFC for LGB individuals within the workplace.

5.8.1.3 Social Support

A number of studies point to the buffering effects of perceived social support on experienced levels of WFC (Carlson et al. 2000; Greenhaus et al. 1987; Schaubroeck et al. 1989). Within a sample of 99 LGB individuals, Huffman et al. (2008) found that supervisor support was positively associated with job satisfaction, coworker support was positively correlated with life satisfaction, and organizational support was positively linked to being “out” at work. It may be that when LGB employees perceive their organization, supervisor, and colleagues as supportive and sensitive to LGB-related issues, they may feel more comfortable disclosing information regarding their LGB identity and family status. Thus, perceptions of support may play a vital role in shaping an organizational culture where LGB families are valued and accepted, thereby removing disclosure disconnects that forcibly separate the work and family domains for LGB employees. When social support is present, LGB employees, like their heterosexual counterparts, may feel free to choose the extent to which they separate or mix aspects of their work and family lives, such that higher levels of social support may be associated with lower levels of LGB identity-based WFC.

5.8.1.4 Organizational Policies and Practices

In addition to social support, organizational policies and practices that are LGB-friendly, including same-sex partner benefits, LGB antidiscrimination policies, and LGB resource support groups, are likely to promote a perception of the organization as supportive and sensitive to LGB-related issues, which in turn may eliminate disclosure disconnects and socially imposed boundaries between the work and family lives of LGB employees. In contrast, organizations that do not institute such policies and practices are likely to promote, whether implicitly or explicitly, an assumption that they do not value or recognize LGB families. Perceptions of discrimination contribute to disclosure disconnects and in turn to higher levels of identity-based WFC among LGB employees. As noted earlier, an organization’s espoused policies regarding LGB-related issues have been shown to be the most powerful predictor of perceived discrimination and various work-related attitudes (Button 2001; Ragins and Cornwell 2001). Overall, then, LGB-friendly organizational policies and practices may be associated with lower levels of LGB identity-based WFC.

5.8.1.5 Centrality of Sexual Identity

It is also likely that the more strongly one sees their sexual identity as being central to their overall identity, the more likely they will report experiencing LGB identity-based WFC. For people who do not attach aspects of their sexuality as strongly to their core identity, the desire to "come out" at work may not be as much an issue as it is for those who place a greater focus on their sexual identity. Such individuals may not experience the same tension between their work and private lives and may be more comfortable keeping these life domains separate. Moreover, centrality of identity has been found to relate to identity salience (Sellers et al. 1998) for race (Griffith and Hebl 2002; Law et al. 2011). Thus, it is possible that it holds for sexuality as well. As a result, greater centrality of sexual identity among LGB individuals may be associated with higher levels of LGB identity-based WFC.

5.8.1.6 Gender

Although patterns of WFC differ by gender in heterosexual samples (Duxbury and Higgins 1991), this same pattern may not hold true for LGB couples. Gay and lesbian couples are found to split household chores and responsibilities for child care in a more egalitarian manner than heterosexual couples (Solomon et al. 2005). In fact, in a study of same-sex couples in civil unions and heterosexual couples in Vermont, Solomon et al. (2005) found that the strongest predictor of couples' division of household labor was sexual orientation, which predicted over and above income differences. Given these findings, it may be the case that LGB couples experience smaller gender discrepancies in identity-based WFC compared to heterosexual couples.

5.9 Implications for Research

Based on our discussion, there are several areas that future research should address. First, in order to begin assessing whether LGB employees experience WFC differently, a first step might be to explore LGB individuals' WFC experiences via qualitative interviews, as well as quantitative analyses of the potentially unique antecedents of LGB identity-based WFC. Such work would lend initial insight into whether or not current measures "work" across LGB populations or whether there are substantive differences in the WFC experiences of LGB individuals. More specifically, participants might be asked how they define and experience WFC and how they interpret items comprising existing scales, as well as to report the extent to which various presumed antecedents of WFC play a role in their experiences of WFC.

Second, if qualitative differences in LGB WFC experiences appear to exist, a necessary second step would be to generate a set of items, based on earlier interviews, that capture the content domain of identity-based conflict and to examine whether these new items and those comprising existing scales demonstrate content validity in representative samples of LGB employees; that is, can LGB individuals adequately classify the new identity-based items and preexisting WFC scale items into their respective dimensions? Consistent with best practices outlined in the scale development literature (e.g., Conway and Huffcut 2003; Ford et al. 1986; Hinkin 1995), it would be necessary to then examine and confirm the underlying dimensionality of this more inclusive measure and determine the extent to which it offers predictive validity over and above existing measures of WFC for LGB individuals.

Third, beyond the work–family domain, our discussion points to a broader need for researchers to examine the common assumptions that may underlie surveys of organizational phenomena. Thinking more inclusively about who constructs a given scale, which groups were included in samples that were used to validate the scale, and which groups the validation process did not include allows researchers to assess various measures from unique and more inclusive perspectives. Indeed, our analysis suggests that LGB family issues have not been considered to the extent that they should be within the existing work–family literature, despite the long-standing history of work–family research. Similarly, other researchers have called attention to the need to reassess many common scales for potential bias. Cole and Sabik (2009), for example, pointed out that racial bias in the measurement of women's self-esteem about appearance may be driving differences between white and ethnic minority women. While the need to re-examine our surveys from a minority perspective is not a difficult concept to grasp, substantive work in this area lags in psychology. However, there are significant gains to be made by thinking about "for whom" our measures work and for whom they do not if we are to understand the complexities underlying the phenomena we study. As such, we hope that this chapter spurs future work that reexamines long-standing constructs in I/O psychology and organizational behavior and asks whether or not these constructs hold in more diverse populations.

Fourth, our discussion highlights the need to examine alternative family structures in greater depth. It may be the case that families who possess other stigmatized identities (disability, size, religion, socioeconomic status, single parent status, etc.) may experience similar identity-based WFC. Examining unique family experiences may lead to a more complete and nuanced conceptualization of the work–family domain. Our definition of identity-based WFC may relate to a range of families with stigmatized identities. However, the examination of LGB families is a logical first step since there appears to be both a stigma attached to an LGB identity (Ragins et al. 2007) and also a visceral negative reaction associated with the realization of this identity for some individuals (Stacey 1998). As such, there may be something particularly unique about an LGB identity that affects the work and family domains in a more negative fashion than other "alternative" families might experience because an LGB identity is often viewed as "controllable". It is possible that this difference produces a greater level of conflict because the stakes for "coming out" about one's stigmatized identity might be higher. Thus, starting with LGB families might provide insight into the more extreme cases in which work and family conflict on the basis of identity, but should also be complemented with work on other stigmatized family identities.

Fifth, while we examine WFC in the present effort, it may be of interest in the future to examine the ways in which work and lifestyle conflict for those LGB individuals who do not consider themselves a part of a family. For example, for single LGB individuals who are not a part of an LGB family, the survey might be administered with the words "life" or "lifestyle" in place of "family." In turn, this may permit researchers to compare and contrast responses of those who are currently in an LGB family/relationship with those who are not. Although much of the literature talks about work-life balance conceptually, scale items still reflect a family focus [as demonstrated in Carlson et al.'s (2000) meta-measure]. While only those who are partnered or consider themselves to be a part of an LGB family are the focus of this chapter, nonpartnered individuals may be included in future research to determine whether or not it is necessary to consider additional issues when measuring LGB identity-based work-life conflict as opposed to LGB identity-based WFC.

Sixth, this chapter provides an impetus for researchers to assess sexuality as part of a standard set of demographics measured within psychological research. While measures of gender or race are staples in most surveys' demographics sections, measures of sexual orientation are not commonly collected. To understand LGB experiences at work, we must begin assessing sexuality in a more standardized way. In particular, and consistent with Intersectionality Theory (Crenshaw 1989), it is possible to examine family identity as a layered construct with multiple pieces. Instead of assuming a unified definition for the term "family", we open the door to realizing how multiple layers of family identity may influence outcomes of interest in unique ways. By beginning to expand our definition of family and becoming cognizant of the multitude of ways that individuals might define family [i.e., "family of choice" (Cherlin 2004)], we are able to better understand how multiple family identities might combine and then, as a result, have a different impact on variables that are important to families, their quality of life and their quality of work.

Finally, we highlight the need for gender researchers to become more heavily invested in examinations of sexuality-based bias within the work–family literature. Because gender and sexuality-based discrimination are inherently intertwined, open dialogue between researchers interested in gender and researchers interested in sexuality will help to develop future work in a more holistic way. By focusing on the intersections of identity and resulting discriminatory or silencing mechanisms, we create more accurate models of the work–family experiences of diverse individuals with potentially diverse or alternative family structures.

5.10 Implications for Practice

The literature reviewed above suggests that organizations may be overlooking the experiences of LGB employees, a significant omission given gay and lesbian employees are estimated to comprise anywhere between 4 to 17% of today's workforce (Gonsiorek and Weinrich 1991; Ragins and Cornwell 2001). It behooves organizations to create better LGB organizational policies and practices (i.e., same-sex partner benefits, LGB partner-friendly social events, LGB resource support groups, and LGB antidiscrimination policies), given that these policies may have the strongest effects on gay and lesbian employees' perceptions of discrimination (Ragins and Cornwell 2001). Thus, by actively assessing LGB identity-based WFC, organizations may allow employers to implement more inclusive work–family policies which address the needs of a historically silenced population within the workplace. These policies may not only prove effective in increasing the perception of acceptance and lowered discrimination, but may also impact important business metrics such as job satisfaction, commitment, and turnover intention (Ragins and Cornwell 2001).

Knowledge of the potentially unique WFC experiences of LGB employees may further serve to inform relevant LGB affinity groups, who might utilize such work to lobby for more effective work–family policies within organizations, such as those related to LGB family benefits, same-sex partner recognition, and more inclusive, LGB-friendly work environments. Including organizational identity politics within a work–family framework may be an effective means for affinity groups to work toward more inclusive organizational policies and practices for LGB families in a way that fits with existing organizational goals.

Finally, because improving WFC may improve job satisfaction (Bruck et al. 2002; Grandey et al. 2005; Kossek and Ozeki 1998), examining LGB identity-based WFC may provide the tools for creating the "business case" for HR professionals interested in decreasing the conflicts between work and family for employees. Creating awareness of the positive effects of decreasing LGB identity-based WFC among those responsible for talent management and human capital programs and solutions within organizations may help to spearhead inclusive work–family policies and practices on a broader scale.

5.11 Concluding Remarks

The present chapter has brought to light the role that heterosexual bias has played thus far in our conceptualizations of WFC. Because gender stereotypes also encompass our assumptions about sexual preferences (i.e., that men are attracted to women and that women are attracted to men), questioning the gendered nature of WFC should also prompt us to question the heteronormative assumptions that exist within the current work–family literature. If our current measures do not allow for or consider the presence of LGB employees and their families, we run the risk of silencing these populations within the WFC domain, both academically and practically. However, urging researchers and employers to consider the plight of LGB individuals when examining and remedying WFC may allow us to collectively create more inclusive studies, measures, and interventions for addressing the needs of LGB families in the future. Decreasing the deficiencies in our current conceptualizations of WFC can only lead to a more nuanced and accurate understanding of the various forms of WFC moving forward—a goal which is preferable for both scientists and practitioners alike.

References

Berlant, L., & Warner, M. (1998). Sex in public. *Critical Inquiry, 24,* 547–566.
Brown, M. P. (2000). *Closet space: Geographies of metaphor from the body to the globe*. London: Routledge.
Bruck, C. S., Allen, T. D., & Spector, P. E. (2002). The relationship between work–family conflict and job satisfaction: A finer grained analysis. *Journal of Vocational Behavior, 60,* 336–353.
Butler, J. (2004). *Undoing gender*. New York: Routledge.
Button, S. B. (2001). Organizational efforts to affirm sexual diversity: A cross-level examination. *Journal of Applied Psychology, 86,* 17–28.
Carlson, D. S., Kacmar, K. M., & Williams, L. J. (2000). Construction and validation of a multidimensional measure of work–family conflict. *Journal of Vocational Behavior, 56,* 249–276.
Cherlin, A. J. (2004). The deinstitutionalization of American marriage. *Journal of Marriage and Family, 66,* 848–861.
Cole, E. R., & Sabik, N. J. (2009). Repairing a broken mirror: Intersectional approaches to diverse women's perception of beauty and bodies. In M. T. Berger & K. Guidroz (Eds.), *The intersectional approach: Transforming the academy through race, class and gender* (pp. 173–192). Chapel Hill: The University of North Carolina Press.
Colgan, F., Creegan, C., McKearney, A., & Wright, T. (2008). Lesbian workers: Personal strategies amid changing organisational responses to 'sexual minorities' in the UK workplaces. *Journal of Lesbian Studies, 12,* 31–45.
Conway, J. M., & Huffcutt, A. I. (2003). A review and evaluation of exploratory factor analysis practices in organizational research. *Organizational Research Methods, 6,* 147–168.
Crenshaw, K. (1989). Demarginalizing the intersection of race and sex: A black feminist critique of antidiscrimination doctrine, feminist theory, and antiracist politics. *University of Chicago Legal Forum, 140,* 139–167.
Croteau, J. M. (1996). Research on the work experiences of lesbian, gay, and bisexual people: An integrative review of methodology and findings. *Journal of Vocational Behavior, 48,* 195–209.
Day, N. E., & Schoenrade, P. (2000). The relationship among reported disclosure of sexual orientation, anti-discrimination policies, top management support, and work attitudes of gay and lesbian employees. *Personnel Review, 29,* 346–363.
Driscoll, J. M., Kelley, F. A., & Fassinger, R. E. (1996). Lesbian identity and disclosure in the workplace: Relation to occupational stress and satisfaction. *Journal of Vocational Behavior, 48,* 229–242.
Duxbury, L. E., & Higgins, C. A. (1991). Gender differences in work–family conflict. *Journal of Applied Psychology, 76,* 60–73.
Ellis, A. L., & Riggle, E. D. B. (1996). The relation of job satisfaction and degree of openness about one's sexual orientation for lesbians and gay men. *Journal of Homosexuality, 30,* 75–85.
Embrick, D. G., Walther, C. S., & Wickens, C. M. (2007). Working class masculinity: Keeping gay men and lesbians out of the workplace. *Sex Roles, 56,* 757–766.
Ferfolja, T. (2009). State of the field review: Stories so far: An overview of the research on lesbian teachers. *Sexualities, 12,* 378–395.
Foldy, E. G., & Creed, W. E. D. (2003). Action learning, fragmentation, and the interaction of single, double, and triple-loop change: A case of gay and lesbian workplace advocacy. In R. J. Ely, E. G. Foldy, & M. A. Scully (Eds.), *Reader in gender, work, and organization* (pp. 242–257). Oxford: Blackwell.
Ford, J. K., MacCallum, R. C., & Tait, M. (1986). The application of exploratory factor analysis in applied psychology: A critical review and analysis. *Personnel Psychology, 39,* 291–314.
Foucault, M. (1992). *The history of sexuality Vol. 2: The use of pleasure*. London: Penguin.
Frone, M. R., Russell, M., & Cooper, M. L. (1992). Antecedents and outcomes of work–family conflict: Testing a model of the work–family interface. *Journal of Applied Psychology, 77,* 65–78.

Frone, M. T., Yardley, J. K., & Markel, K. S. (1997). Developing and testing an integrative model of the work–family interface. *Journal of Vocational Behavior, 50,* 145–167.

Gedro, J. (2007). Conducting research on LGBT issues: Leading the field all over again! *Human Resource Development Quarterly, 18,* 153–158.

Gonsiorek, J. C., & Weinrich, J. D. (1991). The definition and scope of sexual orientation. In J. C. Gonsiorek & J. D. Weinrich (Eds.), *Homosexuality, research implications for public policy* (pp. 161–176). London: Sage.

Gorman, E. H., & Kmec, J. A. (2007). We (have to) try harder: Gender and required work effort in Britain and the United States. *Gender and Society, 21,* 828–856.

Grandey, A. A., Cordiero, B. L., & Crouter, A. C. (2005). A longitudinal and multi-source test of the work–family conflict and job satisfaction relationship. *Journal of Occupational and Organizational Psychology, 78,* 305–323.

Greenhaus, J. H., & Beutell, N. J. (1985). Sources of conflict between work and family roles. *Academy of Management Journal, 10,* 76–88.

Greenhaus, J. H., Bedeian, A. G., & Mossholder, K. W. (1987). Work experiences, job performance, and feelings of personal and family well-being. *Journal of Vocational Behavior, 31,* 200–215.

Greenhaus, J. H., Allen, T. D., & Spector, P. E. (2006). Health consequences of work–family conflict: The dark side of the work–family interface. In P. L. Perrewe & D. C. Ganster (Eds.), *Research in occupational stress and well-being* (Vol. 5, pp. 61–98). Amsterdam: JAI/Elsevier.

Griffin, P. (1992). From hiding to coming out: Empowering lesbian and gay educators. In K. M. Harbeck (Ed.), *Coming out of the classroom* (pp. 167–196). Binghamton: Harrington Park.

Griffith, K. H., & Hebl, M. (2002). The disclosure dilemma for gay men and lesbians: Coming "out" at work. *Journal of Applied Psychology, 87,* 1191–1199.

Hill, R. J. (2009). Incorporating queers: Blowback, backlash, and other forms of resistance to workplace diversity initiatives that support sexual minorities. *Advances in Developing Human Resources, 11,* 37–53.

Hinkin, T. R. (1995). A review of scale development practices in the study of organizations. *Journal of Management, 21,* 967–988.

Huffman, A. H., Watrous-Rodriguez, K. M., & King, E. B. (2008). Supporting a diverse workforce: What type of support is most meaningful for lesbian and gay employees? *Human Resource Management, 47,* 237–253.

Kossek, E. E., & Ozeki, C. (1998). Work-family conflict, policies, and the job-life satisfaction relationship: A review and directions for organizational behavior-human resources research. *Journal of Applied Psychology, 83,* 139–149.

Law, C. L., Martinez, L., Ruggs, E. N., Hebl, M. R., & Akers, E. (2011). Trans-parency in the workplace: How the experiences of transsexual employees can be improved. *Journal of Vocational Behavior, 79,* 710–723.

Lorber, J. (1994). *Paradoxes of gender*. New Haven: Yale University.

MacEwen, K. E., & Barling, J. (1994). Daily consequences of work interference with family and family interference with work. *Work & Stress, 8,* 244–254.

McDermott, E. (2006). Surviving dangerous places: Lesbian identity performances in the workplace, social class, and psychological health. *Feminism Psychology, 16,* 193–211.

Miller, S. L., Forest, K. B., & Jurik, N. (2003). Diversity in blue: Lesbian and gay police officers in a masculine occupation. *Men and Masculinities, 5,* 355–385.

Morin, S. F. (1977). Heterosexual bias in psychological research on lesbianism and male homosexuality. *American Psychologist, 32,* 629–663.

O'Driscoll, M. P., Ilgen, D. R., & Hildreth, K. (1992). Time devoted to job and off-job activities, interrole conflict, and affective experiences. *Journal of Applied Psychology, 77,* 272–297.

Preston, R. C., Fredericksen, R. J., & Herrschaft, D. (2006). The need for change: Bridging employers and business. In M. D. Shankle (Ed.), *The handbook of lesbian, gay, bisexual, and transgender public health: A practitioner's guide to service* (pp. 317–332). Binghamton: The Haworth.

Probst, T. (2003). Changing attitudes over time: Assessing the effectiveness of a workplace diversity course. *Teaching of Psychology, 30,* 236–239.

Ragins, B. R. (2004). Sexual orientation in the workplace: The unique work and career experiences of gay, lesbian and bisexual workers. *Research in Personnel and Human Resources Management, 23,* 35–120.

Ragins, B. R. (2008). Disclosure disconnects: Antecedents and consequences of disclosing invisible stigmas across life domains. *Academy of Management Review, 33,* 194–215.

Ragins, B. R., & Cornwell, J. M. (2001). Pink triangles: Antecedents and consequences of perceived workplace discrimination against gay and lesbian employees. *Journal of Applied Psychology, 86,* 1244–1261.

Ragins, B. R., Singh, R., & Cornwell, J. M. (2007). Making the invisible visible: Fear and disclosure of sexual orientation at work. *Journal of Applied Psychology, 92,* 1103–1118.

Rau, B. L., & Hyland, M. (2006). Role conflict and flexible work arrangements: The effects on applicant attraction. *Personnel Psychology, 55,* 111–136.

Schaubroeck, J., Cotton, J. L., & Jennings, K. R. (1989). Antecedents and consequences of role stress: A covariance structure analysis. *Journal of Organizational Behavior, 10,* 35–58.

Schope, R. D. (2002). The decision to tell: Factors influencing the disclosure of sexual orientation by gay men. *Journal of Gay and Lesbian Social Services, 14,* 1–22.

Sedgwick, E. K. (1988). *Epistemology of the closet.* Berkeley: University of California.

Sellers, R. M., Smith, M. A., Shelton, J. A., Rowley, S. A. J., & Chavous, T. M. (1998). Multidimensional model of racial identity: A reconceptualization of African-American racial identity. *Personality and Social Psychology Review, 2,* 18–39.

Shockley, K. M., & Allen, T. (2007). When flexibility helps: Another look at the availability of flexible work arrangements and work–family conflict. *Journal of Vocational Behavior, 71,* 479–493.

Solomon, S. E., Rothblum, E. D., & Balsam, K. F. (2005). Money, housework, sex, and conflict: Same sex couples in civil unions, those not in civil unions, and heterosexual married siblings. *Sex Roles, 52,* 561–575.

Stacey, J. (1998). The neo-family-values campaign. In R. Lancaster & M. di Leonardo (Eds.), *The gender/sexuality reader* (pp. 453–470). New York: Routledge.

Van Den Bergh, N. (2004). Getting a piece of the pie: Cultural competence for GLBT employees at the workplace. *Journal of Human Behavior and the Social Environment, 8,* 55–73.

Waldo, C. R. (1999). Working in majority context: A structural model of heterosexism as minority stress in the workplace. *Journal of Counseling Psychology, 46,* 218–232.

Warner, L. R. (2008). A best practices guide to intersectional approaches in psychological research. *Sex Roles, 59,* 454–463.

Weeks, J., Heaphy, B., & Donovan, C. (2001). *Same sex intimacies: Families of choice and other life experiments.* London: Routledge.

Williams, K. J., & Alliger, G. M. (1994). Role stressors, mood spillover, and perceptions of work–family conflict in employed parents. *Academy of Management Journal, 37,* 837–868.

Williams, C., Giuffre, P. A., & Dellinger, K. (2009). The gay-friendly closet. *Sexuality Research and Social Policy, 6,* 29–45.

Chapter 6
Gender, Gender-Role Ideology, and the Work–Family Interface: A Cross-Cultural Analysis

Ujvala Rajadhyaksha, Karen Korabik, and Zeynep Aycan

6.1 Overview

The current chapter examines the effects of gender and culture on work–family conflict (WFC) and work–family enrichment (WFE). We first review the literature on WFC and WFE. We then look at the impact of different aspects of gender (including physical gender, gender-role ideology, gender egalitarianism, and gender inequality)[1] on the work–family (W–F) interface. Throughout the chapter we highlight the similarities and differences in relationships between the various aspects of gender and WFC and WFE that have been found in international studies and cross-cultural comparisons. The chapter concludes with a discussion on the agenda for future research.

[1] In this chapter we discuss the impact of several distinct, yet interrelated aspects of gender. We use the term gender to refer to the physical aspect of gender or whether someone is a man or a woman. Gender-role ideology is defined as whether individuals' attitudes about the roles of men and women are traditional versus egalitarian. In contrast to these two individual-level variables, gender egalitarianism and gender inequality are cultural or societal level variables. In cultures with traditional values men are seen primarily as breadwinners and women primarily as caregivers, whereas in cultures with egalitarian values there is less adherence to this traditional division of labor. The term gender inequality is used to refer to differences in power and status between men and women in different countries.

U. Rajadhyaksha (✉)
Department of Business Administration and Economics,
Saint Mary's College, Notre Dame, IN 46556, USA
e-mail: urajadhy@saintmarys.edu

K. Korabik
Centre for Families, Work and Well-Being, University of Guelph,
Guelph, ON N1G2W1, Canada
e-mail: kkorabik@uoguelph.ca

Z. Aycan
Departments of Psychology and Management, Koç University,
Rumeli Fener Road, 34460 Sariyer, Istanbul, Turkey
e-mail: zaycan@ku.edu.tr

M. J. Mills (ed.), *Gender and the Work-Family Experience*,
DOI 10.1007/978-3-319-08891-4_6

6.2 Work–Family Conflict

WFC has become the reality in the lives of many employed adults all over the world. Several factors are associated with the ever-increasing challenge of juggling work and family responsibilities. Some of these include longer work days and international business travel as a result of globalization (Westman et al. 2008); increased participation of women in the workforce and its concomitant impact on gender roles and ways of doing 'work'; changing family structures characterized by a rising number of dual career couples, single-parent families, families with aging parents requiring care; and the growth of a sandwich generation of workers who have to simultaneously care for dependent elders and children (Casper and Bianchi 2002).

WFC arises due to "simultaneous pressures from both work and family that are mutually incompatible in some respect" (Greenhaus and Beutell 1985, p. 77). W–F research has been dominated by Role Theory whereby conflicting expectations from multiple roles create psychological tension and conflict. Underlying the notion of WFC is the 'scarcity hypothesis'—the belief that an individual's time and energy resources are in short supply, and therefore that any resource drain or depletion in one sphere will have negative ramifications for the other sphere (Rothbard 2001). WFC is generally operationalized as a bidirectional and multi-dimensional construct with the possibility of work-interfering-with-family conflict (WIF) and family-interfering-with-work conflict (FIW) occurring along the three dimensions of time, strain, and behavior (e.g., Frone et al. 1992a; Gutek et al. 1991). Further, boundaries between work and family are asymmetrically permeable—the incidence of WIF tends to exceed that of FIW (Frone et al. 1992b; Pleck 1977).

Research on WFC includes many investigations of integrative models that examine how it is related to its antecedents and outcomes (e.g., Frone et al. 1992a). A number of meta-analyses and path analytic meta-analyses of the literature have been carried out (Amstad et al. 2011; Bryon 2005; Ford et al. 2007; Michel et al. 2011; Shockley and Singla 2011). The results have indicated that work domain variables have the potential to impact and create conflict in the work domain as well as cross over boundaries and create conflict in or affect variables in the family domain. Similarly, family domain variables can create conflict in or affect variables in the family domain as well as in the work domain. However, within-domain relationships tend to exceed cross-domain relationships in magnitude (Amstad et al. 2011; Shockley and Singla 2011).

The majority of studies on WFC have been conducted in the context of Anglo English speaking countries (Casper et al. 2007). This is a notable limitation, and pleas have been made for more WFC research to be performed in international contexts (Poelmans et al. 2005). Studies on WFC have been carried out in many areas of the world beyond the United States, including Western Europe and Scandinavia (e.g., Kinnunen and Mauno 1998), Eastern Asia (e.g., Aryee 1992; Aryee et al. 1999; Matsui et al. 1995), and Southern Asia/Africa (e.g., Ayo et al. 2009; Tabassum 2012). However, most of the research conducted outside North America consists of single-country studies that have not specifically accounted for cultural variables or facilitated cross-cultural comparisons (Aycan 2008; Gelfand and Knight 2005;

Shaffer et al. 2011). Recently, there have been more cross-cultural investigations of the W–F interface (e.g., Billing et al. 2014; Joplin et al. 2003; Lapierre et al. 2008; Spector et al. 2004, 2007; Yang et al. 2000), but these have not explicitly focused on the role of gender.

6.3 Work–Family Enrichment

The notion of WFC implies a negative spillover between the work and family domains. This negative thrust has been critiqued with researchers asking for more examination of positive relationships between the work and family domains (Greenhaus and Powell 2006). Positive W–F relationships have been variously referred to as positive spillover, enrichment, enhancement, or facilitation (Greenhaus and Powell 2006; Grzywacz and Marks 2000; Wayne et al. 2006). Essential to all these terms is the idea that the role exchange between work and family is not always detrimental and can have enhancing effects. Following Shockley and Singla (2011), we use the term work–family enrichment (WFE) to refer to positive W–F relationships. Unlike WFC, which is based on the scarcity hypothesis, WFE is based on Role Accumulation Theory, which suggests that participation in multiple roles could produce positive outcomes through opportunities and resources that individuals can use to promote growth and better functioning in different life domains. Similar to WFC, WFE has been found to be bi-directional in nature with work–family enrichment (WFE) occurring along with family-work enrichment (FWE). Relative to WFC, research on WFE is sparse (Frone 2003). While some WFE studies have been conducted outside of the Anglo context (e.g., Baral and Bhargava 2011; Bosmat 2013; Choi and Kim 2012; Ho et al. 2013; Karatepe and Azar 2013; Nasurdin et al. 2013), there are few cross-cultural studies that specifically examine gender and WFE.

Meta-analyses have indicated that both WFE and FWE are related to a number of positive outcomes including affective commitment, physical and mental health, and job and family satisfaction. For example, Haar and Bardoel (2008) looked at positive spillover in 420 Australian employees and found WFE was negatively associated with psychological distress and turnover intentions, while FWE was negatively linked with psychological distress and positively linked with family satisfaction. However, WFE is more strongly related to work-related variables, whereas FWE was more strongly related to non-work related variables (McNall et al. 2010; Shockley and Singla 2011). This is somewhat resonant of the stronger impact of same domain relationships observed in WFC literature (Michel et al. 2011).

6.4 Gender and Work–Family Conflict

The examination of gender is integral to W–F research—both its positive and negative elements—given that gender roles influence how men and women distribute resources across work and family domains. Interestingly, although the boost to work and family research has come from the increasing presence of women in the workforce, few studies have specifically focused on W–F and gender (Parasuraman and Greenhaus 2002). Even when gender has been included as a variable, its treatment has been atheoretical and gender as operationalized by whether someone is a man or a woman has often been used as a proxy for other aspects of gender (Korabik et al. 2008). One drawback of treating gender as a biologically determined variable is that it does not consider the possibility that there may be greater within-gender variation than across-gender variation in roles. Gender is actually a multidimensional phenomenon. Korabik et al. (2008) proposed that rather than considering only physical gender, research should consider intrapsychic aspects of gender that influence not only individuals' identities, but also their behaviors, the roles they choose to enact and how they choose to enact them. One such variable that is pertinent to W–F research is gender-role ideology (GRI) (Korabik et al. 2008). In addition, sociological or cultural conceptions of gender, like gender egalitarianism and gender inequality, can be studied in an effort to better understand the W–F interface (Lyness and Kropf 2005; Powell et al. 2009).

6.4.1 Gender and WFC: Theoretical Approaches

Two perspectives are frequently used in the literature to explain the relationship between gender and WFC. One is the rational viewpoint (Gutek et al. 1991), which posits that the more the hours one spends in a domain, the more potential there is for conflict to occur. This theory predicts that men should experience more WIF than women because they spend more time at work, whereas women should experience more FIW than men because they spend more time at home. A competing theory is Pleck's (1977) gender-role theory. It postulates that family demands will more likely affect work roles for women, whereas work demands will more likely spill over into the family for men. This gender-asymmetrical impact of work and family roles is due to the differential importance given to these roles by men and women. This affects their perceptions of WIF and FIW so that additional hours spent in one's prescribed gender-role domain (family for women and work for men) are not seen as an imposition as much as additional hours spent in the domain associated with the other gender. According to the gender-role perspective, women should report more WIF than men even when they spend the same number of hours in paid work, and men should report more FIW than women even when they devote the same number of hours to family activities.

In their review of WFC studies, Eby et al. (2005) concluded that there is mixed evidence as to whether men and women report different levels of WFC. Their meta-analysis mentions that some research has found no gender differences in WFC (Duxbury and Higgins 1991; Eagle et al. 1997), some studies have found men to report higher WFC than women (Parasurman and Simmers 2001), and other studies have found women to experience higher WFC than men (Frone et al. 1992b) or higher levels on some dimensions of WFC (e.g., Gutek et al. 1991; Loerch et al. 1989).

Regarding Pleck's (1977) hypothesis of gender differences in the permeability of W–F boundaries, support has also been mixed. Gutek et al. (1991) reported more WIF for women than men, but no gender difference in FIW. Other studies have found no significant gender differences at all, though family boundaries were consistently more permeable than work boundaries (Eagle et al. 1997; Frone et al. 1992a, b). Overall it appears that gender has a near zero relationship to WIF and is only weakly related to FIW, suggesting that men and women experience similar levels of interference in both domains (Bryon 2005).

6.4.2 Gender Differences in Antecedents and Consequences of WFC

As with research examining mean differences, studies of gender differences in the antecedents of WFC have produced conflicting results. In an investigation of family-related antecedents of WFC, Loerch et al. (1989) found that family role conflict was a significant predictor of strain- and behavior-based WFC for both genders, and a unique predictor of time-based conflict for men, but not women. Furthermore, family intrusions and total role involvement predicted time-based conflict for women, whereas family intrusions were a unique predictor of strain-based conflict for men.

Focusing on work domain antecedents, Wallace's (1999) study of lawyers found that work involvement variables were not predictive of either time- or strain-based WFC among women, though higher work motivation and working more hours were associated with men's strain- and time-based conflict, respectively. Furthermore, work overload and being in a profit-driven environment had similar effects on time-based WFC for men and women lawyers, while the impact of these antecedents on strain-based WFC was stronger for women as compared to men. Wallace also found that work context was important—working in a law firm setting was associated with greater time- and strain-based conflict for women though not for men. Finally, as the percentage of women lawyers in the workplace increased, men reported greater time-based conflict, but women reported more strain-based conflict. Duxbury and Higgins (1991) examined gender differences in work and family domain antecedents of WFC. They found that work involvement was a stronger predictor of WFC for women, whereas family involvement was a stronger predictor for men. Work expectations, on the other hand, were a more significant predictor of WFC for men, while family expectations were a stronger predictor of family conflict for women. Gutek et al. (1991) examined the effect of hours spent in the home and work domain and found that for women, the number of hours spent on the job was related to WIF. For FIW, no gender effect of hours spent in family work was found. This was contrary to Huffman et al.'s (2003) study of military personnel where time demands measured by the number of hours worked were more strongly related to WFC for men than for women. This gender difference disappeared, however, when time demands were measured via perceptions of workload. McElwain et al. (2005)

used a time demands measure that was a composite of work hours and perceived job demands and found no significant gender differences for the relationships between work time demands and WIF. However, there was a significant gender difference in the relationship between family demands and FIW. Specifically, women tended to experience high levels of FIW when they had high family demands as compared to men. Men's levels of FIW, however, were not dependent on the amount of family demands they had. It would seem that control over work hours plays a significant role in determining women's versus men's WFC rather than work hours per se. In support of this notion, Grönlund (2007) found that in Sweden women in jobs with high demands and high control did not experience more WIF than men, even when working the same hours.

Social support is another important antecedent associated with reduced WFC. Aycan and Eskin (2005) found gender differences in the type of support used by men and women in Turkey. For women, spousal support was associated with reduced WIF and FIW, whereas for men spousal support was associated with reduced FIW and organizational support was associated with reduced WIF. Their finding supported earlier literature suggesting that men needed more social support than women in coping with WFC, because although changing gender roles prescribe men to be more involved in their families, this is still not tolerated by most organizations (cf., Cinnamon and Rich 2002). Furthermore, men do not have as many role models as women do to show them how to cope with WFC, and they do not exhibit help-seeking behavior as much as women do (Addis and Mahalik 2003).

Turning to the outcomes of WFC, although Frone et al. (1996) and Frone et al. (1993) established that higher WFC resulted in poor physical and psychological health, as well as heavy alcohol use, their findings did not support the hypothesized gender differences in the relationship between WFC and outcomes. By contrast, Duxbury and Higgins (1991) found that women were more likely than men to report low quality of work life when they had high WFC, whereas men were more likely than women to report low quality of family life when they had high WFC. In addition, Burley (1995) found that the relationships of WFC to spousal support and marital adjustment were significantly more negative for men than for women.

The results with regard to the moderating effect of gender on the relationships of WIF and FIW to satisfaction are extremely inconsistent. Bagger et al. (2008) found that family identity salience acted as a buffer such that higher FIW was related to higher job distress and lower job satisfaction more so for women than men. By contrast, McElwain et al. (2005) found the negative relationship between FIW and job satisfaction to be stronger for men than for women, but that there was no significant gender difference in the relationship between WIF and family satisfaction. Ford et al.'s (2007) path analytic meta-analysis indicated that the negative correlation between job stress and family satisfaction was less strong for women than for men. However, Shockley and Singla's (2011) meta-analysis showed that the negative correlation between WIF and family satisfaction was stronger for men than women, whereas the negative correlation between FIW and family satisfaction was stronger for women than men.

6.5 Cross-Cultural Studies of Gender Interacting with WFC and WFE

Several studies of gender and WFC have been conducted in individual countries outside of the North American context, including Malaysia (e.g., Hassan et al. 2010), India (e.g., Ramadoss and Rajadhyaksha 2012), Iran (e.g., Namayandeh et al. 2011), Hong Kong (e.g., Fu and Shaffer 2001), Finland (e.g., Väänänen et al. 2004), and Turkey (e.g., Yavas et al. 2008). Some studies have demonstrated within-gender differences in WFC based on ethnicity (e.g., Mahpul and Abdullah 2011), whereas other single-country studies have supported both a 'gender similarity' as well as a 'gender difference' model of WFC depending on the database used for drawing the sample (e.g., Keene and Quadagno 2004). We will not review the results of this research here since a substantial cross-cultural literature exists.

The results of cross-cultural comparisons on gender and WFC have been characterized by the same inconsistency found in the North American literature on gender and WFC. Some studies have revealed no significant gender effects. For instance, in a cross-cultural test of the W–F interface in 48 countries, Hill et al. (2004) found little support for a culture-specific or gender-specific model of WFC. A few of their observed gender differences included marital status being more likely to reduce FIW for women than for men, parental status being associated with significantly more FIW for women than for men, and perceptions of a lack of fit being more strongly related to WIF for women than for men. However, there were no gender differences across cultures. Shaffer et al. (2011) examined 219 studies that used non-USA samples and also found no differences due to gender. Their results indicated that work demands predicted both WIF and FIW in their Anglo, Asian, Nordic, and Western European country clusters. Family stressors were positively related to WFC for countries in the Anglo cluster, to both WIF and FIW for countries in the Asian cluster, and to FIW for countries in the Western European cluster. WIF and FIW were negatively related to work-related affective reactions and positively related to withdrawal outcomes in all country clusters. WIF and FIW were often, but not always, negatively related to family attitudes (e.g., satisfaction) in the Anglo, Asian, and Nordic, East, and West European country clusters.

By contrast, other studies have found gender differences in WFC, but these have not always been consistent. Steibler (2009) examined dual-earner couples in 23 European countries and found that after work hours were controlled, women reported both more time- and strain-based WIF than men. In a study of eight European countries, Simon et al. (2004) found that WIF was higher than FIW in all countries, supporting the notion of asymmetrical boundaries between work and family (Pleck 1977). However, men experienced greater WIF than women in Italy, whereas the reverse was the case in the Netherlands. Mortazavia et al. (2009) conducted a cross-cultural study using samples from Iran, Ukraine, and the USA to examine interactions between gender, nationality, and the cultural values of horizontal individual ism/collectivism measured at the national and individual levels (idiocentrism and allocentrism) on W–F demands and WFC. They found that men reported more WIF than women in all three countries, but there was no significant gender difference in FIW. In a study comparing the USA and China, Yang et al. (2000) reported that men experienced higher levels of WFC than women did in China, whereas a gender difference did not exist in the USA sample. Using data from Project 3535[2], Korabik et al. (2012) found that men reported higher WIF than women in all countries except India, Taiwan, and Turkey where WIF was higher for women than men. Conversely, women reported higher FIW than men in all countries except Australia, China, and the USA, where FIW was higher for men than women. In addition, greater satisfaction with organizational policies was associated with lower WIF for both genders in Australia, Canada, Indonesia, and the USA. This relationship also held for men in Israel and women in Spain and Turkey. Greater satisfaction with organizational policies was also significantly associated with lower turnover intent for both genders in every country except Turkey. Greater satisfaction with organizational policies was significantly associated with higher life satisfaction for both genders in Canada, Indonesia, Israel, Turkey, and the USA. This relationship also held for men in China and India and women in Australia and Taiwan. Greater satisfaction with government policies was significantly associated with higher life satisfaction for both genders in Canada, China, India, and Indonesia. This relationship also held for men in Australia and the USA and for women in Israel. Satisfaction with government policies was less consistently related to intent to turnover, with the strongest correlations evident for men in the USA, women in Spain, and both men and women in Israel (Korabik et al. 2012).

Gender has been largely overlooked in the literature on WFE (Greenhaus and Powell 2006). Studies do show, however, that women tend to perceive higher levels of FWE than men (Grzywacz and Marks 2000; Rothbard 2001). Although in a three-year cross-lagged panel study carried out in Finland (Hakanen et al. 2011) gender was found to be related to WFE the same way for men and women, Shockley and Singla's (2011) meta-analysis indicated that WFE had a greater effect on satisfaction outcomes for women than for men. Moreover, using a sample from Spain, Boz et al. (2009) found that FWE was related to life satisfaction and mental and physical well-being in a different manner for women and men. Their results also showed that women were able to experience FIW and FWE concurrently, while men were more likely to separate their family from their work roles. In addition, when women reported experiencing both FIW and FWE, the positive effect of FWE outweighed the negative consequences of FIW on well-being.

Data from Project 3535 (Korabik et al. 2012) have indicated that women reported higher WFE than men in all countries except China, Spain, and Indonesia where WFE was higher for men than women. Moreover, greater satisfaction with

[2] Project 3535 is a collaborative investigation of the W–F interface among organizationally employed married/cohabiting parents in ten countries (i.e., Australia, Canada, China, India, Indonesia, Israel, Spain, Taiwan, Turkey, and the US). The contributions of the members of the Project 3535 research team to this chapter are gratefully acknowledged. The team consists of: Drs. Zeynep Aycan, Roya Ayman, Anne Bardoel, Tripti Desai, Anat Drach-Zahavy, Leslie B. Hammer, Ting-Pang Huang, Karen Korabik, Donna S. Lero, Artiwadi Mawardi, Steven Poelmans, Ujvala Rajadhyaksha, Anit Somech, and Li Zhang. The project website is www.workfamilyconflict.ca.

organizational policies was associated with higher WFE for both genders in Canada and Turkey. This relationship also held for men in China and women in Australia, Israel, Taiwan, and the USA (Korabik et al. 2012).

6.6 Gender-Role Ideology

Typically, GRI is conceptualized as falling on a unidimensional continuum ranging from traditional to nontraditional or egalitarian (Gibbons et al. 1997). Individuals with a traditional GRI believe that women should give priority to family responsibilities and men to work responsibilities (Gutek et al. 1991). By contrast, nontraditional or egalitarian individuals believe in a more equal role distribution for men and women. The conceptualization of GRI does not make the assumption of biopsychological equivalence, i.e., both men and women can have either traditional or egalitarian attitudes (Korabik et al. 2008).

Research indicates that individuals' GRI can change both between and within generations (Moen et al. 1997; Wentworth and Chell 2005), thus supporting the notion that GRI is shaped by environmental influences. The GRI of individuals also can vary between countries. In a comparative study of gender-role attitudes among the North American countries of Mexico, Canada, and the USA, Harris et al. (2006) found that in general Mexicans were slightly more likely to exhibit traditional attitudes and gender-role behavior that was congruent with their biological gender. Additionally, being a man was slightly more likely to predict traditional GRI than being a woman in Canada and the USA, as compared to Mexico. Goldberg et al. (2012) found that GRI varied between ethnic groups within a country. They studied a large culturally and ethnically diverse sample of students at a US university and found that Asian Americans, especially men and those less acculturated, were more likely to hold more conservative GRI and support gender-role segregation and maternal nonemployment when children are young. Their mothers' employment and own employment status, however, was associated with more positive views about maternal employment overall. Additionally GRI can be shaped by national cultural and economic variables. For instance, Parboteeah et al. (2008) found that managers' traditional gender-role attitudes were positively related to a nation's cultural values of power distance and uncertainty avoidance while being negatively related a nation's cultural values of gender egalitarianism, as well as to degree of regulation of the economy and degree of educational attainment.

Women's exposure to the labor force and to education can foster more egalitarian GRI on account of role expansion (Smith-Lovin and Tickamyer 1978). Individuals in industrialized countries have been found to hold more egalitarian GRIs with more favorable views of married women's labor force participation (Treas and Widmer 2000). In fact, with more women entering the workforce, individuals' attitudes in many societies are experiencing a change from traditional to more egalitarian (Friedman and Weissbrod 2005). However in some transitional societies men's GRI could become more traditional as a backlash. For instance, in a study conducted in urban China, Pimentel (2006) found that husbands had become more traditional in their GRI over cohorts while wives' GRI had stayed constant and was more egalitarian than that of husbands. Pimentel explained this difference in terms of increasing expectations of equality among women and declining job opportunities for men in reformist China, resulting in declining levels of marital satisfaction over time. In a comparison of GRI of women in Taiwan and coastal China, Tu and Liao (2005) found that urbanization had a more significant impact on women's attitudes than on men's attitudes and this effect was more significant in coastal China which has seen more marked changes in development in recent decades, as compared to Taiwan. Also, cohort-effect differences in gender-role attitudes were found to be more significant in coastal China and more so for men than for women.

There can be gender differences in GRI particularly for working individuals. Husbands' and wives' GRIs within working couples can influence each other (Kulik 2004). In a study of dual-earner couples in Sri Lanka, Kailasapathy and Metz (2008) found that spouse's GRI affected the ability to negotiate within the home to reduce WFC. Women's egalitarian GRI in dual-earner marriages could cause them to experience a sense of unfairness when they feel that they do more than their spouse (Frisco and Williams 2003). On the other hand, the more egalitarian the husband's GRI relative to the wife's, the weaker the relationship between job-role quality and distress tends to be (James et al. 1998). The more egalitarian the GRIs of husband-wife pairs, the less likely they are to adopt gender-stereotypic decisions regarding relocation for jobs, i.e., with the wife hesitating from capitalizing on a job move because of the loss that it would mean to the husband (Bielby and Bielby 1992). Along with gender, GRI can moderate the link between spousal support and marital quality. For instance, emotional spousal support has been found to better predict marital satisfaction and less marital conflict for traditional women and egalitarian men, while emotional and instrumental spousal support has been found to better predict marital satisfaction for egalitarian women and traditional men (Mickelson et al. 2006).

6.6.1 GRI and the W–F Interface

Studies have examined relationships between GRI and broad work and family variables. For example, Davis and Pearce (2007) found that adolescents' work–family gender ideologies were linked to their educational attainments. For girls and boys, having more egalitarian views of gendered work and family roles made them more likely to desire a college education and a graduate or professional degree, although the relationship was stronger for girls than for boys. Schwarzwald et al. (2008) in a study of Izraeli married couples found that GRI moderated the relationship between a couple's usage of power tactics and marital satisfaction.

Studies linking GRI and the W–F interface specifically defined as WFC and WFE are relatively few. GRI has been found to be a better predictor of WFC than physical gender (Velgach et al. 2006) which might help explain many of the inconsistent findings in the gender and WFC literature. To the extent that attitudes affect behavior, GRI is likely to impact WFC by influencing the degree to which individuals resort to traditional versus nontraditional division of labor. Thus, it would be expected that working women with traditional GRI would experience more WIF than would working women with egalitarian GRI because their traditional attitude would influence them to exert most of their efforts into their home roles. Conversely, working men with traditional GRI should experience more FIW than working men with egalitarian attitudes as their attitudes would dictate that they should spend their time providing for their family through paid work (Gutek et al. 1991; Korabik et al. 2008).

Empirical examinations of the relationship between GRI and WFC have produced mixed results. No significant differences between those with traditional and egalitarian GRI were found on either WIF or FIW in a study by Chappell et al. (2005) with a sample from Canada or by Drach-Zahavy and Somech (2004) using Project 3535 data from Israel. By contrast, Ayman et al. (2005) found significant negative relationships between GRI and strain-based WIF, time-based WIF, and time-based FIW, indicating that egalitarian individuals experienced lower WFC than traditional individuals on these dimensions. In a sample of working men and women from India gathered as part of Project 3535, Rajadhyaksha and Velgach (2009) found that those with traditional GRI experienced more of both WIF and FIW than those with egalitarian GRI. Moreover, there was an interaction effect between gender and GRI. Women 'traditionals' experienced more FIW than men 'traditionals'. Using Project 3535 data from Israel, Somech and Drach-Zahavy (2007) found an interaction effect between gender and GRI with regard to the relationship between coping strategies and WIF and FIW.

6.6.2 Cross-Cultural Studies of GRI and the W–F Interface

There have been few cross-cultural examinations of the relationship between GRI and WFC, and almost no studies have examined the relationship between GRI and WFE. Steibler's (2009) study of dual-earner couples in 23 European countries showed that men with more egalitarian gender-role attitudes had lower levels of WIF. Using preliminary data from five of the countries (i.e., Canada, India, Taiwan, Spain, and the USA) involved in Project 3535, Poelmans et al. (2006) conducted a cross-cultural analysis of the relationship between GRI and WFC. After controlling for job sector and job level, it was found that in all countries, those with traditional GRI reported greater WIF and greater FIW than those with egalitarian GRI. Somech and Drach-Zahavy (2011) used the data from all ten Project 3535 countries and found that individual coping strategies were related to WIF and FIW as a function of GRI and individualism/collectivism.

6.7 Cross-Cultural Studies of Cultural Gender Egalitarianism, Gender Inequality, and the W–F Interface

There have been relatively few studies that have investigated the impact of cultural gender egalitarianism or societal/national gender inequality on the W–F interface. In a study of managers and professionals from 20 European countries, Lyness and Kropf (2005) found that both national gender equality (measured using the United Nations Gender Development Index) and the proportion of women in senior management positions predicted perceptions of supportiveness of organizational culture which in turn was related to employees' perceptions of greater work–life balance. They suggested that future studies of the W–F interface recognize the importance of the larger context and a nation's standing with regard to gender equality. Öun (2012) looked at data from four Nordic countries and found that overall, women reported higher WFC than men. However, greater gender equity at the household level was related to lower WIF. Further, WFC was higher in Finland compared to the other three Nordic countries of Denmark, Sweden, and Norway. This difference was explained in terms of the relatively greater gender inequity within Finland with lesser integration of women in to the workforce. Beham et al. (2012) conducted a study of how utilization of W–F resources affected work interference with family (WIF) and satisfaction with W–F balance (SWFB) among professional and non-professional service employees across five Western European countries. They found that the utilization of organizational W–F resources varied across welfare state regimes and levels of national gender equality, being highest in Sweden and the Netherlands and lowest in Portugal. Across the five countries, professional employees experienced higher levels of WIF and lower levels of SWFB than non-professional employees and the gap between professionals and non-professionals varied across countries for WIF, but not for SWFB. It was significantly larger in the UK and in Sweden than in the other three countries. Finally, a family-supportive supervisor and a family-supportive organizational culture differentially affected the WIF of professional and non-professional workers, with a family-supportive supervisor being more beneficial to non-professionals and a family-supportive organizational culture being more beneficial to professional employees.

Many national policies that affect working conditions, especially of female workers, play a role in determining women's socioeconomic status and therefore gender inequality (e.g., Guan et al. 2011; Ray et al. 2010). In a recent study conducted across 12 industrialized nations that examined the relationship between WFC and national paid leave policies, Allen et al. (2014) found that of the three forms of paid leave examined—sick, annual, and parental—paid sick leave had a small but significant negative relationship with WFC, while paid parental leave and paid annual leave had very little impact on WFC. Also, the impact of national leave policies on WFC was moderated by employees' perceptions of the family-supportiveness of their organization as well as their supervisor, such that the impact was more beneficial when employees perceived more rather than less support. Clearly, it appears that national gender inequality has the potential to impact the W–F interface directly as well as indirectly through the utilization and/or availability of organizational resources and national policies that affect conditions of work.

Cultural gender egalitarianism has also been found to affect the W–F interface. Steibler (2009) examined 23 European countries and found that those in countries with higher levels of gender egalitarianism as a cultural value had higher levels of strain-based WIF. In a comparison of work–life balance (WLB) perceptions of employees in Indian and American multinational corporations, Chandra (2012) found that within the Indian context, gender socialization led WLB to be perceived as more of a women's issue that needed to be solved at the individual level, and there was greater emphasis on employee welfare schemes to balance work and family. By contrast, within American companies the emphasis of WLB programs was on flexible work arrangements.

A recent study conducted by Lyness and Judiesch (2014) examined the interplay between gender and gender egalitarianism on the W–F interface in 36 countries. Their study used multi-source data as well as multilevel analyses and found that supervisors' perceptions of employees' WLB differed by ratee gender and country context. Supervisors rated women lower than men in WLB in low egalitarian countries, but similar to men in high egalitarian countries, and only appraisals of women (but not men) varied depending on egalitarian context. Societal gender inegalitarianism explained the majority of variation in supervisors' appraisals of women's WLB, whereas women's self-reported balance was linked to objective gender inequalities.

6.8 Conclusion

In a call for more culture sensitive theories of the W–F interface, Powell et al. (2009) suggest gender egalitarianism, among other cultural variables, for inclusion in future research studies. They also refer to several ways in which culture could be examined in W–F research—namely, culture-as-nations, culture-as-referents, and culture-as-dimensions. Poelmans (2003) recommended that we consider the micro-layer, the meso-layer, the macro-layer, and the micromacro-layer while studying the antecedents and consequences of WFC. Ollier-Malaterre et al. (2013) recommended that future W–F research should consider positive and negative aspects of the W–F interface and examine interactions between institutional factors such as national policy contexts in addition to cultural dimensions on individual and organizational levels of analyses.

Our review of the literature indicates that gender-based examinations of the W–F interface built on the notion of 'biological' gender provide a somewhat incomplete understanding of the phenomena of WFC and WFE by yielding mixed results. Future W–F studies should incorporate wider conceptions of gender that account for differences in the ways that gender is enacted in diverse contexts by men and women. GRI could be one such variable that operates between biological and sociological conceptions of gender. Our review of the literature also indicates that there are several interactions and complex relationships between gender and GRI (micro variables) and gender egalitarianism and gender equity (macro variables covering culture and nation). Exploring the relationships between these variables and WFC/WFE may turn out to be the most likely way to plug the many existing lacunae in W–F research.

References

Addis, M. E., & Mahalik, J. R. (2003). Men, masculinity and the contexts of help seeking. *American Psychologist, 58,* 5–14.

Allen, T. D., Lapierre, L. M., Spector, P. E., Poelmans, S. A. Y., O'Driscoll, M., Woo, J., et al. (2014). The link between national paid leave policy and work–family conflict among married working parents. *Applied Psychology: An International Review, 63,* 5–28.

Amstad, F. T., Meier, L., Fasel, U., Elfering, A., & Semmer, N. (2011). A meta-analysis of work–family conflict and various outcomes with a special emphasis on cross-domain versus matching-domain relations. *Journal of Occupational Health Psychology, 16,* 151–169.

Aryee, S. (1992). Antecedents and outcomes of work–family conflict among married professional women: Evidence from Singapore. *Human Relations, 45,* 813–837.

Aryee, S., Luk, V., Leung, A., & Lo, S. (1999). Role stressors, interrole conflict, and well-being: The moderating influence of spousal support and coping behaviors among employed parents in Hong Kong. *Journal of Vocational Behavior, 54,* 259–278.

Aycan, Z. (2008). Cross-cultural approaches to work–family conflict. In K. Korabik, D. S. Lero, & D. L. Whitehead (Eds.), *Handbook of work–family integration: Research, theories, and best practices* (pp. 353–370). San Diego: Elsevier.

Aycan, Z., & Eskin, M. (2005). Childcare, spousal, and organizational support in predicting work–family conflict for females and males in dual-earner families with preschool children. *Sex Roles, 53,* 453–471.

Ayman, R., Velgach, S., & Ishaya, N. (April 2005). *Multi-method approach to investigate work–family conflict.* Poster presented at the meeting of the Society for Industrial and Organizational Psychology, Los Angeles, California, USA.

Ayo, H. T., Henry, A. S., & Taiwo, A. (2009). Psychosocial variables as predictors of work–family conflict among secondary school teachers in Irele local government area, Ondo State, Nigeria. *Pakistan Journal of Social Sciences, 6,* 11–18.

Bagger, J., Li, A., & Gutek, B. A. (2008). How much do you value your family and does it matter? The joint effects of family identity saliency, family-interference-with-work and gender. *Human Relations, 61,* 187–211.

Baral, R., & Bhargava, S. (2011). Examining the moderating influence of gender on the relationships between work–family antecedents and work–family enrichment. *Gender in Management: An International Journal, 26,* 122–147.

Beham, B., Drobnic, S., & Präg, P. (2012). The work–family interface of service sector workers: A comparison of work resources and professional status across five European countries. *Applied Psychology: An International Review, 63,* 29–61.

Bielby, W. T., & Bielby, D. (1992). I will follow him: Family ties, gender-role beliefs, and reluctance to relocate for a better job. *American Journal of Sociology, 97,* 1241–1268.

Billing, T. K., Bhagat, R. S., Babakus, E., Krishnan, B., Ford Jr, D. L., Srivastava, B. N., Rajadhyaksha, U., Shin, M., Kuo, B., Kwantes, C., Setiadi, B., & Nasurdin, A. M. (2014). Work–family conflict and organisationally valued outcomes: The moderating role of decision latitude in five national context. *Applied Psychology: An International Review, 63 (1),* 62–95.

Bosmat, S. (2013). Combining multiple roles among high position women in Israel, as seen by the woman, her husband and a child. *Journal of International Women's Studies, 14,* 69–93.

Boz, M., Martinez, I., & Munduate, L. (2009). Breaking negative consequences of relationship conflicts at work: The moderating role of work family enrichment and supervisor support. *Revista de Psicología del Trabajo y de las Organizaciones, 25,* 113–121.

Bryon, K. (2005). A meta-analytic review of work–family conflict and its antecedents. *Journal of Vocational Behavior, 62,* 169–198.

Burley, K. A. (1995). Family variables as mediators of the relationship between work–family conflict and marital adjustment among dual-career men and women. *Journal of Social Psychology, 135,* 483–497.

Casper, L. M., & Bianchi, S. M. (2002). *Continuity and change in the American family: Anchoring the future*. Thousand Oaks: Sage.

Casper, W., Bordeaux, C., Eby, L., Lockwood, A., & Lambert, D. (2007). A review of research methods in IO/OB work–family research. *Journal of Applied Psychology, 92,* 28–43.

Chandra, V. (2012). Work-life balance: Eastern and western perspectives. *The International Journal of Human Resource Management, 23,* 1040–1056.

Chappell, D., Korabik, K., & McElwain, A. (June 2005). *The effects of gender-role attitudes on work–family conflict and work–family guilt.* Poster presented at the meeting of the Canadian Psychological Association, Montreal, Quebec, Canada.

Choi, H., & Kim, Y. T. (2012). Work-family conflict, work–family facilitation, and job outcomes in the Korean hotel industry. *International Journal of Contemporary Hospitality Management, 24,* 1011–1028.

Cinnamon, R., & Rich, Y. (2002). Gender differences in the importance of work and family roles: Implications for work–family conflict. *Sex Roles, 47,* 531–541.

Davis, S. N., & Pearce, L. P. (2007). Adolescents' work–family gender ideologies and educational expectations. *Sociological Perspectives, 50,* 249–272.

Drach-Zahavy, A., & Somech, A. (July 2004). *Emic and etic characteristics of coping strategies with WFC: The case of Israel.* Paper presented at the International Congress of Cross-Cultural Psychology, Xi'an, China.

Duxbury, L. E., & Higgins, C. A. (1991). Gender differences in work–family conflict. *Journal of Applied Psychology, 76,* 60–73.

Eagle, B. W., Miles, E. W., & Icenogle, M. L. (1997). Interrole conflicts and the permeability of work and family domains: Are there gender differences? *Journal of Vocational Behavior, 50,* 168–184.

Eby, L. T., Casper, W. J., Lockwood, A., Bordeaux, C., & Brinleya, A. (2005). Work and family research in IO/OB: Content analysis and review of the literature (1980–2002). *Journal of Vocational Behavior 66,* 124–197.

Ford, M. T., Heinen, B. A., & Langkamer, K. L. (2007). Work and family satisfaction and conflict: A meta-analysis of cross domain relations. *Journal of Applied Psychology, 92,* 57–80.

Friedman, S. R., & Weissbrod, C. S. (2005). Work and family commitment and decision-making status among emerging adults. *Sex Roles, 53,* 317–325.

Frisco, M. L., & Williams, K. (2003). Perceived housework equity, marital happiness, and divorce in dual-earner households. *Journal of Family Issues, 24,* 51–73.

Frone, M. R. (2003). Work-family balance. In J. C. Quick & L. E. Tetrick (Eds.), *Handbook of occupational health psychology* (pp. 143–162). Washington: American Psychological Association.

Frone, M. R., Russell, M., & Cooper, M. K. (1992a). Antecedents and outcomes of work–family conflict: Testing a model of the work–family interface. *Journal of Applied Psychology, 77,* 65–78.

Frone, M. R., Russell, M., & Cooper, M. L. (1992b). Prevalence of work–family conflict: Are work and family boundaries asymmetrically permeable? *Journal of Organizational Behavior, 13,* 723–729.

Frone, M. R., Russell, M., & Cooper, M. L. (1993). Relationship of work–family conflict, gender, and alcohol expectancies to alcohol use/abuse. *Journal of Organizational Behavior, 14,* 545–558.

Frone, M. R., Russell, M., & Barnes, G. M. (1996). Work-family conflict, gender, and health-related outcomes: A study of employed parents in two community samples. *Journal of Occupational Health Psychology, 1,* 57–69.

Fu, K. C., & Shaffer, M. A. (2001). The tug of work and family: Direct and indirect domain-specific determinants of work–family conflict. *Personnel Review, 30,* 502–522.

Gelfand, M. J., & Knight, A. P. (2005). Cross-cultural perspectives on work–family conflict. In S. A. Y. Poelmans (Ed.), *Work and family: An international research perspective* (pp. 401–414). Mahwah: Erlbaum.

Gibbons, J., Hamby, B., & Dennis, W. (1997). Researching gender-role ideologies internationally and cross-culturally. *Psychology of Women Quarterly, 21,* 151–170.

Goldberg, W. A., Kelly, E., Matthews, N., Kang, H., Li, W., & Sumaroka, M. (2012). The more things change, the more they stay the same: Gender, culture, and college students' views about work and family. *Journal of Social Issues, 68,* 814–838.

Greenhaus, J., & Beutell, N. (1985). Sources of conflict between work and family roles. *Academy of Management Review, 10,* 76–88.

Greenhaus, J. H., & Powell, G. N. (2006). When work and family are allies: A theory of work–family enrichment. *Academy of Management Review, 31,* 72–79.

Grönlund, A. (2007). More control, less conflict? Job demand-control, gender and work–family conflict. *Gender, Work & Organization, 14,* 476–497.

Grzywacz, J. G., & Marks, N. F. (2000). Reconceptualizing the work–family interface: An ecological perspective on the correlates of positive and negative spillover between work and family. *Journal of Occupational Health Psychology, 5,* 111–126.

Guan, J., Rajadhyaksha, U., & McElroy, J. (2011). The relation between work conditions and women's socio-economic status: A global exploratory study. *Journal of Research in Peace, Gender and Development, 1,* 271–285.

Gutek, B. A., Searle, S., & Klepa, L. (1991). Rational versus gender-role explanations for work family conflict. *Journal of Applied Psychology, 76,* 560–568.

Haar, J. M., & Bardoel, E. A. (2008). Positive spillover from the work–family interface: A study of Australian employees. *Asia Pacific Journal of Human Resources, 46,* 275–287.

Hakanen, J. J., Peeters, M., & Perhoniemi, R. (2011). Enrichment processes and gain spirals at work and at home: A 3-year cross-lagged panel study. *Journal of Occupational and Organizational Psychology, 84,* 8–30.

Harris, R. J., Firestone, J. M., & Bryan, P. J. (2006). A comparative analysis of sex-role ideology in Canada, Mexico and the United States. *Advances in Gender Research, 10,* 97–124.

Hassan, Z., Dollard, M. F., & Winefield, A. H. (2010). Work-family conflict in East vs Western countries. *Cross Cultural Management: An International Journal, 17,* 30–49.

Hill, E. J., Yang, C., Hawkins, A. J., & Ferris, M. (2004). A cross-cultural test of the work–family interface in 48 countries. *Journal of Marriage and the Family, 66,* 1300–1316.

Ho, M., Xuefei, C., Cheung, F. M., Liu, H., & Worthington, E. (2013). A dyadic model of the work–family interface: A study of dual-earner couples in China. *Journal of Occupational Health Psychology, 18,* 53–63.

Huffman, A. H., Payne, S., & Castro, C. (April 2003). *Time demands, work–family conflict and turnover: A comparison of men and women.* Poster presented at the Annual meeting of the Society for Industrial and Organizational Psychology, Orlando, Florida, USA.

James, B., Barnett, R., & Brennan, R. T. (1998). The psychological effects of work experiences and disagreements about gender-role beliefs in dual-earner couples: A longitudinal study. *Women's Health: Research on Gender, Behavior and Policy, 4,* 341–368.

Joplin, J. R. W., Shaffer, M. A., Francesco, A. M., & Lau, T. (2003). The macro environment and work–family conflict. Development of a cross-cultural comparative framework. *International Journal of Cross-Cultural Management, 3,* 305–328.

Kailasapathy, P., & Metz, I. (2008). Work-family conflict in Sri Lanka: Negotiations of exchange relationships in family and at work. *Journal of Social Issues, 68,* 790–813.

Karatepe, O., & Azar, A. K. (2013). The effects of work–family conflict and facilitation on turnover intentions: The moderating role of core self-evaluations. *International Journal of Hospitality and Tourism Administration, 14,* 255–281.

Keene, J. R., & Quadagno, J. (2004). Predictors of perceived work–family balance: Gender difference or gender similarity. *Sociological Perspectives, 47,* 1–23.

Kinnunen, U., & Mauno, S. (1998). Antecedents and outcomes of work–family conflict among employed women and men in Finland. *Human Relations, 51,* 157–177.

Korabik, K., McElwain, A., & Chappell, D. (2008). Integrating gender-related issues into research on work and family. In K. Korabik, D. S. Lero, & D. L. Whitehead (Eds.), *Handbook of work–family integration: Research, theory, and best practices* (pp. 215–232). San Diego: Elsevier.

Korabik, K., Lero, D. S., Aycan, Z., & Bardoel, A. (Dec 2012). *HR policies to enhance work–family balance: Fostering organizational sustainability in global context.* Paper presented at the Research Colloquium on Creating Sustainable Organizations: The Human and Social Dimensions, Deakin Management Centre, Victoria, Australia.

Kulik, L. (2004). Predicting gender role ideology among husbands and wives in Israel: A comparative analysis. *Sex Roles, 51,* 575–588.

Lapierre, L. M., Spector, P. E., Allen, T. B., Poelmans, S., Cooper, C. L., O'Driscoll, M. P., Sanchez, J. I., Brough, P., & Kinnunen, U. (2008). Family-supportive organization perceptions, multiple dimensions of work–family conflict, and employee satisfaction: A test of model across five samples. *Journal of Vocational Behavior, 73,* 92–106.

Loerch, K. J., Russell, J. E., & Rush, M. C. (1989). The relationships among family domain variables and work–family conflict for men and women. *Journal of Vocational Behavior, 35,* 288–308.

Lyness, K. S., & Judiesch, M. K. (2014). Gender egalitarianism and work-life balance for managers: Multisource perspectives in 36 Countries. *Applied Psychology: An International Review, 63,* 96–129.

Lyness, K. S., & Kropf, M. B. (2005). The relationships of national gender equality and organizational support with work–family balance: A study of European managers. *Human Relations, 58,* 33–60.

Mahpul, I. H., & Abdullah, N. A. (2011). The prevalence of work–family conflict among mothers in peninsular Malaysia. *International Journal of Humanities and Social Science, 1,* 154–161.

Matsui, T., Ohsawa, T., & Onglatco, M. L. (1995). Work family conflict and the stress buffering effects of husband support and coping behavior among Japanese married workingwomen. *Journal of Vocational Behavior, 47,* 178–192.

McElwain, A., Korabik, K., & Rosin, H. M. (2005). An examination of gender differences in work–family conflict. *Canadian Journal of Behavioural Science, 37,* 269–284.

McNall, L. A., Nicklin, J. M., & Masuda, A. D. (2010). A meta-analytic review of the consequences associated with work–family enrichment. *Journal of Business and Psychology, 25,* 381–396. doi:10.1007/s10869-009-9141-1.

Michel, J. S., Kotrba, L. M., Mitchelson, J. K., Clark, M. A., & Baltes, B. B. (2011). Antecedents of work–family conflict: A meta-analytic review. *Journal of Organizational Behavior, 32,* 689–725.

Mickelson, K. D., Claffey, S. T., & Williams, S. L. (2006). The moderating role of gender and gender role attitudes on the link between spousal support and marital quality. *Sex Roles, 55,* 73–82.

Moen, P., Erickson, M., & Dempster-McClain, D. (1997). Their mother's daughters? The intergenerational transmission of gender attitudes in a world of changing roles. *Journal of Marriage and the Family, 59,* 281–294.

Mortazavia, S., Pedhiwala, N., Shafiro, M., & Hammer, L. (2009). Work-family conflict related to culture and gender. *Community, Work & Family, 12,* 251–273.

Namayandeh, H., Yaacob, S. N., & Juhari, R. (2011). The effect of gender-role orientation on work interference with family (WIF) and family interference with work (FIW) among married female nurses in Shiraz-Iran. *Asian Culture and History, 2,* 165–171.

Nasurdin, A., Ahmad, N. H., & Zainal, M. (2013). Comparing work–family conflict and facilitation among male and female entrepreneurs in Malaysia. *International Journal of Business and Society, 14,* 149–162.

Ollier-Malaterre, A., Valcour, M., Den Dulk, L., & Kossek, E. E. (2013). Theorizing national context to develop comparative work-life research: A review and research agenda. *European Management Journal, 31,* 433–447.

Öun, I. (2012). Work-family conflict in the Nordic countries: A comparative analysis. *Journal of Comparative Family Studies, 43,* 165–184.

Parasuraman, S., & Greenhaus, J. H. (2002). Toward reducing some critical gaps in work family research. *Human Resource Management Review, 12,* 299–312.

Parasurman, S., & Simmers, C. A. (2001). Type of employment, work–family conflict and well-being: A comparative study. *Journal of Organizational Behavior, 22,* 551–568.

Parboteeah, K. P., Hoegl, M., & Cullen, J. B. (2008). Managers' gender-role attitudes: A country institutional profile approach. *Journal of International Business Studies, 39,* 795–813.

Pimentel, E. E. (2006). Gender ideology, household behavior, and backlash in urban China. *Journal of Family Issues, 27,* 341–365.

Pleck, J. H. (1977). The work–family role system. *Social Problems, 24,* 417–427.

Poelmans, S. A. Y. (2003). The multi-level 'fit' model of work and family. *International Journal of Cross Cultural Management, 3,* 267–274.

Poelmans, S. A. Y., O'Driscoll, M., & Beham, B. (2005). An overview of international research on the work–family interface. In S. A. Y. Poelmans (Ed.), *Work and family: An international research perspective* (pp. 3–46). Mahwah: Lawrence Erlbaum.

Poelmans, S. A. Y., Ayman, R., Korabik, K., Rajadhyaksha, U., Huang, T. P., Lero, D. S., & Pande, D. T. (July 2006). *How far is too far?: Comparing Spain, Taiwan, India, US & Canada on work–family conflict.* Paper presented at the 18th Congress of the International Association for Cross-Cultural Psychology, Spetes, Greece.

Powell, G. N., Francesco, A. M., & Ling, Y. (2009). Toward culture-sensitive theories of the work–family interface. *Journal of Organizational Behavior, 30,* 597–616.

Rajadhyaksha, U., & Velgach, S. (Aug 2009). *Gender, gender-role ideology and work–family conflict in India.* Paper presented at the annual meeting of the Academy of Management, Chicago, Illinois, USA.

Ramadoss, K., & Rajadhyaksha, U. (2012). Gender differences in commitment to roles, work–family conflict and spousal support. *Journal of Social Sciences, 33,* 227–233.

Ray, R., Gornick, J. C., & Schmitt, J. (2010). Who cares? Assessing generosity and gender equality in parental leave policy designs in 21 countries. *Journal of European Social Policy, 20,* 196–216.

Rothbard, N. P. (2001). Enriching or depleting: The dynamics of engagement in work and family roles. *Administrative Science Quarterly, 46,* 655–684.

Schwarzwald, J., Koslowsky, M., & Izhak-Nir, E. (2008). Gender-role ideology as a moderator of the relationship between social power tactics and marital satisfaction. *Sex Roles, 59,* 657–670.

Shaffer, M. A., Joplin, J., & Hsu, Y. (2011). Expanding the boundaries of work–family research: Review and agenda for future research. *International Journal of Cross-Cultural Management, 11,* 221–268.

Shockley, K., & Singla, N. (2011). Reconsidering work–family interactions and satisfaction: A meta-analysis. *Journal of Management, 37,* 861–886.

Simon, M., Kümmerling, A., & Hasselhorn, H. M. (2004). Work-home conflict in the European nursing profession. *International Journal of Occupational and Environmental Health, 10,* 384–391.

Smith-Lovin, L., & Tickamyer, A. R. (1978). Nonrecursive models of labor force participation, fertility behavior, and sex role attitudes. *American Sociological Review, 43,* 541–557.

Somech, A., & Drach-Zahavy, A. (2007). Strategies for coping with work–family conflict: The distinctive relationships of gender-role ideology. *Journal of Occupational Health Psychology, 12,* 1–19.

Somech, A., & Drach-Zahavy, A. (July 2011). *Coping with work–family conflict from a cross cultural perspective.* Paper presented at the meeting of the International Association of Cross-Cultural Psychology, Istanbul, Turkey.

Spector, P. E., Allen, T. D., Poelmans, S., Lapierre, L. M., Cooper, C. L., O'Driscoll, M., et al. (2007). Cross-national differences in relationships of work demands, job satisfaction and turnover intentions with work–family conflict. *Personnel Psychology, 60,* 805–835.

Spector, P. E., Cooper, C. L., Poelmans, S., Allen, T. D., O'Drsicoll, M., Sanchez, J. I., Siu, O. L., Dewe, P., Hart, P., Lu, L., Moraes, L. F. R., Ostrognay, G. M., Sparks, K., Wong, P., & Yu, S. (2004). A cross-national comparative study of work–family stressors, working hours, and well-being: China and Latin America versus the Anglo world. *Personnel Psychology, 57,* 119–142.

Steibler, N. (2009). Reported levels of time-based and strain-based conflict between work and family roles in Europe: A multilevel approach. *Social Indicators Research, 93,* 469–488.

Tabassum, A. (2012). The impact of social support on work-to-family and family-to-work conflict: An analysis on the female primary school teachers of Bangladesh. *International Journal of Research Studies in Management, 1,* 67–78.

Treas, J., & Widmer, E. D. (2000). Married women's employment over the life course: Attitudes in cross-national perspective. *Social Forces, 78,* 1409–1436.

Tu, S., & Liao, P. (2005). Gender differences in gender-role attitudes: A comparative analysis of Taiwan. *Journal of Comparative Family Studies, 36,* 545–566.

Väänänen, A., May, K., Ala-Mursula, L., Pentti, J., Kivimäki, M., & Vahtera, J. (2004). The double burden of and negative spillover between paid and domestic work: Associations with health among men and women. *Women & Health, 40,* 1–18.

Velgach, S., Ayman, R., Antani, A., & Ishaya, N. (July 2006). *Impact of GRI on WFC: The case of a health organization in the USA*. Paper presented at the International Congress of Applied Psychology, Athens, Greece.

Wallace, J. E. (1999). Work-to-nonwork conflict among married male and female lawyers. *Journal of Organizational Behavior, 20,* 797–816.

Wayne, J. H., Randel, A. E., & Stevens, J. (2006). The role of identity and work–family support in work–family enrichment and its work related consequences. *Journal of Vocational Behaviour, 69,* 445–461.

Wentworth, D. K., & Chell, R. M. (2005). Gender identity at home: Comparing the role of househusband to housewife. In J. W. Lee (Ed.), *Psychology of gender identity* (pp. 113–126). Hauppauge: Nova Biomedical.

Westman, M., Etzion, D., & Gattenio, E. (2008). International business travels and the work–family interface: A longitudinal study. *Journal of Occupational and Organizational Psychology, 81,* 459–480.

Yang, N., Chen, C., Choi, J., & Zou, Y. (2000). Sources of work–family conflict: A Sino-US comparison of the effects of work and family demands. *Academy of Management Journal, 43,* 113–123.

Yavas, U., Babakus, E., & Karatepe, O. M. (2008). Attitudinal and behavioral consequences of work–family conflict and family-work conflict: Does gender matter? *International Journal of Service Industry Management, 19,* 7–31.

Part II
CONSIDERATIONS FROM THE HOMEFRONT

Chapter 7
Feeling Work at Home: A Transactional Model of Women and Men's Negative Affective Spillover from Work to Family

Melissa E. Mitchell, Lillian T. Eby, and Anna Lorys

7.1 Introduction

Affect is central to individuals' daily experiences at work and with family. Affect is fundamentally tied to those things that are most important to us—our goals, values, and beliefs—and is salient in virtually all of our interactions with others (Lazarus 2006). The most important and memorable moments of our lives are characterized by high emotion, and our attitudes toward our relationships and our jobs are, at least in part, determined by our affective reactions within those domains (Levenson and Gottman 1985; Weiss and Cropanzano 1996). Given the importance of affect in daily experience, it is critical to understand how affective states transfer across life domains. Specifically, how does affect generated at work transmit into the family, who is most likely to experience this transmission, and what are the ways in which the transmission of affect can be regulated? Through the lens of spillover theory (Staines 1980), this chapter examines these questions with a focus on the transmission of negative affect from work to family.

Spillover theory is a dominant paradigm in the work–family literature. The central premise of this theory is that experiences in the work domain spill over into the family domain, and vice versa (e.g., Staines 1980). Several studies find that affect in the work domain is related to affect in the family domain (e.g., Ilies et al. 2009;

M. E. Mitchell (✉)
Department of Psychology, University of Georgia,
Psychology Building, Athens, GA 30602, USA
e-mail: melmitch@uga.edu

L. T. Eby
Department of Psychology and Owens Institute for Behavioral Research,
University of Georgia, 510 Boyd GSRC, Athens, GA 30602, USA
e-mail: leby@uga.edu

A. Lorys
Department of Psychology, University of Georgia,
Psychology Building, Athens, GA 30602, USA
e-mail: lorysa@uga.edu

M. J. Mills (ed.), *Gender and the Work-Family Experience*,
DOI 10.1007/978-3-319-08891-4_7

Judge and Ilies 2004; Song et al. 2008; Sonnentag and Binnewies 2013). Given the importance of the family domain to overall life satisfaction and well-being (e.g., Heller et al. 2004; Proulx et al. 2007), and findings suggesting that negative mood mediates associations between job stressors and family behavior (Story and Repetti 2006), it is crucial for researchers to understand what processes may exacerbate or ameliorate the transfer of negative affect from work to family. However, the existing literature lacks a comprehensive understanding of how the emotion process, including cognitive appraisal and coping, is involved in the transfer of affect from work to family. In addition, it is critical to explore the person and environment factors that make certain work events and emotion processes more or less likely. Thus, the purpose of this chapter is to explore the role of the emotion process in the transfer of work experiences into family life. Guided by Lazarus and Folkman's (1984) seminal transactional model of emotion, we conceptualize affective responses as resulting from the dynamic interplay between characteristics of the person and the environment. In doing so, we respond to Judge and Ilies' (2004) call for an expansion of affective events theory (AET; Weiss and Cropanzano 1996) to include the effects of work events on affective processes with family, and to Allen et al.'s (2012) call for expanded theoretical models of how personal and situational variables interact to predict outcomes in the work and family domains.

Throughout this review, we consider gender as a key antecedent that has downstream effects on the work-to-family spillover process. We conceptualize gender as both a person and an environment variable consisting of gender role expectations, individual differences in masculinity and femininity, and biological sex differences. We suggest that these aspects of gender influence work events, as well as the appraisal and coping processes. By placing gender front and center in the proposed model, we address Story and Repetti's (2006) call for an approach to affective spillover that focuses on cognitive processes and gender.

Although we recognize that there is a growing body of literature on positive affective spillover and family-to-work spillover, this chapter focuses on negative affective work-to-family spillover for several reasons. First, research finds that gender differences are most apparent under conditions of stress (Schulz et al. 2004; Vogel et al. 2003). Second, there is evidence that individuals experience stronger work-to-family spillover than family-to-work spillover (Brotheridge and Lee 2005; Evans and Bartolomé 1984; Williams and Alliger 1994). Third, research suggests that negative spillover is more enduring than positive spillover (Sonnentag and Binnewies 2013). However, we note that it is also important to examine the role of gender and the emotion process in positive affective spillover in order to gain a complete understanding of the spillover process. Although we focus primarily on negative affective spillover in our review, we believe that our model can be extended to capture the unique processes involved in positive affective spillover. We think it would be fruitful for future scholars to examine the person and environment factors that give rise to benign-positive appraisals of work events, and the behaviors that tend to generate and sustain positive affect across domains. In addition, our review focuses on within-person affective spillover rather than between-person crossover (i.e., the transfer of affect from one person to another). Although crossover processes are important to consider, it is excluded from the current review in order to provide an in-depth treatment of within-person spillover.

We begin our review by briefly introducing the transactional model of emotion. Next, we discuss how negative affective work-to-family spillover fits into the transactional framework and present our conceptual model. Then, we discuss person and environment factors that may play roles in the emotion process, and consequently in affective spillover, specifically focusing on how these factors may differ for men and women. This leads to a discussion of the emotion process as a moderator of the association between affective states at work and affective states at home. We conclude our review with suggestions for future research.

7.1.1 Transactional Model of Emotion

Transactional theories of emotion posit that all affective experience is mediated by appraisal: "an evaluation of the personal significance of a particular encounter between the person and the environment" (Lazarus 1991, p. 820). Individuals engage in two types of appraisal when evaluating an event as stressful (Lazarus and Folkman 1984). In primary appraisal, people evaluate whether the event is harmful or beneficial for their well-being. In secondary appraisal, people evaluate their ability to cope with the event. Appraisals are influenced by both person and environment factors, that is, within a particular encounter, characteristics of the person and the environment interact to make certain appraisals more or less likely. Appraisals then give rise to coping behaviors, defined as efforts to manage environmental demands (problem-focused coping) and the emotions generated from those demands (emotion-focused coping). Coping behaviors, in turn, give rise to reappraisals as individuals encounter new information; these reappraisals engender additional coping behaviors. Thus, appraisal and coping reciprocally influence each other throughout an encounter (Lazarus and Folkman 1984).

7.1.2 Transactional Model of Work-to-Family Affective Spillover

Affect is an umbrella term for both mood and emotion; following previous emotion theorists (Lazarus 1991; Weiss and Cropanzano 1996), we conceptualize emotion as distinct from mood in that emotions or affective states arise in response to a specific event, whereas moods are not directed at a particular object or event. A number of studies have found that negative affect at work is related to negative affect at home (e.g., Ilies et al. 2009). Moreover, research suggests that the spillover of negative work experiences into the family domain is mediated by the affective strain resulting from those experiences (Barling and Macewen 1992). Additionally, as discussed above, transactional theories of emotion (e.g., Lazarus and Folkman 1984) suggest that all affective states are mediated by cognitive appraisal. Taken together, prior theory suggests that work events give rise to appraisal processes, which generate negative affective states if (1) the person appraises the event as threatening to their well-being and (2) the person evaluates their coping resources as inadequate for

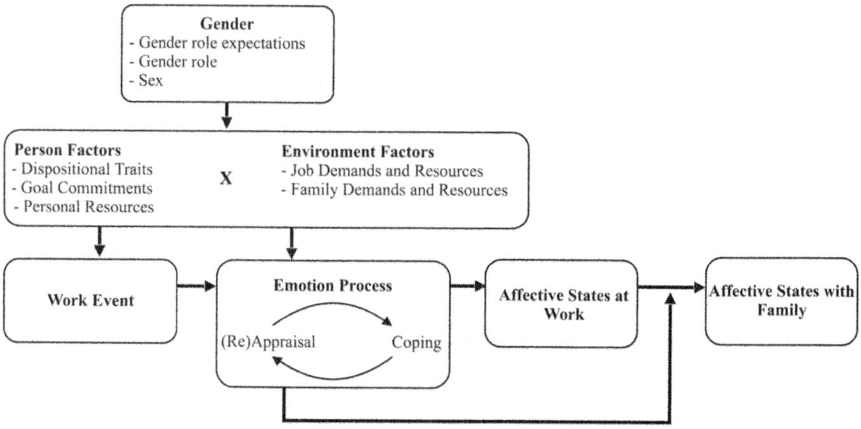

Fig. 7.1 A transactional model of affective work-to-family spillover

managing the event. We propose that these affective states may spill over into the family domain through the reciprocal processes of appraisal and coping. These associations between work events, the emotion process, and affective states at work and with family are depicted in Fig. 7.1.

Our conceptual model follows AET's (Weiss and Cropanzano 1996) tenet that work events lead to affective states at work. However, in accordance with transactional theories of emotion, we conceptualize the emotion process as the critical mediator required for a work event to produce an affective state. In addition, we follow AET's recognition of person and environment factors as causes of work events; however, consistent with transactional theories of emotion, we assert that person and environment factors have interactive effects on the occurrence of work events and appraisals of those events. For example, imagine that Leslie, a local government employee with high career goals, has just finished an important project proposal when her supervisor informs her that the funding for the project has been cut due to government overspending. Because of her high career goals, Leslie appraises this event as highly threatening to her personal well-being, causing her to feel anxious and angry. This example illustrates how person (career goals) and environment factors (government overspending) interact to trigger a work event (loss of funding for valued project), which is appraised as threatening (appraisal), resulting in negative affective states at work (anxiety and anger). Our transactional spillover model acknowledges that work events, appraisals, and resulting affective states derive from a complex interplay of the person and the environment.

A novel contribution of the model is our framing of the emotion process as not just a mediator of the association between work events and affective states, but also as a *moderator* of the association between affective states at work and affective states at home (see Fig. 7.1). In so doing, we contend that certain appraisals and coping behaviors make affective work-to-family spillover more or less likely, and that these processes have a dynamic relationship within a particular transaction. For example, imagine that Ron, an engineer who has low self-esteem, receives negative feedback from a supervisor, which causes him to feel anger and shame at work. Throughout the day, Ron ruminates about the feedback, which only exacerbates his negative emotion. By the time he returns home, Ron is extremely upset and attempts to further cope with his anger by venting to his partner. Thus, the use of rumination as a coping strategy moderates the association between negative affect at work and negative affect at home, such that it exacerbates Ron's negative emotion, and thus his spillover of negative emotion from work to home. This example illustrates the dynamic interplay between coping and appraisal; appraisals influence coping, which in turn influence reappraisals. As such, we propose that these emotion processes hinder or facilitate the transfer of negative affect from work to home.

Although appraisal and coping occur at the individual level, transactional theories of emotion acknowledge that characteristics of the social system also influence (1) the environmental conditions groups of people are exposed to and (2) characteristic ways of reacting to the environment, including appraisals and coping (Lazarus and Folkman 1984; Lazarus 1999). While acknowledging the considerable intragroup and intraindividual variability in appraisal and coping, we suggest that gender plays a role in the stress process by making certain person and environment factors more or less probable for men and women (Lazarus 1999). We suggest that these factors, in turn, have downstream effects on the emotion process and affective spillover from work to home. We view gender as a multifaceted construct composed of socially constructed norms and beliefs about the roles of men and women (i.e., gender role expectations), individual differences in masculinity and femininity, and biological sex differences. Throughout this chapter, we explore the role of gender in the emotion process, specifically as it relates to negative affective spillover from work to family. We suggest that gender role expectations present individuals with social demands (social pressure to act in accordance with gender roles and to hold gendered attitudes) and constraints (social pressure to not act in certain ways in accordance with gender roles) that shape both personal and environmental factors (see Fig. 7.1). These differentiated gender roles are facilitated by biological sex differences, including those resulting from physical specialization (e.g., pregnancy, breastfeeding) and hormones (Wood and Eagly 2002), and individual differences in gender role (Rosenkrantz et al. 1968). Through gender's effects on person and environment factors, we suggest that gender has reverberating effects on the affective spillover process. Thus, we take the position that gender differences in spillover are largely the result of differences in the *meaning* of men's and women's experiences. These meanings, we argue, are derived through the interdependent processes of appraisal, coping, and reappraisal. We now turn our attention to a discussion of specific person and environment factors that affect the emotion process, and consequently negative affective spillover from work to family.

7.2 Person Factors

7.2.1 Dispositional Traits

There are a number of dispositional traits that influence affective experience. However, most research on negative affect at work, and negative spillover more specifically, focus on affective disposition as a predictor of work and nonwork outcomes. A large body of research demonstrates that trait negative affectivity (NA), the tendency to experience negative emotional states (Watson and Clark 1984), consistently influences appraisals of negative events. Research finds that people higher in NA tend to experience negative work events more negatively than those who are lower in NA, and NA has been found to influence mood and interpretations of events at work (Judge and Ilies 2004). Additionally, people who are higher in NA may trigger aversive work and family events through their negative appraisals of the environment (Weiss and Cropanzano 1996). Individuals who are higher in NA and trait anxiety also are more likely to engage in potentially problematic coping behaviors, such as confrontation, disengagement, and avoidance, than those lower in these traits (Carver et al. 1989; O'Brien and DeLongis 1996). Thus, there is considerable support for the idea that NA affects how individuals appraise and cope with life and work events.

There is also evidence that trait-based negative affect plays a role in negative affective work-to-family spillover. For example, Repetti and Wood (1997) found that the associations between workload and parental withdrawal and irritability were particularly strong among mothers with more symptoms of depression and higher trait anxiety, suggesting that individual tendencies to experience negative emotion can have downstream effects on negative affective spillover from work to family. Grzywacz and Marks (2000) also found that negative affective spillover was higher among more neurotic individuals. Similarly, Wang et al. (2011) found that neuroticism exacerbated negative spillover among men, such that the positive association between job stress and negative emotion display with family was stronger among more neurotic men. Collectively, these studies indicate that negative affective spillover is higher among individuals who tend to experience negative emotions, particularly anxiety.

Research suggests that women score higher on negative affectivity and neuroticism than men (e.g., Costa et al. 2001), and report feeling negative emotions more intensely and for longer durations than men (Brody and Hall 2008). Thus, to the extent that negative affectivity is related to greater negative affect, we would expect women to experience more spillover than men. However, the literature in this area is inconsistent. For example, Wang et al. (2011) found that neuroticism exacerbated negative emotion spillover among men, but not women. By contrast, Grzywacz and Marks (2000) found no gender differences in the association between neuroticism and negative spillover, although they found that women experienced more negative spillover than men. Other research finds that men and women may differ in specific emotional reactions to work stress when in the home. For example, Schulz et al.

(2004) found that more negative workdays were associated with more angry marital behavior for women and more withdrawn behavior for men. These results suggest that both men and women experience negative affective spillover from work to family, although their specific affective reactions may differ.

Although women tend to score higher on negative affectivity than men, there is also evidence that women score higher in positive affectivity (Grandey et al. 2002). This suggests that women may be more emotionally reactive than men, regardless of valence (Brody and Hall 2008). Consistent with this idea, Campos et al. (2013) found that mothers displayed both more positive and negative emotion than fathers per day, and Williams and Alliger (1994) found that women experienced both higher negative and positive affective spillover than men. Other researchers have suggested that women's affective range may be broader than men's (Fujita et al. 1991); therefore, women may experience spillover of a broader range of emotions from work to home. In support of this idea, Matjasko and Feldman (2006) found that mothers experienced spillover of happiness, anger, and anxiety from work to home, whereas fathers only experienced anxiety spillover. These findings indicate that women may experience higher levels of negative and positive spillover than men as well as spillover of a greater range of emotions. These gender differences in emotional reactivity may be the result of gender role socialization. In childhood, boys learn to minimize, suppress, and control their expression of vulnerable emotions, whereas girls' emotions are accepted and attended to by others (Brody and Hall 2008). As a result, women learn to express a greater range of emotion across domains than men. As a result, women may be more likely than men to experience spillover of both positive and negative emotion from work to family.

7.2.2 Goal Commitments

According to the transactional model (Lazarus and Folkman 1984; Lazarus 1999), appraisals are influenced by a number of person factors, most importantly goal commitments—defined as those things that are valued, meaningful, and important to an individual. Goal commitments determine the significance of a particular experience to an individual's well-being. Lazarus and Folkman (1984) describe several ways that goal commitments influence appraisal. First, goal commitments affect the activities and situations in which individuals choose to be involved. For example, individuals who are highly committed to work goals will likely spend a lot of time involved in work activities and much of their time thinking about and discussing work (Greenhaus and Beutell 1985). Second, people are more sensitive to those things that are relevant to their goal commitments. For example, an individual who is highly committed to work goals may be more aware of and attentive to potential threats to these goals, and thus more likely to appraise ambiguous work events negatively. Third, goal commitments influence the extent to which individuals are vulnerable to threat and harm, such that the more a person is committed to a particular goal, the greater the potential threat. For example, individuals who are highly committed to work goals may appraise negative work events as particularly distressing. In support of these propositions, Song et al. (2008) found that negative affective work-to-home spillover was higher among those who were higher in work orientation (a strong commitment to the work role).

Historically, it was assumed that men were more likely to be committed to work goals, whereas women were more likely to be committed to family goals due to men and women's differential socialization into sex-stereotypic roles (Pleck 1977). From this perspective, men may be expected to have higher negative work-to-family spillover than women because they are more likely to attend and react to negative work events, given their higher commitment to work goals. Thus, men may experience greater negative affect at work, which may then spill over into the family. However, although some previous research has found that men are more likely to report stressful episodes at work than are women (Folkman and Lazarus 1980; Kendler et al. 2001), and that women tend to be more involved with family and men with work (e.g., Byron 2005), gender differences in work and family goals are often small. Additionally, recent research suggests that as more women have entered the workforce, gender roles have eroded somewhat (Wood and Eagly 2002), and as a result, men and women have become more equally committed to both work and family roles (Barnett and Hyde 2001; Barnett et al. 1993). For example, more than a third of men and women in Cinamon and Rich's (2002) sample viewed both work and family roles as highly important. Additionally, recent research finds that men and women who hold similar jobs report similar levels of job demands (McElwain et al. 2005), suggesting that earlier findings of gender differences in commitment may have had more to do with the differing characteristics of men's and women's jobs than men's greater prioritization of the work role. Moreover, research suggests that gender identity (i.e., description of the self in terms of masculine or feminine traits) may be a better predictor of commitment to the work and family roles than biological sex (Powell and Greenhaus 2010). One potential implication of men and women's greater commitment to goals in both domains is an increase in affective spillover for both genders. This is in line with Williams et al.'s (1991) suggestion that the effects of role juggling may be more severe for those who are highly committed to both their work and family roles, as a compromise in either domain threatens an important role. Given these findings, we suggest that researchers who are interested in affective spillover also carefully consider respondents' commitment to work and family goals.

7.2.3 Personal Resources

According to Lazarus (1999), as well as other prominent theories of job stress (e.g., Job Demands-Resources, Demerouti et al. 2001; Conservation of Resources Theory, Hobfoll 1989), individuals and groups experience stress when the demands of the environment are greater than their resources. Although researchers often include dispositional factors such as self-esteem and locus of control in definitions of personal resources (e.g., Lazarus and Folkman 1984), we define personal resources more narrowly as external sources of support that may be engaged under stress.

From the view of transactional emotion theories, although individuals may have "objective" personal resources, these resources only influence affect through cognitive appraisal; that is, although individuals' appraisals are generally congruent with reality, it is the appraisal of these resources that determines affective reactions rather than the objective situation (Lazarus and Folkman 1984). Thus, individuals who hold the same or similar personal resources may appraise the availability of resources differently. Research has found that personal resources, such as perceived social support, are negatively related to psychological strain (e.g., Vermeulen and Mustard 2000) and are positively related to adaptive coping (Holahan and Moos 1991). Given their effects on the emotion process, personal resources may also influence the extent to which negative affect from work spills over into the family.

Despite advances in women's status in the workplace and society, considerable research finds that men have more financial resources than women. American women working full-time earned 77% of men's earnings in 2012 (DeNavas-Walt et al. 2013). Women's comparatively lower income may increase women's likelihood of experiencing negative affective spillover from work to family. This is because women—particularly those in single-earner households, who earn considerably less money than those in other household structures (DeNavas-Walt et al. 2013)—may appraise work events that threaten their earnings as particularly distressing, resulting in more negative affect at work. This negative affect may be exacerbated to the extent that women are confronted with additional financial demands in their family life. Thus, to the extent that women have fewer financial resources than men, we would predict that women experience greater negative affective spillover from work to family.

Although women may have less access to financial resources than men, women tend to have broader social support networks that may mitigate negative affective spillover from work to home. There is consistent evidence that men and women differ in the desire to affiliate with others during stress. Taylor et al. (2000) argued that women's stress response may be better characterized as "tend-and-befriend" rather than "fight-or-flight"; that is, women tend to seek support during times of stress more than men, particularly from other women. Seeking support may have several benefits, including an expanded network of potential supporters with greater exchange of resources, and increased recovery from stress (Taylor et al. 2000). There is also evidence that social support has a larger impact on negative affect for those with more feminine gender roles; for example, Beehr et al. (2003) found that individuals higher in femininity had a greater decline in psychological strain when their supervisors were supportive than those lower in femininity. Thus, women may have greater access to social support resources than men, potentially mitigating the threat of negative work events, and consequently reducing negative affect.

However, there are also drawbacks to receiving social support. For one, involvement of a supportive network may necessitate both the receipt and provision of support; the provision of social support may be draining and may undermine one's own recovery from stress (Shumaker and Hill 1991). Second, affiliation may increase the likelihood of problematic social coping strategies such as corumination (Haggard et al. 2011). Considerable research has found that women are more likely to focus on and discuss negative affective states (i.e., ruminate), which tends to sustain or amplify negative affect (Nolen-Hoeksema 1987) and cortisol and immune reactivity (Denson et al. 2009). This ruminative tendency may be fostered by intimate affiliative groups, and may paradoxically sustain negative affect rather than ameliorate it. Finally, high social contact also increases the likelihood that one will encounter stressful social situations (Taylor et al. 2000). For example, Kendler et al. (2001) found that women reported higher rates of interpersonal problems within their proximal networks than did men, and that the relationship between experiencing interpersonal problems within one's network and the onset of major depression was stronger among women than men. Clearly, these complex gender differences in personal resources need to be taken into account in further comparisons of men and women's spillover experiences.

7.3 Environmental Factors

7.3.1 Job Demands and Resources

According to AET (Weiss and Cropanzano 1996), features of the work environment may trigger the occurrence of certain work events, leading to specific affective reactions. Considerable research supports the idea that the combination of high job demands and low job resources predict psychological strain (e.g., Demerouti et al. 2001). Thus, to the extent that individuals are employed in jobs that are associated with high job demands and low job resources, we would expect greater appraisal of stress and subsequently greater transfer of negative emotion from work to family. Men and women may differ in the types of jobs they are employed in and therefore in the types of workplace stressors to which they are exposed. These differences may impact appraisal and coping, and consequently influence affective spillover from work to family. That is, gender differences in job demands and resources may have downstream effects on men and women's negative affective spillover from work to family.

Much research has focused on the additional job demands faced by women in organizations. For example, women are more likely to experience gender discrimination and harassment at work than are men (Rotundo et al. 2001). In addition, occupational sex segregation makes certain work demands more salient for women than men. For example, many authors have argued that emotional labor—managing affective displays as part of a work role (Hochschild 1979)—is more commonly expected of women than men (e.g., Guy and Newman 2004). Research finds that surface acting, a component of emotional labor involving faking emotions as part of a work role (Hochschild 1979), is associated with negative affective states at work (Scott and Barnes 2011), which in turn are associated with work–family conflict (Yanchus et al. 2010). Given these associations, it is likely that emotional labor has subsequent effects on work-to-family affective spillover, and that this job demand is faced disproportionately by women. As discussed below, this effect may be compounded given women's arguably greater emotional work in the home domain compared to men (Wharton and Erickson 1993).

Men and women may also differ in job resources. For example, there is some evidence that women have greater access to work–family resources at work. Research suggests that women perceive greater availability of work–family benefits than men (Thompson et al. 1999) and use work–family benefits more than men (Allen 2001). This may be indicative of strong gender norms that discourage men from using the work–family resources that are available to them. For example, Allen and Russell (1999) found that men who took an extended family leave received fewer organizational rewards than those who did not. Similarly, Butler and Skattebo (2004) found that raters viewed men experiencing family conflict as lower performers and gave them lower reward recommendations than those who did not experience family conflict, whereas ratings of women were unaffected by family conflict. This may suggest that men may be less likely to use family supportive resources in order to protect themselves from negative career perceptions and/or outcomes associated with family conflict. Women's greater access to support for work–family benefits may decrease women's negative affective spillover through its effects on appraisal of coping resources; that is, women may perceive greater ability to cope with work stressors due to their greater perceived and actual availability of work–family support. However, although women may receive greater work–family and social support at work, they may also be more affected when they perceive a lack of support. For example, Grzywacz and Marks (2000) found that low social support at work was more strongly associated with negative work-to-family spillover for women than for men.

Other gender differences in job demands and resources may influence how men and women cope with work events. For example, Folkman and Lazarus (1980) found that men were more likely than women to use problem-focused coping (i.e., attempting to change the environment in order to cope with a stressor) at work. They interpreted this difference as resulting from men and women's different job contexts, such that the men in their sample likely had higher-level jobs and thus more opportunities to change their environment through problem-solving than women. It is likely that these gender differences have weakened over time as women's status in the workplace has improved.

7.3.2 Family Demands and Constraints

Research consistently finds that women face greater demands in the home than men. Hochschild and Machung (1989) argue that women face a "second shift" after work that involves housework, childcare, and other domestic duties. As a result of this greater household burden, women may not have the same opportunities as men to recover from job stress through after-work coping behaviors such as withdrawal. As a result, women may experience sustained negative affect from work within the family domain. In addition, several studies have found that women experience less physiological recovery from work compared to men, as indicated by women's higher stress hormone excretion after work and on rest days (e.g., Frankenhauser et al. 1989; Pollard et al. 1996). Thus, due to their higher demands in the home, women may be less able than men to recover from negative affect from work, resulting in women experiencing increased spillover of negative affect from work to home.

Women are the primary providers of socioemotional support in the family domain. This emotion work can be considered an additional household demand that primarily falls on women (Erickson 2005). Considerable research finds that men are more comfortable seeking social support from and disclosing emotion to women than to men, particularly their spouses (Brody and Hall 2008; Erickson 1993). As a result, female partners are often the primary sources of social support for their male partners. As discussed above, providing social support confers both costs and benefits; however, an additional cost of support provision within the family is emotional contagion. Research finds that men's negative emotions tend to crossover to other family members to a greater extent that do women's (Larson and Almeida 1999); one explanation for this finding is that women are expected to respond to their male partners with empathy and support, and therefore, are more likely to "catch" their partners' negative emotions (Brody and Hall 2008). Thus, women are expected to manage emotions both at work and with family to a greater extent than men. This additional burden may exacerbate women's negative affective spillover from work to home.

7.4 The Emotion Process as a Moderator of the Work-to-Family Spillover Process

Throughout this chapter, we have argued that gender has direct effects on person and environment factors, which in turn influence the emotion process. Further, we argued that this process has downstream effects on affective work-to-family spillover. We also contend that affective spillover from work to home is moderated by the emotion process—specifically, the appraisals and coping strategies involved in the response to a work event. We have already discussed how gender influences the person and environment factors that give rise to work events and appraisals of those events. To the extent that individuals appraise work events as more threatening to well-being and taxing to their resources, we would predict greater negative affective work-to-family spillover based on higher levels of negative affective states at work. However, we also argue that some coping strategies are likely to lead to further negative reappraisals, and thus greater negative spillover from work to family. Specifically, certain coping behaviors, and subsequent reappraisals resulting from coping behaviors, may moderate the association between affective states at work and affective states at home, such that affective spillover is ameliorated or enhanced depending on the strategy used.

One common strategy for coping with negative work events is withdrawal. Although both men and women tend to withdraw at home after stressful workdays (Repetti 1989; Repetti and Wood 1997), some research suggests that this strategy is more common among men. For example, Schulz et al. (2004) found that husbands, but not wives, were more likely to withdraw from their partners in the evening after feeling negative affect at the end of the workday. In the short term, withdrawal behavior may be beneficial for well-being (Repetti 1992). Research finds that psychological detachment from work attenuates negative affective spillover (Sonnentag and Binnewies 2013); thus, withdrawing or detaching may be one way that individuals use to minimize the extent to which negative affect from work spills over into the home.

However, although withdrawal may be an adaptive coping strategy in the short-term, such behavior may be problematic for family relationships. Women may be particularly distressed by their male partners' withdrawal behavior due to their greater preference for affiliation and emotional engagement (Levenson and Gottman 1985). This is consistent with Schulz et al.'s (2004) finding that wives whose husbands tended to withdraw in the evening had lower marital satisfaction than wives whose husbands did not withdraw. Since women tend to prefer to cope with strain in affiliative ways by discussing problems with others (Taylor et al. 2000), husbands' tendencies to withdraw from marital interaction may result in wives' feeling unsupported and rejected. Among heterosexual dual-earner couples, men's tendencies to withdraw to cope with negative work events may be problematic when combined with women's desire to affiliate. These gendered patterns of coping with stress may not only undermine both partners' ability to minimize negative affective spillover, but may also trigger additional negative events (e.g., arguments) within the family domain.

Other ways of coping may lessen negative affective spillover from work to home. For example, Wiese et al. (2010) found that individuals who were told to think about a positive family-related experience after thinking about a job-related failure showed faster emotional recovery than those told to think about a positive job-related experience. These results suggest that negative spillover can be ameliorated to the extent that individuals cope with negative work events by reflecting on positive experiences in their family lives. As discussed earlier, other coping behaviors, such as rumination and co-rumination, may amplify negative spillover by sustaining negative affective states (Nolen-Hoeksema 1987). Future research is needed to examine the specific coping strategies individuals can use to change their appraisals of negative work events and reduce negative affective spillover.

7.5 Conclusions and Directions for Future Research

Throughout this chapter, we emphasized the importance of the emotion process to negative affective work-to-family spillover. Although research demonstrates the affective links between the work and family domains, more research is needed to examine how specific discrete emotions experienced at work are associated with discrete emotions at home. For example, an initial anger reaction at work may change over the course of the day and interactions with others, and may develop into a different emotion as the individual engages in coping behaviors and reappraises the work event. Thus, affective states at work may develop into quite different affective states at home. An expanded focus on the spillover of discrete emotions is consistent with Lazarus' (1999) view of emotions as distinct "stories" of how a person appraises and copes with a particular transaction. However, a focus on discrete emotions requires more complex methodologies, particularly when it comes to physiological measures. Recent research suggests that typical physiological measures of stress, such as cortisol, differ depending on the specific emotion experienced and the coping strategy used (Denson et al. 2009). Thus, future research is needed to examine spillover processes at the discrete emotion level.

Another direction for future research is an examination of how family characteristics affect the spillover process. The research on spillover consistently finds that the quality of family life can ameliorate or exacerbate negative affective spillover. For example, relationship satisfaction can protect against negative emotions resulting from work events (Campos et al. 2013). Likewise, Story and Repetti (2006) found that positive associations between workload and anger were strongest in conflictual family environments. Extending these findings, it would be interesting to explore the types of behaviors that spouses and children engage in to help reduce their family members' negative affect, and the short- and long-term consequences of these behaviors on relationship satisfaction and stability.

Following Judge et al. (2006), we also encourage more research on the functionality of negative emotions in the work and family domain. Negative affective spillover may have adaptive value as a signal to family that something is wrong and that caretaking behaviors should be mobilized. For example, research indicates that preschool children behave in a less aversive and more positive manner on days when mothers are rated as more withdrawn (Repetti and Wood 1997). In addition, Repetti (1989) found that husbands were more withdrawn when wives engaged in more supportive behavior, perhaps suggesting that wives' support enabled men to psychologically detach from work. Likewise, negative affective spillover may motivate employees to engage in more effective coping strategies to reduce negative spillover, such as negotiating housework with a partner or exercising. These findings underscore the need to study affective spillover from a family systems perspective by focusing on the ways that family members inhibit and encourage negative affective spillover.

Although the focus of this chapter was negative affective spillover, it is important for researchers to examine the roles of gender and the emotion process in positive affective spillover. Recent research finds that positive affect at work is related to positive affect at home (e.g., Judge and Ilies 2004; Ilies et al. 2009; Song et al. 2008); however, less research has examined the mechanisms and antecedents involved in the positive affective spillover process. Aspects of our model may be applicable to positive spillover. For example, personal factors that encourage appraisal of stressors as challenges rather than threats—such as resilience, optimism, and self-efficacy beliefs—may encourage the spillover of positive affect from work to home through the emotion process. Job resources, such as supportive supervision or mentoring support, may also result in positive affective spillover from work to home. This would be in line with previous research documenting that autonomy, learning opportunities, respect, and meaningful work are positively related to work–family facilitation (Voydanoff 2004). It would be interesting to examine the implications of such job resources for the emotion process; perhaps when job resources are high, environmental events are appraised benevolently, generating positive affect. There is also some evidence that experiencing stressors can bolster subsequent positive affect; for example, Bolger et al. (1989) found that mood was more positive on days following a stressful event than it would have been if a stressful event was not experienced. This suggests that there may be some time-lagged affective gains associated with successful coping with stress. Future research should examine how individual differences in protective traits like resilience and optimism may encourage gains in positive affect following stressful work events.

Although coping is discussed as a response to threat appraisals in the transactional model, there may be analogous behaviors that sustain positive affect across work and family domains. For example, savoring can be considered an analog to rumination for positive events, whereby individuals recall and reminisce about positive events in ways that tend to sustain and amplify positive affect (Sonnentag and Grant 2012). To the extent that individuals savor positive work experiences throughout the day, we would expect them to experience greater positive affective spillover from work to home. Additionally, capitalization—sharing positive events with others (Gable et al. 2004)—can be considered an analog to co-rumination about positive events. Previous research has found that capitalization is associated with increases in positive affect beyond experiencing the event itself (Lambert et al. 2013; Langston 1994), suggesting that positive affective spillover may be enhanced to the extent that individuals share positive work events with their family members. This is consistent with research finding that capitalization about work events strengthens the positive association between daily work engagement and work–family facilitation (Culbertson et al. 2012), and that capitalization about work events is positively related to life satisfaction and positive affect (Ilies et al. in press). Future research should also explore the role of gender in these cognitive and social processes; it may be that behaviors such as capitalization are more common among women, given their greater preferences for affiliation (Taylor et al. 2000). This propensity may lead women to experience greater spillover of positive and negative emotions, depending on how work events are appraised. This is consistent with evidence that women experience higher levels of both work–family conflict and facilitation compared to men (Grzywacz and Marks 2000; Powell and Greenhaus 2010; van Steenbergen et al. 2007).

Consistent with previous critiques of the use of gender as an explanatory variable, we encourage researchers to measure the proposed mechanisms underlying sex and gender differences using strong theoretical rationale. Some potential mechanisms proposed in this chapter include differences in goal commitment, personal resources, job and family demands and resources, and choice of coping behaviors. With this said, it is important to note that there is usually greater variability within gender than between genders, and that gender differences in emotion and behavior often depend on the context (Brody and Hall 2008). We suggest that researchers focus on understanding these contextual features when examining gender and the spillover process. Wood and Eagly (2002) suggest that gender differences in behavior are driven by a gendered division of labor; thus, to the extent that work and family responsibilities become more equitable across genders, we should expect gender differences to become smaller. Meta-analytic work on gender differences in work attitudes and work–family conflict across time would be a welcome addition to the often inconsistent literature in this area.

We acknowledge that given the reciprocal associations within the emotion process, depicted in Fig. 7.1, and our focus on work events as primary causes of affective reactions, our proposed model will be difficult to fully test. We support Lazarus' (1999) suggestion that researchers shift their measurement of emotion from self-report surveys to narratives; narrative methodologies allow individuals to describe how a particular transaction unfolds in terms of appraisal, coping, and reappraisal, while drawing on their past experiences, goal commitments, and resources. In combination with experience sampling methodologies, narratives of emotion would be a fruitful approach to a person-centered understanding of affective spillover.

In conclusion, given the importance of affect and the work–family interface to individuals' everyday lives, an approach to spillover that focuses on the how characteristics of the person and the environment jointly affect the emotion process is important and necessary. Throughout this chapter, gender was discussed as an important antecedent variable that has downstream effects on negative affective spillover from work to family. It is hoped that the proposed model offers a theory-based framework for additional empirical and conceptual work on the intersection of gender, the emotion process, and affective spillover from work to family.

References

Allen, T. D. (2001). Family-supportive work environments: The role of organizational perceptions. *Journal of Vocational Behavior, 58,* 414–435.

Allen, T. D., & Russell, J. E. (1999). Parental leave of absence: Some not so family-friendly implications. *Journal of Applied Social Psychology, 29,* 166–191.

Allen, T. D., Johnson, R. C., Saboe, K. N., Cho, E., Dumani, S., & Evans, S. (2012). Dispositional variables and work–family conflict: A meta-analysis. *Journal of Vocational Behavior, 80,* 17–26.

Barling, J., & Macewen, K. E. (1992). Linking work experiences to facets of marital functioning. *Journal of Organizational Behavior, 13,* 573–583.

Barnett, R. C., & Hyde, J. S. (2001). Women, men, work, and family. *American Psychologist, 56,* 781–796.

Barnett, R. C., Marshall, N. L., Raudenbush, S. W., & Brennan, R. T. (1993). Gender and the relationship between job experiences and psychological distress: A study of dual-earner couples. *Journal of Personality and Social Psychology, 64,* 794–806.

Beehr, T. A., Farmer, S. J., Glazer, S., Gudanowski, D. M., & Nair, V. N. (2003). The enigma of social support and occupational stress: Source congruence and gender role effects. *Journal of Occupational Health Psychology, 8,* 220–231.

Bolger, N., DeLongis, A., Kessler, R. C., & Wethington, E. (1989). The contagion of stress across multiple roles. *Journal of Marriage and the Family, 51,* 175–183.

Brody, L. R., & Hall, J. A. (2008). Gender and emotion in context. In M. Lewis, J. M. Haviland-Jones, & L. Feldman Barrett (Eds.), *Handbook of emotions* (pp. 395–408). New York: Guilford.

Brotheridge, C. M., & Lee, R. T. (2005). Impact of work–family interference on general well-being: A replication and extension. *International Journal of Stress Management, 12,* 203–221.

Butler, A. B., & Skattebo, A. (2004). What is acceptable for women may not be for men: The effect of family conflicts with work on job performance ratings. *Journal of Occupational and Organizational Psychology, 77,* 553–564.

Byron, K. (2005). A meta-analytic review of work–family conflict and its antecedents. *Journal of Vocational Behavior, 67,* 169–198.

Campos, B., Wang, S. W., Plaksina, T., Repetti, R. L., Schoebi, D., Ochs, E., et al. (2013). Positive and negative emotion in the daily life of dual-earner couples with children. *Journal of Family Psychology, 27,* 76–85.

Carver, C. S., Scheier, M. F., & Weintraub, J. K. (1989). Assessing coping strategies: A theoretically based approach. *Journal of Personality and Social Psychology, 56,* 267–283.

Cinamon, R. G., & Rich, Y. (2002). Gender differences in the importance of work and family roles: Implications for work–family conflict. *Sex Roles, 47,* 531–541.

Costa Jr, P., Terracciano, A., & McCrae, R. R. (2001). Gender differences in personality traits across cultures: Robust and surprising findings. *Journal of Personality and Social Psychology, 81,* 322–331.

Culbertson, S. S., Mills, M. J., & Fullagar, C. J. (2012). Work engagement and work–family facilitation: Making homes happier through positive affective spillover. *Human Relations, 65,* 1155–1177.

Demerouti, E., Bakker, A. B., Nachreiner, F., & Schaufeli, W. B. (2001). The job demands-resources model of burnout. *Journal of Applied Psychology, 86,* 499–512.

DeNavas-Walt, C., Proctor, B. D., Smith, J. C. (2013). Income, poverty, and health insurance coverage in the United States: 2012. Resource document. U.S. Census Bureau. www.census.gov/prod/2013pubs/p60-245.pdf.

Denson, T. F., Spanovic, M., & Miller, N. (2009). Cognitive appraisals and emotions predict cortisol and immune responses: A meta-analysis of acute laboratory social stressors and emotion inductions. *Psychological Bulletin, 135,* 823–953.

Erickson, R. J. (1993). Reconceptualizing family work: The effect of emotion work on perceptions of marital quality. *Journal of Marriage and Family, 55,* 888–900.

Erickson, R. J. (2005). Why emotion work matters: Sex, gender and the division of household labor. *Journal of Marriage and Family, 67,* 337–351.

Evans, P., & Bartolomé, F. (1984). The changing pictures of the relationship between career and family. *Journal of Organizational Behavior, 5,* 9–21.

Folkman, S., & Lazarus, R. S. (1980). An analysis of coping in a middle-aged community sample. *Journal of Health and Social Behavior, 21,* 219–239.

Frankenhauser, M., Lundberg, U., Fredrikson, M., Melin, B., Tuomisto. M., Myrsten, A. L., et al. (1989). Stress on and off the job as related to sex and occupational status in white-collar workers. *Journal of Organizational Behavior, 10,* 321–346.

Fujita, F., Diener, E., & Sandvik, E. (1991). Gender differences in negative affect and well-being: The case for emotional intensity. *Journal of Personality and Social Psychology, 61,* 427–434.

Gable, S. L., Reis, H. T., Impett, E. A., & Asher, E. R. (2004). What do you do when things go right? The intrapersonal and interpersonal benefits of sharing positive events. *Journal of Personality and Social Psychology, 87,* 228–245.

Grandey, A. A., Tam, A., & Brauburger, A. (2002). Affective states and traits in the workplace: Diary and survey data from young workers. *Motivation and Emotion, 26,* 31–55.

Greenhaus, J. H., & Beutell, N. J. (1985). Sources of conflict between work and family roles. *Academy of Management Review, 10,* 76–88.

Grzywacz, J. G., & Marks, N. F. (2000). Reconceptualizing the work–family interface: An ecological perspective on the correlates of positive and negative spillover between work and family. *Journal of Occupational Health Psychology, 5,* 111–126.

Guy, M., & Newman, M. A. (2004). Women jobs, men's jobs: Sex segregation and emotional labor. *Public Administration Review, 64,* 289–298.

Haggard, D. L., Robert, C., & Rose, A. J. (2011). Co-rumination in the workplace: Adjustment trade-offs for men and women who engage in excessive discussions of workplace problems. *Journal of Business and Psychology, 26,* 27–40.

Heller, D., Watson, D., & Ilies, R. (2004). The role of person versus situation in life satisfaction: A critical examination. *Psychological Bulletin, 130,* 574–600.

Hobfoll, S. E. (1989). Conservation of resources: A new attempt at conceptualizing stress. *American Psychologist, 44,* 513–524.

Hochschild, A. R. (1979). Emotion work, feeling rules, and social structure. *American Journal of Sociology, 85,* 551–575.

Hochschild, A., & Machung, A. (1989). *The second shift: Working parents and the revolution at home*. New York: Viking.

Holahan, C. J., & Moos, R. H. (1991). Life stressors, personal and social resources, and depression: A 4-year structural model. *Journal of Abnormal Psychology, 100,* 31–38.

Ilies, R., Wilson, K. S., & Wagner, D. T. (2009). The spillover of daily job satisfaction onto employees' family lives: The facilitating role of work–family integration. *Academy of Management Journal, 52,* 87–102.

Judge, T. A., & Ilies, R. (2004). Affect and job satisfaction: A study of their relationship at work and at home. *Journal of Applied Psychology, 89,* 661–673.

Judge, T. A., Ilies, R., & Scott, B. A. (2006). Work–family conflict and emotions: Effects at work and at home. *Personnel Psychology, 59,* 779–814.

Kendler, K. S., Thornton, L. M., & Prescott, C. A. (2001). Gender differences in the rates of exposure to stressful life events and sensitivity to their depressogenic effects. *American Journal of Psychiatry, 158,* 587–593.

Lambert, N. M., Gwinn, A. M., Baumeister, R. F., Strachman, A., Washburn, I. J., Gable, S. L., et al. (2013). A boost of positive affect: The perks of sharing positive experiences. *Journal of Social and Personal Relationships, 30,* 24–43.

Langston, C. A. (1994). Capitalizing on and coping with daily-life events: Expressive responses to positive events. *Journal of Personality and Social Psychology, 67,* 1112–1125.

Larson, R. W., & Almeida, D. M. (1999). Emotional transmission in the daily lives of families: A new paradigm for studying family process. *Journal of Marriage and Family, 61,* 5–20.

Lazarus, R. S. (1991). Progress on a cognitive-motivational-relational theory of emotion. *American Psychologist, 46,* 819–834.

Lazarus, R. S. (1999) *Stress and emotion: A new synthesis*. New York: Springer.

Lazarus, R. S. (2006). Emotions and interpersonal relationships: Toward a person-centered conceptualization of emotions and coping. *Journal of Personality, 74,* 9–46.

Lazarus, R. S., & Folkman, S. (1984). *Stress, appraisal, and coping*. New York: Springer.

Levenson, R.W., & Gottman, J. M. (1985). Physiological and affective predictors of change in relationship satisfaction. *Journal of Personality and Social Psychology, 49,* 85–94.

Matjasko, J. L., & Feldman, A. F. (2006). Bringing work home: The emotional experiences of mothers and fathers. *Journal of Family Psychology, 20,* 47–55.

McElwain, A. K., Korabik, K., & Rosin, H. M. (2005). An examination of gender differences in work–family conflict. *Canadian Journal of Behavioural Science, 37,* 283–298.

Nolen-Hoeksema, S. (1987). Sex differences in unipolar depression: Evidence and theory. *Psychological Bulletin, 101,* 259–282.

O'Brien, T. B., & DeLongis, A. (1996). The interactional context of problem, emotion- and relationship-focused coping: The role of the big five personality factors. *Journal of Personality, 64,* 775–813.

Pleck, J. H. (1977). The work–family role system. *Social Problems, 24,* 417–427.

Pollard, T., Ungpakorn, G., Harrison, G., & Parkes, K. (1996). Epinephrine and cortisol responses to work. *Annals of Behavioral Medicine, 18,* 229–237.

Powell, G. N., & Greenhaus, J. H. (2010). Sex, gender, and the work-to-family interface: Exploring negative and positive interdependencies. *Academy of Management Journal, 53,* 513–534.

Proulx, C. M., Helms, H. M., & Buehler, C. (2007). Marital quality and personal well-being: A meta-analysis. *Journal of Marriage and Family, 69,* 576–593.
Repetti, R. L. (1989). Effects of daily workload on subsequent behavior during marital interaction: The roles of social withdrawal and spouse support. *Journal of Personality and Social Psychology, 57,* 651–659.
Repetti, R. L. (1992) Social withdrawal as a short-term coping response to daily stressors. In H. S. Friedman (Ed.), *Hostility, coping, and health* (pp. 151–165). Washington, D.C.: American Psychological Association.
Repetti, R. L., & Wood, J. (1997). Effects of daily stress at work on mothers' interactions with preschoolers. *Journal of Family Psychology, 11,* 90–108.
Rotundo, M., Nguyen, D., & Sackett, P. (2001). A meta-analytic review of gender differences in perceptions of sexual harassment. *Journal of Applied Psychology, 86,* 914–922.
Rosenkrantz, P., Vogel, S., Bee, H., Broverman, I., & Broverman, D. M. (1968). Sex-role stereotypes and self-concepts in college students. *Journal of Consulting and Clinical Psychology, 32,* 287–295.
Schulz, M. S., Cowan, P. A., Cowan, C., & Brennan, R. T. (2004). Coming home upset: Gender, marital satisfaction, and the daily spillover of workday experience into couple interactions. *Journal of Family Psychology, 18,* 250–263.
Scott, B. A., & Barnes, C. M. (2011). A multilevel field investigation of emotional labor, affect, work withdrawal, and gender. *Academy of Management Journal, 54,* 116–136.
Shumaker, S. A., & Hill, D. R. (1991). Gender differences in social support and physical health. *Health Psychology, 10,* 102–111.
Song, Z., Foo, M. D., & Uy, M. A. (2008). Mood spillover and crossover among dual-earner couples: A cell phone event sampling study. *Journal of Applied Psychology, 93,* 443–452.
Sonnentag, S., & Binnewies, C. (2013). Daily affect spillover from work to home: Detachment from work and sleep as moderators. *Journal of Vocational Behavior, 83,* 198–208.
Sonnentag, S., & Grant, A. M. (2012). Doing good at work feels good at home, but not right away: When and why perceived prosocial impact predicts positive affect. *Personnel Psychology, 65,* 495–530.
Staines, G. L. (1980). Spillover versus compensation: A review of the literature on the relationship between work and nonwork. *Human Relations, 33,* 111–129.
Story, L. B., & Repetti, R. (2006). Daily occupational stressors and marital behavior. *Journal of Family Psychology, 20,* 690–700.
Taylor, S. E., Klein, L. C., Lewis, B. P., Gruenewald, T. L., Gurung, R. A., & Updegraff, J. A. (2000). Biobehavioral responses to stress in females: Tend-and-befriend, not fight-or-flight. *Psychological Review, 107,* 411–429.
Thompson, C. A., Beauvais, L. L., & Lyness, K. S. (1999). When work–family benefits are not enough: The influence of work–family culture on benefit utilization, organizational attachment, and work–family conflict. *Journal of Vocational Behavior, 54,* 392–415.
van Steenbergen, E. F., Ellemers, N., & Mooijaart, A. (2007). How work and family can facilitate each other: Distinct types of work–family facilitation and outcomes for women and men. *Journal of Occupational Health Psychology, 12,* 279–300.
Vermeulen, M., & Mustard, C. (2000). Gender differences in job strain, social support at work, and psychological distress. *Journal of Occupational Health Psychology, 5,* 428–440.
Vogel, D. L., Wester, S. R., Heesacker, M., & Madon, S. (2003). Confirming gender stereotypes: A social role perspective. *Sex Roles, 48,* 519–528.
Voydanoff, P. (2004). The effects of work demands and resources on work-to-family conflict and facilitation. *Journal of Marriage and Family, 66,* 398–412.
Wang, S. W., Repetti, R. L., & Campos, B. (2011). Job stress and family social behavior: The moderating role of neuroticism. *Journal of Occupational Health Psychology, 16,* 441–456.
Watson, D., & Clark, L. A. (1984). Negative affectivity: The disposition to experience aversive emotional states. *Psychological Bulletin, 96,* 465–490.
Weiss, H. M., & Cropanzano, R. (1996). Affective Events Theory: A theoretical discussion of the structure, causes and consequences of affective experiences at work. In B. M. Staw &

L. L. Cummings (Eds.), *Research in organizational behavior: An annual series of analytical essays and critical review* (Vol. 18, pp. 1–74). New York: JAI.
Wharton, A. S., & Erickson, R. I. (1993). Managing emotions on the job and at home: Understanding the consequences of multiple emotional roles. *Academy of Management Review, 18,* 457–486.
Wiese, B. S., Seiger, C. P., Schmid, C. M., & Freund, A. M. (2010). Beyond conflict: Functional facets of the work–family interplay. *Journal of Vocational Behavior, 77,* 104–117.
Williams, K. J., & Alliger, G. (1994). Role stressors, mood spillover, and perceptions of work–family conflict in employed parents. *Academy of Management Journal, 37,* 837–868.
Williams, K. J., Suls, J., Alliger, G. M., Learner, S. M., & Wan, C. K. (1991). Multiple role juggling and daily mood states in working mothers: An experience sampling study. *Journal of Applied Psychology, 76,* 664–674.
Wood, W., & Eagly, A. H. (2002). A cross-cultural analysis of the behavior of women and men: Implications for the origins of sex differences. *Psychological Bulletin, 128,* 699–727.
Yanchus, N. J., Eby, L. T., Lance, C. E., & Drollinger, S. (2010). The impact of emotional labor on work–family outcomes. *Journal of Vocational Behavior, 76,* 105–117.

Chapter 8
The Intersection of Gender and Work–Family Guilt

Karen Korabik

8.1 The Problem

> I always feel as though I am failing in some way, as though I am cheating my children, my husband, and myself. The guilt is very difficult to deal with. (McElwain 2008)

As this quote from a working mother illustrates, work–family (W–F) guilt is not only pervasive, but it can also be extremely detrimental to the well-being of workers and their families. As illustrated by the following quote, there is a common perception that women are more likely to suffer from W–F guilt than men.

> I do think men and women experience guilt differently. I believe…women feel more guilt about the work/family balance—perhaps it's innate…perhaps it's because of the traditional roles men and women have had in the home. I know my husband is sad that he doesn't get to spend as much time with his family as he would like, but I don't think he struggles with the same degree of guilt. (McElwain 2008)

Guilt arising from attempting to balance work and family has been a frequent topic of interest in the media and popular press (Bort et al. 2005; Chapman 1987), as well as in the organizational behavior literature. Despite this, until recently, research on W–F guilt has been very limited (Seagram and Daniluk 2002). In this chapter, I review the empirical evidence pertaining to the intersection of gender and W–F guilt.

8.2 Definition and Conceptualizations of W–F Guilt

Most theory and research on guilt has focused on guilt in general rather than on guilt as it applies specifically to the W–F interface. In the general guilt literature, guilt is viewed as a negative emotion that arises when individuals violate their internalized standards about what constitutes proper behavior (Kubany 1994). Thus, when

K. Korabik (✉)
Centre for Families, Work and Well-Being, University of Guelph,
Guelph, ON N1G2W1, Canada
e-mail: kkorabik@uoguelph.ca

M. J. Mills (ed.), *Gender and the Work-Family Experience*,
DOI 10.1007/978-3-319-08891-4_8

individuals believe they should have thought, felt, or acted differently, it can result in feelings of guilt (Kubany 1994; Zahn-Waxler et al. 1990). Guilt has been conceptualized as consisting of a cognitive component, which consists of the recognition that one has harmed another; an affective component, which refers to the unpleasant feelings that are experienced; and a motivational component, which is the desire to undo the harm that has been caused (Hoffman 1982). Kubany et al. (1996) propose that more guilt will be experienced to the extent that individuals act in a way that violates their values, feel their actions are unjustified, feel responsible for what happened, and/or believe that they could have foreseen and prevented the outcome.

Many different definitions of W–F guilt can be found in the literature (McElwain and Korabik 2004). Most of them emphasize one or more of the aspects of general guilt discussed above. Thus, W–F guilt is often seen as resulting from having to make a choice between work and family (Conlin 2000; Pollock 1997), allowing work to interfere with family life (Glavin et al. 2011), or failing to adequately balance work and family roles (Napholz 2000). Similarly, W–F guilt has been defined as a discrepancy between one's preferred and actual level of role participation at home versus at work (Hochwarter et al. 2007). Another view is that W–F guilt arises from the perceived failure to adequately fulfill prescribed gender-role norms (Livingston and Judge 2008; Simon 1995). Finally, some authors have speculated that W–F guilt stems from attempts to deal with the double standards that are placed on women as compared to men (Banarjee 2003; Bui 1999).

8.3 The Measurement of W–F Guilt

Research into W–F guilt has been hampered by a lack of reliable and valid measurement instruments (McElwain and Korabik 2004). As a result, many studies in this area have been qualitative in nature. Some quantitative investigations exist, but mostly these have relied on single-item (e.g., "In the past seven days, how many days have you felt guilty?") or multi-item measures of general guilt.

Recent meta-analytic results have demonstrated that W–F-specific support constructs are more strongly related to W–F conflict than are the more general constructs of supervisor support and perceived organizational support (Kossek et al. 2011). It is likely that this is also the case for guilt. However, hardly any measures of guilt specific to the W–F context exist and many of these consist of single items (e.g., "I feel guilty that I don't spend enough time with my family").

Among the few multi-item measures that are specific to W–F guilt is the Feelings of Guilt about Parenting Scale (Martinez et al. 2011). This 14-item measure was developed and validated in Spain. It assesses situations that could evoke guilt in employed parents (e.g., "Playing with my child for less time than I would like") on a scale ranging from 1 = *not at all guilty* to 4 = *very guilty*. The Spanish version of the scale has excellent internal consistency reliability, and confirmatory factor analysis has indicated that it appears to be unidimensional.

Another measure is an employment-related guilt scale constructed based on the results of interviews and focus groups conducted in Turkey (Aycan and Eskin

2005). The items (e.g., "I feel guilty for not being able to spend as much time as I wish with my children") are rated on a scale ranging from 1 = *strongly disagree* to 5 = *strongly agree*. The internal consistency reliability of the English version is excellent. A similar employment-related guilt scale (Hochwarter et al. 2007) has three items (e.g., "I feel guilty about the time that I am unable to spend with my family due to work") that are rated on a scale ranging from 1 = *strongly disagree* to 5 = *strongly agree*. The measure has good internal consistency reliability.

The W–F guilt scale (WFGS; McElwain 2008; McElwain et al. 2005a) consists of seven items. It differs from the previously discussed measures in that, analogous to the W–F conflict literature, W–F guilt is viewed as being bidirectional. Thus, four of the items assess work interference with family guilt (e.g., "I regret not being around for my family as much as I would like to") and three assess family interference with work guilt (e.g., "I feel bad because I frequently have to take time away from work to deal with issues happening at home"). The items are rated on a scale ranging from 1 = *strongly disagree* to 6 = *strongly agree*. The measure and its subscales have excellent internal consistency reliability and very good test-retest reliability over a 3-month interval. A confirmatory factor analysis established the existence of a two-factor structure with work interference with family guilt (WIFG) and family interference with work guilt (FIWG) as separate dimensions. The WFGS has excellent convergent and discriminant validity. The scale was included in the survey for Project 3535[1]. Measurement equivalence for culture was established across all ten countries (Korabik and van Rhijn 2014). Measurement equivalence for gender has also been found for the Canadian subsample, indicating that men and women attribute the same meaning to the scale items (McElwain 2008).

McElwain (2008) also created a 24-item faceted version of the W–F guilt scale (WFGS-R). It has six subscales assessing physical, emotional, and psychological WIFG and FIWG. Physical W–F guilt refers to guilt from one's inability to be physically present to attend to both work and family duties, e.g., "I regret missing family (work) events because of work (family) responsibilities". Emotional W–F guilt refers to the negative feelings experienced due to W–F conflicts, e.g., "I regret when I take out my frustrations from my work (family) on my family (at work)". Psychological W–F guilt refers to the psychological spillover from one role to the other, e.g., "I feel guilty for having my family (work) on my mind while at work (spending time with my family)". Items are rated on a scale ranging from 1 = *never* to 7 = *always*. Thus far, the WFGS-R has only been validated on a sample of women. Despite this, the results look very promising. The internal consistency reliability was excellent. A confirmatory factor analysis verified a structure with two higher order factors (WIFG and FIWG), each with three lower order factors (physical, emotional, and psychological guilt). The measure also has excellent con-

[1] Project 3535 is a collaborative investigation of the W–F interface among employed married/cohabiting parents in ten countries (i.e., Australia, Canada, China, India, Indonesia, Israel, Spain, Taiwan, Turkey, and the USA). The contributions of the members of the Project 3535 research team to this chapter are gratefully acknowledged. The team consists of: Dr. Zeynep Aycan, Dr. Roya Ayman, Dr. Anne Bardoel, Dr. Tripti Desai, Dr. Anat Drach-Zahavy, Dr. Leslie B. Hammer, Dr. Ting-Pang Huang, Dr. Karen Korabik, Dr. Donna S. Lero, Dr. Artiwadi Mawardi, Dr. Steven Poelmans, Dr. Ujvala Rajadhyaksha, Dr. Anit Somech, and Dr. Li Zhang.

tent, convergent, and discriminant validity in the contexts in which it was evaluated (McElwain 2008). There is a high positive correlation between the WIFG subscale from the WFGS-R and the WIFG subscale from the WFGS; however, there is only a moderate positive correlation between the FIWG subscale from the WFGS-R and the FIWG subscale from the WFGS (McElwain 2008).

8.4 Guilt and the W–F Interface

Several studies have shown that W–F conflict and W–F guilt are interrelated. Aycan and Eskin (2005) found that work interference with family (WIF), but not family interference with work (FIW), was positively correlated with employment-related guilt. Similarly, data from Canada indicate that for both the WFGS and the WFGS-R, significant positive correlations exist between the WIF and WIFG, as well as between the FIW and FIWG subscales. Despite this, scores on W–F guilt do not correlate so highly with those on W–F conflict as to indicate redundancy between these constructs (Korabik and Lero 2004; McElwain 2008; McElwain et al. 2005a, b). As this research is correlational in nature, however, it cannot be determined whether W–F guilt is an antecedent or an outcome of W–F conflict.

Employment-related guilt has been found to be associated with a variety of negative consequences including time inflexibility, depression, and lower satisfaction with life, organizational policies, parenthood, and time spent with children (Aycan and Eskin 2005). Hochwarter et al. (2007) examined whether the ability to manage resources at work could enhance personal control and help to reduce the negative effects of work-induced guilt. They conducted two studies using business school students and public employees as participants, respectively. They found that work-induced guilt had detrimental effects on job and life satisfaction when individuals did not have the ability to manage resources. However, the unfavorable effects of work-related guilt on job and life satisfaction were neutralized when there was an ability to manage resources.

8.5 Physical Gender and W–F Guilt

Gender is a multidimensional construct consisting of physical and demographic gender,[2] as well as a range of socialized gender-role characteristics such as gender-role orientation, attitudes, and behaviors (Korabik et al. 2008b). The vast majority

[2] Physical gender (whether someone is, or considers themselves to be, a man or a woman) refers to the psychological ramifications of biological sex (whether someone is biologically male or female). This terminology avoids assumptions of biopsychological equivalence (equating sex and gender with one another) and biological essentialism (the belief that behavior is solely attributable to biological causes). In self-report studies, physical gender is not directly observed, rather it is assessed by proxy as a demographic category. For simplicity's sake, in this chapter the term gender is used to refer to physical and demographic gender in contrast to the term gender-role which is used to refer to gender-role orientation, attitudes, ideology, etc.

of studies into the effects of gender on the W–F interface have focused solely on physical or demographic gender.

In terms of general guilt proneness, gender differences in guilt have been found as early as 33 months. Zahn-Waxler and Kochanska (1988) reported that preschool-aged girls exhibited guilt-related behaviors when they either observed or committed a transgression. Furthermore, girls have been found to be more affected by their wrongdoings than boys (Kochanska et al. 2002). Many other studies have indicated that general guilt levels are higher in women than men (e.g., Kubany and Watson 2003). It is believed that this may stem from the stereotype that women are more interpersonally sensitive than men (Zahn-Waxler et al. 1990), making them more vulnerable to guilt feelings (Zahn-Waxler and Kochanska 1988).

8.5.1 *Qualitative Research*

Most of the research on guilt as it specifically applies to the W–F interface has been qualitative in nature, and much of it has employed samples consisting solely of women. For example, Napholz (2000) interviewed eight employed Native American women. They were asked to offer explanations for the feelings of guilt that arose due to their multiple roles. One participant stated that women felt obligated to fix everything and felt guilty when they couldn't handle all of the demands placed on them. Another respondent said that guilt had driven her to spend more time with her family because she constantly felt like she should be doing more. She admitted to being so preoccupied with guilt that she was unable to properly complete the tasks on which she was working. Some of the women tried to make amends for the guilt by being a "cool" mother or by spending more time with their children.

In another study, Elvin-Nowak (1999) examined W–F guilt in 13 working mothers in Sweden. Participants' feelings of guilt stemmed from their perceived failure in responsibility toward caring for others. This was due primarily to their lack of control over circumstances which resulted in their inability to balance the demands from their different life spheres. While the mothers felt the most guilt in regard to their children, they also expressed guilt feelings toward their husbands, parents, friends, and coworkers. For example, because these women felt that they should be responsible for mothering their children, they felt guilty when delegating this to someone else (e.g., a babysitter). The women also reported experiencing aggression and anger in reaction to the burden of their guilt feelings. They tried to alleviate the guilt by devising strategies that would allow them to justify putting their own needs first.

Guendouzi (2006) investigated women teachers in the UK, finding that W–F guilt stemmed from trying to achieve an ideal balance between personal and social needs. In addition, she found that guilt resulted from the social pressure placed on mothers to be constantly available and accessible (i.e., the intensive mothering norm). On a related note, Seagram and Daniluk (2002) studied maternal guilt in eight mothers of preadolescent children. They found that the mothers felt a connection or bond with their children and a sense of responsibility for their children's well-being. This manifested itself both in feeling that they needed to prepare their children for life's challenges and in fearing their children might come to harm. The participants' maternal guilt resulted in a sense of inadequacy and emotional depletion (e.g., feelings of anger, frustration, exhaustion, and resentment).

One component of Project 3535 was to collect qualitative data. The findings revealed that women from a variety of countries mentioned W–F guilt during focus group discussions about W–F balance. These included Australia (Bardoel 2004), Canada (Korabik and Lero 2004; McElwain et al. 2005a), India (Desai and Rajadhyaksha 2004), Indonesia (Mawardi 2004), Israel (Drach-Zahavy and Somech 2004), Taiwan (Huang 2004), and the USA (Velgach et al. 2005). Although there were many similarities, women in different countries tended to emphasize somewhat different themes when speaking about what made them feel guilty. Women in Australia and India were most likely to report experiencing guilt due to their inability to be superwomen (Bardoel 2004; Korabik 2005). Women in the USA mentioned feeling guilty about having to put their jobs before their families and their inability to be in two places at one time (Velgach et al. 2005). By contrast, women in India appeared to experience guilt more when they ignored the academic achievement of their children (Desai and Rajadhyaksha 2004). Women in Indonesia, Taiwan, and the Arab women in Israel spoke about feeling guilty for not fulfilling their traditional gender roles (Korabik 2005). Four of the seven Jewish Israeli women, however, felt that they had moved from guilt to positive spillover as a function of their life stage (Drach-Zahavy and Somech 2004).

More recently, there has been recognition that fathers are not immune from experiencing guilt due to having to deal with the stresses of balancing work and family life (Daly 2001; Martinez et al. 2011). As a result, some qualitative studies have included both men and women as participants. My colleagues and I obtained data from online focus groups with both male and female parents employed by Canadian organizations (Korabik and Lero 2004; Korabik et al. 2007; McElwain et al. 2005a, 2007). When asked if they felt W–F guilt, all participants except one man overwhelmingly indicated that this was a common occurrence. The majority of both men and women said that although they felt guilt both toward balancing their work roles and their family roles, the guilt was strongest in regard to their family responsibilities. Moreover, respondents reported feeling more guilt about their children than their spouses/partners due to a greater sense of responsibility regarding the well-being of their children. Respondents also reported experiencing guilt when their coworkers made them feel that they were not "pulling their weight" at work.

The men and the women were very similar to one another both in the extent to which they admitted experiencing W–F guilt and in the things that made them feel guilty. Despite this, most participants, both men and women alike, *believed* that there were gender differences in W–F guilt, such that women were more prone to feelings of guilt than men. Some respondents felt that men and women experienced W–F guilt differently either because women were more emotionally sensitive than men or because women were more able to verbalize their feelings than men were.

Other participants felt that these gender differences stemmed from societal expectations that men and women should fulfill traditionally prescribed gender roles. Both men and women felt that higher expectations were put on women than on men. Although some men realized that they were currently "getting off easy" compared to women, they did worry that they might have to pay a price later in life for their current neglect of their families.

In another study from Canada, Daly (2001) investigated men and women in both dual-earner and single-parent families. The participants reported feeling guilty about what they were unable to do. The contradiction between their ideal aspirations and the reality of their lives resulted in chronic guilt. More specifically, both women and men felt guilty for working too much, not spending enough time with their children, leaving their children with babysitters, and taking time for themselves. Many had given up on trying to rid themselves of the guilt and had focused on how to live with it.

Simon (1995) compared 40 men and women in dual-earner couples who were employed full-time and had a child under the age of 18 living at home. Eighty-five percent of the women reported feeling guilty because their work took time away from their families and made them feel like they were neglecting their children and spouses. Men, on the other hand, did not report feeling guilty or a feeling of being pulled in different directions. Men's guilt appeared to stem more from their inability to fulfill their breadwinner role.

In summary, it appears that in many countries around the world women report experiencing W–F guilt. Although there are some cultural differences, their stories have many similar themes. There also seem to be few differences between the extent to which men and women report feeling guilty. Despite this, both men and women hold the stereotype that women are more prone to W–F guilt than are men.

8.5.2 Quantitative Research

The quantitative research on physical/demographic gender and W–F guilt is still quite sparse. In an early study with a sample of all women, Nevill and Damico (1977) found that those between the ages of 25 and 39 reported significantly higher levels of guilt due to the stress experienced from competing role demands than women at other ages. They suggested that because older women had older children who required less supervision, they were more able to pursue their individual goals without feeling as though they were doing so at the expense of others.

8.5.2.1 Mean Gender Differences in W–F Guilt

Among the few studies that have examined whether W–F guilt is more prevalent in men or women, the results have been mixed. Aycan and Eskin (2005) found that women reported significantly higher levels of employment-related guilt than did men. However, there was still a significant relationship between W–F conflict and guilt for men. By contrast, Hochwarter et al. (2007) found no correlation between gender and employment-related guilt in either of their samples. Martinez et al. (2011) found that mothers and fathers of preschoolers in Spain were similar in reporting high levels of guilt on the Guilt About Parenting Scale. Both mothers and fathers felt guilty that they could not pay as much attention to their children as they wanted and because they had to delegate some parenting tasks to others. However, mothers' guilt was more related to their fear that they were not being a "good" mother, whereas fathers' guilt was more related to their conflict between their desire to be involved with their children and their need to be breadwinners.

Data on the WFGS from Project 3535 indicated no significant overall main effect for gender or gender by country interaction for either WIFG or FIWG. However, in the Canadian subsample men scored significantly higher than women on WIFG (McElwain 2008), whereas in the Israeli subsample women scored significantly higher than men on FIWG.

8.5.2.2 Gender Differences in How W–F Guilt Relates to Antecedents and Outcomes

My colleagues and I conducted research examining the antecedents and outcomes of W–F guilt (Korabik and McElwain 2011; Korabik et al. 2009). We collected data from two samples of employed parents in Canada. The first consisted of 171 employed women who completed both the WFGS and the WFGS-R along with measures of antecedent (i.e., demands, W–F conflict) and outcome (e.g., satisfaction, turnover intent) variables on one occasion. The second sample consisted of 264 men and 180 women who were employed and who were married/cohabiting parents. They completed the WFGS and measures of the antecedent and outcome variables. Data on the outcome variables were also collected three months later from a subsample of this group (122 men and 138 women).

We carried out a variety of structural equation modeling analyses on the data to try to understand what was driving the effects (i.e., the gender composition of the sample, the version of W–F guilt scale used, or use of a cross sectional versus prospective design). The results can be found in Table 8.1. Column 1 displays the effects for the all-women sample on the WFGS-R using a cross-sectional design, whereas Column 2 displays the effects for the same sample and design, but using the WFGS as the measure. Column 3 displays the effects for the mixed gender sample ($N=444$) on the WFGS using a cross-sectional design. Column 4 displays the effects for the mixed gender subsample ($N=260$) on the WFGS using a prospective design.

As can be seen, except for the fact that higher FIWG did not significantly predict a lack of family satisfaction or greater psychological distress, most of the relationships were significant in the expected direction. Moreover, most of the relationships were consistent across samples, measures, and designs. The exception was

Table 8.1 Results of analyses with different samples, measures, and designs

	Results of analyses			
Relationships among variables	**1**	**2**	**3**	**4**
Job demands[a] → WIF conflict	+	+	+	+
Family demands[a] → FIW conflict	+	+	+	+
WIF conflict → WIFG	+	+	+	+
FIW conflict → FIWG	+	+	+	+
WIF conflict → Job satisfaction	–	–	–	–
WIF conflict → Turnover intent	+	+	+	+
FIW conflict → Family satisfaction	–	–	–	–
WIFG → Job satisfaction	–	–	–	ns
WIFG → turnover intent	+	+	+	ns
FIWG → Family satisfaction	ns	ns	ns	ns
Job satisfaction → Life satisfaction	+	+	+	+
Family satisfaction → Life satisfaction	+	+	+	+
WIF conflict → Psychological distress	N/A	N/A	+	+
FIW conflict → Psychological distress	N/A	N/A	+	+
WIFG → Psychological distress	N/A	N/A	+	+
FIWG → Psychological distress	N/A	N/A	ns	ns

[a] Job and family demands were used as predictors only in models where turnover intent was the outcome variable; Column 1 = 171 women, WFGS-R, cross-sectional design; Column 2 = 171 women, WFGS, cross-sectional design; Column 3 = 448 men and women, WFGS, cross-sectional design; Column 4 = 360 men and women, WFGS, prospective design

that higher WIFG did not predict lower job satisfaction or higher turnover intentions when a prospective design was used. This pattern of effects indicates that the gender composition of the sample (all women versus mixed gender) did not have an impact on the results. This may have been due to the fact that many extraneous factors that often produce spurious gender effects had been controlled (Korabik et al. 2008b). For example, in the mixed gender sample, the men and women were similar to one another in that they were all employed parents who were married/cohabiting. However, although the results appear similar for men and women, additional analyses on the mixed gender sample data specifically testing whether the men's and women's models differ significantly from one another are necessary before firm conclusions can be drawn regarding a lack of gender differences.

8.5.2.3 Gender in Context

Shields (2013) has argued that we need to move away from studying whether men and women are different from one another and toward studying gender in context or what factors accentuate or diminish gender differences. In this regard, Glavin et al. (2011) examined the impact of work interruptions outside of work hours. In their large sample of employed American adults, they found that women reported higher levels of general guilt than men. Moreover, among women, but not men, the frequency of work interruptions outside of work hours was positively correlated with guilt, and guilt mediated the association between work contact outside of work hours and psychological distress even after W–F conflict was controlled. In a similar study, Offer and Schneider (2011) examined mothers and fathers in dual-earner families in the USA. They found no gender differences on their single-item family time guilt measure. However, for mothers, but not fathers, greater frequency of W–F multitasking at work and in public places was associated with more family time guilt. Dealing with work interruptions outside of work hours and engaging in W–F multitasking are circumstances that are characterized by low control coupled with high demands/overload. In the literature on W–F guilt, issues related to demands, overload, and control have often been mentioned as being important (Aycan and Eskin 2005; Elvin-Nowak 1999; Hochwarter et al. 2007; Napholz 2000). Thus, the relationship between gender and W–F guilt may be impacted by contextual variables such as overload and control.

To address this possibility, my colleagues and I used the WFGS with samples of employees from the USA (Ishaya et al. 2013) and Canada (Ewles et al. 2013). We examined the effects of gender, work and family overload, and job and family control on WIFG and FIWG, respectively. For both men and women in Canada, higher work overload predicted higher WIFG. However, in the USA, WIF moderated this relationship. A lack of job control was predictive of higher WIFG for both genders in the USA, but was not a significant predictor in the Canadian sample. In both the USA and Canada, greater family overload was related to higher WIFG for both genders. A lack of family control predicted higher WIFG for both genders in the USA, but this held true only for women in Canada. Finally, in both the USA and Canada, higher family overload was associated with greater FIWG for men, but not for women. It is difficult to reconcile the disparate findings about how gender interacts with overload and control to impact W–F guilt. This is because the various studies carried out thus far differ as to their samples, their designs, and the measures of W–F guilt used.

Social support has been found to help alleviate the negative effects of W–F conflict (Ayman and Antani 2008). Aycan and Eskin (2005) found that for women, but not men, supervisory support and emotional spousal support were associated with lower work-induced guilt. We (Ewles et al. 2014) used the WFGS to examine gender differences in how received social support from work and nonwork sources was related to W–F guilt. Support from work-related sources (supervisors and coworkers) for work-related issues was not significantly related to WIFG, but it was associated with significantly lower FIWG for those of both genders. In terms of support for family-related issues, when supervisors provided support for household tasks, men were more likely than women to report higher WIFG. By contrast, the more the supervisors and coworkers provided encouragement and appreciation regarding the family, the lower the FIWG for both men and women. Greater support for work-related duties by spouses/partners, neighbors, relatives, and friends was associated with greater WIFG for both genders. Conversely, for both men and women there was no significant association between the support received from nonwork sources for work-related issues and FIWG. However, when their parents/in-laws provided support for both work and family issues, women were significantly more likely than men to report higher WIFG. Furthermore, when they received appreciation from their spouses/partners regarding their work or family life or from their children regarding their family life, men reported significantly lower WIFG than women. Finally, for both genders, the more often children, neighbors, relatives, and friends listened to and discussed family-related problems, the lower the FIWG. These results indicated that the effects of gender and social support on W–F guilt are complex and depend upon the source, domain, type of support, and the direction of W–F guilt examined.

8.6 Gender-Role Attitudes/Ideology and W–F Guilt

Gender-role ideology (GRI) refers to the attitudes or beliefs an individual holds about the proper roles of men and women in society. It is generally conceptualized as a unidimensional construct with traditional attitudes at one pole and egalitarian attitudes at the other. Chappell et al. (2005) studied a small sample of dual-earner parents from Canada using the WFGS. They found that men with egalitarian GRI reported experiencing more FIWG than traditional men. Egalitarian men also reported higher levels of FIWG than egalitarian women. No significant results were found for WIFG. The Project 3535 data, however, showed a different pattern of results. Those with egalitarian attitudes had lower WIFG than those with traditional attitudes in every country except China (where there was no significant difference) and Turkey (where traditionals had lower WIFG than egalitarians). For FIWG, those with egalitarian attitudes were also lower than those with traditional attitudes in every country except Spain (where there was no significant difference) and Turkey (where traditionals had lower FIWG than egalitarians). Over all countries, both men and women with egalitarian attitudes reported lower FIWG than those with traditional attitudes. However, for WIFG there was an interaction between gender and GRI such that egalitarian men scored higher than traditional men, whereas traditional women scored higher than egalitarian women.

The Project 3535 data from India, Indonesia, and Taiwan were examined by Rajadhyaksha et al. (2011). They established that their GRI scale had measurement equivalence for culture, and found no differences in the gender-role attitudes of men and women in each country. In structural equation models, GRI was treated as an antecedent variable that impacted WIFG via work overload and WIF and impacted FIWG via family overload and FIW. GRI predicted W–F guilt in the same way in each country such that more traditional GRI was associated with higher WIFG and FIWG.

Livingston and Judge (2008) looked at how traditional/egalitarian attitudes and W–F conflict were related to general guilt. They found that there was a stronger positive relationship between WIF and guilt for those with more egalitarian gender role attitudes than for those with more traditional attitudes. By contrast, there was a stronger positive relationship between FIW and guilt for those with traditional gender-role attitudes than for those with egalitarian gender-role attitudes. However, there was an interaction between gender and FIW. Traditional men reported the highest levels of guilt and this was exacerbated when FIW was high. By contrast, egalitarian men reported the lowest levels of guilt, and this was particularly so when FIW was high. Traditional and egalitarian women reported moderate levels of guilt.

8.7 Gender-Role Orientation and W–F Guilt

Gender-role orientation refers to those personality characteristics in the instrumental/agentic and expressive/communal domains that are acquired through gender-role socialization. McElwain et al. (2004) used the WFGS to examine W–F conflict and W–F guilt with respect to gender-role orientation as assessed by the Extended Personal Attributes Questionnaire. Participants were dual-earner employed parents from Canada. W–F guilt was significantly related only to the instrumentality aspect of gender-role orientation such that those lower in instrumentality (feminine and undifferentiated individuals) had higher levels of FIWG than those higher in instrumentality (masculine and androgynous individuals). There were no significant differences between those in the different gender role groups in their levels of WIFG.

8.8 Summary and Critique of the Literature

Research on gender and W–F guilt is still in its infancy. Despite a tremendous interest in the issue, empirical research on the subject is very limited. Mirroring the literature on gender and emotions (Shields 2013), the overall picture is currently one of few gender differences and many inconsistent results. Where differences have been found, results are often congruent with the stereotype of women as being more guilt-prone than men. What's more, such findings have been more frequent when global, nonspecific measures of self-reported guilt have been used and when women have been sampled from the general population regardless of their employment, marital, or parental status. This may be because under such circumstances societal gender stereotypes are more likely to influence self-construals to produce stereotyped gender differences on self-reports about emotions (Shields 2013).

Research in this area may also be characterized by a lack of meaningful and consistent results because it suffers from a number of other methodological limitations. First, many studies on W–F guilt have employed qualitative methodologies, and most of these have used samples comprised solely of women. Not only can conclusions about gender differences not be drawn from such data, but an implicit assumption behind such research is that W–F guilt is a woman's problem that does not pertain to men.

Second, when comparative research has been carried out, it has consisted almost exclusively of atheoretical studies of physical/demographic gender. This is particularly problematic when it pertains to gender and emotions. If a theoretical reason for why gender differences exist is not provided, the categories of man/woman can become reified and used as the explanation (Shields 2013). Moreover, this can produce conceptual confusion and result in physical gender being employed as a proxy for some other variable, something that introduces confounds into the research (Korabik et al. 2008b). For example, physical gender is frequently used as a proxy for gender role variables like gender-role orientation. In this case, findings regarding W–F guilt can be mistakenly attributed to whether someone is a man or woman instead of to the degree of instrumentality and expressivity in their personality. Moreover, in our society, physical gender is a status marker. Because of this, when research fails to control for status-related variables (e.g., job level), differences in W–F guilt may be mistakenly attributed to whether someone is a man or a woman rather than to gender-related status differences (Korabik et al. 2008b).

A third problem is that W–F guilt has often been assessed with one-item measures of unsupported reliability and validity or with measures of general guilt, which are only moderately correlated with W–F specific measures like the WFGS (McElwain 2008). Fourth, a wide variety of different operationalizations, measures, samples, and designs have been used, making it very difficult to compare the results of different studies to one another.

8.9 Future Directions

Clearly, much more research on the topic of gender and W–F guilt is necessary. This should include studies that focus not only on physical gender, but also on gender role constructs. Researchers should be careful to articulate their theory about why they expect gender differences to exist and to use gender-related constructs that are appropriate to the underlying processes that they are studying (i.e., intrapsychic, interpersonal, or social structural) (Korabik et al. 2008b). In addition, more attention needs to be paid to making sure that confounding variables are controlled and to examining gender in context (Korabik et al. 2008b; Shields 2013).

Future research should employ multi-item bidirectional measures created specifically to assess W–F guilt. For example, the WFGS has been shown to be psychometrically sound and to evidence measurement equivalence across a number of cultures. It is also essential to establish the measurement equivalence for gender of any W–F guilt measure before going on to draw any conclusions regarding gender differences. If this is not done, any differences found may be due to the different meaning that men and women attribute to the scale items rather than to actual gender differences.

Thus far, most quantitative research on gender and W–F guilt has been correlational in nature, making it impossible to draw strong inferences about causality. Furthermore, W–F guilt has been variously conceptualized as an antecedent to W–F conflict, as an outcome of W–F conflict, and as a mediator of the relationships between WIF and FIW and outcomes. Longitudinal data is necessary to understand the place of W–F guilt in the larger context of the W–F interface.

8.10 Conclusion

W–F guilt is frequently discussed in the literature on W–F conflict as being an important phenomenon. Gender-related effects in this area appear to be complex and dependent upon participant characteristics (e.g., marital, parental, and employment status), culture, and the direction of W–F guilt assessed (WIFG versus FIWG). In addition, it appears that variables such as the degree of control, overload, and social support in the work and family domains may be important moderators.

When it comes to gender, it is crucial that we do not fall into the traps of viewing W–F guilt as primarily a woman's concern or of accepting gender-related stereotypes as reality (Shields 2013). In addition, it is important not to overgeneralize results so as to emphasize between-gender differences at the expense of within-gender variability (Shields 2013). For example, we must recognize that not all mothers are the same, nor are all fathers, and that many different types of families exist. Likewise, the potential impact of race and culture cannot be underestimated.

Dealing with the combined pressures of work and family is a major issue for employees in today's global workforce (Korabik et al. 2008a). The ensuing stress can result in W–F guilt, a negative emotional state that is associated with a variety of consequences detrimental to individual workers as well as to their organizations, including decreased job and life satisfaction and increased psychological distress, depression, and turnover intentions. Understanding what makes people feel guilty, why they feel guilty, under what circumstances they feel guilty, and the gender dynamics underlying these processes will assist us in designing interventions that will improve the well-being of individual workers and the bottom line of organizations.

References

Aycan, Z., & Eskin, M. (2005). Relative contribution of childcare, spousal, and organizational support in reducing work–family conflict for males and females: The case of Turkey. *Sex Roles, 53,* 453–471.

Ayman, R., & Antani, A. (2008). Social support and work–family conflict. In K. Korabik, D. S. Lero, & D. L. Whitehead (Eds.), *Handbook of work–family integration: Research, theory, and best practices* (pp. 287–304). San Diego: Elseiver.

Banarjee, S. (1–3 Nov 2003). Double standards. *Businessline.*

Bardoel, A. (April 2004). *Work family conflict in Anglo-Saxon and European cultural context: The case of Australia.* Paper presented at the Society for Industrial and Organizational Psychology, Chicago, Illinois, USA.

Bort, J., Pflock, A., & Renner, D. (2005). *Mommy guilt: Learn to worry less, focus on what matters most, and raise happier kids.* New York: American Management Association.

Bui, L. S. (1999). Mothers in public relations: How are they balancing career and family? *Public Relations Quarterly, 44,* 23–26.

Chapman, F. S. (Feb 1987). Executive guilt: Who's taking care of the children? *Fortune, 115* (4), 30–37.

Chappell, D. B., Korabik, K., & McElwain, A. (June 2005). *The effects of gender-role attitudes on work–family conflict and work–family guilt.* Poster presented at the Canadian Psychological Association, Montreal, Quebec, Canada.

Conlin, M. (2000). The new debate over working moms: As more moms choose to stay home, office life is again under fire. *Business Week, 3699,* 102–104.
Daly, K. J. (2001). Deconstructing family time: From ideology to lived experience. *Journal of Marriage and Family, 63,* 283–294.
Desai, T. P., & Rajadhyaksha, U. (April 2004). *Work family conflict in the Asian cultural context: The case of India.* Paper presented at the Society for Industrial and Organizational Psychology, Chicago, Illinois, USA.
Drach-Zahavy, A., & Somech, A. (April 2004). *Work family conflict in the Middle Eastern cultural context: The case of Israel.* Paper presented at the Society for Industrial and Organizational Psychology, Chicago, Illinois, USA.
Elvin-Nowak, Y. (1999). The meaning of guilt: A phenomenological description of employed mothers' experiences of guilt. *Scandinavian Journal of Psychology, 40,* 73–83.
Ewles, G., Korabik, K., & Lero, D. S. (June 2013). *Work–family guilt: The role of overload and control.* Poster presented at the Canadian Psychological Association, Quebec City, Quebec, Canada.
Ewles, G., Korabik, K., & Lero, D. S. (June 2014). *Social support and work–family guilt: The role of gender differences.* Poster presented at the Canadian Psychological Association, Vancouver, British Columbia, Canada.
Glavin, P., Scheiman, S., & Reid, S. (2011). Boundary spanning work demands and their consequences for work and psychological distress. *Journal of Health and Social Behavior, 52,* 43–57.
Guendouzi, J. (2006). "The guilt thing": Balancing domestic and professional roles. *Journal of Marriage and Family, 68,* 901–909.
Hochwarter, W. A., Perrewé, P. L., Meurs, J. A., & Kacmar, C. (2007). The interactive effects of work-induced guilt and ability to manage resources on job and life satisfaction. *Journal of Occupational Health Psychology, 12,* 125–135.
Hoffman, M. L. (1982). Development of prosocial motivation: Empathy and guilt. In N. Eisenberg (Ed.), *The development of prosocial behaviour.* New York: Academic.
Huang, T. P. (Aug 2004). *Work–family conflict of employees in business organizations in Taiwan.* Paper presented at the International Association of Cross-Cultural Psychology, Xi'an, China.
Ishaya, N., Ayman, R., & Korabik, K. (April 2013). *Why so much guilt? Investigating how overload hurts, and why control may help.* Paper presented at the Society for Industrial and Organizational Psychology, Houston, Texas, USA.
Kochanska, G., Gross, J., Lin, M., & Nichols, K. (2002). Guilt in young children: Development, determinants, and relations with a broader system of standards. *Child Development, 73,* 461–482.
Korabik, K. (July 2005). *Alleviating work–family conflict for women managers in a global context.* Paper presented at the Eastern Academy of Management, Cape Town, South Africa.
Korabik, K., & Lero, D. S. (Aug 2004). *A cross-cultural research project on the work–family interface: Preliminary findings.* Paper presented at the International Association of Cross-Cultural Psychology, Xi'an, China.
Korabik, K., & McElwain, A. (April 2011). *The role of work–family guilt in work–family conflict.* Paper presented at the Society for Industrial and Organizational Psychology, Chicago, Illinois, USA.
Korabik, K., & van Rhijn, T. R. (May 2014). *Examining the cross-cultural measurement equivalence of work–family interface measures.* Paper presented at the Society for Industrial and Organizational Psychology, Honolulu, Hawaii, USA.
Korabik, K., McElwain, A., Warner, M., & Lero, D. S. (July 2007). *The impact of coworker support and resentment on work–family conflict.* Paper presented at IESE Conference on Work and Family, Barcelona, Spain.
Korabik, K., Lero, D. S., & Whitehead, D. L. (Eds). (2008a). *Handbook of work–family integration: Research, theory, and best practices.* San Diego: Elseiver.
Korabik, K., McElwain, A., & Chappell, D. B. (2008b). Integrating gender-related issues into research on work and family. In K. Korabik, D. S. Lero, & D. L. Whitehead (Eds), *Handbook*

of work–family integration: Research, theories, and best practices (pp. 215–232). San Diego: Elsevier.

Korabik, K., McElwain, A., & Lero, D. S. (Nov 2009). *Does work–family guilt mediate relationships between work–family conflict and outcome variables?* Paper presented at the Work, Stress and Health Conference, San Juan, Puerto Rico.

Kossek, E., Pichler, S., Bodner, T., & Hammer, L. (2011). Workplace social support and work–family conflict: A meta-analysis clarifying the influence of general and work–family-specific supervisor and organizational support. *Personnel Psychology, 64,* 289–313.

Kubany, E. S. (1994). A cognitive model of guilt typology in combat-related PTSD. *Journal of Traumatic Stress, 7,* 3–19.

Kubany, E. S., Haynes, S. N., Abueg, F. R., Manke, F. P., Brennan, J. M., & Starhura, C. (1996). Development and validation of the Trauma-Related Guilt Inventory (TRGI). *Psychological Assessment, 5,* 428–444.

Kubany, E. S., & Watson, S. B. (2003). Guilt: Elaboration of a multidimensional model. *The Psychological Record, 53,* 51–90.

Livingston, B. A., & Judge, T. A. (2008). Emotional responses to work–family conflict: An examination of gender role orientation among working men and women. *Journal of Applied Psychology, 93,* 207–216.

Martinez, P., Carrasco, M. J., Aza, G., Blanco, A., & Espinar, I. (2011). Family gender role and guilt in Spanish dual earner families. *Sex Roles, 65,* 813–826.

Mawardi, A. (April 2004). *Work–family conflict in an Asian cultural context: The case of Indonesia.* Paper presented at the Society for Industrial and Organizational Psychology, Chicago, Illinois, USA.

McElwain, A. (2008). *An examination of the reliability and validity of the Work–family Guilt Scale.* (Unpublished doctoral dissertation), University of Guelph, Guelph, Ontario, Canada.

McElwain, A., & Korabik, K. (2004). Work–family guilt. In M. Pitt-Catsouphes & E. Kossek (Eds.). *Work and Family Encyclopedia Online.* Chestnut Hill, MA: Sloan Work and Family Research Network. Retrieved February 16, 2009, from http://wfnetwork.bc.edu/encyclopedia_entry.php?id=871&area=All.

McElwain, A., Korabik, K., & Chappell, D. B. (Aug 2004). *Beyond gender: Re-examining work–family conflict and work–family guilt in the context of gender-role orientation.* Paper presented at the International Society for the Study of Work and Organizational Values, New Orleans, Louisiana, USA.

McElwain, A., Korabik, K., & Chappell, D. B. (June 2005a). *The work–family guilt scale.* Poster presented at the Canadian Psychological Association, Montreal, Quebec, Canada.

McElwain, A., Korabik, K., & Chappell, D. B. (June 2005b). *The impact of work–family conflict on work–family guilt.* Poster presented at the Canadian Psychological Association, Montreal, Quebec, Canada.

McElwain, A., Korabik, K., & Lero, D. S. (June 2007). *Coping mechanisms in work–family conflict.* Paper presented at the Canadian Psychological Association. Ottawa, Ontario, Canada.

Napholz, L. (2000). Balancing multiple roles among a group of urban midlife American Indian working women. *Health Care for Women International, 27,* 255–266.

Nevill, D., & Damico, S. (1977). Developmental components of role conflict in women. *The Journal of Psychology, 95,* 195–198.

Offer, S., & Schneider, B. (2011). Revisitng the gender gap in time use patterns: Multitasking and well-being among mothers and fathers in dual-earner families. *American Sociological Review, 76,* 809–833.

Pollock, E. J. (10–13 March 1997). Work and family (a special report): Regaining a balance—This is home; This is work. *Wall Street Journal (Eastern Edition).*

Rajadhyaksha, U., Huang, T. P., Mawardi, A., & Desai, T. P. (July 2011). *Gender-role ideology, work–family overload, conflict and guilt: Examining a path analysis model in three Asian countries.* Paper presented at the International Association of Cross-Cultural Psychology, Istanbul, Turkey.

Seagram, S., & Daniluk, J. C. (2002). It goes with the territory: The meaning and experience of maternal guilt for mothers of preadolescent children. *Women and Therapy, 25,* 61–88.

Shields, S. A. (2013). Gender and emotions: What we think we know, what we need to know, and why it matters. *Psychology of Women Quarterly, 37,* 423–435.

Simon, R. W. (1995). Gender, multiple roles, role meaning, and mental health. *Journal of Health and Social Behaviour, 36,* 182–194.

Velgach, S., Ishaya, N., & Ayman, R. (April 2005). *A multi-method approach to investigate work–family conflict.* Paper presented at the Society for Industrial and Organizational Psychology, Los Angeles, California, USA.

Zahn-Waxler, C., & Kochanska, G. (1988). The origins of guilt. In R. A. Thompson (Ed.), *Nebraska Symposium on Motivation: Vol. 36. Sociometric Development* (pp. 183–258). Lincoln: University of Nebraska Press.

Zahn-Waxler, C., Kochanska, G., Krupnick, J., & McKnew, D. (1990). Patterns of guilt in children of depressed and well mothers. *Developmental Psychology, 26,* 51–59.

Chapter 9
Gender, Accuracy About Partners' Work–Family Conflict, and Relationship Quality

Kei Nomaguchi and Melissa A. Milkie

9.1 Overview

For employed women and men in a dual-earner marriage or partnership, every day is truly a balancing act—of the regular demands that are related to two paid work positions, of an often complex relationship with each other, and for many pairs, the endless dance of emotions and labor that relate to owning a home or raising children. Two jobs means that both adults have a multitude of day-to-day issues at home to deal with—mundane but vital things like having clean clothing to wear to work, having meals ready, and making sure that the household and any children stay afloat during the days, weeks, and months, as dishes, laundry, repairs, and bills pile up seemingly endlessly. At the same time, demands and strains from the job, such as an overload of tasks or hours, coworker problems, and unreasonable clients, often "spill over" into the home domain (Pearlin and McCall 1990). Not surprisingly, then, many employed adults feel that their work and family lives interfere with one

Author Note: Earlier versions of this chapter were presented at Pilot Data Conference, National Center for Family and Marriage Research at Bowling Green State University, Ohio, August 4, 2011, and the Work and Family Researchers Network Inaugural Conference, New York City, June 14–16, 2012. The data were collected with support from a grant to the National Center for Family and Marriage Research, Bowling Green State University from the U.S. Department of Health and Human Services, Office of the Assistant Secretary for Planning and Evaluation (5 UOI AEOOOOOI-03). This research was supported in part by the Center for Family and Demographic Research, Bowling Green State University, which has core funding from the Eunice Kennedy Shriver National Institute of Child Health and Human Development (R24HD050959-07).

K. Nomaguchi (✉)
Department of Sociology, Bowling Green State University, 213 Williams Hall,
Bowling Green, OH 43403, USA
e-mail: knomagu@bgsu.edu

M. A. Milkie
Department of Sociology, University of Toronto, 725 Spadina Avenue,
Toronto, ON, M5S 2J4, Canada
e-mail: melissa.milkie@utoronto.ca

M. J. Mills (ed.), *Gender and the Work-Family Experience*,
DOI 10.1007/978-3-319-08891-4_9

another (Bellavia and Frone 2005; Nomaguchi 2009; Schieman et al. 2009; Young et al. 2014). Accordingly, scholars have focused a great deal of attention on this topic (for reviews see Bellavia and Frone 2005; Bianchi and Milkie 2010).

Partners are at the epicenter of conflicts. As Pearlin (1983) noted, families have a "uniquely pivotal position" in the stress process because they not only generate their own stressors, but are also the backdrop for problems that enter from the outside world. And yet, how a partner's problems with balancing work and family come into the awareness of the other partner may be anything but straightforward. Of course, there are often clear work–family conflicts displayed—for example, he may openly discuss how being passed over for a promotion at work disrupts his sleep; she may be visibly upset about an absence from an important school event that other parents are present for. These provide some clues about how the partner's world outside the home conflicts with his or her home life. But what a partner understands from the other partner is likely to be incomplete. This is because some conflicts are not easily observable given that the partners' respective places of work are typically separate. Sometimes partners may purposely try to segregate job stresses and concerns from their partner in order to protect their spouse, or perhaps because they have not received supportive feedback in the past (Pearlin and McCall 1990). Moreover, within relationships, even the same reality—of a wife's or husband's low or high level of work–family conflict—may be viewed quite differently. As Bernard (1972) insightfully observed years ago, there is not "a" marriage, but "his" and "hers" marriages. She notes that even many questions about basic components of life together, such as how long partners have been together, or who did the dishes yesterday, generate very different responses from spouses. Thus, in terms of work–family conflict, even things that can be directly observed by partners—perhaps exasperation or frustration at work demands spilling over—are not likely to be fully appreciated or understood in the same way by the other spouse.

Especially when information is incomplete, a gender perspective (Ridgeway 2011) posits that a partner's views about the amount and kinds of conflict that a wife or husband experiences is filtered through a gendered lens about what that spouse "should" be expected to feel. Thus, what a husband does observe of the problems his wife is experiencing in balancing work and family—and what a wife observes about her husband's conflicts—sits against a cultural backdrop of work and family ideology that remains highly gendered (Correll et al. 2007; Cotter et al. 2011; Milkie 2010; Milkie and Peltola 1999). In an era of blurred boundaries and insecurities in work and family roles, then, an important and under-examined question about couples' work–family conflict centers on how accurate people are about their partner's level of conflict and how patterns may be gendered.

Do inaccuracies matter for relationship quality? The question of the consequences of inaccuracies in assessing how the partner is balancing work and family is important to investigate. If misunderstandings cause dissatisfaction in relationships, then it becomes crucial to try to increase understanding, especially as partners make work decisions that affect one another. To maximize both partners' ability to meet workplace and family obligations, dual-earner couples employ various adaptive and coping strategies (Moen and Wethington 1992) and these decisions and strategies about their combined work and family roles tend to be made at the couple level

(Becker and Moen 1999). Understanding each other's work–family conflict accurately may help couples make decisions about their adaptive strategies that both partners find to be fair and to enhance the relationship.

In this chapter, we ask two questions: First, how accurately do members of US dual-earner heterosexual couples assess their partner's level of work–family conflict? As part of this question, we ask whether inaccuracies are systematically gendered, i.e., do men tend to overestimate the level of conflict wives feel whereas women tend to underestimate men's conflicts? Second, is a partner's inaccuracy related to relationship quality? How? For each question, we develop a framework for examining the question, provide a brief review of prior empirical studies, and state our predictions. Then we assess our predictions with dual-earner couples in *The Married and Cohabiting Couples 2010 Study* (see the Appendix for methodological notes).

9.2 Gender and Inaccuracy in Estimating Partners' Work–Family Conflict

Why might dual-earner couples inaccurately estimate each other's work–family conflict? A gender perspective suggests that individuals' perceptions are largely influenced by cultural meanings of what men and women "should" do and be like (Correll et al. 2007; Milkie 1999; Ridgeway 2011). In the area of work and family responsibilities, a series of qualitative studies have emphasized that although dual-earner relationships have become the norm, cultural scripts of the division of labor remain gendered. Women are assumed to be better and more interested in care work—i.e., the tasks and mental activities in which a person meets the needs of others—and to feel greater family responsibilities than men (Blair-Loy 2003; Hays 1996), whereas men are believed to feel greater breadwinning responsibilities than women (Townsend 2002). Because employed wives may feel responsible for overseeing what is happening at home, perhaps they are believed to feel a strong domestic pull, and thus feel a high level of work–family conflict whenever they are employed. Employed husbands are seen to "help" their employed wives around the house and with childcare, but rely on their wives for the overall responsibility of the home and thus may not feel a substantial degree of work–family conflict (Doucet 2006; Hays 1996; Hochschild 1989).

In contrast, recent quantitative research has shown that husbands' and wives' work–family conflicts are relatively similar, indicating that the cultural images of stressed women and slacker men may be somewhat inaccurate. Bianchi et al. (2006) found that there was little difference between married mothers' and married fathers' total work time (i.e., time for market work and nonmarket work). Additional studies show few or no gender differences in work–family conflict and balance (Grzywacz and Marks 2000; Gutek et al. 1991; Milkie and Peltola 1999; Schieman et al. 2009). Notably, it may be that women may not report more work–family conflict than men in part because they may be pushed toward employing various strategies or tradeoffs in order to balance work and family responsibilities (Milkie and Peltola 1999), as unfriendly workplaces and cultural expectations degrading them as "bad mothers" push them to reduce employment hours (Correll et al. 2007; Ridgeway 2011; Stone 2007). For men, unlike the cultural image, the sense of work–family conflict has increased in recent cohorts. Nomaguchi (2009) found that work–family conflict increased significantly more among men in dual-earner marriages than among women in dual-earner marriages between 1977 and 1997.

We argue that the discrepancy between qualitative and quantitative findings suggests the possibility that there may be an increasing gap between the gendered cultural script of work–family conflict and actual work–family conflict that men and women are experiencing. Specifically, we expect that men are more likely to overestimate their partners' work–family conflict due to cultural scripts that employed women "should" feel a pull toward the home, whereas their female partners may not feel as much conflict as those cultural scripts suggest they should. In addition, we expect that women are more likely to underestimate their partners' work–family conflict due to cultural scripts that men's "hearts" are in breadwinning and they do not feel primarily responsibility toward family, whereas their male partners actually feel more work–family conflict than the cultural scripts suggest. Thus, on the basis of a potential gap between gendered cultural scripts and reality, we predict that male partners are more likely to overestimate than underestimate female partners' work–family conflict, and female partners are more likely to underestimate than overestimate male partners' work–family conflict.

To date, only a handful of studies have examined accuracies of couples' perceptions of each other's work–family conflict. Using a sample of 191 dual-earner parents collected in the Netherlands, Demerouti et al. (2005) found that the average ratings that women provided for their partners' work–family conflict were higher than the average ratings that their partners reported as their own work–family conflict (2.06 vs. 1.98 ranging from 1–5), suggesting women *overestimated* their partners' work–family conflict, a finding opposite from our prediction. They found no difference between men's average rating of their partners' work–family conflict and their partners' average self-rating of conflict (1.76 vs. 1.76). In contrast, using 224 dual-earner couples (married, cohabiting, or in a serious relationship) from a 1989 random sample of residents in Erie County, New York, Streich et al. (2008) found that the average scores that women provided for their partners' work–family conflict were *lower* than the average scores that their partners provided as their own work–family conflict (2.45 vs. 2.72 with a range from 1–5), indicating that women were *underestimating* their partners' work–family conflict, as we predict. There was little gap between men's reports of their partners' work–family conflict and their partners' self-reports of work–family conflict (2.47 vs. 2.41).

These studies measured the inaccuracies in partners' perceptions of work–family conflict at the aggregated individual level, not by matching a pair of partners and calculating the differences at the couple level. Thus, it is not clear what percentage of men and women overestimate or underestimate their partners' work–family conflict. In addition, because the US study by Streich et al. (2008) used a regional sample, it is not clear to what extent the findings could be generalized. In this

Table 9.1 Cross-tabulations between respondents' perception of partner's work–family conflict (WFC) and partner's self-report of WFC for men and women (%). (Source: *The Married and Cohabiting Couples 2010 Study* (*N*=545))

	Male partner's report of female partner's WFC				
	Not at all	Not too much	Some	A lot	Great deal
	(1)	(2)	(3)	(3)	(4)
Female partner's self-report					
Not at all (1)	13.3	7.6[a]	5.3[a]	0.4[a]	0.2[a]
Not too much (2)	7.0[b]	13.4	13.0[a]	1.6[a]	0.0[a]
Some (3)	2.0[b]	6.7[b]	14.2	4.7[a]	0.1[a]
A lot (4)	0.6[b]	0.9[b]	3.6[b]	2.9	0.5[a]
Great deal (5)	0.0[b]	1.0[b]	0.5[b]	0.3[b]	0.2
	Female partner's report of male partner's WFC				
	Not at all	Not too much	Some	A lot	Great deal
	(1)	(2)	(3)	(4)	(5)
Male partner's self-report					
Not at all (1)	10.4	8.0[c]	1.9[c]	0.0[c]	0.2[c]
Not too much (2)	11.0[d]	18.9	10.8[c]	0.6[c]	0.8[c]
Some (3)	3.4[d]	9.1[d]	14.2	3.3[c]	0.3[c]
A lot (4)	0.8[d]	0.9[d]	3.2[d]	1.1	0.4[c]
Great deal (5)	0.0[d]	0.3[d]	0.3[d]	0.1[d]	0.4

[a] Male partner overestimating female partner's WFC=33.4%
[b] Male partner underestimating female partner's WFC=22.6%
[c] Female partner overestimating male partner's WFC=26.1%
[d] Female partner underestimating male partner's WFC=28.9%

regard, *The Married and Cohabiting Couples 2010 Study* is useful because it offers couple-level data—that is, data were collected from each partner of the couple—from a national sample of married and cohabiting couples in the USA. The couple-level data allow us to more clearly examine how accurately US dual-earner couples perceive each other's work–family conflict.

In *The Married and Cohabiting Couples 2010 Study*, each partner rated his/her own work–family conflict by responding to the question, "How much conflict do you face in balancing your paid work and family life?" (1=*not at all*, 2=*not too much*, 3=*some*, 4=*a lot*, 5=*a great deal*). The mean scores for men and women's self-report of work–family conflict were very similar—2.3 and 2.2 (range 1–5), respectively. Each partner also rated his/her partner's work–family conflict via the question, "How much conflict does your partner/spouse face in balancing his/her paid work and family life (1=*not at all* 2=*not too much*, 3=*some*, 4=*a lot*, 5=*a great deal*)?" On average, men rated perceptions of their partners' work–family conflict higher than did women (2.4 vs. 2.2).

Taking advantage of these two pieces of information, we assessed whether couples accurately perceive each other's work–family conflict. Table 9.1 shows two cross-tabulations, one for male partners' report of female partners' work–family conflict by female partners' self-report of work–family conflict, and the other for female partners' report of male partners' work–family conflict by male partners' self-report of work–family conflict. These tabulations show how we created measures

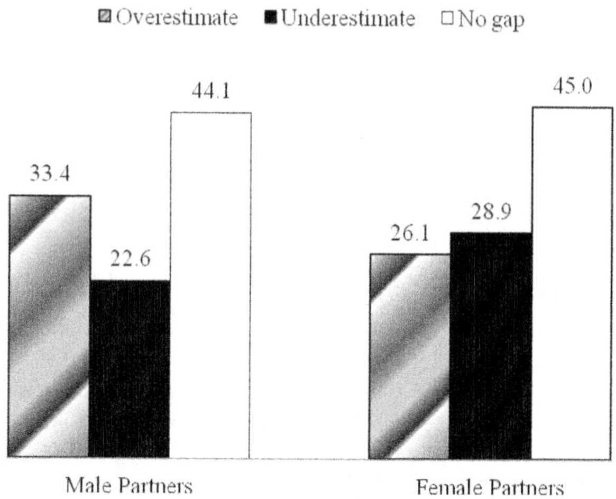

Fig. 9.1 Percentage distributions for overestimating or underestimating partners' work–family conflict. (Source: *The Married and Cohabiting Couples 2010 Study*)

of inaccuracies of partners' work–family conflict. First, male partners' accuracies or inaccuracies of female partners' work–family conflict was measured by taking men's perceptions of their partners' work–family conflict and subtracting their partners' self-report of work–family conflict. We created three categories. If the value was less than 0, men were underestimating their partners' work–family conflict. If the value was more than 0, men were overestimating their partners' work–family conflict. If the value was 0, men were accurately estimating their partners' work–family conflict. For example, if a husband reports that his wife experiences a "great deal" of conflict (5), whereas the wife herself reports "some" (3), ($5-3=2$; $2>0$), he would receive a score of "1" for the dummy "overestimating," a score of 0 for "underestimating," and a score of 0 for "accurately estimating." Likewise, the same three groups were created for female partners' underestimating, overestimating, and accurately estimating partners' work–family conflict.

The percentage distributions of these three groups—overestimating, underestimating, and no discrepancy—are presented in Fig. 9.1. Less than half of male partners (44.1 %) and female partners (45.0 %) were accurate in their report of their partners' work–family conflict. One third (33.4 %) of male partners overestimated female partners' work–family conflict, whereas 22.6 % underestimated it. About one fourth (26.1 %) of female partners overestimated male partners' work–family conflict, and slightly more female partners (28.9 %) underestimated male partners' work–family conflict. As expected, male partners were more likely to overestimate than underestimate female partners' work–family conflict, while female partners were only slightly more likely to underestimate than overestimate male partners' work–family conflict. Differences between male partners and female partners in these distributions were statistically significant.[1]

[1] Chi-square test ($\chi^2=55.20$, $df=4$, $p<0.001$)

9.3 Does Inaccuracy Matter for Relationship Quality?

How are accuracies or inaccuracies of partners' estimates of each other's work–family conflict related to their relationship quality? Prior work has shown that individuals' work–family conflict is related to family-relationship qualities, such as lower family satisfaction (Frone et al. 1994) and lower marital satisfaction (Coverman 1989). However, we do not know much about how couples' inaccuracies of each other's work–family conflict are related to relationship quality, nor of the influence of actual level of work–family conflict on relationship quality. We are particularly interested in the patterns wherein partners' estimates are biased in the direction that reflects the possibility that there has been an increasing gap between the gendered cultural script of work–family conflict and actual work–family conflict that men and women experience, i.e., male partners expecting more work–family conflict for female partners and female partners expecting less work–family conflict for male partners.

On the basis of prior research on relationship quality, we expect that a male partner's overestimating of his female partner's work–family conflict may be linked to both the male partner's and female partner's perceptions of *better* relationship quality, because it is indicative of an acknowledgment of and openness to her difficulties. For example, Thompson (1991) found that husbands' appreciation and understanding of wives' juggling paid work and housework is important for wives' sense of fairness and relationship happiness. In contrast, women's underestimating their partners' work–family conflict may be linked to their partners' perception of poorer relationship quality, because male partners may feel as though their female partners do not understand or appreciate their sense of being torn between paid work and family life. Wilkie et al. (1998) found that a higher sense of being understood by one's partner was related to a higher level of marital satisfaction for husbands. Underestimating their partners' conflicts may also relate to women's own perception of poorer relationship quality, because women may perceive it as unfair that their husbands work at their paid jobs without (from their perspective) feeling guilty or torn. Other research has shown that a sense of fairness in the division of labor is related to a higher level of marital satisfaction for wives (Frisco and Williams 2003; Wilkie et al. 1998).

To our knowledge, there have been no published studies that have examined the associations between partners' inaccuracies in understanding each other's work–family conflict and their relationship quality with empirical data. For example, Streich et al. (2008), mentioned earlier, examined organizational commitment as an outcome of inaccuracies, but not relationship quality. Thus, our assessment using data from dual-earner couples in *The Married and Cohabiting Couples 2010 Study* is one of the first studies to examine this question. We focused on three aspects of couples' relationship quality—emotional support, enchantment[2], and global relationship happiness (for measurement specifics, see the Appendix). These three aspects of relationship quality are known as strong indicators of divorce (Booth et al. 1985; Bradbury et al. 2000; Huston et al. 2001). In general, we found that couples tended to highly rate each of these aspects of relationship quality. The average

[2] Enchantment is an opposite state of disillusionment (Huston et al. 2001), which involves one's sense of still being in love with his/her partner.

rating for emotional support was 4.5 for male partners and 4.4 for female partners (range 1–5); average rating for enchantment was 4.2 (range 1–5) for male partners and 4.2 for female partners; average rating for relationship happiness was 8.7 (range 1–10) for male partners and 8.6 for female partners.

First, we examined whether male partners' overestimating or underestimating of female partners' work–family conflict was related to male partners' and female partners' reports of relationship quality respectively. As shown in Panel A of Table 9.2, compared to male partners who accurately estimated female partners' work–family conflict, male partners who overestimated female partners' work–family conflict reported higher ratings of enchantment and global quality. However, male partners' underestimating of their female partners' work–family conflict, compared to their accurately estimating it, was not related to their own report of relationship quality. Panel B, which predicted female partners' reports of relationship quality, indicates that male partners' inaccuracies about female partners' work–family conflict—either overestimating or underestimating—were not related to female partners' reports of relationship quality.[3]

Second, we examined whether female partners' overestimating or underestimating of male partner's work–family conflict was related to their own as well as their partner's reports of relationship quality respectively. Panel A in Table 9.3 shows that female partners who underestimated male partners' work–family conflict were more likely than those who accurately estimated male partners' work–family conflict to report lower emotional support. However, female partners' overestimating male partners' work–family conflict was not related to their own perceptions of relationship quality. As shown in Panel B, female partners' underestimating of male partners' work–family conflict was related to male partners' lower rating of enchantment. Female partners' overestimating of male partners' work–family conflict was not related to male partners' report of relationship quality. In sum, our findings indicate that male partners' overestimating female partners' work–family conflict was related to their own—but not their female partners'—perceptions of *better* relationship quality. Female partners' underestimating male partners' work–family conflict was related to their own *and* male partners' reports of *poorer* relationship quality.

9.4 Discussion

9.4.1 Do Men and Women Differ in Inaccurately Estimating Their Partners' Work–Family Conflict?

With increasing complexities and insecurities related to work and family life, and blurring boundaries between these spheres, knowing a partner's work–family conflicts may be fraught with difficulty. How much do American spouses know about

[3] See the Appendix for a discussion of controls included in the analyses.

Table 9.2 Unstandardized coefficients from ordinary-least-squared (OLS) regression models predicting the associations between male partner's underestimating or overestimating female partner's work–family conflict (WFC) and male partner's and female partner's reports of relationship quality. (Source: The Married and Cohabiting Couples 2010 Study)

	Emotional support			Enchantment			Relationship happiness		
	b	SE		b	SE		b	SE	
Panel A. Male partner's reports of relationship quality									
Male partner overestimating female partner's WFC	0.109	0.056		0.230	0.073	**	0.426	0.144	**
Male partner underestimating female partner's WFC	−0.099	0.060		−0.028	0.076		−0.113	0.150	
Male partner accurately estimating female partner's WFC	–	–		–	–		–	–	
Controls									
Male partner's WFC	−0.061	0.028	*	−0.133	0.036	***	−0.219	0.070	**
Male partner's report of female partner's WFC	−0.165	0.029	***	−0.243	0.037	***	−0.379	0.073	***
Male partner's age	−0.006	0.002	**	−0.007	0.003	*	−0.010	0.006	
Male partner nonwhite	−0.008	0.051		−0.114	0.066		0.024	0.129	
Male partner's relationship type									
First marriage	–	–		–	–		–	–	
Remarriage	0.244	0.068	***	0.272	0.088	**	0.591	0.173	***
Cohabiting	−0.092	0.064		−0.100	0.083		−0.240	0.162	
Have children < 18 (male partner's report)	−0.098	0.048	*	−0.024	0.062		−0.089	0.122	
Male partner college educated	0.053	0.055		-0.005	0.069		0.055	0.137	
Female partner college educated	0.057	0.053		0.203	0.068	**	0.127	0.133	
Male partner self-employed	−0.029	0.067		−0.146	0.087		−0.140	0.171	
Female partner self-employed	0.147	0.068	*	0.119	0.089		0.316	0.174	
Intercept	5.257	0.132	***	5.316	0.171	***	10.335	0.338	***
R^2	0.146***			0.185**			0.129***		
N	530			520			536		
Panel B. Female partner's reports of relationship quality									
Male partner overestimating female partner's WFC	−0.010	0.066		−0.051	0.079		−0.009	0.154	
Male partner underestimating female partner's WFC	−0.036	0.080		0.139	0.095		0.054	0.186	

Table 9.2 (continued)

	Emotional support			Enchantment			Relationship happiness		
	b	SE		b	SE		b	SE	
Male partner accurately estimating female partner's WFC	–	–		–	–		–	–	
Controls									
Female partner's WFC	−0.202	0.038	***	−0.274	0.046	***	−0.376	0.089	***
Female partner's report of male partner's WFC	0.034	0.037		0.003	0.044		−0.077	0.086	
Female partner's age	−0.003	0.003		−0.007	0.003	*	−0.008	0.006	
Female partner nonwhite	0.019	0.069		-0.109	0.081		0.064	0.159	
Female partner's relationship type									
First marriage	–	–		–	–		–	–	
Remarriage	−0.166	0.061	**	−0.226	0.073	**	−0.527	0.143	***
Cohabiting	0.145	0.083		0.288	0.098	**	0.452	0.193	*
Have children < 18 (female partner's report)	−0.095	0.084		−0.148	0.100		−0.368	0.196	
Male partner college educated	0.042	0.069		0.115	0.082		−0.126	0.160	
Female partner college educated	0.203	0.068	**	0.108	0.079		0.314	0.156	*
Male partner self-employed	−0.030	0.082		−0.200	0.098	*	−0.344	0.191	
Female partner self-employed	−0.001	0.085		−0.052	0.102		0.117	0.199	
Intercept	4.833	0.173	***	5.117	0.200	***	10.061	0.393	***
R^2	0.121***			0.155***			0.131***		
N	528			516			532		

*$p<0.05$; **$p<0.01$; ***$p<0.001$

their "other half," particularly their wives' or husbands' level of felt work–family conflict? The findings from *The Married and Cohabiting Couples 2010 Study* discussed in this chapter suggest that more than half of partners are at least somewhat inaccurate in their estimates of their partners' work–family conflict. It is not an easy or even "normal" process to see things exactly as a partner does, especially when one realm (the partner's workplace) is most often outside of the purview of the other's vision. Consistent with the predictions of a gap between gendered cultural scripts and reality in men's and women's work–family conflict, our findings indicate that male partners are more likely to overestimate than underestimate their female partners' work–family conflict and, although to a smaller degree, female

Table 9.3 Unstandardized coefficients from ordinary-least-squared (OLS) regression models predicting the associations between female partner's underestimating or overestimating male partner's work–family conflict (WFC) and female partner's and male partner's reports of relationship quality. (Source: The Married and Cohabiting Couples 2010 Study)

	Emotional support			Enchantment			Relationship happiness		
	b	SE		b	SE		b	SE	
Panel A. Female partner's reports of relationship quality									
Female partner overestimating male partner's WFC	−0.019	0.077		−0.010	0.092		0.017	0.177	
Female partner underestimating male partner's WFC	−0.174	0.072	*	−0.091	0.086		−0.295	0.165	
Female partner accurately estimating male partner's WFC	–	–		–	–		–	–	
Controls									
Female partner's WFC	−0.202	0.035	***	−0.233	0.042	***	−0.357	0.080	***
Female partner's report of male partner's WFC	0.000	0.044		−0.013	0.052		−0.169	0.101	
Female partner's age	−0.003	0.003		−0.007	0.003	*	−0.011	0.006	
Female partner nonwhite	0.019	0.070		−0.084	0.082		−0.011	0.160	
Female partner's relationship type									
First marriage	–	–		–	–		–	–	
Remarriage	0.160	0.082		0.272	0.098	**	0.498	0.190	**
Cohabiting	−0.124	0.085		−0.190	0.102		−0.404	0.196	*
Have children < 18 (female partner's report)	−0.160	0.062	*	−0.207	0.074	**	−0.568	0.142	***
Male partner college educated	0.063	0.069		0.110	0.081		−0.080	0.157	
Female partner college educated	0.213	0.068	**	0.106	0.080		0.365	0.155	*
Male partner self-employed	−0.021	0.082		−0.209	0.099	*	−0.332	0.190	
Female partner self-employed	0.027	0.085		−0.050	0.102		0.201	0.197	
Intercept	4.958	0.175	***	5.082	0.207	***	10.395	0.401	***
R^2	0.133***			0.143***			0.149***		
N	526			514			530		
Panel B. Male partner's reports of relationship quality									
Female partner overestimating male partner's WFC	−0.029	0.057		−0.018	0.072		−0.101	0.145	

Table 9.3 (continued)

	Emotional support			Enchantment			Relationship happiness		
	b	SE		b	SE		b	SE	
Female partner underestimating male partner's WFC	−0.038	0.059		−0.239	0.076	**	−0.193	0.150	
Female partner accurately estimating male partner's WFC	–	–		–	–		–	–	
Controls									
Male partner's WFC	−0.065	0.032	*	−0.084	0.041	*	−0.211	0.081	**
Male partner's report of female partner's WFC	−0.122	0.025	***	−0.189	0.033	***	−0.268	0.065	***
Male partner's age	−0.006	0.002	**	−0.005	0.003		−0.007	0.006	
Male partner nonwhite	−0.007	0.052		−0.130	0.067		0.002	0.131	
Male partner's relationship type									
First marriage	–	–		–	–		–	–	
Remarriage	−0.107	0.048	*	−0.039	0.061		−0.115	0.122	
Cohabiting	0.233	0.068	***	0.242	0.088	**	0.502	0.175	**
Have children < 18 at home (male partner's report)	−0.092	0.065		−0.103	0.084		−0.229	0.164	
Male partner college educated	0.078	0.055		0.008	0.069		0.104	0.138	
Female partner college educated	0.040	0.053		0.176	0.068	**	0.101	0.134	
Male partner self-employed	−0.050	0.067		−0.188	0.086	*	−0.202	0.171	
Female partner self-employed	0.167	0.068	*	0.171	0.088		0.397	0.174	*
Intercept	5.198	0.137	***	5.155	0.175	***	10.172	0.349	***
R^2	0.132***			0.181***			0.116***		
N	526			516			531		

*$p<0.05$; ** $p<0.01$; *** $p<0.001$;
SE Standard Error

partners are more likely to underestimate than overestimate their male partners' conflict. We are cautious in our conclusions, however, because we recognize that one third of male partners and less than one third of female partners show these patterns. A majority of couples' reports do not reflect the patterns that the thesis about a gap between cultural scripts and reality suggests. Of this group, most agree with each other, but there were also some who are inaccurate but in the direction opposite from predictions. Investigation of these patterns is warranted in future research.

9.4.2 Do Inaccuracies Matter for Relationship Quality?

Our evidence suggests that partners' over- or under-estimating the others' work–family conflict level is related to couples' relationship quality (and notably, higher levels of one's own actual work–family conflicts are detrimental to relationship quality too). Although future research should address how over- and under-estimating relate to relationship qualities with more refined measures, we provide some speculative interpretations. Male partners' overestimates of female partners' work–family conflict seems to be related to their own perceptions of better relationship quality. It may be that when male partners see their female partner as quite torn between work and family responsibilities, they may see her as trying to fulfill as many home responsibilities as she can, as cultural lore suggests, giving her the benefit of the doubt in home investment level. In these cases, male partners report better relationship quality, perhaps signaling their appreciation for what the woman does. On the flip side, female partners' underestimates of male partners' work–family conflict relates to their own and male partners' reports of poorer relationship quality. In essence, when a female sees her partner in the traditional light of breadwinning masculinity, believing that he is less conflicted between work and family worlds than he really is, both the female and her partner feel worse about their relationship. Our findings are consistent with the findings of prior research, which show that a sense of fairness in the division of labor, a partner's empathy, and a greater sense of being understood by a partner on difficult issues, are related to higher relationship satisfaction (Wilkie et al. 1998).

9.4.3 Future Directions

The Married and Cohabiting Couples 2010 Study offered insight into understanding inaccuracies of couples' perceptions of each other's work–family conflict and their implications for relationship quality. Yet, there are several questions that we were unable to examine with this data set that future research should address. First, we examined the global measure of work–family conflict that does not distinguish differences between work-to-family conflict and family-to-work conflict. As such, future research using more detailed measures of the bidirectional nature of such conflict is warranted. Second, *The Married and Cohabiting Couples 2010 Study* did not include detailed information about conditions of paid work, such as hours of employment, job autonomy, and workplace flexibility, which are related to work–family conflict (Bakker and Guerts 2004; Schieman and Young 2010). Third, this data was cross-sectional and therefore precluded causal assessments of the associations between partners' inaccuracies in each other's work–family conflict and relationship quality. Although we argue that being inaccurate in underestimating difficulty about a partner's work–family conflict can lead to worse relationship quality, it is also possible that having a poorer relationship at the outset makes one less aware of the partner's (difficult) subjective experience across work–family domains. Likewise, having better relationship quality could influence male partners to misestimates that skew, in a sense, in a "positive" way; perhaps male partners who are more empathetic and loving are more aware of the employed women's "plight" and thus believe their partners have it harder than they do in reality. While the current data preclude adjudication among these possibilities, we hope to propel future research to address such nuanced questions about couples' work–family conflicts and the meanings attached to gender, work, and family.

9.5 Conclusion

The landscape of work–family conflict among dual-earner couples is changing—in many ways. Work worlds may be becoming more complex, as globalization and technology may make some workers' time and space more fluid, and boundaries as to when work ends and when "family life" begins are in flux. Gender spheres, too, are changing, as the cultural landscape regarding what men and women, husbands and wives, fathers and mothers "should do" responds to and challenges workplace policies and practices, and may create new exigencies for future generations. Assessing a partner's level of work–family conflict, and what it means for relationship quality, may be even more complex in such a future. Research in this nascent area is warranted as gender schemas shift, and as dual-earner couples attempt to negotiate their work and family lives in a complex and changing societal context.

Appendix: Methodological Notes on The Married and Cohabiting Couples 2010 study

Data and Sample

The Married and Cohabiting Couples 2010 Study (MCC2010) is a web-based household survey that was obtained through a collaboration between the National Center for Family & Marriage Research (NCFMR) at Bowling Green State University and Knowledge Networks (KN). KN maintains a national panel of potential respondents, called KnowledgePanel (KP), who were selected by using random digit dialing sampling and address-based sampling methodology. Among the KN, individuals who do not already have Internet access are provided free Internet access and a laptop computer. Those who already have Internet access are given points redeemable for cash as incentives for their participation. KP consists of about 50,000 adult members (ages 18 and older) and includes persons living in cell phone only households as well as persons who have a landline phone. The KP members completed a demographic profile that determined eligibility for inclusion in specific studies. When selected, members receive a notification email letting them know there is a new survey available for them to take (Knowledge Networks 2010).

Table 9.4 Means (*SD*) or % distributions for variables for dual-earner couples in *The Marriage and Cohabiting Couples 2010 Study* ($N=545$)

	Male partners		Female partners	
Age (*M*)	42.7	(10.7)	42.2	(11.1)
Nonwhite (%)	28.1		23.0	
Relationship status (%)				
First marriage	69.5		69.3	
Remarriage	13.8		15.3	
Cohabiting	16.6		15.3	
Have children < 18 (%)	45.1		41.4	
College education (%)	33.6		39.1	
Self-employed (%)	13.9		13.4	
Work–family conflict (WFC) (*M*, range: 1–5)				
Self	2.3	(0.9)	2.2	(0.9)
Partner	2.4	(0.9)	2.2	(0.9)
Relationship Quality (*M*):				
Emotional support (1–5)	4.5	(0.5)	4.4	(0.7)
Enchantment (1–5)	4.2	(0.8)	4.2	(0.8)
Relationship happiness (1–10)	8.7	(1.3)	8.6	(1.5)

Data are weighted

For the MCC2010 study, a nationally representative sample of US heterosexual married and cohabiting adults aged 18–64 was selected from active KP members with a supplement of cohabiting adults aged 18–64 from an opt-in panel ($n=1075$). The survey was conducted from July to October 2010. The data and a field report that describes the sampling design are publicly available through the Inter-university Consortium for Political and Social Research (ICPSR 2013). For this chapter, we selected dual-earner couples ($N=545$), including 391 married and 154 cohabiting couples. Using household ID numbers and gender of respondents, we created couple-level data. KN provides study-specific post-stratification weights to adjust the data to the distributions provided by the Current Population Survey for male partners and female partners respectively. We used these weights in our statistical analyses. Appendix Table 9.4 shows sample characteristics.

Measures of Relationship Quality

Emotional support was an average of four questions ($\alpha=0.85$): (a) "My spouse/partner shows love and affection toward me"; (b) My spouse/partner encourages me to do things that are important to me"; (c) "My spouse/partner will not cheat on me"; and (d) "My spouse/partner listens when I need someone to talk to" (1 = *strongly disagree* to 5 = *strongly agree*).

Enchantment was a scale created using 11 items of "marital disillusionment scale" (Huston et al. 2001) ($\alpha=0.95$): (a) "My marriage/relationship hasn't gone quite as perfectly as I thought it might"; (b) "I'm beginning to see my spouse/partner in a somewhat more negative light"; (c) "I'm beginning to see my marriage/relationship in a somewhat more negative light"; (d) "Marriage/Life together is not as enjoyable as I had expected it to be"; (e) "Our relationship has changed for the worse"; (f) "I no longer really like my spouse/partner as a person"; (g) "My marriage/relationship is no longer as important to me as it used to be"; (h) "I am very disappointed in my marriage/relationship";(i) I feel tricked, cheated, or deceived by love"; (j) "I feel no longer quite as positively about my spouse/partner as I once did"; and (k) "If I could go back in time, I would not marry my spouse/live with my partner again" (1 = *strongly agree* to 5 = *strongly disagree*). Each item was reverse-coded and we averaged the scores of 11 items to create an enchantment scale.

Global relationship happiness was measured by one question, "Taking all things together, how satisfied are you with your relationship with your spouse or partner?" (1 = *very dissatisfied* to 5 = *very satisfied*).

Controls

In our analyses of the associations between inaccuracies in partners' perceptions of each other's work–family conflict and relationship quality, we took demographic and socioeconomic characteristics into account, such as age, race/ethnicity (white vs. nonwhite), education (whether they have a college degree or not), self–employment, relationship status (first marriage, remarriage, or cohabiting), and parental status (whether they had at least one child under age 18 living in the household), because these characteristics are related to gender ideology (Thornton and Young-DeMarco 2001), work–family conflict (Milkie and Peltola 1999; Schieman et al. 2009), and relationship quality (Amato et al. 2003). We also accounted for the effects of the *levels* of partners' own work–family conflict and their perceptions of the other partner's work–family conflict while we focus on how *discrepancies* between partners' perceptions are related to relationship quality. These characteristics were included as controls in regression models (see Tables 9.2, 9.3).

References

Amato, P. R., Johnson, R., D., R., Booth, A., & Rogers, S. J. (2003). Continuity and change in marital quality between 1980 and 2000. *Journal of Marriage and Family, 65,* 1–22.

Bakker, A. B., & Geurts, S. A. E. (2004). Toward a dual-process model of work-home interference. *Work and Occupations, 31,* 345–366.

Becker, P. E., & Moen, P. (1999). Scaling back: Dual-earner couples' work–family conflict. *Journal of Marriage and the Family, 61,* 995–1007.

Bernard, J. (1972). *The future of marriage*. New York: Bantam.

Bellavia, G. M., & Frone, M. R. (2005). Work-family conflict. In J. Barling, E. K. Kelloway, & M. R. Frone (Eds.), *Handbook of work stress* (pp. 113–147). Thousand Oaks: Sage.

Bianchi, S. M., & Milkie, M. A. (2010). Work and family research in the first decade of the 21st century. *Journal of Marriage and Family, 72,* 705–725.
Bianchi, S. M., Robinson, J. P., & Milkie, M. A. (2006). *Changing rhythms of American family life*. New York: Russell Sage.
Blair-Loy, M. (2003). *Competing devotions*. Cambridge: Harvard University Press.
Booth, A., Johnson, D. R., White, L. K., & Edwards, J. N. (1985). Predicting divorce and permanent separation. *Journal of Family Issues, 6,* 331–346.
Bradbury, T. N., Fincham, F. D., & Beach, S. R. H. (2000). Research on the nature and determinants of marital satisfaction: A decade in review. *Journal of Marriage and the Family, 62,* 964–980.
Correll, S. J., Benard, S., & Paik, I. (2007). Getting a job: Is there a motherhood penalty? *American Journal of Sociology, 112,* 1297–1338.
Cotter, D., Hermsen, J. M., & Vanneman, R. (2011). The end of the gender revolution? Gender role attitudes from 1977 to 2008. *American Journal of Sociology, 117,* 259–289.
Coverman, S. (1989). Role overload, role conflict, and stress: Addressing consequences of multiple role demands. *Social Forces, 67,* 965–982.
Demerouti, E., Bakker, A. B., & Schaufeli, W. B. (2005). Spillover and crossover of exhaustion and life satisfaction among dual-earner parents. *Journal of Vocational Behavior, 67,* 266–298.
Doucet, A. (2006). *Do men mother?* Toronto: University of Toronto Press.
Frisco, M. L., & Williams, K. (2003). Perceived housework equity, marital happiness, and divorce in dual-earner household. *Journal of Family Issues, 24,* 51–73.
Frone, M. R., Barnes, G. M., & Farrell, M. P. (1994). Relationship of work–family conflict to substance use among employed mothers: The role of negative affect. *Journal of Marriage and the Family, 56,* 1019–1030.
Grzywacz, J. G., & Marks, N. F. (2000). Reconceptualizing the work–family interface: An ecological perspective on the correlates of positive and negative spillover between work and family. *Journal of Occupational Health Psychology, 5,* 111–126.
Gutek, B. A., Searle, S., & Klepa, L. (1991). Rational versus gender role explanations for work–family conflict. *Journal of Applied Psychology, 76,* 560–568.
Hays, S. (1996). *The cultural contradictions of motherhood*. New Haven: Yale University Press.
Hochschild, A. R. (1989). *The second shift*. New York: Quill.
Huston, T. L., Caughlim, J. P., Houts, R. M., Smith, S. E., & George, L. J. (2001). The connubial crucible: Newlywed years and predictors of marital delight, distress, and divorce. *Journal Personality and Social Psychology, 80,* 237–252.
ICPSR. (2013). Study no. 31322. Retrieved from http://www.icpsr.umich.edu/icpsrweb/DSDR/studies/31322/version/1. Accessed 17 March 2012.
Knowledge Networks. (2010). Knowledge panel design summary. Retrieved from http://www.knowledgenetworks.com/knpanel/docs/KnowledgePanel(R)-*Design-Summary-Description.pdf*. Accessed 29 June 2011.
Milkie, M. A. (1999). Social comparisons, reflected appraisals and mass media: The impact of pervasive beauty images on black and white girls' self-concepts. *Social Psychology Quarterly, 62,* 190–210.
Milkie, M. A. (2010). The stress process: Some family-level considerations. In W. R. Avison, C. S. Aneshensel, S. Schieman, & B. Wheaton (Eds.), *Advances in the conceptualization of the stress process: Essays in honor of Leonard I. Pearlin* (pp. 93–108). New York: Springer.
Milkie, M. A., & Peltola, P. (1999). Playing all the roles: Gender and the work–family balancing act. *Journal of Marriage and the Family, 61,* 476–490.
Moen, P., & Wethington, E. (1992). The concept of family adaptive strategies. *Annual Review of Sociology, 18,* 233–251.
Nomaguchi, K. M. (2009). Change in work–family conflict among employed parents between 1977 and 1997. *Journal of Marriage and Family, 71,* 15–32.
Pearlin, L. (1983). Role strains and personal stress. In H. B. Kaplan (Ed.), *Psychosocial stress: Trends in theory and research* (pp. 3–32). New York: Academic.

Pearlin, L. I., & McCall, M. E. (1990). Occupational stress and marital support: A description of microprocesses. In J. Eckenrode & S. Gore (Eds.), *Stress between work and family* (pp. 39–60). New York: Plenum.

Ridgeway, C. L. (2011). *Framed by gender*. Oxford: Oxford University Press.

Schieman, S., & Young, M. (2010). The demands of creative work: Implications for the stress in the work–family interface. *Social Science Research, 39,* 246–259.

Schieman, S., Milkie, M. A., & Glavin, P. (2009). When work interferes with life: The social distribution of work-nonwork interference and the influence of work-related demands and resources. *American Sociological Review, 74,* 966–988.

Stone, P. (2007). *Opting out? Why women really quit careers and head home*. Berkeley: University of California Press.

Streich, M., Caspter, W. J., & Salvaggio, A. N. (2008). Examining couple agreement about -family conflict. *Journal of Managerial Psychology, 23,* 252–272.

Thompson, L. (1991). Family work: Women's sense of fairness. *Journal of Family Issues, 12,* 181–196.

Thornton, A., & Young-DeMarco, L. (2001). Four decades of trends in attitudes toward family issues in the United States: The 1960s through the 1990s. *Journal of Marriage and Family, 63,* 1009–1037.

Townsend, N. W. (2002). *The package deal: Marriage, work, and fatherhood in men's lives*. Philadelphia: Temple University Press.

Wilkie, J. R., Ferree, M. M., & Ratcliff, K. S. (1998). Gender and fairness: Marital satisfaction in two-earner couples. *Journal of Marriage and the Family, 60,* 577–594.

Young, M., Schieman, S., & Milkie, M. A. (2014). Spouse's work-to-family conflict, family stressors, and mental health among dual-earner mothers and fathers. *Society and Mental Health, 4,* 1–20.

Chapter 10
Work–Life Equality: The Importance of a Level Playing Field at Home

Jeanette N. Cleveland, Gwenith G. Fisher, and Katina B. Sawyer

10.1 Introduction

Men and women increasingly participate at similar rates in the workforce (U.S. Bureau of Labor Statistics 2012a), with women holding half of managerial and professional jobs. Yet little appears to have changed at home in the USA as women continue to perform more housework than men. The division of household labor is important as women's participation in the workforce continues to increase, with 53.6% of women in the USA working in 2010 (U.S. Current Population Survey 2011). The division of household chores is one of the greatest sources of conflict and dissatisfaction among married couples (Kluwer et al. 1996, 2000; Kluwer 1998). For example, almost a quarter of women and men report the division of household chores as a key factor in divorce; currently, nearly double the percentage reported in the 1950s and 1960s (de Graaf and Kalmijn 2006). Importantly, the gender gap in the reporting of division of labor problems has increased, with women reporting greater problems than men (de Graaf and Kalmijn 2006). Therefore, whether paid or unpaid, both inside and outside of the home, the division of housework has important implications for working couples.

The goal of this chapter is to demonstrate the way in which couples divide paid work and housework is significantly guided by gender norms. Further, the division

---

J. N. Cleveland (✉)
Department of Psychology, Colorado State University, 225 Behavioral Sciences Building, 1876 Campus Delivery, Fort Collins, CO 80523, USA
e-mail: jeanette.cleveland@colostate.edu

G. G. Fisher
Department of Psychology, Colorado State University, 228 Behavioral Sciences Building, 1876 Campus Delivery, Fort Collins, CO 80523, USA
e-mail: gwen.fisher@colostate.edu

K. B. Sawyer
Department of Psychology, Villanova University, St. Mary's Hall, Suite 119, 800 Lancaster Avenue, Villanova, PA 19085, USA
e-mail: katina.sawyer@villanova.edu

M. J. Mills (ed.), *Gender and the Work-Family Experience*,
DOI 10.1007/978-3-319-08891-4_10

of paid work and housework has significant implications for the upward mobility of women in the workforce while placing tension on and jeopardizing the health and well-being of individuals and families. First, we highlight the importance of housework as an important work/life issue and describe it in the context of extant work/life research. Second, the methodological issues complicating this research area are identified, including construct deficiency and measurement bias. Next, we discuss gender specialization and describe various theories related to household division of labor. Finally, we conclude the chapter with a discussion of individual-, couple-, and organizational-level strategies that can level the playing field at home as well as suggestions for future research.

10.2 Work/Life Conflict

At the heart of the issue of work/life equality is the issue of work/life conflict, or interference between work and nonwork roles (Greenhaus and Beutell 1985). Work/life conflict is important for both individuals and organizations because there are many negative attitudinal, behavioral, and other outcomes of work/life conflict including lower levels of job satisfaction and organizational commitment (Ernst Kossek and Ozeki 1998), higher levels of absenteeism and turnover and lower levels of job performance, higher levels of stress and burnout (Anderson et al. 2002; Wayne et al. 2004), lower levels of marital satisfaction, poor physical health (Allen et al. 2000), and cognitive problems including poor concentration and low alertness (MacEwen and Barling 1994).

10.2.1 Work/Life Criterion Deficiency

The construct of work/life conflict, as currently measured, may be deficient in a number of ways. The vast majority of research that has examined work and nonwork roles has (1) focused on *family* in the nonwork domain, and (2) examined *conflict* between these roles. Although the notion of family is unquestioningly important to most workers, the topic of household labor in the nonwork domain extends the construct domain beyond caregiving roles. Although the work/life literature has contributed a great deal to our understanding of work and family issues, as well as the role of gender in determining participation in work and family spheres, Tetrick and Buffardi (2006) highlighted a number of measurement problems within the work–family domain. One issue in particular is that work/life conflict has focused heavily on *family* within the nonwork domain, without considering the potential nonfamily related conflicts which may arise within the more general life sphere. Fisher et al. (2009) developed a measure of work/nonwork interference based on the notion that, although family is important, traditional work/family measures may be too narrow for measuring the interface between work and nonwork roles. To more accurately understand the impact of work on nonwork roles and vice-versa, important aspects of life at home may be missed or ignored if too much emphasis is placed on only family roles (e.g., with child care being predominant). Additional research is needed to articulate more specific nonfamily roles in the nonwork domain to improve our understanding of how work relates to nonwork roles in a more thorough manner.

While this chapter will primarily focus on the ways in which couples divide housework, including child care, it is also possible that the burden may fall on women to perform a variety of life-related (but not family-related) tasks as well. For example, women may be expected to purchase gifts for friends, keep track of social schedules, or participate more heavily in exercise and grooming activities. As such, future research should examine the impact of gender on the division of life-related activities outside of the family sphere.

10.3 Importance of Housework and Workforce Participation

Although historically, the division of housework was of little academic interest outside the field of home economics (Ehrenreich and English 1978), the dramatic increase in working women especially among married, divorced, and separated women has brought this issue into more prominent view. For example, in 2010, 53.6 % of women and 63.7 % of men overall were working (Current Population Survey 2011). The proportion of working women is even higher among women who are married (57.4 %), divorced (61.1 %), or separated (56.5 %). This is a dramatic increase compared to previous generations; in 1970, only 40.8 % of women were employed (Current Population Survey 2011). In addition, women continue to work largely in gendered jobs with lower salary, benefits, and flexibility. For example, women are more likely than men to work in nonmanagement positions (26.9 % women vs 17.9 % men), service occupations (21.3 % women vs 14.5 % men), and in education and health services (36 % women vs 11 % men; Current Population Survey 2011). Of the only 17 % of board positions in Fortune 500 companies that are occupied by women, fewer than 25 are Fortune 500 CEOs, and only 18 % have been elected to senior legislative positions (Catalyst 2012). Further, more women hold multiple jobs than men do (5.4 % vs 4.5 %) (Current Population Survey 2010) and since 1970, women on average have increased their contributions to the family income from 2.6% to 37.1 % (Current Population Survey 2011). Finally, during the last 20 years, the proportion of wives who earn more than their husbands (among dual-earner couples) has increased from 17.8 % in 1987 to 28.9 % in 2009 (Current Population Survey 2011).

10.3.1 Why Focus on Housework?

In spite of the changes in recent decades, men are typically the breadwinners. Women's time spent doing housework is related to paid work involvement

(Bianchi et al. 2000). The popular press, including recent books such as *Lean In* (Sandberg 2013) have also highlighted continued gender gaps at work and home in spite of the narrowed gap between men and women in labor force participation rates. Gender equality theorists argue that these differences in gender roles underlie inequality, placing women at a distinct disadvantage at home and at work (Budig 2004). Even though both women and men report that they want to spend more time with their children, women are the ones who are more likely to actually scale back on their work time to prioritize family (Becker and Moen 1999). Women are then penalized for this prioritization of family over work, evidenced by lower earnings and having primary responsibility for the bulk of tasks related to child rearing (Budig and England 2001). For example, only 9% of working mothers between the ages of 25 and 44 spend more than 50 hours per week at work (Williams 2013). Although this increases to 13.9% when only considering those with at least a college degree, this is still a small percentage overall (Williams 2013). Ely and Padavic (2013) indicated that the low proportion of women at the highest levels is due to the long hours required of such jobs and that many women (mothers) are unwilling to work in jobs that require such long hours. An alternative explanation is that women *are* willing to work in jobs with long hours yet *cannot* when they disproportionately bear the burden of housework responsibility.

10.3.1.1 Childcare and Division of Labor

While it is important to compare men and women overall when discussing household labor division, it is also important to focus directly on those with children. The presence of children adds to the level of necessary housework, particularly laundry, cleaning, and meal preparation (Jacobs and Gerson 2004). Two trends have emerged regarding time in relation to parental caregiving responsibilities. First, the amount of parents' primary childcare time has increased since 1965 among western industrialized countries (Jacobs and Gerson 2004). Second, gender variations in parental care have narrowed. Specifically, fathers' time spent attending to childcare responsibilities has increased significantly, with proportionately smaller increases among mothers' childcare time (Bianchi et al. 2006; Sayer et al. 2004). Fathers have shifted some of their time from sleep and leisure to spend more time with their children while mothers have reduced some of their housework time and increased time spent attending to childcare responsibilities (Gauthier et al. 2004; Sayer 2005).

This is an encouraging pattern due to the increase in time spent on childcare overall. Yet the increased participation of men in the childcare domain may not make significant changes in the amount of time women are spending in childcare related activities. For this reason, it is important to consider the increased time commitments to the home domain experienced by parents (and particularly mothers, who are also more likely to be responsible for the bulk of home duties) in comparison with those who do not have childcare responsibilities.

10.4 Housework: Actual and Perceived Division of Labor

Women continue to do more housework or household labor than men (Liss 2013). Even when employed full-time outside of the home, women continue to spend more hours doing housework than their husbands (Blair and Lichter 1991). Further, in addition to this 'double shift' of housework and paid employment, women spend more time on tedious house tasks in addition to bearing the bulk of hours spent in child rearing. Although since 1965, the proportion of time that women contribute to housework has declined while men's has increased (Bianchi et al. 2000), women continue to do more regardless of how the division of household labor is measured.

In order to properly understand the nuances associated with the division of household labor, it is important to understand how these constructs are determined and assessed methodologically, as well as how they are perceived by those individuals completing the tasks. In this section, we briefly review the types of tasks which are performed in the household and by whom, methodological issues regarding how the division of housework is assessed, including perceptions of hours spent in household labor, and the role of fairness in housework labor division.

10.4.1 Measuring Household Work

A number of studies have sought to quantify the amount of housework performed by men vs. women. Interview studies suggest that women work 15 hours more than men each week when paid and unpaid work is combined (Hochschild and Machung 1989). More recent diary studies show that when paid and unpaid labor are combined, men and women work equal number of hours (Sayer et al. 2009). Employed mothers with young children, however, work more total hours than men do. Using time diaries where people report what they are doing with their time, generally women report less leisure time per day than men (Mattingly and Liana 2006), averaging approximately 30 minutes less. On the other hand, when researchers actually followed dual-earner couples who worked more than 30 hours per week, they found that men spent significantly more time engaged in leisure activities than women and women spent significantly more time on housework (Saxbe et al. 2011). These results highlight important differences in methodologies used to measure household work.

There are two key methodological issues regarding the measurement of housework and division of housework within couples. The first issue involves defining the construct: what exactly is the domain of housework tasks? Some research has highlighted the blurry boundaries between routine and leisure activities (Coltrane 2000). As indicated previously, although women perform more housework than men, the degree of imbalance among such work varies by the type of housework tasks (Blair and Lichter 1991). According to Twiggs et al. (1999), housework tasks are gendered and there is a hierarchy within the gender-typed tasks. For example, women are largely responsible for routine and repetitive tasks such as laundry or washing dishes. These tasks take up the majority of housework time. Further, although both laundry and washing dishes are considered routine female housework activities, men are less likely to do the laundry than the dishes. Housework assessments then reflect not only the amount of time spent but also responsibility for a given (historically, often gendered) task and is measured either through estimates of the actual time spent or as a report on who is more frequently responsible for the task.

The second issue pertains to quantifying the amount of time spent performing housework. For example, while individuals may engage in one task at a time, they may also multitask by performing two or more tasks at once (e.g., laundry and picking up around the house), making the reporting of time spent in household labor difficult to estimate. Relatedly, there is the potential for recollection problems for participants as housework is so routine to daily life that they may not be as salient as nonroutine events. In other words, participants may not be consciously aware of or be able to accurately recall how much time they actually spent doing these tasks.

Three approaches to measuring housework and division of domestic labor have been compared by Juster et al. (2003) and Lee and Waite (2005). The most frequently used measure is respondents' retrospective reports of housework. Specifically, either one or both partners are asked to report time spent on total housework over a specific time period (e.g., last week, month, etc.) or about the time spent on one specific activity. The measure is easily implemented and therefore popular. However, combining housework time across all tasks into one overall measure may not capture the nuanced differences in the types of housework completed or in linking the completion of specific types of housework tasks to assessments of well-being. The second measurement method is use of a "time diary" in which respondents are asked to record their actual time use for all activities (usually measured with reference to the previous day). Such measures are viewed as more accurate than retrospective report survey questions, yet they are also more time-consuming and expensive to implement. In addition, the time diary approach assumes that the previous day is an accurate representation of how participants *usually* spend their time. Results using both survey questions and time diary measures do correlate closely especially when tasks are those that are performed regularly and are externally structured (Juster et al. 2003).

A third measure related to the time diary approach is the experience sampling method (ESM; Lee and Waite 2005). In ESM, respondents report their primary and secondary activities eight times a day, often at random intervals when prompted to do so by a device. Compared to survey measures, ESM-based measures produce lower housework time estimates. Further, the gender gap between husbands and wives reports of activities is smallest based on ESM estimates (for primary activities only) and largest based on wives' retrospective survey reports (Lee and Waite 2005). Thus, it is important to examine the extent to which gender discrepancies exist as a function of the measurement tool used to capture housework hours.

10.4.2 Gender Discrepancies in Reporting Housework

Most research on housework relies on retrospective survey-based measures or diary studies in which only one person reports about the division of housework. When information is collected from both partners, there is often a discrepancy (Coltrane 2000). Although both men and women in the USA tend to inflate their reports of time spent, men do so more than women (Coltrane 1996, 2000; Press and Townsley 1998). There are a number of reasons for reporting differences. First, social desirability may influence the reporting depending upon the extent to which the task may be considered more gendered. Men may overestimate their contribution in order to reflect a more supportive husband or due to lack of information on how much the partner is contributing (Kamo 2000). Finally, wives' and husbands' differences in reporting may reflect domestic harmony or disharmony or couple marital conflict. In other words, differences in reporting may be more apparent when members of a couple do not agree on how work is being done or should be done.

10.4.3 Fairness Perceptions

Fairness perceptions are important because they have implications for a range of emotions and well-being and, additionally, whether one feels that they are being fair (or unfair) to their partner (Lively et al. 2008). However, fairness is a subjective experience and differs from reports of equal division of labor. Men report that division of housework is fair if they contribute 36% or more, while women perceive housework as fair if they do 66% or less (Lennon and Rosenfield 1994). Women are more likely to feel that the division of housework is unfair to them while men are more likely to report the distribution of tasks as fair (DeMaris and Longmore 1996).

10.5 Gender Specialization: The Role of Separate Spheres

Traditional gender stereotypes create circumstances in which women are expected to perform nearly all of the household duties, while men are expected to perform most of the paid work. Thus, when women contribute little to the household in terms of income, it may be an indicator of traditional gender roles operating within the family unit (Bittman et al. 2003; Brines 1994; Greenstein 2000; Prince-Cooke 2006). While "gender specialization" is decreasing in prevalence, it was viewed historically as beneficial to both men and women, because it resulted in mutual dependence within couples (Prince-Cooke 2006). Specifically, when women specialize in the home domain and men specialize in the work domain, both partners depend upon each another because neither partner is able to perform the necessary tasks and duties required for success in the opposite domain. This gendered division of labor has been labeled the two "separate spheres," one of work (which is male) and one of the home (which is female) (Lundberg and Pollak 1993). When husbands and wives are responsible for separate and distinct sets of work activities (Lundberg and Pollak 1996), they no longer must coordinate or compromise with one another. This arrangement is assumed to create optimal conditions for both husbands and wives, because each individual is able to complete their activities independently and without negotiation.

However, the viability of gendered division of labor appears to be diminishing significantly within our current economy. Demographic data suggest that traditional gendered arrangements occur less frequently today because both men and women increasingly participate in the labor force (U.S. Bureau of Labor Statistics 2012b). As a result, women and men participate in both work and family spheres. As such, couples increasingly need to negotiate with one another about the extent to which they participate in the work domain versus the nonwork domain, creating a new set of circumstances for them to consider when navigating the work–life interface. Further, research shows that when either member of a couple perceives unfairness in arrangements either inside or outside of the home, greater levels of marital conflict and lower marital satisfaction are reported, and may contribute to divorce (Lavee and Katz 2002; Prince-Cooke 2006). Thus, a key factor to maintain healthy relationships is for couples to successfully negotiate or communicate with each other to arrive at a consensus regarding their work and family arrangements.

While it is important to investigate perceptions of and measurements related to the amount of paid work and family labor completed by males and females, it is also necessary to examine the underlying theoretical frameworks which may be driving these perceptions and their related antecedents and consequences. Further, we review a sampling of theories which help to shed light on the mechanisms through which work and family negotiations may occur. While this is not an exhaustive review, the theories outlined below are particularly relevant when considering how paid work and family labor are split among partners, allowing for a closer examination of the role of gender and household politics in determining levels of work–life conflict within couples. As such, we review a sample of theories that highlight the key drivers of work–life negotiations between partners, both at home and at work.

10.6 Theoretical Approaches to Household Division of Labor

10.6.1 Exchange Theory: The Division of Paid Work and Housework

One underlying explanation for gender specialization is exchange theory (Bittman et al. 2003; Molm and Cook 1995). According to this theory, one partner (e.g., economically dependent) within a couple contributes to the relationship by providing nonmonetary goods (e.g., household labor, child care) and, in return, receives monetary goods (e.g., income, property) from the economically independent partner. The dependent partner relies on the independent partner for economic resources and thus, is unlikely to leave the relationship as a result. Further, because the dependent partner is financially tied to the relationship, the independent partner has little reason to contribute additional nonmonetary resources in exchange for their contributions. Given that women often make smaller economic contributions in relationships compared to men (as evidenced by the gender pay gap and the lower representation of women in high powered positions in the workplace, U.S. Bureau of Labor Statistics 2012a, b), women are more likely to occupy the dependent partner role. Further, because the independent partner does not feel the need to increase their contributions to the relationship, women may feel pressured to contribute increasingly to the household domain, while receiving static levels of assistance in exchange.

10.6.2 Bargaining Theory: The Division of Paid Work and Housework

A related theoretical perspective regarding family and work negotiation is bargaining theory. Bargaining theory describes the exchanges between partners as primarily based around "threat points" (Bittman et al. 2003; McElroy 1990). A threat point is determined by the resources that each individual in the relationship independently acquires and can use at his/her discretion in the event that the relationship ends. Thus, threat points are constantly balancing in a relationship, in anticipation of a potential divorce. For example, if a woman does not contribute monetarily to a relationship, yet her partner does, then (in terms of resources) her partner does not need to fear that the relationship might end. He would, in essence, have more bargaining power over his partner, and therefore, more power to create the conditions in the marriage that are more favorable to him. In this way, the "threat point" is used to exert power over the more dependent member of a relationship because the dependent member lacks personal resources available for use in the event of a divorce. Again, because the less economically powerful person in a relationship is more likely to be a woman (as measured by income differentials and power differentials in the workplace; U.S. Bureau of Labor Statistics 2012a, b), women are at greater risk for potential oppression and power misuse than men. However, when a woman is employed in paid work, she assumes a better exchange/bargaining position with her husband. Thus, there is an incentive for women to join the labor force: to gain valuable resources, and maintain threat point balance.

10.6.3 Understanding Equitable Exchanges

The challenges associated with the division of paid and household work may become easier as partners view each other as either contributing wholly to one sphere (work or the home) or as equal contributors to the paid work sphere (spending similar hours and/or earning similar salaries in the paid workforce). Research shows that women who work fewer hours than their partner outside of the home are likely to do more household work (Brines 1994; Greenstein 2000) and also report greater fairness in the distribution of household labor (Lennon and Rosenfield 1994). Women who perform all of the housework while their husband performs all of the work outside of the home report the highest levels of fairness (Lennon and Rosenfield

1994). These women may perceive the gender specialization of tasks (Bittman et al. 2003) as fair (e.g., husband takes care of work outside of the home, while wife takes care of work inside of the home). Thus, perceptions of fairness, in this case, are not based on actual hours worked in the home, but rather how these hours are perceived in light of the overall contribution of both partners to the marriage. However, there is evidence that as couples increasingly equally share the division of paid work, they begin to divide the household labor more equally as well (Bittman et al. 2003; Brines 1994; Greenstein 2000; Prince-Cooke 2006). This implies that as partners begin to contribute equally in terms of income and hours worked outside of the home, these equitable practices are also maintained inside the home.

To this end, equity theory, which states that unfair exchanges decrease satisfaction for both parties (Klumb et al. 2006), is a theoretical framework which enables us to better understand the psychological undercurrents between partners when they perceive that they are completing either more or less than their equitable share. Similar to exchange and bargaining theories, equity theory focuses on the exchange of or bargaining for paid labor versus household labor between partners. Yet, equity theory diverges from exchange and bargaining theories and predicts that neither person in the relationship will be happy when exchanges are inequitable, regardless of the amount of power one holds.

Equally sharing work, on the other hand, may be associated with lower distress for both parties. While exchange and bargaining theories revolve around the maintenance of power within relationships, the elimination of this power struggle may alleviate tension for couples engaged in this struggle. In fact, according to exchange, bargaining, and equity theories, equality between individuals may be beneficial for both partners' well-being, particularly because it is associated with a lower risk of divorce (Prince-Cooke 2006). Further, perceptions of unfairness in the division of household labor are linked with marital conflict and marital dissatisfaction (Lavee and Katz 2002).

10.6.4 Gender Role Attitudes: The Effects of Traditional and Nontraditional Attitudes on the Division of Labor

While equity theory may serve to better understand outcomes associated with the division of housework, there may be limits to its usefulness in prediction. When members of a couple strongly subscribe to traditional gender roles, tenets of bargaining and exchange theories may be more valid. Research demonstrates that among couples, adherence to traditional gender roles is associated with a more traditional division of labor inside the home (Lu et al. 2000). Further, traditional gender ideology has been found to predict the unequal distribution of labor in the home to a greater degree than the wife's nonparticipation in the paid workforce (Pina and Bengston 1993). Husbands' gender ideology also has been shown to be a predictor of the division of household labor, with wives completing a greater percentage of housework when husbands adhered to traditional norms (Pyke and Coltrane 1996).

In conjunction, women with traditional gender ideologies report greater role clarity both inside and outside of the home because they feel that well-developed roles (lack of participation in paid labor, high levels of participation in household labor) are available to them (Buunk et al. 2000).

Further, the ways in which women or men identify themselves outside home can influence the division of household labor. For example, husbands and wives that consider themselves "co-breadwinners" are more likely to share labor in the household (Deutsch 2001). On the other hand, couples who identified more strongly with traditional masculine and feminine traits continued to maintain traditional gender identities by reporting that the male was the breadwinner (Deutsch and Saxon 1998) even though they actually had nontraditional work arrangements. The women who reported employment in paid work due solely to financial pressure continued to report that being a mother was their primary role (Deutsch and Saxon 1998). Therefore, gender ideology influences the ways in which individuals divide and also perceive their labor contributions within a couple, even if objective information about income and hours worked indicates that they are equally sharing paid labor.

10.6.5 Gender Deviance Neutralization and the Division of Household Labor

Incorporating the influence of gender ideology, Brines (1994) and Greenstein (2000) proposed two related theories: gender display theory and deviance neutralization theory, respectively, as explanations for the ways that couples divide household labor. According to these theories, couples divide routine household activities consistent with their adherence to gender norms. For example, among couples with more traditional gender views and similar relative employment hours, husbands spend less time doing female sex-typed household tasks, such as laundry or washing dishes (Atkinson and Huston 1984). Similarly, the opposite pattern would be found for those with less traditional gender norms. Therefore, Brines (1994) and Greenstein (2000) assert that gender ideology may be one guiding mechanism behind the division of household labor. The context of their research focused upon couples in which the women were the primary breadwinners (e.g., either the sole income or earning a higher income than her spouse). Within such couples (woman as breadwinner), the predictions based on equity theory, bargaining theory, and exchange theory do not appear to be supported.

According to equity theory, when the wife is the primary economic contributor, the husband should perform more housework. However, the evidence shows the opposite pattern (Perry-Jenkins and Folk 1994; Van Willigen and Drentea 2001). Specifically, husbands with wives who work full-time do no more housework than husbands with wives who are full-time homemakers. Men's work inside the home increases as the relative proportion of hours worked outside the home decreases, until it reaches equity with their partner. This finding is consistent with equity theory predictions. However, as men's paid work hours continue to become proportionately less than their wives', men's participation in the household also decreases. Therefore, when the number of hours spent in the labor force by a woman proportionally exceeds that of a male, the increase in paid work hours and income by females are associated with lower levels of help from males in the household.

Other research (Hochshild and Machung 1989) showed that one-fifth of husbands who earn more than their wives share the housework (although husbands were more likely to do male sex-typed chores, such as mowing the lawn, car maintenance, and cleaning the garage). Within couples where the husband and wife earn the same amount, one third of the husbands shared the housework. However, in couples where husbands earn less than their wives, none of the husbands performed the majority of housework. Brines (1994) suggested that this finding among female breadwinner couples is associated with men's unwillingness to be further feminized by participating in housework when they are not the major economic provider.

Further, with wives complicit in the process, women and men may attempt to neutralize the nontraditional gender behaviors that occur outside of the home (e.g., wife as breadwinner) by engaging in more traditional gendered behaviors within the home and through housework (Greenstein 2000). In addition to their responsibility as the primary provider outside the home, female breadwinners with traditional gender ideologies are expected to and likely perform the majority of household tasks. This pattern predicts an increased risk for role and stress overload for female breadwinners. Additionally, the finding is inconsistent with the predictions of exchange theory or bargaining theory because, according to these theories, the female breadwinner should have greater resources and greater bargaining power, and therefore, a greater opportunity to negotiate preferable household arrangements. Yet, these women (who work more hours and/or are paid more than their husbands) contribute more hours to housework than their husbands.

While exchange, bargaining, or equity theories cannot fully account for these findings, the role of gender norms may explain the phenomenon which occurs within female breadwinner couples (Brines 1994; Greenstein 2000). As women increase hours spent in the workforce relative to their husbands, traditional gender roles may be threatened. Because the notion of a female breadwinner does not fit with traditional gender stereotypes, women and men who hold more traditional gender views may feel that they must counteract the perceived violation of traditional gender norms outside of the home. This "gender deviance neutralization" (Bittman et al. 2003) predicts that women will perform the majority of housework in order to feel as though they are, in a sense, still fulfilling their "womanly duties." Similarly, husbands of female breadwinners may believe that they have violated or failed in their masculine role by not being the primary economic provider. Thus, if husbands of female breadwinners do not believe they are adequately fulfilling their masculine role outside the home, they may preserve their masculinity by opting out of household duties, thereby diffusing feelings of gender deviance.

Overall, exchange, equity, and bargaining theory can explain instances where traditional gender roles are enacted or the situation is gender neutral. However, when gender roles are violated, gender deviance neutralization appears to provide a more complete or nuanced explanation (Bittman et al. 2003; Brines 1994;

Greenstein 2000) for the division of household labor. Neutralizing gender deviance does not necessarily account for the potential negative effects that female breadwinners may experience as a result of completing more than their fair share of housework, as well as working long hours outside of the home. The finding that female breadwinners often shoulder the bulk of the labor, both inside and outside of the home, is indicative of the influence that traditional gender roles may have on the division of paid and household labor (Weber 1998). Taken together, these theories help to better explain the outcomes associated with the division of labor between partners, as well as the effects of traditional gender roles on the interplay between males' and females' participation in the paid and household labor domains. Thus, it is important to consider the role of traditional gender norms in determining which spheres partners have historically specialized in, the exchanges and bargains which may exist to hold these spheres in place, and the outcomes related with violations of these norms, which may have serious implications for burdens placed on working women. These competing pressures may add to work–family conflict for women in the workforce, compared to their male counterparts, which we discuss in greater detail below.

10.7 Addressing Perceptions and Leveling the Playing Field

In 1996, the National Committee on Pay Equity established Equal Pay Day in order to emphasize the fact that women must work more than 15 months in order to earn the same salary that a man earns in 1 year (York 2013). As this chapter and other chapters in this book attest, the correlates or causes of this gender gap in pay are many, including differences in occupational distribution (with women clustered in lower paying occupations), differences in the human capital accumulation, and both intentional and unintentional gender discrimination. In work organizations, there have been significant legal and organizational changes that have begun to level the field of work among women and men. These changes have been crucial and necessary, yet they are not sufficient. We continue to find that women do not rise to the top of organizations nor seek or secure significant leadership positions. Most often these findings are attributed to women themselves, as either due to their lack of qualifications, motivation, or interest in such positions, or because these positions require long hours. However, even if all of these work issues were eliminated or managed, women (and men) would still face at least one societal or cultural issue that significantly affects male–female differences in work experiences and outcomes—i.e., that women spend a greater number of hours doing household (and caregiving) work, which in turn decreases the time and energy they can devote to work for pay (York 2013).

Similar to the workplace changes that resulted in greater diversity awareness and inclusion, enduring and pervasive changes in the 'private' sphere of home and housework must be implemented at multiple levels (e.g., individual, critical pairs or groups, organizations, communities) and in formal as well as informal ways (e.g., observable task changes, norms, power sharing, etc.) to provide a truly more level playing field for men and women at work and home. As we have noted throughout this chapter, work–life tension and scarce time and economic resources are at the heart of work and nonwork gender bias and discrimination. Drawing from this literature, and extending it to the domain of household labor, there are a number of ways that work–life conflict or interference might be addressed via the division of household labor. Using a framework of target and/or source of change and formality of change (e.g., 3 × 2), we describe some suggestions for formal and informal changes at a number of levels.

10.7.1 Individual-Level Changes

In order to begin to engage in the process of improving the gendered nature of work and family participation levels, we believe that it is important to focus on potential formal as well as informal changes at the individual level. We will discuss the implications of both of these individual-level changes below.

10.7.1.1 Informal Changes

Most of us are guided by societal norms, including gender norms, interpreted and conveyed to us by our families and social context. However, both women and men as individuals must consciously examine and re-examine the relevance and usefulness of specific norms as they apply to themselves and within their evolving couple or family structures. Both women and men benefit by making clear choices and identifying what beliefs guide their behavior solely or largely by tradition or gender norms/stereotypes, and whether or not they feel comfortable continuing to engage in those behaviors or, alternatively, changing these norms. For example, men are still socialized into breadwinner roles and women into caretaker roles. If a child or an elderly parent becomes ill and someone needs to take a day off from work, the gendered assumption is that the woman will make this sacrifice, as opposed to the man. For some individuals, this might work very well, but it is certainly worthwhile for both men and women to consider whether this is the best way for them individually to handle this situation.

We assert that the process of examining gender norms and expectations begins with individual self-awareness, and this process can be initiated well before formally entering the workplace full-time (e.g., during high school and college, if not before). This, of course, begs the question: Does this fall within the domain of work psychologists? We believe that it is absolutely a workplace psychology issue, and can be accomplished through assessments of vocational interests and assumptions, career counseling and self-assessments and self-awareness exercises. Work psychologists are well-positioned to design and develop tools to assist individuals in understanding the nature and the implications of their beliefs, assumptions, and norms regarding the roles of men and women at work and at home.

10.7.1.2 Formal Changes

At a more systemic level, there would be real and immediate benefits that could be realized by training women and men in effective decision-making, setting priorities, time management, and negotiation and conflict management, as they apply in work and nonwork settings. For example, it would be useful for both men and women to develop individual skills to navigate household labor, community service, and other roles, and to develop the ability to translate or apply work skills to the home domain. In particular, women and men can be trained to listen, depersonalize a situation, and step back (or empathize) to identify and address the important and unimportant household tasks and potential configurations for the division of these tasks. It would be useful to train men and women on how to develop methods and divide up tasks based on skill level, liking/enjoyment, and avoiding the assignment of repetitive, time consuming tasks to one person (for example, by rotating these tasks or delegating them to a third party). Men and women will also benefit from developing the perspective that household work division will not be a fixed phenomenon, but rather is likely to change as work or life situations change. For example, the demands on men's and women's time and energy will vary depending on developmental stages of children, or changes in the frequency of certain tasks (e.g., less laundry, more eating out, etc.).

10.7.2 Couple-Level Changes

In addition to individual-level changes, there are a variety of informal and formal changes at the couple-level that can contribute to a more even distribution of work and nonwork responsibilities. We outline these couple-level changes below.

10.7.2.1 Informal Changes

Prior to engaging in a formal relationship, couples can benefit substantially by discussing the division of tasks in a gender neutral way, particularly if the members of a couple have interests or preferences that might be accommodated by divisions of responsibility that are not strictly traditional (e.g., many men like to cook, but this is often stereotyped as a female activity). Couples can benefit by developing superordinate goals together which consider the division of paid and unpaid work as contributions to the well-being of the pair, and eventually the family, with the presence of children or expanded family needs. As children or elder care needs increase, couples can revisit the division of household labor; gender roles often firmly reassert themselves once children (or elderly parents) arrive.

In considering how to develop more equitable roles for women, it is important to recognize that this sort of change creates special challenges for men, particularly if they have been socialized to cultures that emphasize rigid gender norms. A critical issue to negotiate is the best way to mitigate men's feelings of loss of a favored gender role (i.e., the more powerful role).

It is very useful to identify the tasks that can be completed with flexibility in terms of time and place (paying bills, etc.), to identify nonessential tasks, and to lengthen time between task completion (bi-weekly house cleaning vs weekly; weekly market shopping vs daily or thrice weekly, etc.). It also helps to identify core times that all family adults meet to divide or delegate household work. Secondly, it is also very useful for men and women to communicate openly and clearly about task roles and responsibilities, rather than making assumptions regarding what one or the other will do or is expected to do especially if these assumptions are based on traditional gender stereotypes.

10.7.2.2 Formal Changes

Drawing from work–life interventions in organizations, skills developed in paid work can be applied to navigating nonwork domains as well, especially in terms of seeking support and collaboration from one's spouse during potentially stressful times, much in the same way one might do with a supervisor at work. Supervisory support as well as coworker support are critical facets in mitigating work/life conflicts and strains (Cleveland et al. 2006). It is important to develop skills to identify when one needs spousal support in managing housework and how to effectively obtain this support, as well as planning a course of action and a timeframe for accomplishing tasks.

10.7.3 Work and Organization-Level Changes

Changes at both the formal and informal level in organizations can complement individual- and couple-level changes to provide a balanced workplace. If we begin to address the systemic issues related to gender, work, family, and community, we can create a society which is more equitable for men and for women alike.

10.7.3.1 Informal Changes

Work group members have beliefs and assumptions about work and family roles that can substantially influence the success or failure of attempts to create an equitable balance. It is important to recognize that these beliefs and assumptions are likely to vary, and that no one set of beliefs is necessarily right or correct. Coworkers can be a surprising source of resistance to efforts to change the balance of work and nonwork responsibilities. For example, suppose a husband increases his nonwork responsibilities and is not able to be present or engaged at work quite as often as in the past. Coworkers, particularly those who are socialized to more traditional work role expectations, might resent this and feel that they will have to pick up the slack. It is important for men and women who are trying to make changes in their relative responsibilities to recognize that their coworkers' concerns are not necessarily unreasonable, and to address them in realistic and respectful ways. Much in the same ways that the members of a couple often have to negotiate roles and responsibilities, members of work groups are likely to benefit from explicit and honest discussions of how changes in one person's workload might affect others he or she works with, and how challenges that might arise from these changes can be mitigated.

10.7.3.2 Formal Changes

Organizations are increasingly confronted with requests for flexibility. A great deal of empirical research has demonstrated that flexible work practices (e.g., offering flexibility in when and/or where one works) offer many benefits (Baltes et al. 1999; Halpern 2005). Yet the simple implementation of flextime may lead to unintended consequences such as perceptions of inequity or complications in negotiating work vs. nonwork roles. For example, technological advances, increases in flexible work policies, and increases in telecommuting have culminated in the blurring of boundaries between work and home life. This is relevant to the division of labor in the household as gender role expectations may interact with time and location of work. Individuals who work at home may encounter situations in which "being" physically in their home for work results in their spouse or partner expecting that they will perform more domestic labor. In addition, among dual-career couples, the individual with a more flexible schedule may experience more family interference with work, because it is assumed that this member will have more time to complete household tasks. It is often the case that an individual with more flexibility is more likely to miss work and stay home to deal with family demands (e.g., a sick child). Hammer et al. (2005) conducted a longitudinal study to examine the role of using family-friendly workplace supports in relation to work and family outcomes. Their results indicated that women's use of workplace supports was related to higher levels of family-to-work conflict. Therefore, we suggest that although flexible work arrangements can be beneficial, they can also have a disproportionately negative effect in some situations.

Another limitation of flexible work arrangements is that they are only available to a minority of the workforce (Bulger and Fisher 2012; Golden 2001). Golden (2001) indicated that availability of flexible work practices varies in important ways by demographic, work, and job characteristics. Individuals in lower-level jobs, who are more likely to be women and ethnic minorities and less likely to be educated, are less likely to have flexibility. Men and women in higher level professional jobs may have more flexibility, but with higher level jobs come longer work hours and/or have higher levels of responsibility such that it may be more difficult to use benefits.

Part-time work would seem to offer a good solution to many of the problems of balancing work and nonwork responsibilities. It seems intuitive that working fewer hours should be associated with lower levels of work-to-family conflict and that one potential solution is to reduce work hours. However, organizations, particularly in the United States, do not offer many part-time options, particularly for professional occupations. Further, Barnett and Gareis (2002) suggest that "success" of part-time work in improving marital quality depends on the amount of control one has over nonwork tasks. Thus, part-time jobs may only help to deflate work–family conflict if one has more control within the family sphere.

Supporting the idea that work and family domains may be dependent on one another in terms of overall time spent and the outcomes associated with time spent in either domain, Duxbury and Higgins (1991) found that the hours an individual works are not just those recorded on a time sheet, but rather reflect a range of responsibilities at the individual and family levels. Unfortunately, the demands of individuals, couples, families and organizations are not always in sync. At work, there are teams, committees, and departments with coworkers and others who depend on individual employees (and upon whom the individual employee depends as well). Therefore, there are times when "face time" (being physically present at work) is simply essential, and other times where it is a norm or more subtle expectation but not a genuine requirement. Similarly, in nonwork settings some activities may be put off or shared with other family members, but other activities must be completed by a given family member at a given point in time (e.g., mothers engaging in breastfeeding).

One of the best ways to approach potential conflicts between the demands of different spheres is with frequent, tempered and informed communication. Many conflicts can be defused by working through questions of whether the circumstances that drive conflict come about because of what is essential vs. what is customary. For example, suppose staff meetings have always been held at 3 pm. If some workers take on responsibility for school-age children, this can be a source of time-based conflict, because it coincides with the time many children are dismissed from school. If this meeting time is customary, but another can be reasonably found, it might be possible to reduce or even eliminate the conflict by changing the meeting time. However, it is worth recognizing that asking people to change, even when there is little real cost to making a change, may *feel* like an imposition. Thus, these feelings should be recognized and respected.

10.8 Future Research

Based on the issues and empirical research described in this chapter, we offer a few recommendations for additional research. First, we issue a call for more work-life research to investigate nonwork roles and responsibilities in addition to family caregiving. Much of the extant research has focused on family roles, but seems criterion deficient in understanding the true scope of the impact of work on workers' nonwork lives, as well as how nonfamily-related issues may interfere with work. It may be helpful to understand the specific household tasks or chores in which work is more likely to interfere, or that may be more likely to interfere with work.

Secondly, additional research is needed among workers in nonmanagerial and professional occupations. This is due to the fact that a preponderance of work/family research focuses on workers in managerial and professional occupations.

Workers in hourly and nonprofessional settings are likely to have *less* flexibility in time and location of work, which may serve to exacerbate problems navigating the division of household labor. Although some work-life research has studied workers in nonprofessional jobs (e.g., Grzywacz et al. 2002, who found higher rates of conflict among workers in service jobs; Grzywacz et al. 2006, who studied work–family issues among Mexican migrant farmworkers; and Grandey et al. 2007, who studied male blue-collar hourly workers), additional work is needed.

Next, the majority of work/life research has focused on individuals. In the past decade, work/family research has expanded a great deal to study couples or dyads (e.g., spillover from one spouse to another; Westman 2001; Westman and Etzion 2005). The issues of work and the household division of labor point to a critical need to study households as a unit. Therefore, it is important to consider multiple units or levels of analysis when posing our research questions.

As previously described, empirical evidence points to the efficacy of flexible work arrangements as being beneficial to help individuals manage work and life demands. However, workers with more flexibility may end up managing *more* domestic and caregiving responsibilities. Additional research is needed to increase our understanding about boundary conditions regarding when flexibility helps vs. hinders. The meta-analysis by Baltes et al. (1999) indicated that too much flexibility about flexible work practices is associated with more negative outcomes than more rigid or structured flexible work arrangements. Additional research is needed to examine the impact of flexible work arrangements within the home and, specifically, with the division of household responsibilities. Systematic evaluation of organizational interventions designed to reduce work-to-life conflict and life-to-work conflict are needed. The issues discussed in this chapter point to the need for attention to more than just family caregiving roles, but household tasks as well.

Finally, additional research should be conducted to identify individual differences and processes that are related to successfully managing and negotiating household division of labor. What are the factors that make for equality and peace on the home front? Learning this may be fruitful for helping to offer additional recommendations on narrowing the gender gap at home.

10.9 Conclusion

Is the glass half full (progress) or half empty (gender inequalities and disparities)? Although we have begun to level the playing field between men and women with regard to educational attainment and labor force participation, research still highlights inequality on the home front. Women are more likely than men to spend more time caring for other family members, in addition to performing more household tasks. The trend is moving in a positive direction toward more balance or equity between men and women, but there is still a great deal of room for improvement. Time is a finite resource. As long as women have more caregiving responsibilities and spend more time involved in domestic work than men, it is unlikely that the gender discrepancies will disappear.

References

Allen, T. D., Herst, D. L., Bruck, C. S., & Sutton, M. (2000). Consequences associated with work-to-family conflict: A review and agenda for future research. *Journal of Occupational Health Psychology, 5,* 278–308.

Anderson, S. E., Coffey, B. S., & Byerly, R. T. (2002). Formal organizational initiatives and informal workplace practices: Links to work–family conflict and job-related outcomes. *Journal of Management, 28,* 787–810.

Atkinson, J., & Huston, T. L. (1984). Sex role orientation and division of labor early in marriage. *Journal of Personality and Social Psychology, 46,* 330–345.

Baltes, B. B., Briggs, T. E., Huff, J. W., Wright, J. A., & Neuman, G. A. (1999). Flexible and compressed workweek schedules: A meta-analysis of their effects on work-related criteria. *Journal of Applied Psychology, 84,* 496–513.

Barnett, R. C., & Gareis, K. C. (2002). Full-time and reduced-hours work schedules and marital quality: A study of female physicians with young children. *Work and Occupations, 29,* 364–379.

Becker, P. E., & Moen, P. (1999). Scaling back: Dual-earner couples work–family strategies. *Journal of Marriage and the Family, 61,* 995–1007.

Bianchi, S. M., Milkie, M., Sayer, L. C., & Robinson, J. (2000). Is anyone doing the housework? Trends in the gender division of household labor. *Social Forces, 79,* 191–228.

Bianchi, S. M., Robinson, J. P., & Milkie, M. A. (2006). Changing rhythms of American life. New York: Russell Sage.

Bittman, M., England, P., Sayer, L., Folbre, N., & Matheson, G. (2003). When does gender trump money? Bargaining and time in household work. *American Journal of Sociology, 109,* 186–214.

Blair, S. L., & Lichter, D. (1991). Measuring the division of household labor: Gender segregation of housework among American couples. *Journal of Family Issues, 12,* 91–113.

Brines, J. (1994). Economic dependency, gender, and the division of labor at home. *The American Journal of Sociology, 100,* 652–688.

Budig, M. (2004). Feminism and the family. In J. Scott, J. Treas, & M. Richards (Eds.), *The Blackwell companion to the sociology of families* (pp. 416–434). Oxford: Blackwell.

Budig, M., & England, P. (2001). The wage penalty for motherhood. *American Sociological Review, 66,* 204–224.

Bulger, C. A., & Fisher, G. G. (2012). Ethical imperatives of work-life balance. In N. P. Reilly, M. J. Sirgy, & C. A. Gorman (Eds.), *Work and quality of life: Ethical practices in organizations* (pp. 181–200). New York: Springer.

Buunk, B. P., Kluwer, E. S., Schuurman, M. K., & Siero, F. W. (2000). The division of labor among egalitarian and traditional women: Differences in discontent, social comparison, and false consensus. *Journal of Applied Social Psychology, 30,* 759–779.

Catalyst. (2012). 2012 Catalyst census: Fortune 500 women board directors. http://www.catalyst.org/knowledge/2012-catalyst-census-fortune-500. Accessed 4 Jan 2014.

Cleveland, J. N., McCarthy, A., & Jones, A. (September 2006). The influence of managerial support and family structure on work–family outcomes. Presented at the Irish Academy of Management conference, Cork, Ireland.

Coltrane, S. (1996). *Family man: Fatherhood, housework and gender equity*. Oxford: Oxford University.

Coltrane, S. (2000). Research on household labor: Modeling and measuring the social embeddedness of routine family work. *Journal of Marriage and the Family, 62,* 1208–1233.

Current Population Survey. (2011). Laborforce statistics from the currently population survey. http://www.bls.gov/cps/. Accessed 15 Dec 2013.

de Graaf, P. M., & Kalmijn, M. (2006). Divorce motives in a period of rising divorce: Evidence from a Dutch life-history survey. *Journal of Family Issues, 27,* 487–505.

DeMaris, A., & Longmore, M. A. (1996). Ideology, power, and equity: Testing competing explanations for the perceptions of fairness in household labor. *Social Forces, 74,* 1043–1071.
Deutsch, F. M. (2001). Equally shared parenting. *Current Directions in Psychological Science, 10,* 25–28.
Deutsch, F. M., & Saxon, S. E. (1998). Traditional ideologies, nontraditional lives. *Sex Roles, 38,* 331–362.
Duxbury, L. E., & Higgins, C. A. (1991). Gender differences in work–family conflict. *Journal of Applied Psychology, 76,* 60–74. doi:10.1037/0021-9010.76.1.60.
Ehrenreich, B., & English, D. (1978). *For her own good: Two centuries of the experts' advice to women*. New York: Random House.
Ely, R., & Padavic, I. (2013). Work-family conflict is not the problem: Overwork is. Blog for The Huffington Post and Stanford University's Michelle R. Clayman Institute for gender research in conjunction with the latter's redesigning, redefining work summit (November, 7). http://gender.stanford.edu/news/2013/work–family-conflict-not-problem-overwork.
Ernst Kossek, E., & Ozeki, C. (1998). Work-family conflict, policies, and the job-life satisfaction relationship: A review and directions for organizational behavior-human resources research. *Journal of Applied Psychology, 83,* 139–149.
Fisher, G. G., Bulger, C. A., & Smith, C. S. (2009). Beyond work and family: A measure of work/non-work interference and enhancement. *Journal of Occupational Health Psychology, 14,* 441–456.
Gauthier, A. H., Smeeding, T. M., & Furstenberg, F. F. (2004). Are parents investing less time in children? Trends in selected industrialized countries. *Population and Development Review, 30,* 647–671.
Golden, L. (2001). Flexible work schedules: Which workers get them? *American Behavioral Scientist, 44,* 1157–1178.
Grandey, A. A., Cordeiro, B. L., & Michael, J. H. (2007). Work-family supportiveness organizational perceptions: Important for the well-being of male blue-collar hourly workers?. *Journal of Vocational Behavior, 71,* 460–478.
Greenhaus, J. H., & Beutell, N. J. (1985). Sources and conflict between work and family roles. *Academy of Management Review, 10,* 76–88.
Greenstein, T. N. (2000). Economic dependence, gender, and the division of labor in the home: A replication and extension. *Journal of Marriage and the Family, 62,* 322–335.
Grzywacz, J. G., Almeida, D. M., & McDonald, D. A. (2002). Work-family spillover and daily reports of work and family stress in the adult labor force. *Family Relations, 51,* 28–36.
Grzywacz, J. G., Quandt, S. A., Early, J., Tapia, J., Graham, C. N., & Arcury, T. A. (2006). Leaving family for work: Ambivalence and mental health among Mexican migrant farmworker men. *Journal of Immigrant and Minority Health, 8,* 85–97.
Halpern, D. F. (2005). How time-flexible work policies can reduce stress, improve health, and save money. *Stress and Health, 21,* 157–168.
Hammer, L. B., Neal, M. B., Newsom, J., Brockwood, K. J., & Colton, C. (2005). A longitudinal study of the effects of dual-earner couples' utilization of family-friendly workplace support on work and family outcomes. *Journal of Applied Psychology, 90,* 799–810.
Hochschild, A. R., & Machung, A. (1989). *The second shift: Working parents and the revolution at home*. New York: Penguin.
Jacobs, J. A., & Gerson, K. (2004). *The time divide: Work, family, and gender equality*. Cambridge: Harvard University Press.
Juster, F. T., Ono, H., & Stafford, F. P. (2003). An assessment of alternative measures of time use. *Sociological Methodology, 33,* 19–54.
Kamo, Y. (2000). "He said, she said": Assessing discrepancies in husbands' and wives' reports on the division of household labor. *Social Science Research, 29,* 459–476.
Klumb, P., Hoppmann, C., & Staats, M. (2006). Division of labor in German dual-earner families: Testing equity theoretical hypotheses. *Journal of Marriage and the Family, 68,* 870–882.
Kluwer, E. S. (1998). Responses to gender inequality in the division of family work: The status quo effect. *Social Justice Research, 11,* 337–357.

Kluwer, E. S., Heesink, J. A. M., & Van de Vliert, E. (1996). Marital conflict about the division of household labor and paid work. *Journal of Marriage and the Family, 58,* 958–969.
Kluwer, E. S., Heesink, J. A. M., & Van de Vliert, E. (2000). The division of labor in close relationships: An asymmetrical conflict issue. *Personal Relationships, 7,* 263–282.
Lavee, Y., & Katz, R. (2002). Division of labor, perceived fairness, and marital quality: The effect of gender ideology. *Journal of Marriage and the Family, 64,* 27–39.
Lee, Y., & Waite, L. J., (2005). Husbands' and wives' time spent in housework: A comparison of measures. *Journal of Marriage and the Family, 67,* 328–336.
Lennon, M. C., & Rosenfield, S. (1994). Relative fairness and the division of housework: The important of options. *American Journal of Sociology, 100,* 506–531.
Liss, M. (2013). Inequality in the division of household labor and child care: Cause, consequences, and how to change. In M. A. Paludi (Ed.), *Psychology for business success: Juggling, balancing, and integrating work and family roles and responsibilities* (pp. 19–42). Denver: Praeger.
Lively, K. J., Powell, B., Geist, C., & Steelman, L. C. (2008). Equity among intimates: Applying equity theory to the family. *Advances in group processes, 25,* 87–115.
Lu, Z., Maume, D. J., & Bellas, M. L. (2000). Chinese husbands' participation in household labor. *Journal of Comparative Family Studies, 31,* 191–215.
Lundberg, S., & Pollak, R. A. (1993). Separate spheres bargaining and the marriage market. *The Journal of Political Economy, 101,* 988–1010.
Lundberg, S., & Pollak, R. A. (1996). Bargaining and distribution in marriage. *Journal of Economic Perspectives, 10,* 139–158.
MacEwen, K. E., & Barling, J. (1994). Daily consequences of work interference with family and family interference with work. *Work & Stress, 8,* 244–254.
Mattingly, M., & Liana, C. S. (2006). Under pressure: Gender difference in the relationship between free time and feeling rushed. *Journal of Marriage and the Family, 68,* 205–221.
McElroy, M. (1990). The empirical content of Nash-bargained household behavior. *Journal of Human Resources, 25,* 559–583.
Molm, L., & Cook, K. (1995). Social exchange and exchange networks. In K. Cook, G. Fine, & J. House (Eds.), *Sociological perspectives on social psychology* (pp. 209–235). Needham Heights: Allyn & Bacon.
Perry-Jenkins, M., & Folk, K. (1994). Class, couples, and conflict: Effects of the division of labor on assessments of marriage in dual-earner families. *Journal of Marriage and the Family, 56,* 165–180.
Pina, D. L., & Bengston, V. L. (1993). The division of household labor and wives' happiness: Ideology, employment, and perceptions of support. *Journal of Marriage and the Family, 55,* 901–912.
Press, J., & Townsley, E. (1998). Wives' and husbands' housework reporting: Gender, class, and social desirability. *Gender and Society, 12,* 188–218.
Prince-Cooke, L. (2006). "Doing" gender in context: Household bargaining and risk of divorce in Germany and the United States. *American Journal of Sociology, 112,* 442–472.
Pyke, K., & Coltrane, S. (1996). Entitlement, obligation, and gratitude in family work. *Journal of Family Issues, 17,* 60–82.
Sandberg, S. (2013). *Lean in: Women, work, and the will to lead.* New York: Random House.
Saxbe, D. E., Repetti, R., & Graesch, A. (2011). Time spent in housework and leisure: Links with parent's physiological recovery from work. *Journal of Family Psychology, 25,* 271–282.
Sayer, L. C. (2005). Gender, time and inequality: Trends in women's and men's paid work, unpaid work and free time. *Social Forces, 84,* 289–303.
Sayer, L. C., Bianchi, S. M., & Robinson, J. P. (2004). Are parents investing less in children? Trends in mothers' and fathers' time with children. *American Journal of Sociology, 110,* 1–43.
Sayer, L. C., England, P, Bittman, M., & Bianchi, S. M. (2009). How long is the second (plus first) shift? Gender differences in paid, unpaid, and total work time in Australia and the United States. *Journal of Comparative Family Studies, 40,* 523–545.

Tetrick, L. E., & Buffardi, L. C. (2006). Measurement issues in research on the work-home interface. In F. Jones, R. J. Burke, M. Westman (Eds.), *Work-life balance: A psychological perspective* (pp. 90–114). New York: Psychology Press.

Twiggs, J. E., McQuillan, J., & Ferree, M. M. (1999). Meaning and measurement: Reconceptualizing measure of the division of household labor. *Journal of Marriage and the Family, 61,* 712–724.

U.S. Bureau of Labor Statistics. (2012a). http://www.bls.gov/opub/ted/2012/ted_20120110.htm. Accessed 30 Dec 2013.

U.S. Bureau of Labor Statistics. (2012b). http://www.bls.gov/opub/ted/2009/ted_20090807.htm. Accessed 30 Dec 2013.

Van Willigen, M., & Drentea, P. (2001). Benefits of equitable relationships: The impact of sense and fairness, household division of labor, and decision making power on perceived social support. *Sex Roles, 44,* 571–597.

Wayne, J., Musisca, N., & Fleeson, W. (2004). Considering the role of personality in the work–family experience: Relationships of the big five to work–family conflict and facilitation. *Journal of Vocational Behavior, 64,* 108–130.

Weber, L. (1998). A conceptual framework for understanding race, class, gender, and sexuality. *Psychology of Women Quarterly, 22,* 13–32.

Westman, M. (2001). Stress and strain crossover. *Human Relations, 54,* 717–751.

Westman, M., & Etzion, D. (2005). The crossover of work–family conflict from one spouse to the other. *Journal of Applied Social Psychology, 35,* 1936–1957.

Williams, J. C. (2013). Why men work so many hours. Harvard Business Review. HBR Blog Network. http://hbrorg/2013/05/why-men-work-so-many-hours/. Accessed 4 Jan 2014.

York, A. (2013). Why men should share equally in housework. Special to CNN. http://www.cnn.com/2013/04/08/opinion/york-equal-housework/.

Chapter 11
On-Demand: When Work Intrudes upon Employees' Personal Time—Does Gender Matter?

Angela R. Grotto

11.1 Introduction

Executive, managerial, and professional jobs (EMPs) are often accompanied by high earnings, job autonomy, and responsibility. Not surprisingly, the average weekly work hours for EMPs exceeds that of other employees. According to the Current Populations Survey (CPS) (2012), the average weekly work hours for both men and women in managerial and professional occupations was the highest compared to all other occupations, at 45 and 42 hours per week, respectively. Not only do EMPs work the most weekly hours, but they also have excessive work hours, that is, 49 plus hours per week (Jacobs and Gerson 2004; Kuhn and Lozano 2008). In fact, the 2012 CPS shows that 21 % of men and 14 % of women in managerial and professional jobs worked 49 plus hours per week, compared to just 14 % for men and 7 % for women in all other occupations. Furthermore, when comparing 2012 CPS data to 2010 CPS data (2010), the weekly work hours of both male and female EMPs have increased over the past 10 years.

The high level of responsibility associated with these occupations certainly requires long work hours, but that alone cannot account for such excessive levels. Are EMPs choosing to work long hours? If so, what motivates them and allows them to do so? Or is the changing nature of their work forcing them to work more? What other external conditions might be to blame? Many companies encourage a culture of "face time"—an organizational norm for visibility in the workplace with employees' physical presence indicating their true level of commitment or contribution to organizations (Bailyn 1993; Perlow 1995). Employees working for these time-demanding companies may feel pressure to put in long hours at the office. However, EMP work is no longer limited to the physical workplace (i.e., the office). Radical advancements in communicative technologies (CT; e.g., smartphones) have dramatically increased the flexibility of jobs but also allow work to

A. R. Grotto (✉)
Department of Management and Marketing, Manhattan College, De La Salle Hall 507,
4513 Manhattan College Parkway, Riverdale, NY 10471, USA
e-mail: angela.grotto@manhattan.edu

M. J. Mills (ed.), *Gender and the Work-Family Experience*,
DOI 10.1007/978-3-319-08891-4_11

intrude on employees' personal time, making face time far less relevant. EMPs who use technology on a daily basis essentially work "boundaryless" jobs (Voydanoff 2009) with no limits, which can lead to excessive work hours.

A study conducted by the Center for Creative Leadership (CCL) revealed that managers and professionals who use CT extend their work beyond normal work hours (Deal 2013). Managers and professionals who carry smartphones reported interacting with work 13.5 hours each work day and 72 hours per week (Deal 2013). Among managers and professionals working 50 plus hours per week with their smartphones, 15% reported working 7 days a week, with just over half of men (52%) and 42% of women working on weekends (Deal 2013).

Despite the fact that flexible jobs may help employees balance their work roles with their various personal roles (e.g., parent, spouse, friend, community member; e.g., Kossek et al. 2009), the CCL survey results clearly demonstrate that job flexibility can be quite dysfunctional (Clark 2000). Smartphones allow for relentless "boundary violations" at home, as work constantly breaches the boundaries surrounding employees' personal lives (Kreiner et al. 2009). The use of CT in jobs that are already very flexible exacerbates organizational norms for EMPs to work long hours, morphing face time into something far worse. Presently, EMPs are working in "on-demand" jobs—jobs that require employees to be constantly available and accessible to their employers and clients during nonwork hours via technology. Visibility at the office seems no longer sufficient for EMPs to demonstrate their loyalty and thus advance and be rewarded. On-demand is the new face time.

The current chapter dissects the factors giving rise to on-demand jobs and whether these factors differ for men and women in EMP jobs. The focus is placed on EMPs because of the demanding nature of their work and their excessive work hours. Other employees experience work intrusions during their personal time via technology, but the pressure to respond to these intrusions is not nearly as great as that of EMPs. Also discussed are the consequences of being on-demand and whether there are gender differences. On-demand jobs can be likened to being on-call. Regardless of whether the employee is actually called in or not, the mere possibility of being disturbed by work-related matters during personal time has been linked with negative consequences such as negative moods (Bamberg et al. 2012). Similarly, when work calls and e-mails intrude on evenings and weekends, it may significantly undermine employees' personal lives (e.g., emotional exhaustion) and work lives (e.g., decreased productivity). This chapter argues that the strains of on-demand jobs transcend gender, and so both men and women suffer the consequences. As individuals can only do so much to manage their on-demands jobs, companies must intervene to help ease the pressure.

11.2 The Weakening of Borders Surrounding Work and Personal life

The changing boundaries surrounding the worlds of work and nonwork play a critical role in the rise of on-demand jobs. Three different types of boundaries exist around work (Ashforth et al. 2000; Clark 2000; Nippert-Eng 1996). Spatial boundaries define *where* work behavior takes place (e.g., work duties are performed at the office). Temporal boundaries define *when* the work role is performed (e.g., jobs are performed between 9:00 a.m. and 5:00 p.m.). Psychological boundaries dictate when and where work thoughts, behaviors, and emotions are appropriate (e.g., assertiveness is appropriate at the office but not at home).

The flexibility and permeability of a work boundary determines its strength. Flexible work boundaries allow jobs to be to be carried out in various settings at various times, while inflexible boundaries constrain when and where work can be performed (e.g., Beach 1989; Ritchter 1992). For instance, most nurses perform their jobs within the boundaries of hospitals, and manufacturing workers perform their jobs within factories. Permeable borders surrounding various nonwork domains allow an individual to be involved in the work role while physically located in a nonwork domain (e.g., the home; Ashforth et al. 2000; Nippert-Eng 1996). For instance, a permeable home boundary allows an individual to receive job-related phone calls or e-mails while at home. Together, flexible and permeable (i.e., weak) boundaries allows work to permeate other life domains.

Economic, organizational, and job-related changes are responsible for the weakening of employees' work and nonwork boundaries. First, the flexible nature of jobs coupled with sophisticated CT give employees the *ability* to be on-demand. Second, EMPs who are heavily invested in their jobs are *willing* to use CT to be on-demand. Lastly, economic instability, employers' high expectations, and intense work pressures compel EMPs to be on-demand. I argue that the on-demand experiences of men and women in EMP roles are more similar than different. Not only are both male and female EMPs equally exposed to economic, organizational, and job-related pressures, but they also tend to hold egalitarian attitudes toward gender roles, use CT as part of their jobs, and highly value their jobs. These attributes make EMPs more willing and able to be on-demand, regardless of their gender.

11.3 On-Demand Jobs: Willing and Able

11.3.1 The Ability to be On-Demand

Two key aspects of work have weakened job borders and thereby give EMPs the ability to be on-demand. Job flexibility (i.e., control over where and when one works) and advanced CT and have made EMP jobs substantially more flexible. EMPs have always had a considerable amount of autonomy over how they get their jobs done (Voydanoff 1988, 2004). But many EMPs have newer forms of autonomy: place autonomy (control over work locations) and time autonomy (control over work scheduling; Kossek et al. 2006). Place and time autonomy give EMPs the ability to work in various settings (e.g., home, car, outdoors) and at various times (e.g., evenings, weekends, during vacation). Changes in the nature of work and CT are largely responsible for these newer forms of autonomy.

Many jobs are now knowledge-based, requiring complex mental skills (Kelloway and Barling 2000). Jobs that require the use of equipment or materials at the worksite (e.g., manufacturing jobs) and work that involves the use of technical or manual skills in addition to mental skills (e.g., health care) are typically restricted to the workplace (Finegold and Frenkel 2006). However, work that primarily involves cognitive skills can easily be performed outside of the workplace and beyond normal work hours (Ezzedeen and Swiercz 2007). The work of EMPs tends to be highly knowledge-intensive. For instance, the strategic nature of executive jobs requires very complex mental proficiencies, such as the ability to forecast. Professionals possess high-levels of cognitive skills in specialized areas of knowledge, such as information systems data analysts. These skills can be used anywhere and at any time. Since knowledge work is not restricted to the workplace, EMPs can be involved in their work while in other life domains (e.g., home) during nonwork hours (e.g., evenings). For instance, the information systems data analyst can use his laptop to perform his job while sitting on the couch with his family during movie night.

Major advancements in CT have radically enhanced the flexibility of EMP jobs (e.g., Jackson 2002). For example, while at home, EMPs can connect to a virtual network to access work files. Also, most EMPs today have smartphones that allow them to be constantly connected to their work e-mail accounts. So CT makes jobs mobile, allowing employees to perform their work in various nonwork locations (e.g., home, cars, airplanes, gyms, restaurants, hotels, etc.) during any hour of the day (e.g., early mornings, late nights, weekends; e.g., Wikstrom et al. 1998). Indeed, 60 % of EMPs who use a smartphone for business work between 13.5 and 18.5 hours per day, while only 29 % of those who do not use a smartphone are connected with work that many hours on average (Deal 2013). This significant job flexibility also means that EMPs can be on-demand to their employers and clients via CT. In summary, the growth of knowledge work and advancements in CT have drastically increased the flexibility of EMP jobs, thereby creating on-demand EMP jobs.

11.3.2 Gender Differences in On-Demand Abilities

When considering employees at all job levels, men report more job autonomy than women (Day et al. 2012; Park and Jex 2011). But are there gender differences at the highest ranks? Given that common job features impinge on the lives of both men and women in similar ways (Jacobs and Gerson 2004), female EMPs should possess the same level of job autonomy as their male counterparts. Indeed, past research has shown that male and female EMPs have the ability to work long hours beyond the workplace (e.g., Mennino et al. 2005; Schieman and Reid 2008). These findings suggest that men and women in EMP jobs have similar levels of autonomy that give them the ability to be on-demand.

Similarly, CT gives all EMPs the ability to push the limits of their work roles, regardless of their gender. Although there is evidence suggesting that men are more likely to use job-related CT while at home (e.g., Day et al. 2012; Park and Jex 2011), none of the extant research has focused on EMPs exclusively. Given the broad responsibilities and high demands of EMP jobs, men and women may be equally likely to use CT to perform their EMP roles beyond the workplace. In fact, the results of a CCL survey of managers and professionals showed no gender differences in job-related smartphone use (Deal 2013). Together, extensive job autonomy and frequent CT use during off-hours enable both male and female EMPs to be on-demand.

Some may argue that despite technology and job flexibility, the demands that women face at home may prevent them from being on-demand to their jobs. However, employment tends to be associated with egalitarian attitudes toward gender roles at home among women (Fan and Marini 2000). In fact, employed women who are highly paid and well-educated are more likely to equally share household labor with their partners, as they have more power in their personal relationships (Cunningham 2007; Mannino and Deutsch 2007; Parkman 2004). So, rather than being the primary caretaker, these women are more likely to equally share their domestic roles with their partners. When both partners are unwilling to follow gender-normed behavior, it is even more likely that housework and child care duties are shared (Donald and Linington 2008). This team-based approach at home means that female EMPs can devote time and energy to their valued work roles during nonwork hours, which includes responding to work-related phone calls and e-mails. Nevertheless, although male and female EMPs are both *able* to be on-demand, their *willingness* to do so may vary, based on personal preferences (Park et al. 2011).

11.3.3 The Willingness to be On-Demand: Role Identities

As work is able to exceedingly intrude on personal life, employees must decide whether to allow these intrusions or not. Some employees make conscious efforts to keep work separated from nonwork through the creation and maintenance of boundaries (e.g., Lambert 1990). For example, an accountant who prefers to keep her work separated from her home life might choose to turn off her e-mail notifications during the weekends. She may also have a personal rule that she is always home by 6:00 p.m. on work days. She might even avoid thinking about work while at home (a psychological boundary). This active maintenance of boundaries can help employees uphold order in their interdependent work and nonwork lives (e.g., Weick 1979).

Who might keep work separated from their personal life? Based on an individual's beliefs and values about what roles do and do not belong in a particular domain, one may idiosyncratically construct boundaries (Douglas 1975). For instance, individuals who highly value their time with family may believe that work does not belong at home and therefore devise strategies to prevent job contacts while at home. For example, these individuals might leave their company-provided smartphones at the office over the weekend, or they might send messages to their coworkers letting them know that they will be unavailable over the weekend. Indeed, a recent study showed that employees who preferred to keep their work lives separated from their home lives were more likely to psychologically detach from their work roles during off-hours compared to those who preferred to integrate their roles (Hahn and Dormann 2013).

Conversely, individuals who prefer to integrate work with their personal lives do not tie their jobs to the workplace (Ashforth et al. 2000; Nippert-Eng 1996). Instead, these individuals may consider it acceptable for work to interrupt their personal time and thus are quite willing to be on-demand during evenings and weekends. Who might prefer to integrate work and nonwork roles? Individuals who strongly identify with their work roles choose to be highly involved in their work, meaning they are cognitively preoccupied with, engaged in, and concerned with their jobs (Paullay et al. 1994). These individuals are internally motivated to extend their workdays by spending more effort on work-related activities and working longer hours (Fenner and Renn 2004). In fact, research has shown that employees who are highly involved in their jobs were more likely to use CT after work hours to perform work-related activities and allow work intrusions at home (Hecht and Allen 2009; Major et al. 2002), and they allowed work to permeate into other areas of their lives (Olson-Buchanan and Boswell 2006). Given the high-status of their work roles and their investments in their careers, EMPs should highly identify with their work roles, making them very willing to use CT during nonwork hours and be involved in their jobs at all hours of the day.

11.3.4 Gender Differences in Work Role Identity Among EMPs

Are there gender differences in the extent to which male and female EMPs identify with their high-status work roles? Women have historically prioritized family over work, while men often prioritized their jobs over others aspects of their lives (Blair-Loy 2009; Kelly et al. 2010; Moen and Roehling 2005). Many women today still assume the role of primary caretaker, whether for children or the elderly, even if they are working full-time (Milkie et al. 2002). This perspective suggests that men are more willing to be available to work during their personal time than women. Yet, individuals in high-status careers, regardless of gender, tend to highly identify with their work roles, suggesting that female EMPs are just as willing as male EMPs to be on-demand. Research in this area is contradictory, with some studies showing that women prefer to integrate roles more than men (Kossek et al. 2009) and others showing women with a greater desire for role segmentation (Rothbard et al. 2005). But no studies have focused on EMPs, so it is not clear whether men and women in high-status positions differ in their role identities and thus their willingness to integrate work and nonwork roles.

Gender roles may be more relevant than gender when considering the relationship between role identity and on-demand behavior among EMPs. Egalitarian individuals tend to believe that men and women should identify equally with their work and personal life roles, which includes devoting equal time to paid work and housework (Hochschild 1989). As employed women are likely to hold egalitarian attitudes toward gender roles, particularly those who are highly paid and highly educated, it is plausible that female EMPs are just as willing as male EMPs to engage in on-demand behavior during nonwork hours.

11.3.5 The Willingness to be On-Demand: Organization-Based Self-Esteem

Executives, managers, and professionals may be willing to be on-demand during nonwork hours based on their individual needs. Organization-based self-esteem (OBSE) is a specific form of self-esteem that considers employees' self-evaluations specifically within the context of work. Employees with high OBSE believe that they can satisfy their needs by participating in roles within the organization (Pierce et al. 1989), and they also believe in their self-worth and competence as organizational members (Bowling 2010). Individuals in high-status positions at work may have higher levels of OBSE than others. Given the autonomy, complexity, and challenge of EMP jobs, these individuals are likely to believe that they are competent, valuable, and capable members of their organizations (Pierce et al. 1989). The work roles of EMPs not only fulfill basic needs (e.g., my work role serves an economic need), but satisfy higher-level needs (e.g., being a psychologist is fulfilling; Ashforth et al. 2000). As the work role serves as a source of esteem and fulfills higher-level needs, EMPs with high OBSE may be willing to invest a lot of their personal time into their jobs.

Compensation may be another source of OBSE for EMPs, as it can communicate to an individual his/her worth or value to the organization (Thierry 2001). Moreover, pay-level might influence an employee's beliefs about his/her worthiness as an organizational member. In a study that took into account employees' length of company tenure and changes in pay, pay-level was significantly related to OBSE (Gardner et al. 2004). EMPs are at a higher pay-level than most other employees, and these high pay-levels might trigger feelings of self-worth that motivate them to invest personal time in their work roles.

On-demand behavior can be very reinforcing for EMPs. After-hour job contacts can make them feel needed, engendering feelings of self-worth (Bowling 2010). Each time an EMP is contacted after-hours for help, his/her self-esteem gets a boost and thus she/he is further motivated to invest in the work role. Also, in a recent study, employees who perceived intruding work matters as important reported high-levels of OBSE (Grotto 2013). When EMPs attend to important work matters after-hours, the interactions may boost their self-esteem (Bowling 2010), further reinforcing the on-demand behavior.

11.3.6 Gender Differences in OBSE Among EMPs

Do male EMPs have stronger beliefs in their self-worth and competence compared to their female counterparts? If so, then men in EMP roles may be more willing to fulfill their work-related needs through on-demand behavior. But gender differences in self-esteem seem to diminish with age (Reitzes and Mutran 1994). Rather than gender, commitment to various life roles (e.g., worker, parent, and spouse) has been related to self-esteem for employed men and women. Additionally, income, education, and occupational status have positive effects on self-esteem for both men and women. This research suggests that aspects of the work role are more important for self-esteem than gender. There is an abundance of evidence indicating no gender differences in OBSE levels (e.g., Bowling 2010; Grotto 2013; Lapointe et al. 2011). Perhaps the prestige associated with high-status positions within organizations helps women overcome any doubts in their self-worth or competence. If so, then both men and women in EMP roles are expected to have high-levels of OBSE and thus will want to expend great effort in their work roles. Being on-demand is one way that they can demonstrate their efforts and contribute to their organizations. Therefore, gender may be less of a factor when looking at employees specifically in the upper-ranks of organizations.

11.3.7 The Willingness to be On-Demand: Perceptions of On-Demand Work

The perceived legitimacy of the work that intrudes on personal time is another underlying factor that may influence someone's willingness to be on-demand. Illegitimate work tasks are not part of an individual's core work role requirements and thus constitute "identity stressors" that violate one's professional identity (Thoits 1991). Given someone's role within an organization (e.g., director of finance), there are certain tasks that one may expected to do (e.g., approve budgets) and tasks that one may *not* be expected to fulfill (e.g., write the budget). Being asked to perform a work task that an individual considers to be incompatible with his/her work role may be perceived as an identity-threatening stressor and an "offense to the self" (Semmer et al. 2007). Although EMP employees are very eager to be on-demand for reasons discussed earlier, they may not be willing to perform work tasks during nonwork hours that threaten their identity rather than boost their self-esteem. Furthermore, EMPs may not be willing to take on illegitimate work tasks in an effort to conserve their time and energy for more legitimate work matters during off-hours.

Work tasks that are considered unreasonable or unnecessary may also be perceived as illegitimate (Semmer et al. 2010). Unreasonable tasks are beyond the scope of someone's responsibility, such as when an expert is asked to perform a task that is far below his/her ability level, or when a leader is asked to perform a task that is not commensurate with his/her rank. Likewise, EMPs may not be willing to perform unreasonable tasks during their personal time. For example, a senior software engineer may consider checking someone else's code as beneath her ability and think her time is better spent developing new code. A director of finance who approves departmental budgets may consider drafting the budget an unreasonable task for himself.

An unnecessary task is one that does not have to be performed. EMPs may also not be willing to perform unnecessary tasks during their personal time. For instance, if a CEO calls her director of human resources (HR) at 8:00 p.m. on a Thursday night asking him to join an 11:00 p.m. call with the China team, but the HR director does not believe his attendance on the call is necessary given the agenda, he may not be willing to participate.

Not all work tasks are of equal value, and employees may consider some work tasks a "waste of time" or low-value work (Galinsky et al. 2004). Employees want to do work that will make a difference, especially when it is on their personal time. Low-value work may not be perceived as urgent or important enough to expend limited personal resources during their nonwork time, so individuals may be less willing to perform this type of work during nonwork hours. Similar to the perceived legitimacy of the work tasks, the use of scare personal resources during one's personal time must be well-justified, especially for EMPs whose time is quite scarce due to their demanding jobs.

11.3.8 Gender Differences in Perceptions of On-Demand Work

There is little prior research on gender differences in the perceptions of work tasks. In a study of Swedish government sector managerial workers, women reported more illegitimate work tasks than men (Björk et al. 2013). However, it is unclear whether this relationship would hold for employees working in private companies, which are not as bureaucratic as government agencies. One study that examined employees at different job levels from various companies and industries did not find any gender differences in the perceived importance, urgency, or necessity of work intrusions during personal time (Grotto 2013).

This is clearly a promising area for future research. The time of EMPs is very valuable, regardless of their gender. EMPs embedded within very time-demanding organizations must be very selective about how much of their scare time, energy, and attention is expended on work-related tasks during their precious nonwork hours. It is highly expected that both men and women in EMP roles would not be willing to take the time to respond to work e-mails or telephone calls during their off-hours if it involves illegitimate, unnecessary, or low-value work. Therefore, the nature of the work that is intruding into the personal lives of EMPs may affect their willingness to be on-demand. But there are other factors to consider. Perhaps there are certain clients who are known for intruding on a manager's personal time with unnecessary questions and illegitimate requests, and so the manager purposely does not make herself available to this client. Conversely, the manager's boss might frequently contact her during the evenings with pressing questions about urgent client deliverables, and in this case the manager is willing to accept these interruptions. When taking into consideration the nature of the intruding work task, we start moving away from factors that are under the individual's control to external circumstances that may create expectations for EMPs to be on-demand to their employers and clients 24/7.

11.4 The Pressure to be On-Demand

Despite most managers and professionals showing appreciation for the flexibility a smartphone affords them (Deal 2013), certain aspects of their jobs pressure them to be available during nonwork hours and respond to technological work intrusions. Within a global service economy, intense jobs are embedded in high-performing companies that are constantly restructuring, making employees feel incredibly insecure about their jobs. Thus, several workplace conditions may pressure employees to be on-demand.

11.4.1 Workplace Structures, Culture, and Rewards

The global service economy has grown tremendously over the past few decades, spurring intense competition for customers. In response to the need to provide 24/7 service to clients, many companies have shifted to global structures with global job roles (Presser 2003, 2005). Global roles increase time pressures for employees by changing the temporal nature of their work (Kanter 1999). Traditional 9:00 to 5:00 work schedules used to dictate when employees were expected to work. But EMPs with global roles must work in different time zones and manage multiple clocks, depending on where their team members and clients are located (Moen et al. 2013). They frequently work during evenings and weekends to manage global teams, be available to global clients, participate in global meetings, and meet deadlines in other time zones. Accordingly, global EMPs must now decide when they are *not* working (Goodrick and Reay 2011; Moen et al. 2013). This "always on" mentality requires EMPs to be continually connected to work outside of normal work hours, regardless of their willingness to do so.

The economic recession has forced companies to cut costs. Many employees have had first-hand or vicarious experiences with downsizing, which can create concerns about their future with a company (Sverke et al. 2002). Perceived or anticipated layoffs have been linked with feelings of job insecurity (Kalimo et al. 2003; Sverke and Hellgren 2002; Taris et al. 2006). In fact, during a past economic recession, 25 % of workers in the USA have reported at least "moderate" risk for job loss because of company actions to manage finances in the economic downturn (Probst et al. 2002).

Job insecurity is a source of stress (Ashford et al. 1989; Sverke et al. 2002) that can engender low-levels of work effort and withdrawal behaviors such as turnover (e.g., low-levels of organizational commitment, employee absences, and employee turnover; Cheng and Chan 2008; Sverke et al. 2002). However, the relationship of job insecurity with actual employee behaviors is complex within the present economic context. When employees perceive few alternative job opportunities, this creates an economic need to work (e.g., Brockner et al. 1992). So employees who feel at risk for job loss may actually work more in an effort to avoid job loss (Brandes et al. 2008; Brockner et al. 1992). These work efforts might extend beyond the workplace to on-demand behavior.

Even employees who have survived layoffs may feel insecure about their jobs. Layoff survivors tend to feel that their work roles are threatened (Brockner et al. 1992; Sverke and Hellgren 2002). In fact, a 2008 study found that, following a layoff, employees perceived their work environments as insecure, which was related to increased work efforts among employees (Brandes et al. 2008). Thus, the threat of job loss may compel employees to stay connected to work via CT during their personal time, to show their commitment and dedication. This is especially expected among managers who may be concerned about whether layers of management will be eliminated as a result of downsizing.

Downsizing also has widened job scopes and increased responsibilities for many employees (Presser 2003, 2005), contributing to work extensification, or work that is highly demanding, fast paced, and requires long hours (Currie and Eveline 2011; Jarvis and Pratt 2006; Lu 2009). Many workers accept the extensification of work as status quo (Moen et al. 2013), perhaps because they see it as the only way to keep pace with their heavy workloads and avoid falling behind in their careers. Being on-demand to their jobs is one way for EMPs to persevere.

Certain aspects of a company's culture may also pressurize employees to be on-demand. In Slaughter's (Slaughter 2012) popular article in *The Atlantic*, "Why Women Still Can't Have It All," she blames the persistence of a time-demanding culture on the relentless competition to work harder in a global and unstable economy, which translates into working earlier, later, and longer. Indeed, organizational expectations to work long hours tend to result in long work hours (Kossek and Ozeki 1999; Thompson et al. 1999). This type of workplace culture takes advantage of EMPs whose additional work hours do not cost additional wages for employers. Essentially, companies have little incentive to limit the work hours of EMPs (Jacobs and Gerson 2004), but plenty of reasons to overwork them (e.g., stay ahead of the competition).

Employees are most likely to be subjected to an "always on" culture when embedded within a high-commitment culture. Based on the ideas of social exchange theory (Blau 1964), there is an inherent psychological contract in high-commitment workplaces. Employees are given a great deal of job autonomy, and in return are expected to demonstrate commitment by making work a central part of their lives (Moen et al. 2013). So the perks of job autonomy and flexibility signal to employees that their employers are invested in them, compelling them to prioritize work over personal life and work long hours (Bailyn 1993; Blair-Loy and Wharton 2002, 2004; Schor 1991). Thus, there is a growing lack of clarity on what is considered "normal working hours" (Moen et al. 2013). Employees working in these environments may feel as though they owe it to their employers be on-demand 24/7.

High-commitment workplaces further enable an "always on" culture by providing employees with smartphones, which not only creates pressure to respond to work interruptions during nonwork hours, but to respond immediately (Dikkers et al. 2007). In return for their high-status, job flexibility, and autonomy, EMPs working in high-commitment workplaces may feel particularly driven to show their commitment by being on-demand. So although high-commitment workplaces give EMPs considerable flexibility, the perks come with a price.

Evidence suggests that the extension of acceptable work hours is often viewed unfavorably by workers (Harrison et al. 2004). Yet many employees still succumb to the pressure because they are motivated by the anticipated rewards (Lobel 1991) as well as fear of negative consequences (Thompson et al. 1999). For instance, EMPs may respond to work interruptions after-hours because of incentives such as career advancement (e.g., promotions) and financial rewards (e.g., bonuses; Jacobs and Gerson 2004). In high-commitment companies, the exchange of long work hours and high-work efforts for advancement and compensation reinforces the belief that employees are appreciated by their employers (Osterman 2000; Konrad and Mangel 2000). As most EMPs are typically generously rewarded for their experience, expertise, and dedication, they may be more willing than others to invest their personal time in their jobs. Basically, EMPs believe that if they are accessible via CT during their personal time, then they will have even more opportunities to contribute to their organizations, thereby further increasing their rewards.

For individuals who do not give in to on-demand pressures, there is a fear of being left behind. Two decades ago when face time served as the primary indicator of an employee's commitment, research showed that a lack of time spent at the office did indeed lead to being passed over for promotions (Schor 1991). Another study showed that advancement in management was in fact associated with working long hours (Judge et al. 1995). Employees may not want to risk ignoring e-mails or job-related phone calls during the evenings or weekends, as it might lessen their chances of being promoted or translate into smaller bonus payments. The repercussions for deviating from the norm to be on-demand may be strongest for EMPs (e.g., Blair-Loy 2003; Stone 2007; Xie and Shauman 2003). With incredibly flexible jobs and company smartphones that allow them to be on-demand, EMPs may strive to differentiate themselves from those who simply put in their time only when at the office.

11.4.2 The "Stress of Higher Status" Perspective

The nature of EMP work itself creates on-demand expectations. According to the "stress of higher status" perspective (Schieman et al. 2009), the autonomous nature of EMP jobs increases the permeability of the borders surrounding personal life. So the great degree of schedule control afforded to these individuals may be both a blessing and a curse. Although job control allows EMPs to work whenever they want, it also engenders expectations of undivided dedication to one's career and organization (Blair-Loy 2003; Schieman et al. 2009). The time-demanding nature of EMP work is not limited to the physical workplace, but spills over to other life domains via CT. To prove their commitment, EMPs may feel pressure to prioritize work over their personal responsibilities and be available 24/7. Ample evidence suggests that the nature of EMP work creates expectations to be on-demand, as job authority, excessive work pressures, schedule control, and decision-making latitude have all been linked with blurring of work and nonwork roles (Schieman et al. 2009).

11.4.3 Gender Differences in Workplace and Job Pressures

Are men or women more likely to find themselves in time-demanding organizations and intense jobs? In general, males report higher workloads, more feelings of work overload, and higher expectations to be available during their personal time (Day et al. 2012). But are there differences among men and women in EMP positions with respect to the demands of their organizations and the intensity of their jobs?

Given that job features encroach equally on men and women (Jacobs and Gerson 2004), the pressures of a high-commitment workplace and the stress of high status are likely to affect men and women in similar ways. Female EMPs in high-commitment workplaces are likely to confront the same excessive time demands and pressures as their male counterparts. Likewise, male EMPs are just as likely as female EMPs to work in fast paced, demanding jobs with long work hours. It is the nature of their high-ranking and specialized positions that engenders on-demand behavior. Research does suggest that the corporate work conditions and intense job demands associated with high-commitment workplaces and high-status jobs make it difficult for EMPs of both genders to lead balanced lives (Blair-Loy and Wharton 2004; Wharton and Blair-Loy 2006).

Yet gender may be a factor when taking into consideration the lack of women in leadership positions (Cha 2013). In companies with fewer women in the higher ranks, there tends to be a lack of support for work–life balance. A study by Wharton and Blair-Loy (2006) showed that women reported higher-levels of work-to-family conflict within global financial service firms, which have some of the lowest percentages of females in the C-suite. Also, women in companies that value overwork are more likely to leave their jobs than men (Stone 2007). Parental status may compound the situation in male-dominated industries that do not support work–life balance. In fact, mothers in male-dominated industries were more likely to leave their jobs and the labor force when they experienced conflicting time demands between work and family (Cha 2013). So it is important to consider the responsibilities of men and women beyond their intense jobs.

Even though many EMP men and women may have selected themselves into highly demanding companies and jobs and may even thrive in these environments, responsibilities outside of work can complicate matters. In particular, the job of being a parent is 24/7. So whether the EMP is a man or a woman, the extent of involvement in the parental role may influence their on-demand behavior. Combining such an intense and time-demanding personal life role with an intense and time-demanding work role may push some employees to their limits.

11.5 The Consequences of On-Demand Jobs

Research suggests that employees who are constantly connected to work during their nonwork hours are vulnerable to a number of health consequences. Much of this prior research has focused on the consequences of blurring the work role with other life roles and a lack of psychological detachment (i.e., mental distance) from work during nonwork hours. By remaining psychologically attached to the work role during their personal time, employees drain their personal resources (e.g., energy; Edwards and Rothbard 2000) and do not give themselves a chance to recover from their work day demands (Meijman and Mulder 1998). If employees remain on-demand for long periods of time, psychological health problems such as chronic stress could develop (Geurts and Sonnentag 2006). If recovery remains insufficient for an extended period of time, psychological health problems can develop into serious physical health risks, such as increased risk of cardiovascular problems (von Thiele et al. 2006).

Indeed, a number of psychological health problems have been reported by employees who have not had the chance to fully recover from their work day demands. Emotional exhaustion is commonly reported by employees who blur their work and nonwork roles and inadequately detach from work during nonwork hours (de Jonge et al. 2012). Employee interviews revealed that specific episodes of work intruding on personal time (e.g., an unexpected phone call from a boss during the weekend) engendered negative feelings, such as anger (Grotto 2013). A potential psychological outcome of on-demand jobs are feelings of work interfering with other life roles (e.g., Schieman and Young 2013). Employees who reported demands to use CT and persistently used CT during nonwork hours also reported poor psychological well-being (Chesley 2005) and feelings of strain, stress, and job burnout (Day et al. 2012). On-demand employees may also be at risk for poor physical health. When specific work events conflicted with family, employees have reported subsequent increases in heart rate (Shockley and Allen 2013). Also, employees who reported work intrusions or a lack of detachment from work also reported physical health complaints (de Jonge et al. 2012; Schieman and Young 2013), psychosomatic complaints (e.g., feelings of dizziness and fatigue; Sonnentag et al. 2010), and a need for recovery (e.g., feeling too tired to for personal activities; Sonnentag et al. 2010).

All of these health consequences can negatively impact work behavior and attitudes. For instance, employees who used CT during nonwork hours and then reported feelings of work interfering with personal life also reported lower-levels of work satisfaction (Diaz et al. 2012). Also, continual lack of recovery can eventually lead to less effort at work and poor job performance (Fritz and Sonnentag 2006; Sonnentag et al. 2010). Yet some individuals still choose to be on-demand to their jobs, perhaps for personal reasons that were discussed earlier or because they are rewarded for this behavior. However, given the potential for negative consequences, there may be a limit to how much one can and should be on-demand. Perhaps attachment to the work role during nonwork hours is beneficial to individuals, but only up to a certain point, regardless of personal preferences or how the intrusions are perceived (e.g., important or not).

Indeed, the sheer number of work intrusions reported during nonwork time was linked with self-reported negative health complaints, despite many of the intrusions being perceived as important by individuals (Grotto 2013). So although employees may believe that prioritizing work over other life roles leads to a successful career (Moen and Roehling 2005), it may be a very unhealthy approach to work. Given the ample evidence suggesting how on-demand employees may suffer, success at work may come at the expense of a healthy personal life (Amichai-Hamburger 2009). Even the benefits of intrinsic personal rewards (e.g., feelings of accomplishment) and extrinsic work rewards (e.g., promotions) that result from employees' endless involvement in work may have its limits once it takes a toll on physical and mental health.

11.5.1 Gender Differences in the Consequences of On-Demand Jobs

When a 24/7 job is integrated with other demanding life roles, the health consequences may be severe. Who has more demanding roles at home—men or women? The 24/7 job of being a parent still primarily falls on the shoulders of women, as men's careers continue to take precedence (Milkie et al. 2002). But over time, men, particularly those with egalitarian attitudes, are sharing the burden of unpaid work at home with their partners (Bulanda 2004; Cunningham 2007). Also, women in EMP roles tend to more equally divide household labor with their partners (Cunningham 2007; Mannino and Deutsch 2007). It seems that dual-earner couples veer away from gender-normed behavior (Donald and Linington 2008) and work as a team at home (Marks 2006). So gender may be somewhat irrelevant when deciding on the share of household labor. This approach can be advantageous for on-demand employees who are either willing or feel pressured to invest much of their personal time in work-related activities.

Even employees who share domestic responsibilities with their partners may suffer from on-demand work. EMPs of both genders who are exposed to high-work expectations and intense time demands have reported feeling imbalanced or conflicted in life (Blair-Loy and Wharton 2004; Schieman et al. 2006; Wharton and Blair-Loy 2006). Moreover, those who combine such intense and demanding work roles with demanding personal roles (e.g., parent) may be pushed to their limits, even if the negative effects are not realized immediately. For instance, among employees with children living at home, high-job demands and an inability to withdraw from work during their personal time were associated with fatigue six months later (von Thiele 2011).

EMPs are a unique group. Given their high-status at work and their high-commitment to their workplaces, these individuals are very likely to be on-demand to their employees and clients, making them vulnerable to a number of health consequences. Their egalitarian approach to household labor might help buffer some of these negative effects. However, if these employees have children, the situation is more complicated. Since the parent role is very time-demanding, even EMPs who are willing to be on-demand may eventually see their health suffer.

11.6 Conclusions and Recommendations

There is much reason to believe that increasingly flexible jobs and readily available CT are responsible for the rise of on-demand jobs. However, the intense manner in which EMPs are working and the way they are using CT are the real underlying issues, and these issues similarly affect men and women. There is a strong need to limit how much the job and CT dictate how employees live their lives (Jacobs and Gerson 2004). Employees in high-commitment workplaces are given abundant freedom to work when and where they want with the aid of CT and are rewarded for their on-demand behavior. But they clearly lack a different type of control.

Based on the job demands-control model (Karasek and Theorell 1990), it is not the level of job demands that create stress or strain, but whether employees feel they can exert control over the demands they confront. EMPs do have considerable control over their jobs, but they have less control over the intense conditions of their work (Allvin et al. 2011). So even though EMPs are willing and able to invest their personal time in their work roles, most lack control over the work demands that are constantly intruding into their personal lives via technology. How much EMPs work during their personal time is heavily affected by what is happening at work (e.g., client deadlines, crises, needy clients, demanding bosses). Although EMPs can decide whether or not to respond to work interruptions during nonwork hours, they have much less control over the interruptions themselves. Even if one has the authority to ignore a work e-mail during nonwork hours, lacking control over the intrusion can still be problematic. In support of this, a recent study found that the more frequently work intruded into employees' personal time, the more they reported poor physical health complaints (Grotto 2013). Therefore, communicative technologies, time-demanding employers and clients, and intense jobs give EMPs very little power over when and how often their work demands invade their personal life.

Realistically, we will never return to the old ways of work, with the job being left at the office once the employee leaves for the day, especially for EMPs. Perhaps intertwined work and nonwork roles would be somewhat manageable if the world still operated with traditional gender roles, with men as the primary wage earners and wives dedicated to domestic work. Then men could continue to focus on their work roles even while at home. But many households today are comprised of dual-earner couples, with men and women participating in multiple life roles, some of which can be very demanding (e.g., parent). Yet, many corporate cultures continue to operate as if employees have no commitments outside of work (Moen et al. 2013; Thompson et al. 2006).

Some may argue that employees are at fault. Many workers seem to accept unreasonable demands for their time because they value the rewards they get in return, including job perks (e.g., onsite child care, free gym memberships), career advancement opportunities, and pay raises. But these rewards may not matter if employees burn out, under-perform, or leave. As companies continue to encroach on employees' personal time in an effort to keep up with competitors in the short-term, they may be hurting long-term performance. Corporations are slowly chipping away at their most highly valued workers. So what can be done about it?

Given the potential for negative impacts on employee and organizational health, on-demand work is a very public issue, yet companies expect employees to manage it on their own (Cha 2013). Accordingly, many individuals have devised their own strategies. Some scholars claim that individuals act as active agents, setting their own boundaries around their personal life (Allvin et al. 2011). The maintenance of these boundaries can be beneficial for employees' psychological feelings of role interference (Park et al. 2011). For example, employees who keep their work roles separated from other life domains are able to psychologically detach from their work role (Park et al. 2011), which contributes to their well-being (Hahn and Dormann 2013). But this is not always realistic, especially for EMPs.

Given the lack of control that today's employees have over their work demands, employee are actually active reactors who are forced to respond to and manage their work demands rather than actively controlling or preventing them (Moen et al. 2013). These strategies involve making personal efforts to allow or not allow a particular work intrusion during nonwork time (Flaherty 2003). However, employees using these strategies have only so much control, as the structural conditions of their jobs and the temporal norms of their companies constrain their options. Thus, the burden is ultimately on employees to react and adjust to their on-demand jobs. This approach does not necessarily give employees control over their job demands. These employees rarely have the chance to fully detach from their work roles and recover from the day's work demands. For example, EMPs might block 2 hours during the evening to focus on family time, but this timeframe is only a temporary break from work (Moen et al. 2013).

Individual strategies may not be sufficient to mitigate the negative effects of on-demand work (Butler et al. 2009). Corporations need to pitch in as well. Some time-demanding companies help employees maintain a sense of work–life balance by providing benefits at the worksite, such as onsite childcare. But only the employees who are fortunate enough to work for these supportive companies have access to these resources. There are no national mandates to provide work–life resources to all employees. Also, resources and support provided by companies or the government do not address the root issue—intense time-demands. It is apparently not healthy for employees to work 24/7, which warrants company and national policies that dictate acceptable work hours for EMPs.

There are many benefits to giving employees time to psychologically detach from work, such as positive effects on health and creativity (de Jonge et al. 2012). So high-commitment companies need to reevaluate their cultures and strongly consider reshaping their norms to encourage mental disengagement from work during off-hours, including interventions training employees on how to do so. But broad organizational policies may not be practical for some EMPs. In these cases, employers should reconsider the legitimacy of the on-demand work, as the cognitive appraisal of a work task can be a strong factor in how employees are impacted by work intrusions (Lazarus and Folkman 1984). An event is stressful when the demands of the environment are perceived as exceeding one's resources and thus endangering one's well-being. When work intrudes on personal time, employees assess their relative job demands and the availability of their resources (e.g., time, energy). If the job demands exceed their available resources, then on-demand work may negatively impact them. If employers can minimize illegitimate work during employees' personal time, then employees would have more time to keep up with the most important work matters (Galinsky et al. 2004). For instance, when a boss sends an e-mail, she can be clear how important or urgent the work issue is so that the receiver can decide whether to protect his/her personal time or not.

It is critical to re-examine the need for on-demand jobs, as a lack of recovery from work during personal time may not only negatively impact employees' personal lives and health, but also their task performance, personal initiative, and work effort; so organizational performance can suffer as well. Individual strategies and organizational policies and interventions can help address these issues, and future exploration of the causes and consequences of on-demand work will be important for employees' quality of life and organizational health.

References

Amichai-Hamburger, Y. (2009). Technology and well-being: Designing the future. In Y. Amichai-Hamburger (Ed.), *Technology and psychological well-being* (pp. 260–278). New York: Cambridge University Press.

Allvin, M., Aronsson, G., Hagstrom, T., Johansson, G., & Lundberg, U. (2011). *Work without boundaries: Psychological perspectives on the new working life*. Oxford: Wiley-Blackwell.

Ashford, S. J., Lee, C., & Bobko, P. (1989). Content, causes, and consequences of job insecurity: A theory-based measure and substantive test. *Academy of Management Journal, 32,* 803–829.

Ashforth, B. E., Kreiner, G. E., & Fugate, M. (2000). All in a day's work: Boundaries and micro role transitions. *Academy of Management Review, 25,* 472–491.

Bamberg, E., Dettmers, J., Funck, H., Krähe, B., & Vahle-Hinz, T. (2012). Effects of on-call work on well-being: Results of a daily survey. *Applied Psychology: Health and Well-Being, 4,* 299–320.

Bailyn, L. (1993). *Breaking the mold: Women, men, and time in the new corporate world.* New York: Free Press.

Beach, B. (1989). *Integrating work and family life*. Albany: State University of New York Press.

Björk, L., Bejerot, E., Jacobshagen, N., & Härenstam, A. (2013). I shouldn't have to do this: Illegitimate tasks as a stressor in relation to organizational control and resource deficits. *Work & Stress, 27,* 262–277.

Blair-Loy, M. (2003). *Competing devotions*. Cambridge: Harvard University Press.

Blair-Loy, M. (2009). Work without end? Scheduling flexibility and work-to-family conflict among stockbrokers. *Work and Occupations, 36,* 279–317.

Blair-Loy, M., & Wharton, A. S. (2002). Employees' use of work–family policies and the workplace social context. *Social Forces, 80,* 813–846.

Blau, P. (1964). *Exchanges and power in social life*. New York: Wiley.

Blair-Loy, M., & Wharton, A. S. (2004). Organizational commitment and constraints on work–family policy use: Corporate flexibility policies in a global firm. *Sociological Perspectives, 47,* 243–267.

Bowling, N. A. (2010). Effects of job satisfaction and conscientiousness on extra-role behaviors. *Journal of Business and Psychology, 25,* 119–130.

Brandes, P., Castro, S. L., James, M. S. L., Martinez, A. D., Matherly, T. A., Ferris, G. R., & Hochwarter, W. A. (2008). The interactive effects of job insecurity and organizational cynicism on work effort following a layoff. *Journal of Leadership & Organizational Studies, 14,* 233–247.

Brockner, J., Grover, S., Reed, T. F., & DeWitt, R. L. (1992). Layoffs, job insecurity, and survivors' work effort: Evidence of an inverted-U relationship. *Academy of Management Journal, 35,* 413–425.
Bulanda, R. E. (2004). Paternal involvement with children: The influence of gender ideologies. *Journal of Marriage and Family, 66,* 40–45.
Butler, A. B., Bass, B. L., & Grzywacz, J. G. (2009). Job demands, spousal support, and work–family balance: A daily analysis of the work–family interface. In D. R. Crane & E. J. Hill (Eds.), *Handbook of families and work* (pp. 9–30). Lanham: University Press of America.
Cha, Y. (2013). Overwork and the persistence of gender segregation in occupations. *Gender & Society, 27,* 158–184.
Cheng, G. H., & Chan, D. K. (2008). Who suffers more from job insecurity? A meta-analytic review. *Applied Psychology: An International Review, 57,* 272–303.
Chesley, N. (2005). Blurring boundaries? Linking technology use, spillover, individual distress, and family satisfaction. *Journal of Marriage and Family, 67,* 1237–1248.
Clark, S. C. (2000). Work/family border theory: A new theory of work/family balance. *Human Relations, 53,* 747–770.
Cunningham, M. (2007). Influences of women's employment on the gendered division of household labor over the life course: Evidence from a 31-year panel study. *Journal of Family Issues, 28,* 422–444.
Current Populations Survey. (2010). U.S. Bureau of Labor Statistics, unpublished data. http://www.bls.gov/cps/aa2010/aat23.txt. Accessed 17 Dec 2013.
Current Populations Survey (CPS). (2012). U.S. Bureau of Labor Statistics, unpublished data. http://www.bls.gov/cps/aa2012/cpsaat23.htm. Accessed 20 Dec 2013.
Currie, J., & Eveline, J. (2011). E-technology and work/life balance for academics with young children. *Higher Education, 62,* 533–550.
Day, A., Paquet, S., Scott, N., & Hambley, L. (2012). Perceived information and communication technology (ICT) demands on employee outcomes: The moderating effect of organizational ICT support. *Journal of Occupational Health Psychology, 17,* 473–491.
de Jonge, J., Spoor, E., Sonnentag, S., Dormann, C., & van den Tooren, M. (2012). "Take a break?!" off-job recovery, job demands, and job resources as predictors of health, active learning, and creativity. *European Journal of Work and Organizational Psychology, 21,* 321–348.
Deal, J. J. (2013). Always on, never done? Don't blame the smartphone. http://www.ccl.org/leadership/pdf/research/AlwaysOn.pdf. Accessed 16 Dec 2013.
Diaz, I., Chiaburu, D. S., Zimmerman, R. D., & Boswell, W. R. (2012). Communication technology: Pros and cons of constant connection to work. *Journal of Vocational Behavior, 80,* 500–508.
Dikkers, J. S., Geurts, S. A., Den Dulk, L., Peper, B., Taris, T. W., & Kompier, M. A. (2007). Dimensions of work-home culture and their relations with the use of work-home arrangements and work-home interaction. *Work & Stress, 21,* 155–172.
Donald, F., & Linington, J. (2008). Work/family border theory and gender role orientation in male managers. *South African Journal of Psychology, 38,* 659–671.
Douglas, M. (1975). *Implicit meanings: Essays in anthropology*. London: Routledge and Paul.
Edwards, J. R., & Rothbard, N. P. (2000). Mechanisms linking work and family: Clarifying the relationship between work and family constructs. *Academy of Management Review, 25,* 178–199.
Ezzedeen, S. R., & Swiercz, P. M. (2007). Development and initial validation of a cognitive-based work-nonwork conflict scale. *Psychological Reports, 100,* 979–999.
Fan, P. L., & Marini, M. M. (2000). Influences on gender-role attitudes during the transition to adulthood. *Social Science Research, 29,* 258–283.
Fenner, G. H., & Renn, R. W. (2004). Technology-assisted supplemental work: Construct definition and a research framework. *Human Resource Management, 43,* 179–200.
Finegold, D., & Frenkel, S. (2006). Managing people where people really matter: The management of human resources in biotech companies. *International Journal of Human Resource Management, 17,* 1–24.

Flaherty, M. G. (2003). Time work: Customizing temporal experience. *Social Psychology Quarterly, 66,* 17–33.
Fritz, C., & Sonnentag, S. (2006). Recovery, well-being, and performance-related outcomes: The role of workload and vacation experiences. *Journal of Applied Psychology, 91,* 936–945.
Galinsky, E., Bond, J. T., Kim, S. S., Backon, L., Brownfield, E., & Sakai, K. (2004). Overwork in America: When the way we work becomes too much. http://familiesandwork.org/site/research/reports/OverWorkInAmerica.pdf. Accessed 17 Dec 2013.
Gardner, D. G., Van Dyne, L., & Pierce, J. L. (2004). The effects of pay level on organization-based self-esteem and performance: A field study. *Journal of Occupational and Organizational Psychology, 77,* 307–322.
Goodrick, E., & Reay, T. (2011). Constellations of institutional logics: Changes in the professional work of pharmacists. *Work and Occupations, 38,* 372–416.
Grotto, A. R. (2013). Unexpected work intrusions into employees' personal lives: Investigation, measure development, and exploration of causes and consequences. Unpublished doctoral dissertation. Baruch College and the Graduate Center at the City University of New York, NY: New York.
Geurts, S., & Sonnentag, S. (2006). Recovery as an explanatory mechanism in the relation between acute stress reactions and chronic health impairment. *Scandinavian Journal of Work, Environment & Health, 32,* 482–492.
Hahn, V. C., & Dormann, C. (2013). The role of partners and children for employees' psychological detachment from work and well-being. *Journal of Applied Psychology, 98,* 26–36.
Harrison, A., Wheeler, P., & Whitehead, C. (2004). *The distributed workplace*. London: Spon Press.
Hecht, T. D., & Allen, N. J. (2009). A longitudinal examination of the work-nonwork boundary strength construct. *Journal of Organizational Behavior, 30,* 839–862.
Hochschild, A. R. (1989). *The second shift: Working parents and the revolution at home*. New York: Viking Penguin.
Jacobs, J. A., & Gerson, K. (2004). *The time divide: Work, family, and gender inequality*. Cambridge: Harvard University Press.
Jackson, M. (2002). *What's happening to home? Balancing work, life and refuge in the information age*. Notre Dame: Sorin Books.
Jarvis, H., & Pratt, A. C. (2006). Bringing it all back home: The extensification and 'overflowing' of work, the case of San Francisco's new media households. *Geoforum, 37,* 331–339.
Judge, T. A., Cable, D. M., Boudreau, J. W., & Bretz, R. D. (1995). An empirical investigation of the predictors of executive career success. *Personnel Psychology, 48,* 485.
Kalimo, R., Taris, T. W., & Schaufeli, W. B. (2003). The effects of past and anticipated future downsizing on survivor well-being: An equity perspective. *Journal of Occupational Health Psychology, 8,* 91–109.
Kanter, R. M. (1999). Change is everyone's job: Managing the extended enterprise in a globally connected world. *Organizational Dynamics, 28,* 7–23.
Karasek, R. A., & Theorell, T. (1990). *Healthy work*. New York: Basic Books.
Kelloway, E. K., & Barling, J. (2000). Knowledge work as organizational behavior. *International Journal of Management Reviews, 2,* 287–304.
Kelly, E., Ammons, S., Chermack, K., & Moen, P. (2010). Gendered challenge, gendered response: Confronting the ideal worker norm in a white-collar organization. *Gender & Society, 24,* 281–303.
Konrad, A., & Mangel, R. (2000). The impact of work-life programs on firm productivity. *Strategic Management Journal, 21,* 1225–1237.
Kossek, E. E., & Ozeki, C. (1999). Bridging the work–family policy and productivity gap: A literature review. *Community, Work & Family, 2,* 7–32.
Kossek, E. E., Lautsch, B. A., & Eaton, S. C. (2006). Telecommuting, control, and boundary management: Correlates of policy use and practice, job control, and work–family effectiveness. *Journal of Vocational Behavior, 68,* 347–367.

Kossek, E. E., Lautsch, B. A., & Eaton, S. C. (2009). "Good teleworking": Under what conditions does teleworking enhance employees' well-being? In Y. Amichai-Hamburger (Ed.), *Technology and psychological well-being* (pp. 148–173). New York: Cambridge University Press

Kreiner, G. E., Hollensbe, E. C., & Sheep, M. L. (2009). Balancing borders and bridges: Negotiating the work-home interface via boundary work tactics. *Academy of Management Journal, 52,* 704–730.

Kuhn, P., & Lozano, F. (2008). The expanding workweek? Understanding trends in long work hours among U.S. men, 1979–2006. *Journal of Labor Economics, 26,* 311–43.

Lambert, S. J. (1990). Processes linking work and family: A critical review and research agenda. *Human Relations, 43,* 239–257.

Lapointe, E., Vandenberghe, C., & Panaccio, A. (2011). Organizational commitment, organization-based self-esteem, emotional exhaustion and turnover: A conservation of resources perspective. *Human Relations, 64,* 1609–1631.

Lazarus, R. S., & Folkman, S. (1984). *Stress, appraisal, and coping.* New York: Springer.

Lobel, S. A. (1991). Allocation of investment in work and family roles: Alternative theories and implications for research. *Academy of Management Review, 16,* 507–521.

Lu, J. L. (2009). Effect of work intensification and work extensification on women's health in the globalized labour market. *Journal of International Women's Studies, 10,* 111–126.

Major, V. S., Klein, K. J., & Ehrhard, M. G. (2002). Work time, work interference with family, and psychological distress. *Journal of Applied Psychology, 87,* 427–436.

Mannino, C. A., & Deutsch, F. M. (2007). Changing the division of household labor: A negotiated process between partners. *Sex Roles, 56,* 309–324.

Marks, S. R. (2006). Understanding diversity of families in the 21st century and its impact on the work–family area of study. In M. Pitt-Catsouphes, E. E. Kossek, & S. Sweet (Eds.), *The work and family handbook: Multi-disciplinary perspectives and approaches* (pp. 41–65). Mahwah: Lawrence Erlbaum.

Meijman, T. F., & Mulder, G. (1998). Psychological aspects of workload. In P. J. D. Drenth, H. Thierry, & C. J. de Wolff (Eds.), *Handbook of work and organizational, Vol. 2: Work psychology* (pp. 5–33). Hove: Psychology Press.

Mennino, S. F., Rubin, B. A., & Brayfield, A. (2005). Home-to-job and job-to-home spillover: The impact of company policies and workplace culture. *Sociological Quarterly, 46,* 107–135.

Milkie, M. A., Bianchi, S. M., Mattingly, M. J., & Robinson, J. P. (2002). Gendered division of childrearing: Ideals, realities, and the relationship to parental well-being. *Sex Roles, 47,* 21–38.

Moen, P., & Roehling, P. (2005). *The career mystique: Cracks in the American dream.* Boulder: Rowman & Littlefield.

Moen, P., Lam, J., Ammons, S., & Kelly, E. L. (2013). Time work by overworked professionals: Strategies in response to the stress of higher status. *Work and Occupations, 40,* 79–114

Nippert-Eng, C. (1996). Calendars and keys: The classification of 'home' and 'work'. *Sociological Forum, 11,* 563–582.

Olson-Buchanan, J. B., & Boswell, W. R. (2006). Blurring boundaries: Correlates of integration and segmentation between work and nonwork. *Journal of Vocational Behavior, 68,* 432–445.

Osterman, P. (2000). Work reorganization in an era of restructuring: Trends in diffusion and effects on employee welfare. *Industrial and Labor Relations Review, 53,* 179–196.

Park, Y., & Jex, S. M. (2011). Work-home boundary management using communication and information technology. *International Journal of Stress Management, 18,* 133–152.

Park, Y., Fritz, C., & Jex, S. M. (2011). Relationships between work-home segmentation and psychological detachment from work: The role of communication technology use at home. *Journal of Occupational Health Psychology, 16,* 457–467.

Parkman, A. M. (2004). Bargaining over housework: The frustrating situation of secondary wage earners. *American Journal of Economics and Sociology, 63,* 765–794.

Paullay, I. M., Alliger, G. M., & Stone-Romero, E. F. (1994). Construct validation of two instruments designed to measure job involvement and work centrality. *Journal of Applied Psychology, 79,* 224–228.

Perlow, L. A. (1995). Putting the work back into work/family. *Group & Organization Management, 20,* 227–239.
Pierce, J. L., Gardner, D. G., Cummings, L. L., & Dunham, R. B. (1989). Organization-based self-esteem: Construct definition, measurement, and validation. *Academy of Management Journal, 32,* 622–648.
Presser, H. B. (2003). *Working in a 24/7 economy*. New York: Russell Sage.
Presser, H. B. (2005). Embracing complexity: Work schedules and family life in a 24/7 economy. In S. M. Bianchi, L. M. Casper, & B. R. King (Eds.), *Work, family, health, and well-being* (pp. 43–48). Mahwah: Lawrence Erlbaum.
Probst, T. M., Brett, J. M., & Drasgow, F. (2002). The impact of job insecurity on employee work attitudes, job adaptation, and organizational withdrawal behaviors. In J. M. Brett & F. Drasgow (Eds.), *The psychology of work: Theoretically based empirical research* (pp. 141–168). Mahwah: Lawrence Erlbaum.
Reitzes, D. C., & Mutran, E. J. (1994). Multiple roles and identities: Factors influencing self-esteem among middle-aged working men and women. *Social Psychology Quarterly, 57,* 313–325.
Ritchter, J. (1992). Balancing work and family in Israel. In S. Zedeck (Ed.), *Work, families, and organizations*. San Francisco: Jossey-Bass.
Rothbard, N. P., Phillips, K. W., & Dumas, T. L. (2005). Managing multiple roles: Work-family policies and individuals' desires for segmentation. *Organization Science, 16,* 243–258.
Schieman, S., & Reid, S. (2008). Job authority and interpersonal conflict in the workplace. *Work and Occupations, 35,* 296–326.
Schieman, S., & Young, M. C. (2013). Are communications about work outside regular working hours associated with work-to-family conflict, psychological distress and sleep problems? *Work & Stress, 27,* 244–261.
Schieman, S., Whitestone, Y., & Van Gundy, K. (2006). The nature of work and the stress of higher status. *Journal of Health and Social Behavior, 47,* 242–257.
Schieman, S., Milkie, M. A., & Glavin, P. (2009). When work interferes with life: Work-nonwork interference and the influence of work-related demands and resources. *American Sociological Review, 74,* 966–988.
Schor, J. B. (1991). *The overworked American: The unexpected decline of leisure*. New York: Basic Books.
Semmer, N. K., Jacobshagen, N., Meier, L. L., & Elfering, A. (2007). Occupational stress research: The "Stress-As-Offense-to-Self" perspective. In J. Houdmont & S. McIntyre (Eds.), *Occupational health psychology: European perspectives on research, education and practice* (pp. 43–60). Maia: ISMAI Publishing.
Semmer, N. K., Tschan, F., Meier, L. L., Facchin, S., & Jacobshagen, N. (2010). Illegitimate tasks and counterproductive work behavior. *Applied Psychology: An International Review, 59,* 70–96.
Shockley, K. M., & Allen, T. D. (2013). Episodic work–family conflict, cardiovascular indicators, and social support: An experience sampling approach. *Journal of Occupational Health Psychology, 18,* 262–275.
Slaughter, A. M. (2012). Why women still can't have it all. The Atlantic. http://www.theatlantic.com/magazine/archive/2012/07/why-women-still-cant-have-it-all/309020/. Accessed 20 Dec 2013.
Sonnentag, S., Kuttler, I., & Fritz, C. (2010). Job stressors, emotional exhaustion, and need for recovery: A multi-source study on the benefits of psychological detachment. *Journal of Vocational Behavior, 76,* 355–365.
Stone, P. (2007). *Opting out?: Why women really quit careers and head home*. Berkeley: University of California Press.
Sverke, M., & Hellgren, J. (2002). The nature of job insecurity: Understanding employment uncertainty on the brink of a new millennium. *Applied Psychology: An International Review, 51,* 23–42.
Sverke, M., Hellgren, J., & Naswall, K. (2002). No security: A meta-analysis and review of job insecurity and its consequences. *Journal of Occupational Health Psychology, 7,* 242–264.

Taris, T. W., Beckers, D. G. J., Verhoeven, L. C., Geurts, S., Kompier, M., & van der Linden, D. (2006). Recovery opportunities, work-home interference, and well-being among managers. *European Journal of Work and Organizational Psychology, 15,* 139–157.

Thierry, H. (2001). The reflection theory on compensation. In M. Erez, U. Kleinbeck, & H. Thierry (Eds.), *Work motivation in the context of a globalizing economy* (pp. 149–166). Mahwah: Lawrence Erlbaum.

Thoits, P. A. (1991). On merging identity theory and stress research. *Social Psychology Quarterly, 54,* 101–112.

Thompson, C. A., Beauvais, L. L., & Lyness, K. S. (1999). When work–family benefits are not enough: The influences of work–family culture on benefit utilization, organizational attachment, and work–family conflict. *Journal of Vocational Behavior, 54,* 392–415.

Thompson, C. A., Beauvais, L. L. & Allen, T. D. (2006). Work and family from an industrial/organizational psychology perspective. In M. Pitt-Catsouphes, E. E. Kossek, & S. Sweet (Eds.), *The work and family handbook: Multi-disciplinary perspectives and approaches* (pp. 283–307). Mahwah: Lawrence Erlbaum.

Weick, K. E. (1979). *The social psychology of organizing* (2nd ed.). Reading: Addison-Wesley.

Wharton, A. S., & Blair-Loy, M. (2006). Long work hours and family life: A cross-national study of employees' concerns. *Journal of Family Issues, 27,* 415–436.

Wikstrom, T., Palm Linden, K., & Michelson, M. (1998). *Hub of events or splendid isolation: Teleworkers and the home.* Stockholm: Swedish Transport and Communications Research Board.

von Thiele, U. (2011). Inability to withdraw from work as related to poor next-day recovery and fatigue among women. *Applied Psychology: An International Review, 60,* 377–396.

von Thiele, U., Lindfors, P., & Lundberg, U. (2006). Self-rated recovery from work stress and allostatic load in women. *Journal of Psychosomatic Research, 61,* 237–242.

Voydanoff, P. (1988). Work role characteristics, family structure demands, and work/family conflict. *Journal of Marriage & the Family, 50,* 749–761.

Voydanoff, P. (2004). The effects of work demands and resources on work-to-family conflict and facilitation. *Journal of Marriage & Family, 66,* 398–412.

Voydanoff, P. (2009). The interaction of work and family demands and resources: Linking mechanisms and boundary-spanning strategies. In D. R. Crane & E. J. Hill (Eds.), *Handbook of families and work* (pp. 141–171). Lanham: University Press of America.

Xie, Y., & Shauman, K. A. (2003). *Women in science: Career processes and outcomes.* Cambridge: Harvard University Press.

Part III
CAREER & ORGANIZATIONAL CONSIDERATIONS

Chapter 12
Family-Friendly Organizational Policies, Practices, and Benefits through the Gender Lens

Justin M. Sprung, Tatiana H. Toumbeva, and Russell A. Matthews

12.1 Introduction

Concern for employees' family and leisure time is by no means a new point of interest. Recently, however, with almost 80% of workers reporting an increased desire for workplace flexibility (Galinsky et al. 2004), organizational leaders are increasingly realizing the need for providing appealing and effective family-friendly benefits. This amplified interest in work–family issues has been brought about, in part, due to the increase in numbers of full-time working women and dual-earner couples in the past few decades (Hammer and Zimmerman 2011). Although the percentages of working men and women in the USA today are roughly equal, with women comprising 46.9% of the workforce (Bureau of Labor Statistics 2013), gender still seems to influence a variety of factors within the work environment. One of the most publicized and contentious gender differences in the workplace concerns perceptions and usage of family-friendly benefits. In fact, the *Journal of Social Issues* recently dedicated an entire special issue to this topic—"The Flexibility Stigma" (Williams et al. 2013)—exploring how gender and social class contribute to the stigma surrounding flexible work arrangements. Therefore, although traditional gender norms are thought to be fading, they still appear to actively influence today's workforce, especially when it comes to the use of, and access to, family-friendly benefits.

Our goal in the present chapter is to summarize how gender contributes to the overall efficacy of family-friendly benefits by focusing on two primary aims.

J. M. Sprung (✉)
Department of Psychology, Luther College, 700 College Drive, Decorah, IA 52101, USA
e-mail: spruju01@luther.edu

T. H. Toumbeva
Department of Psychology, Bowling Green State University, Bowling Green, OH 43403, USA
e-mail: ttoumbe@bgsu.edu

R. A. Matthews
Department of Psychology, Bowling Green State University, Bowling Green, OH 43403, USA
e-mail: ramatth@bgsu.edu

M. J. Mills (ed.), *Gender and the Work-Family Experience*,
DOI 10.1007/978-3-319-08891-4_12

First, we review the literature on gender differences in employee utilization and awareness of available family-friendly benefits, followed by a discussion of why these discrepancies may exist. Second, we briefly summarize the literature on the general effectiveness of benefit availability and utilization for improving important employee outcomes. Given the major role that the supervisor plays in the lives of workers (Kossek and Distelberg 2009), our main focus in this section centers around the interplay between supervisor gender and perceived supervisor supportiveness of employee family life. To help further contextualize the effect of gender, we consistently address underlying individual characteristics that may contribute to the existence of gender differences within our two areas of focus. We conclude the chapter by documenting several areas for future inquiry.

12.2 Family-Friendly Benefits

Although there are a variety of family-friendly benefits offered within the USA, the 1993 Family and Medical Leave Act (FMLA) represents the only legal obligation that US employers have regarding work–family issues. The FMLA stipulates that employers with 50 or more employees must provide up to 12 weeks of unpaid leave to employees in order for them to deal with a family or medical issue, as long as the employee has worked at the organization for a minimum of 1250 hours (United States Department of Labor 2013). Because of the limited amount of federal legislation in this area, the majority of family-related benefits are typically provided at the employer's discretion and generally considered a component of an organization's plan for implementing strategic human resource (HR) practices (Bloom et al. 2011).

Outside of the FMLA, the amount and types of discretionary family-friendly benefits vary across organizations, but typically include some form of flexible work arrangements and/or dependent care support. Flexible work arrangements (FWA) come in a variety of forms, but share the common objective of allowing employees to have enhanced control over when and where they complete their work (Major and Germano 2006). Commonly recognized FWAs include telecommuting, flextime, a compressed work week, part-time schedules, and job sharing (for an in-depth review of different types of FWAs, see Kossek and Michel 2011). Whereas FWAs provide flexibility in work scheduling, dependent care support programs offer financial and/or instrumental assistance (e.g., on-site childcare, caregiving referrals, paid leave) to employees for their childcare or eldercare responsibilities (Major and Germano 2006). Both FWAs and dependent care support programs are tools intended to assist employees in balancing their work and family lives. These discretionary benefits are often viewed as a sign of the organization's commitment toward creating a family-friendly workplace (Grzywacz and Butler 2008).

According to a recent study conducted by the Society for Human Resource Management (SHRM), 57% of organizations offer some form of telecommuting (either part- or full-time) whereas 53% offer flextime opportunities. In addition, 17% of organizations provide childcare referral services and 10% offer eldercare referral services (SHRM 2012). Although family-friendly benefits have become increasingly common in the USA, the actual use of these benefits has lagged behind (Galinsky et al. 2008). Multiple studies demonstrate that employees may not perceive these benefits as a viable option due to informal regulations and/or a fear of negative consequences as a result of their use (e.g., Eaton 2003; Thompson et al. 1999). In addition, even though these benefits are expected to promote gender equality and workplace inclusion, there is mixed evidence as to whether they are achieving that goal. In fact, some scholars have even suggested that the availability and usage of these benefits may be exacerbating the very problems they were expected to prevent (e.g., Ryan and Kossek 2008; Rudman and Mescher 2013). We can gain a better understanding of how and why these benefits may be having counterintuitive effects by examining their associated gender differences.

12.3 Benefit Usage

Despite the increased availability of family-friendly benefits, simply offering these benefits does not necessarily result in their use. For example, in 2012, only 16% of all employees who were eligible for FMLA leave actually took it (Klerman et al. 2013). Similarly, several studies examining discretionary family-friendly benefits reveal rather low overall usage rates, regardless of their increased availability (e.g., Blair-Loy and Wharton 2002; Galinsky et al. 2008). For both the FMLA and discretionary family-friendly benefits, gender has been a primary point of interest regarding usage rates of available benefits.

Since the origin of the FMLA in 1993, men have consistently taken leave less often and tend to take significantly shorter leaves than women (Armenia and Gerstel 2006; Gerstel and Armenia 2009; Waldfogel 2001). According to the most recent FMLA survey conducted by the Department of Labor, women (21%) were significantly more likely than men (16%) to take parental leave within the past 18 months. Although the gender gap in leave-taking still exists, it has slightly decreased over time (7% in 1995 to 5% in 2012; Klerman et al. 2013), suggesting that slow progress is being made toward gender equality in the prevalence of leave-taking. In addition, there is preliminary evidence to suggest that although men are less likely than women to take leaves for newborns, men are nearly as likely as women to take leaves for seriously ill children or parents, and just as likely to take leave to care for a sick spouse (Armenia and Gerstel 2006). However, more research is necessary to make any firm conclusions regarding gender equality (and the closing of the gender usage gap). Even if men and women are approaching a similar prevalence rate in leave-taking, women still tend to take significantly longer leaves regardless of the reason for leave (Klerman et al. 2013). Thus, there is a consistent gender gap in leave-taking and leave length, especially when the reason for leave is childbirth.

These discrepancies (i.e., leave-taking and leave length) may be partially due to the fact that women on maternity leave are more likely to receive some form of replacement pay than men on paternity leave (Galinsky et al. 2008; Matos and

Galinsky 2012). At the same time, however, the opportunity for at least some form of pay during parental leave has remained rather low for both men and women in the USA over the past 20 years (Van Giezen 2013). As such, other forces are likely influencing this discrepancy. Men's lower use may also be due to traditional gender norms, as there seems to be a larger social stigma associated with men taking paternity leave than there is for women taking maternity leave (Berdahl and Moon 2013), an issue we will discuss later in the chapter. In addition, economic factors may come into play. Specifically, excluding cases of adoption or surrogacy, women must take at least some time off in order to physically have the child. If the husband also takes leave, the likelihood of there being any money coming in for that family is, based on the data available, low. Thus, regardless of any social stigma, this economic reality can have a large impact on the decisions that people make and should not be ignored by researchers examining this issue.

As for gender differences in usage rates of discretionary family-friendly benefits, the evidence is even less clear. Consistent with popular perception, the majority of studies provide evidence suggesting that women use flexible schedules, work from home, and make use of childcare referral more often than men (e.g., Galinsky et al. 2004; Hammer et al. 2005; Hill et al. 2003; Singley and Hynes 2005). However, recent findings suggest that there may be no clear gender difference in the usage of discretionary family-friendly benefits as a whole. According to McMenamin (2007), men and women use flexible benefits equally, with the percentage of men and women using flexible schedules remaining comparable over the past 20 years. The difference between men and women may, however, lie in the type of flexibility that they prefer.

For example, a recent popular press article suggested that men and women do not differ in usage of flexible work options that permit face time within the organization (i.e., flexible arrival and departure times), but women tend to be more likely to telecommute than men (Fondas 2013). Thus, women may be more willing to use benefits in which they would sacrifice face time, while men are less willing to do so. This is congruent with empirical research suggesting that telecommuting is an arrangement that is preferred by women (e.g., Raghuram et al. 2003; Singh et al. 2013). This is also consistent with traditional gender roles regarding work and family responsibilities which, in turn, may help to contribute to the career penalties that women face as a result of using family-friendly benefits.

It should be noted, however, that the majority of research on family-friendly benefits focuses on perceptions about the availability and perceived outcomes of these benefits rather than gender differences in their actual use. Accordingly, it is difficult to draw firm conclusions regarding gender differences in the usage of discretionary family-friendly benefits. Due to the mixed findings, and paired with the fact that usage rates tend to be low for both men and women, further research would be beneficial to form a clear picture regarding the actual usage of discretionary family-friendly benefits and whether men and women prefer different forms of benefits. Another specific area for future research may be to examine potential gender differences in eldercare assistance given the growing number of employees with both child and eldercare responsibilities.

12.4 Benefit Awareness

One of the most proximal barriers to employee utilization is employees' awareness (or lack thereof) of available benefits. The FMLA, in particular, suffers from ignorance of its provisions. According to the Department of Labor, only 66.2 % of employees have heard of FMLA in 2012, which is only 7 % higher than the year 2000 (Klerman et al. 2013). Given that men tend to use FMLA benefits significantly less than women do, it should come as no surprise that men are also less aware of the benefits available to them. In fact, gender has been suggested as one of the strongest predictors of employees' knowledge and awareness of FMLA regulations, with women purported as being 3–6 times more likely than men to be aware of their eligibility for FMLA parental leave (Kramer 2008). Similarly, evidence based on a nationally representative sample indicated that among eligible employees, men were significantly less likely than women (72 % compared to 91 %, respectively) to report that they had access to FMLA parental leave regardless of various sociodemographic factors (i.e., race, marital status, children, firm size, and authority level; Baird and Reynolds 2004). Consequently, this lack of awareness among male workers may contribute to the gender discrepancy in the usage of FMLA leave.

Regarding discretionary family-friendly benefits, although the evidence is mixed in terms of gender differences in actual utilization, studies assessing employee awareness consistently provide similar findings to results within the FMLA literature. Specifically, multiple studies demonstrate that women are more likely to have knowledge and awareness of discretionary family-friendly benefits offered by their employers (e.g., Martenengo et al. 2010; Prottas et al. 2007; Villablanca et al. 2011). Therefore, a clear gender gap emerges from the available evidence with men being less aware of both legal and discretionary family-friendly benefit options.

This lack of awareness may be a contributing factor to why a large majority of people do not use the benefits available to them. A promising area for future research may be an identification of effective strategies for increasing benefit awareness among employees. Klerman et al. (2013) state that the most common sources of knowledge for the FMLA are posters and communication from the HR department; however, no evidence is presented as to whether certain strategies are utilized to a greater extent—or more effective—for men compared to women. It would be interesting to examine whether HR professionals put forth more effort in advertising benefits to female employees, and whether these strategies are actually (possibly unintentionally) contributing to the gender discrepancy in awareness. Regardless of gender differences, raising employee awareness would likely be beneficial for all eligible employees.

12.4.1 Intentions of Using Benefits

Men's general lack of awareness of family-friendly benefits, compared to women, seems to suggest that improved awareness might lead to increased usage of the available benefits. Multiple studies assessing intentions to seek out and/or use family-friendly benefits, however, suggest that this may not be the case. For example, Gerstel and McGonagle (1999) found that women (25 %) were more likely than men (16 %) to report that they need to take a leave from a job for reasons covered by the FMLA, regardless of whether they actually took the leave. Similarly, Klerman et al. (2013) reported that women were nearly twice as likely as men to report a need for FMLA-related leave that was unmet. Therefore, even though men tend to be using leaves less often, evidence from the FMLA literature suggests that men may still be having their needs met more-so than women. As such, men may be less aware of the FMLA simply because they do not seek out family friendly-benefits as often.

On a related note, a recent survey of college students indicated that although men and women placed equal value on work flexibility and work–life balance, men were significantly less likely to seek flexible arrangements upon entering the workforce, primarily due to traditional gender stereotypes (Vandello et al. 2013). This is congruent with Butler et al.'s (2004) findings demonstrating that even when men report that they have positive work outcome expectancies associated with family-friendly benefits, this does not increase their intentions of using them. Thus, although both men and women are motivated to achieve work–life balance, men seem reluctant to use family-friendly benefits to achieve that goal. Therefore, factors other than awareness (i.e., gender norms) may be more important to consider regarding the gap between policy availability and utilization for both men and women.

12.5 Benefit Accessibility

Some have proposed that gender, in and of itself, contributes to the accessibility of family-friendly benefits, yet, empirical evidence is mixed. Some findings indicate that women have greater access to FWAs (e.g., Glauber 2011; McNamara et al. 2012) whereas others suggest that men have greater access (e.g., Golden 2009; McCrate 2005). Taking the previous literature together as a whole, accessibility to discretionary family-friendly benefits seems much closer to "gender neutral" than benefit awareness. For example, even though Glauber (2011) reported that men are less likely to have access to formal flexible work scheduling than women overall, the discrepancy (52 % compared to 56 %) was not very large and may be due to other factors (i.e., size of organization). Moreover, a factor that makes this research less straightforward than the awareness literature is the fact that some studies examined formal flexibility policies alone, whereas other studies include informal flexibility offered on a case-by-case basis.

Taking into account the "formality" of FWAs, there is more consensus regarding gender differences. For example, although Golden (2009) and Glauber's (2011) overall conclusions regarding gender and access to FWAs contrast, both acknowledge that women may be more likely to have access to formal FWAs offered by the organization while men tend to be more likely to benefit from informal flexibility given on a case-by-case basis. Therefore, many organizations may selectively implement FWAs as a function of formalized discretion of managers to grant or deny requests based on a case-by-case system rather than a universal policy (Kelly and Kalev 2006). Due to this gender discrepancy between formal versus informal accessibility, it has been suggested that implementation of more formal programs—rather than the case-by-case system—would likely promote more gender equity in access to family-friendly benefits (Golden 2009). To this end, we discuss the importance of the supervisor in the perceived availability, implementation, and effectiveness of family-friendly benefits later in this chapter given the integral role supervisors play in this process.

Although the evidence regarding who has greater access to family-friendly benefits is mixed, some workers may be at a clear disadvantage when it comes to accessing these benefits regardless of gender. For example, employees that are less privileged (i.e., lower wages, lower education levels, and hourly work) have restricted access to family-friendly benefits compared to their more privileged counterparts (Galinsky et al. 2011; Swanberg et al. 2005). In addition, men and women who are married, have children, and work in managerial positions appear to have somewhat greater access to flexibility in work scheduling (Golden 2009). There has also been speculation that race plays a role, with white employees proposed as having greater access to family-friendly benefits than African–Americans (e.g., Golden 2008, 2009). Though a full review of this area is beyond the scope of this chapter, it is important to note that many factors other than gender are likely to play a critical role in the perceived accessibility and subsequent usage of family-friendly benefits.

12.5.1 Organizational Gender Composition

A seemingly common assumption is that jobs with a greater composition of women employees offer more family-friendly benefits. This assumption is supported by many studies (e.g., Davis and Kalleberg 2006; Gerstel and Aremenia 2009; Lowen and Sicilian 2009). Recent evidence on this topic, however, is not so clear cut. For example, Glauber (2011) suggests that gender-integrated occupations (40–60 % female) have the greatest access to flexible scheduling, with male-dominated occupations (greater than 70 % male) having the least access and female-dominated occupations (greater than 70 % female) falling between the two. Furthermore, in the 2012 National Study of Employers, Matos and Galinsky (2012) suggested that employers that were larger, nonprofit, and have more women and racial/ethnic minorities *in top positions* were more likely to offer flexibility and dependent care assistance to their employees. Therefore, access may not necessarily be dependent on the gender composition of the organization as a whole but the size of the organization and gender composition of the employees who are in a position of power.

Interestingly, organizational size may have a differential impact on men and women. Glauber (2011) found that men tend to have the greatest access to flexible scheduling when they work in small organizations whereas women have the greatest access when they work in large organizations. This may be due to women's access to formal benefits in larger organizations and men's access to informal benefits in smaller organizations (Glauber 2011). This is consistent with a previous study suggesting that women may have greater access to formal benefits whereas men may have greater access to informal benefits (Golden 2009), and further illustrates the importance of supervisors allowing all employees the same opportunity for FWAs regardless of whether the benefits are formally or informally offered.

12.6 Gender Norms and the Flexibility Stigma

Perhaps the most important influence on whether or not employees view family-friendly benefits as a viable resource is the *perceived* accessibility and usefulness of these resources. Although it is debatable whether firm conclusions can be made regarding gender differences in actual accessibility and usage of family-friendly benefits, it is clear that the overall usage rates of family-friendly benefits are low, compared to their availability, regardless of gender (Galinsky et al. 2008, 2011). Whereas awareness and formal accessibility may influence actual usage of available benefits, many informal and unspoken norms play a large role as well. One of the most powerful contributors to perceived accessibility is traditional gender norms.

Although gender equality has become an overarching societal goal, gender stereotypes continue to serve as a powerful influence on human behavior (Prentice and Carranza 2002). For example, traditional gender norms and expectations (i.e., male as provider, female as housekeeper) are still often prescribed today; men are commonly expected to be dominant, career-focused, and independent while women are often perceived as more caring, interdependent, and modest than men. When men or women do not conform to these stereotypes, they often suffer from social and professional consequences (e.g., Moss-Racusin et al. 2010; Rudman and Phelan 2008). Experiencing "backlash" as a result of gender norm-breaking reinforces typical gender norms. In turn, both men and women may be prevented from breaking these norms, thereby maintaining the gender status quo (Rudman and Fairchild 2004). This maintenance of the gender status quo appears to be playing a key role in employees' perceptions and usage of family-friendly benefits.

Even though formal benefits may recognize the growing needs of today's families, there are many informal regulations and processes that determine the extent to which these benefits are perceived as available to the employees (Eaton 2003). In fact, these informal practices may, knowingly or unknowingly, stigmatize workers who take advantage of family-friendly benefits. This is referred to as the flexibility stigma, and is often based on typical gender stereotypes (Bornstein 2013). Both men and women can suffer from stigmatization associated with perceptions and usage of family-friendly benefits, albeit in different ways. As described below, the flexibility stigma for men is based on gender non-conforming behavior whereas the stigma for women stems from gender-conforming behavior (Williams et al. 2013).

12.6.1 Stigma for Women

Multiple studies highlight the negative outcomes that working women with children encounter. It has been well established that working mothers face a “maternal wall” when it comes to various workplace decisions. The reason for this may be that female employees, especially low-wage workers, are penalized for motherhood through perceived incompetence and reduced consideration for promotions regardless of their actual work qualifications (e.g., Crosby et al. 2004; Heilman and Okimoto 2008; Dodson 2013). This stigmatization of mothers stems from the ideal worker norm, which states that ideal workers place more emphasis on work obligations than unpaid family responsibilities (Kelly et al. 2010). As a result, mothers are probably more likely to be seen as a “risk” for making use of a family-related benefit due to the stereotypical gender expectation that they will be preoccupied with family care responsibilities. Although the option of family-friendly benefits may be available to help women balance work and family, Williams et al. (2013) suggest that making use of a family-friendly benefit may be interpreted by other professionals, as well as the individual employee herself, as a form of moral violation for not living up to one’s work demands and expectations. As a result, because women are traditionally thought of as the primary caregiver, their careers may be negatively impacted when they have to fulfill family responsibilities.

Women may be discounted not only within the workplace but outside of it as well. Working women may be viewed as less effective parents than non-working mothers (e.g., Eataugh and Folger 1998; Gorman and Fritzsche 2002), especially when working in a stereotypically male-gendered occupation (Berdahl and Moon 2013; Okimoto and Heilman 2012). Therefore, although women may suffer career penalties for being a mother, they are also likely to suffer social consequences (i.e., being viewed as a bad mother) if they are not the primary caregiver. Herein lies the conundrum for women: if they have children or family responsibilities, they are expected to take leave and/or use available benefits, for which their careers are penalized. At the same time, if they choose to focus on their careers by avoiding the use of family-friendly benefits, they may be ostracized for not conforming to what a woman “should” do. In terms of using family-friendly benefits, women seem to potentially be at a disadvantage either way.

12.6.2 Stigma for Men

On the other hand, it has also been well established that men who are seen as less masculine are respected less and suffer more negative consequences than men judged as more masculine (e.g., Funk and Werhun 2011; Heilman and Wallen 2010; Judge et al. 2012). Thus, although simply having family responsibilities does not result in as many negative consequences for men as it does for women (Fuegen et al. 2004), the act of caring for children and/or publicizing their family responsibilities may result in stigmatization. For men, requesting a family leave or some form of flexibility to care for a dependent is violating their traditional gender norm of placing work as their primary priority, and may be seen as a sign of weakness or low status. Multiple studies suggest that men experience more negative reactions from others than women when asking for a family leave (e.g., Allen and Russell 1999; Wayne and Codeiro 2003), experiencing family conflict (Butler and Skattebo 2004), and working fewer hours in order to balance family responsibilities (Vinkenburg et al. 2012). Unlike women who get penalized for conforming to their gender role, men get penalized for *not* conforming to their traditional gender role. Thus, though the mechanism is different, both men and women's careers may be penalized for making use of available benefits.

Similar to women, men are also socially stigmatized for breaking gender norms, as demonstrated in two recent studies. Berdahl and Moon (2013) found that men who were more involved in domestic-related tasks and caregiving for their children experienced more harassment (i.e., being seen as "not man enough") than men who spent less time caring for their children. Similarly, Rudman and Mescher (2013, p. 325) demonstrated that male employees who request family leave suffer from a femininity stigma and are punished for "acting like a woman." Interestingly, both men and women were equally likely to feminize male leave requesters, viewing them as weaker than men who did not ask for leave. This finding is congruent with previous research suggesting that men who act modestly (rather than dominantly) tend to suffer more prejudice from both men and women due to a perceived violation of their gender-prescribed behavior (Moss-Racusin et al. 2010). Therefore, even though women tend to report more acceptance of gender norm-breaking (e.g., Coleman and Franiuk 2011; Goldberg et al. 2012), men who utilize family-friendly benefits are not only subjected to harassment by other men but women as well. As such, traditional gender norms regarding benefit use are being perpetuated by both men and women.

12.6.3 Gender Norm Summary

As can be seen, both men and women suffer career and social consequences, albeit in different ways, as a result of the flexibility stigma. In fact, Berdahl and Moon (2013) suggest that gender performance may drive workplace mistreatment more than work performance. Unfortunately, being perceived as a lesser man and/or a lesser worker for using family-friendly benefits or violating gender norms is not all that uncommon (cf., Bornstein 2013; Stone and Hernandez 2013). These stereotypes, in turn, may undermine worker's use of available benefits: men may be less likely to use benefits to maintain their status of masculinity whereas women may be hesitant to utilize benefits for fear of being stigmatized as less competent (Correll et al. 2007). Therefore, the potential for improving work–life balance among all employees continues to be limited by persisting traditional gender norms.

Although there is some evidence that gendered perceptions regarding the flexibility stigma may be changing for the better among young adults (e.g., Coleman and Franiuk 2011), other evidence suggests that perceptions regarding gender roles and work–family responsibilities has remained fairly constant since the 1980s (Goldberg et al. 2012). Poelmans (2012) notes that these norms are deeply rooted in several layers of socio-cultural values (i.e., dyadic, organizational, societal, and cultural), and will take a tremendous amount of time and effort to change. Given that we know gender stereotyping and traditional gender norms still persist when it comes to family-friendly benefits, future research should examine how to potentially reduce the negative perceptions associated with breaking gender norms and will likely result in a better understanding of how to encourage utilization of family-friendly benefits.

12.7 Outcomes Associated with Family-Friendly Benefits

The negative career and social penalties, the flexibility stigma, and the perpetuation of traditional gender norms represent some of the unintended negative consequences associated with family-friendly benefits. It has been well established that both men and women may forego utilizing family-friendly benefits for fear of negative career consequences and/or due to financial necessity (e.g., Klerman et al. 2013). However, the overarching goal of these benefits is to help employees balance work and family responsibilities and to improve worker satisfaction. In this section, we will provide a brief overview of the effectiveness of family-friendly benefits at promoting positive outcomes, and whether benefit effectiveness differs between men and women. Given the importance of the supervisor in determining employee outcomes—as well as the fact that supervisor support may serve as an important family-friendly benefit in and of itself—the majority of this section focuses on the worker-supervisor interaction in contributing to positive employee outcomes.

12.7.1 General Effectiveness

One of the most immediate effects of offering family-friendly benefits concerns the attractiveness of the organization for potential and current employees. Both men and women value work-life balance (Vandello et al. 2013). Not surprisingly, organizations that offer family-friendly benefits are often perceived as more supportive and desirable among job applicants of both genders (e.g., Bourhis and Mekkaoui 2010; Wayne and Casper 2012). Therefore, the organization's reputation concerning family-friendly policy availability serves as a beneficial recruiting tool, irrespective of gender.

In terms of positive individual and organizational consequences, family-supportive benefits have been shown to be associated with a variety of favorable outcomes for employees and the organization as a whole. For example, multiple studies have demonstrated that the availability and use of family-friendly benefits tends to be associated with positive work attitudes (i.e., commitment, job satisfaction, and intentions to stay in the organization; e.g., Allen 2001; Breaugh and Frye 2007; Casper and Harris 2008), increased performance (e.g., Bloom et al. 2011; Jones and Murrell 2001), and reduced conflict between the work and family domains (e.g., Butts et al. 2013; Kossek et al. 2011; Thompson et al. 1999). Although not all studies find beneficial effects associated with family-friendly benefits (e.g., De Menezes and Kelliher 2011), a review of the literature suggests that family-friendly benefits can, and often do, benefit employees.

Studies that have examined gender differences, however, suggest that the magnitude of these positive effects may not be universal. For example, Butts et al. (2013) report in their meta-analysis that in samples with more women, the relation between policy availability and job satisfaction, as well as the relation between policy use and work–family conflict (i.e., a form of inter-role conflict characterized by incompatibility between the work and family domains; Greenhaus and Beutell 1985), were weaker compared to samples with more men. The authors speculated that available benefits may be more beneficial to men because they have fewer caregiving responsibilities whereas women's needs are less likely to be met due to their greater caregiving workload. However, Carlson et al. (2010) found that women benefit more from using flexible schedules than men, as women experienced less work–family conflict. Still, Hammer et al. (2005) found that usage of family-friendly benefits may not reduce work–family conflict and may actually lead to increased conflict for women, reasoning that women's usage may lead to the expectation of taking on even more family responsibilities.

In addition, there is evidence suggesting that men and women may possibly judge the utility of family-friendly benefits based on different criteria. For example, Sharpe et al. (2002) found that women were more likely to use FWAs to reduce work–family conflict whereas men were more likely to report using the benefits to enhance personal productivity (i.e., structure and routine in work and personal life). This implies that men may be more likely to judge the effectiveness of FWAs based on their job performance whereas women may be more likely to judge their effectiveness based on the ability to reduce work–family conflict. Future research would be beneficial in determining whether this is indeed the case.

The majority of recent studies on the effectiveness of family-friendly benefits mention supervisor support as a crucial factor in whether these benefits will be effective and/or perceived as useful. For example, Breaugh and Farabee (2012) noted that telecommuting and other FWAs are not quick fixes, and require supervisor support to be effective. In terms of performance, although Bloom et al. (2011) found that family-friendly benefits were positively related to organizational performance, this relation disappeared once the authors controlled for the quality of management practices. In fact, some have even questioned whether work–life balance is actually a matter of choice for the employee. Gregory and Milner (2009) suggest that work–life balance may be constrained by the culture created within the organization due to the enabling of traditional gender roles; in turn, the organizational culture may limit the employees' perceptions of what benefits they can actually use. Accordingly, to better understand the effectiveness of family-friendly benefits for producing positive employee outcomes, it is important to also understand the supervisors' role in the process of administering these benefits.

12.8 Importance of Supervisor

In an attempt to enhance employees' ability to manage the work–family interface, many organizational initiatives involve the development and maintenance of a family-supportive workplace. Thomas and Ganster (1995) identify family-supportive supervision as one of the two components comprising a family-supportive workplace environment, with the other component being family-friendly benefits. Despite the importance of offering formal workplace supports such as competitive family-friendly benefits, informal supports (i.e., direct supervisor support) are perhaps even more critical to the overall success of family-supportive workplace initiatives. For example, Behson (2005) demonstrated that supportive supervision explained more variance in job satisfaction, work–family conflict, and turnover intentions than formal support. Furthermore, unsupportive supervisors can act to undermine the effect of family-friendly benefits and offset any potential positive impact of benefit utilization (Kossek 2005). Despite the importance of supervisor support, the role of family-friendly benefits should not be downplayed. Foley et al. (2006) found that family-supportive organizations are a boundary condition under which family-supportive supervision can occur. In other words, supervisors are less likely to provide family-specific support to employees in the absence of a family-supportive organizational culture, as evidenced by formal family-friendly benefits.

As already noted, scholars have offered multiple explanations for the counterintuitive evidence surrounding organizational family-friendly benefits, such as underutilization due to lack of awareness about what is available and concerns about possible negative repercussions associated with their use (e.g., Kossek 2005; Neal and Hammer 2007). Consistently, however, the role of direct supervision has been presented as a critical determinant of benefit usage and efficacy. Immediate supervisors are in a unique position to facilitate employees' management of work and family roles, especially given that the simple presence of family-friendly benefits is not sufficient to alleviate the experience of work–family conflict (Allen 2001; Kossek 2005).

A great deal of evidence exists that links supervisor support and the experience of work–family conflict (e.g., Byron 2005; Hammer et al. 2007), and the negative impact of work–family conflict has been demonstrated on an array of individual and organizational outcomes (e.g., job and family satisfaction, job performance, turnover intentions, organizational commitment, physical and mental health; Allen 2001; Allen et al. 2000; Ford et al. 2007; Grzywacz and Bass 2003; Hammer et al. 2005). Employees who perceive their supervisors as being supportive of personal work–family management needs are likely to experience reduced levels of work–family conflict (cf., Kossek et al. 2011). Family-supportive supervisors engage in behaviors such as provision of emotional support (e.g., listening, empathizing), instrumental support (e.g., accommodating flexible work schedules), role modeling, and brainstorming creative work–family management strategies with employees to help them manage work and non-work demands (Hammer et al. 2009). Supervisors who exhibit such family-supportive supervisor behaviors (FSSB) tend to be perceived as more accommodating of employees' non-work responsibilities than supervisors who do not exhibit these behaviors. In a recent study, Matthews et al. (2014) provided preliminary evidence that FSSB explain incremental variance in employee work engagement above and beyond perceptions of general managerial effectiveness and organizational support. In addition, work engagement was found to mediate the relationship between employee perceptions of FSSB and subjective wellbeing.

Ways in which family-supportive supervisors can help employees reduce the experience of work–family conflict include: fostering a high-quality exchange relationship with their subordinates (Liden and Graen 1980), demonstrating family-supportive behaviors (Hammer et al. 2009), championing the use of family-friendly benefits (Hammer et al. 2007), and helping create or maintain a family-friendly organizational culture (Thompson et al. 1999). Supervisors are typically viewed as representatives of organizational practices and top leadership, and as such, they can influence employee attitudes and outcomes (e.g., wellbeing, affective organizational commitment, turnover intentions, work–family conflict; Allen 2001; Major and Lauzun 2010; Thompson et al. 1999). As such, the power of the supervisors should be harnessed to enhance the utilization and efficacy of family-friendly benefits. For an expanded discussion on the role of supervisor support in the management of the work–family interface, see Matthews et al. (2013).

12.8.1 Supervisor Support and Gender Differences

Given the importance of supervisor support in helping employees manage the work–family interface, it is surprising that the supervisor–employee dyad has not been examined in greater depth in the literature. Specifically, as it pertains to benefit utilization, supervisor gender is a key contextual factor that can help further explain why family-friendly benefits do not always have the intended positive results.

To address this gap in the literature, researchers have begun to examine the issue of supervisor gender as it relates to work–family management. Anecdotally, female supervisors are typically considered as more supportive of work–family management needs than male supervisors. Research seems to support this general belief (Hopkins 2002; Parker and Allen 2002). For example, supervisors often provide differential support to employees based on gender, with female supervisors offering higher levels of family-specific support (i.e., making referrals to employee assistance programs) to female employees (Gerstein et al. 1993). Perhaps one reason for this comes from research by Foley et al. (2006) who found that employees feel more comfortable requesting family-related help from same-gender, compared to cross-gender supervisors. Interestingly, Foley et al. noted this gender effect did not weaken in the presence of a highly family-supportive organizational culture. Although the gender effect they found explained less variance in family-supportive supervision and family-supportive culture, gender differences present a critical issue that should not be overlooked in future research.

Consistent with Foley et al.'s (2006) findings, Hopkins (2002) showed that female employees are more likely to seek assistance for family and personal problems from same-gender supervisors. Hopkins also provided support for the interaction between employee and supervisor gender with respect to important family- and work-related outcomes. Specifically, female supervisors were more likely to provide formal support referrals to male employees. Interestingly, however, Hopkins also noted that female employees perceived their male supervisor to be more supportive (i.e., understanding and flexible) than did female employees with female supervisors. A potential caveat that could help explain this seemingly contradictory finding is the gender composition of the organization. Specifically, in organizations where female employees are under-represented relative to male employees, female employees perceive their female supervisor as less supportive than their male supervisors (Ryan et al. 2012). This finding is inconsistent with most anecdotal and scholarly evidence, and highlights the need to always consider important contextual and organizational environments within which supervisor–employee dyads are nested.

Further highlighting the role that supervisor gender plays in widening the gender gap associated with supervisory support, recent findings by Raghuram et al. (2012) demonstrated that the difference in stress levels for male versus female immigrants was twice as large when the supervisor was perceived as unsupportive. Taking a more granular approach, Winfield and Rushing (2005) examined whether gender influenced the type of support provided and found that when the direct supervisor was of the same gender, employees were likely to receive interactional but not instrumental support.

Li and Bagger (2011) extended the issue of supervisor–employee dyad similarity to encompass similarity in not only gender but also childcare responsibilities. Specifically, the authors suggested that within cross-gender dyads, provision of family-specific support was dependent on the amount of supervisor childcare responsibilities such that supervisors with higher levels of childcare responsibilities relative to their employees provided higher levels of family-supportive supervision. These effects, however, were not supported for same-gender supervisor–employee dyads, perhaps due to the unconditional provision of support within same-gendered dyads regardless of any differences (or similarities) in childcare responsibilities. As such, in addition to consideration of gender, dependent care responsibilities should be examined as another factor that may play a role in perpetuating the gender gap.

These findings indicate that supervisors may in fact be key perpetrators of the development and maintenance of a gender gap as it pertains to utilization and efficacy of family-friendly benefits. Well-known social psychology phenomena such as favoritism, interpersonal attraction, and similarity bias may be the primary culprits for this gender-driven differential provision of support (Foley et al. 2006). Future research should continue to devote efforts to further delineate how supervisor demographic characteristics such as gender can act to facilitate or impede the success of family-friendly benefits and employees' ability to effectively manage the work–family interface.

12.8.2 I-Deals and the Gender Gap

Idiosyncratic deals (i.e., i-deals) have been widely promoted as a best practice in strategic management (e.g., Hornung et al. 2008). Major and Lauzun (2010) extended the i-deal framework to the work–family context by drawing on previous qualitative research demonstrating that many of the work–life needs and requests employees make of supervisors were highly idiosyncratic in nature (e.g., childcare, eldercare, flextime; Morganson et al. 2007). The work–family i-deal is defined as a "voluntary, personalized agreement in which an aspect or aspects of the employment arrangement are negotiated between an individual employee and the employer expressly for the mutual benefit derived from reduced work–family conflict" (Major and Lauzun 2009, p. 6). Major and Lauzun argue that when supervisors foster high-quality leader-member exchange (i.e., LMX; unique relationships ranging from low to high-quality based on exchange of resources; Liden and Graen 1980) with their employees, they are more likely to engage in constructive negotiation of the work–family i-deal that would address specific employee work–family needs.

Encouraging supervisors to negotiate i-deals with each of their employees is one way to reduce the gender gap that occurs with respect to utilization and effectiveness of family-friendly benefits. Furthermore, and in light of Kossek et al.'s (2011) meta-analytic findings suggesting that perceptions of family-supportive supervision are more important in helping to alleviate employee work–family conflict compared to perceptions of generally supportive supervision, i-deals could be harnessed to match the type of provided supervisor support to the unique employee work–family situation, irrespective of gender. A "one-size-fits-all" approach in the provision of family-specific supervision should be discouraged as it is considered ineffective work–family management (Major et al. 2008). As such, and extending previous recommendations for supervisor training programs (e.g., Major and Lauzun 2009), future intervention work should aim to educate supervisors on how to effectively negotiate i-deals with both male and female employees. Specifically, supervisors should become aware of relevant gender differences, biases, and stereotypes and learn how to overcome them, and as a result, become well-equipped to recognize the idiosyncrasies specific to each individual employee.

12.8.3 Importance of Supervisor Summary

There is irrefutable evidence that supervisors are crucial to the success of family-friendly benefits and the employees' ability to effectively manage the work–family interface. Although studies on the supervisor–employee dyad are limited, empirical and theoretical support exists for the effect of supervisor–employee gender similarity on the experience of supportive supervision and various employee outcomes. Given that supervisors can serve as a communication channel connecting various levels within an organization, they should be encouraged to champion family-friendly benefits and provide fair and idiosyncratic family-specific support that is free of gender biases and stereotypes.

12.9 Future Directions

Because gender plays a large role in the utilization and effectiveness of family-friendly benefits, we can greatly benefit from future research on the subject. Although the intersection of gender and family-friendly benefits has been widely researched of late, there are many areas for future inquiry. First of all, further examination of employer practices regarding advertisement of family-friendly benefits is warranted. In particular, we suggest exploration into whether certain practices are advertised on a gendered basis, i.e., are some benefits advertised more to women than men, and vice versa. Second, assessing potential gender differences in strategies to obtain work–life balance is another valuable avenue to investigate. For example, as previously noted, the evidence concerning gender preferences for particular benefits is mixed. Researchers should aim to examine whether men and women use these benefits for different reasons, and whether men and women differ in their tendency to seek out formal versus informal benefits. Due to the stigmatization associated with these benefits, employees may be covert in seeking out support for their family life.

Similarly, it would be constructive to examine whether men and women judge the effectiveness of family friendly-benefits based on different criteria. As Sharpe et al. (2002) noted, men and women may put more emphasis on performance and work–family conflict, respectively. Is this indeed the case, or are men and women simply reporting in a way that is congruent with traditional gender stereotypes? This leads to perhaps the most significant area for future investigation—how to reduce the negative perceptions associated with breaking gender norms. There is a desperate need for future research in this area, as gendered stigmatization is evident for both men and women. Finally, a topic that can work in concert with that mentioned previously is future investigation into the supervisor–employee dyad. Preliminary evidence suggests the importance of considering gender as a large contributor to employee perceptions and supervisor decisions related to family-friendly benefits. Given that supervisors may reinforce traditional gender norms (Kelly 2010)—thereby discouraging some employees from utilizing benefits while possibly encouraging others—future research should continue to explore this dynamic.

12.10 Conclusion

Gender norms and expectations are still alive and well in the workplace today, particularly when it comes to family-friendly benefits. As a result, both men and women are at risk for social and professional stigmatization. Although many organizational benefits and procedures advertise gender equality, these claims appear to be superficial due to the persistent ideals of how men and women "should" act in their work and family domains. Until employees, supervisors, and organizations put forth a genuine effort to enforce gender equality by overcoming traditional gendered expectations, in both formal and informal procedures, family-friendly benefits will continue to show a mix of positive and negative outcomes. It is hoped that this chapter will stimulate interest in the topic and therefore encourage progress toward the goal of gender equality.

References

Allen, T. D. (2001). Family-supportive work environments: The role of organizational perceptions. *Journal of Vocational Behavior, 58,* 414–435.
Allen, T. D., & Russell, J. E. (1999). Parental leave of absence: Some not so family-friendly implications. *Journal of Applied Social Psychology, 29,* 166–191.
Allen, T. D., Herst, D. E. L., Bruck, C. S., & Sutton, M. (2000). Consequences associated with work-to-family conflict: A review and agenda for future research. *Journal of Occupational Health Psychology, 5,* 278–308.
Armenia, A., & Gerstel, N. (2006). Family leaves, the FMLA, and gender neutrality: The intersection of race and gender. *Social Science Research, 35,* 871–891.
Baird, C. L., & Reynolds, J. R. (2004). Employee awareness of family leave benefits: The effects of family, work, and gender. *Sociological Quarterly, 45,* 325–353.
Behson, S. J. (2005). The relative contribution of formal and informal organizational work–family support. *Journal of Vocational Behavior, 66,* 487–500.
Berdahl, J. L., & Moon, S. H. (2013). Workplace mistreatment of middle class workers based on sex, parenthood, and caregiving. *Journal of Social Issues, 69,* 341–366.
Blair-Loy, M., & Wharton, A. S. (2002). Employees' use of work–family policies and the workplace social context. *Social Forces, 80,* 813–845.
Bloom, N., Kretschmer, T., & Van Reenen, J. (2011). Are family-friendly workplace practices a valuable firm resource? *Strategic Management Journal, 32,* 343–367.
Bornstein, S. (2013). The legal and policy implications of the "flexibility stigma". *Journal of Social Issues, 69,* 389–405.
Bourhis, M., & Mekkaoui, R. (2010). Beyond work–family balance: Are family-friendly organizations more attractive? *Industrial Relations, 65,* 98–117.
Breaugh, J. A., & Farabee, A. M. (2012). Telecommuting and flexible work hours: Alternative work arrangements that can improve the quality of work life. In N. P. Reilly, M. J. Sirgy, & C. A. Gorman (Eds.), *Work and quality life: Ethical practices in organizations* (pp. 251–274). New York: Springer.
Breaugh, J. A., & Frye, N. K. (2007). An examination of the antecedents and consequences of the use of family-friendly benefits. *Journal of Managerial Issues, 19,* 35–52.
Byron, K. (2005). A meta-analytic review of work–family conflict and its antecedents. *Journal of Vocational Behavior, 67,* 169–198.
Bureau of Labor Statistics. (2013). Labor force statistics from the Current Population Survey. Annual average data. Retrieved from http://www.bls.gov/cps/tables.htm.
Butler, A., Gasser, M., & Smart, L. (2004). A social-cognitive perspective on using family-friendly benefits. *Journal of Vocational Behavior, 65,* 57–70.
Butler, A., & Skattebo, A. (2004). What is acceptable for women may not be for men: The effect of family conflicts with work on job-performance ratings. *Journal of Occupational and Organizational Psychology, 77,* 553–564.
Butts, M. M., Casper, W. J., & Yang, T. S. (2013). How important are work–family support policies? A meta-analytic investigation of their effects on employee outcomes. *Journal of Applied Psychology, 98,* 1–25.
Carlson, D. S., Grzywacz, J. G., & Kacmar, K. M. (2010). The relationship of schedule flexibility and outcomes via the work–family interface. *Journal of Managerial Psychology, 25,* 330–355.
Casper, W. J., & Harris, C. M. (2008). Work-life benefits and organizational attachment: Self-interest utility and signaling theory models. *Journal of Vocational Behavior, 72,* 95–109.

Coleman, J. M., & Franiuk, R. (2011). Perceptions of mothers and fathers who take temporary leave. *Sex Roles, 64,* 311–323.
Correll, S. J., Benard, S., & Paik, I. (2007). Getting a job: Is there a motherhood penalty? *American Journal of Sociology, 112,* 1297–1339.
Crosby, F. J., Williams, J. C., & Biernat, M. (2004). The maternal wall. *Journal of Social Issues, 60,* 675–682.
Davis, A. E., & Kalleberg, A. L. (2006). Family-friendly organizations? Work and family programs in the 1990s. *Work and Occupations, 33,* 191–223.
De Menezes, L. M., & Kelliher, C. (2011). Flexible working and performance: A systematic review of the evidence for a business case. *International Journal of Management Reviews, 13,* 452–474.
Dodson, L. (2013). Stereotyping low-wage mothers who have work and family conflicts. *Journal of Social Issues, 69,* 257–278.
Eataugh, C., & Folger, D. (1998). Perceptions of parents whose work and parenting behaviors deviate from role expectations. *Sex Roles, 39,* 215–223.
Eaton, S. C. (2003). If you can use them: Flexibility policies, organizational commitment, and perceived performance. *Industrial Relations: A Journal of Economy and Society, 42,* 145–167.
Foley, S., Linnehan, F., Greenhaus, J. H., & Weer, C. H. (2006). The impact of gender similarity, racial similarity, and work culture on family-supportive supervision. *Group & Organization Management, 31,* 420–442.
Fondas, N. (2013). How women and men use flexible work policies. The Atlantic. Retrieved from http://www.theatlantic.com/sexes/archive/2013/07/how-women-and-men-use-flexible-work-policies-differently/277954/.
Ford, M. T., Heinen, B. A., & Langkamer, K. L. (2007). Work and family satisfaction and conflict: A meta-analysis of cross-domain relations. *Journal of Applied Psychology, 92,* 57–80.
Fuegen, K., Biernat, M., Haines, E., & Deaux, K. (2004). Mothers and fathers in the workplace: How gender and parental status influence judgements of job-related competence. *Journal of Social Issues, 60,* 737–754.
Funk, L. C., & Werhun, C. D. (2011). "You're such a girl!" The psychological drain of the gender-role harassment of men. *Sex Roles, 65,* 13–22.
Galinsky, E., Bond, J. T., & Hill, E. J. (2004). *A status report on workplace flexibility: Who has it? Who wants it? What difference does it make?* New York: Families and Work Institute.
Galinsky, E., Bond, J. T., & Sakai, K. (2008). *2008 national study of employers.* New York: Families and Work Institute.
Galinsky, E., Sakai, K., & Wigton, T. (2011). Workplace flexibility: From research to action. *The Future of Children, 21,* 141–161.
Gerstein, L., Moore, D., Duffy, K., & Daina, C. (1993). The effects of biological sex and ethnicity on EAP utilization and referrals. *Consulting Psychology Journal, 45,* 23–27.
Gerstel, N., & Armenia, A. (2009). Giving and taking family leaves: Right or privilege? *Yale Journal of Law & Feminism, 21,* 161–184.
Gerstel, N., & McGonagle, K. (1999). Job leaves and the limits of the Family and Medical Leave Act: The effects of gender, race, and family. *Work and Occupations, 26,* 510–534.
Glauber, R. (2011). Limited access: Gender, occupational composition, and flexible work scheduling. *The Sociological Quarterly, 52,* 472–494.
Goldberg, W. A., Kelly, E., Matthews, N. L., Kang, H., Li, W., & Sumaroka, M. (2012). The more things change, the more they stay the same: Gender, culture, and college students' views about work and family. *Journal of Social Issues, 68,* 814–837.
Golden, L. (2008). Limited access: Disparities in flexible work schedules and work-at-home. *Journal of Economic Issues, 29,* 86–109.
Golden, L. (2009). Flexible daily work schedules in U.S. jobs: Formal introductions needed? *Industrial Relations: A Journal of Economy and Society, 48,* 27–54.
Gorman, K. A., & Fritzsche, B. A. (2002). The good-mother stereotype: Stay at home (or wish that you did!). *Journal of Applied Social Psychology, 32,* 2190–2201.

Greenhaus, J. H., & Beutell, N. J. (1985). Sources of conflict between work and family roles. *Academy of Management Review, 10,* 76–88.
Gregory, A., & Milner, S. (2009). Work-life balance: A matter of choice? *Gender, Work, and Organization, 16,* 1–13.
Grzywacz, J. G., & Bass, B. L. (2003). Work, family, and mental health: Testing different models of work–family fit. *Journal of Marriage & Family, 65,* 248–261.
Grzywacz, J. G., & Butler, A. B. (2008). Work-family conflict. In J. Barling & C. L. Cooper (Eds.), *The Sage handbook of organizational behavior* (pp. 451–468). Los Angeles: Sage.
Hammer, L. B., Kossek, E. E., Yragui, N. L., Bodner, T. E., & Hanson, G. C. (2009). Development and validation of a multidimensional measure of family supportive supervisor behaviors (FSSB). *Journal of Management, 35,* 837–856.
Hammer, L. B., Kossek, E. E., Zimmerman, K., & Daniels, R. (2007). Clarifying the construct of family-supportive supervisory behaviors (FSSB): A multilevel perspective. In P. L. Perrewé, D. C. Ganster, P. L. Perrewé, & D. C. Ganster (Eds.), *Exploring the work and non-work interface* (pp. 165–204). Bingley: Emerald.
Hammer, L. B., Neal, M. B., Newsom, J. T., Brockwood, K. J., & Colton, C. L. (2005). A longitudinal study of the effects of dual-earner couples' utilization of family-friendly workplace supports on work and family outcomes. *Journal of Applied Psychology, 90,* 799–810.
Hammer, L. B., & Zimmerman, K. L. (2011). Quality of work life. In S. Zedeck (Ed.), *American Psychological Association handbook of industrial and organizational psychology* (pp. 391–431). Washington, DC.: American Psychological Association.
Heilman, M. E., & Okimoto, T. G. (2008). Motherhood: A potential source of bias in employment decisions. *Journal of Applied Psychology, 93,* 189–198.
Heilman, M. E., & Wallen, A. S. (2010). Wimpy and undeserving of respect: Penalties for men's gender-inconsistent success. *Journal of Experimental Social Psychology, 46,* 664–667.
Hill, E. J., Hawkins, A. J., Martinson, V., & Ferris, M. (2003). Studying "working fathers": Comparing fathers' and mothers' work–family conflict, fit, and adaptive strategies in a global high-tech company. *Men's Studies Press, 1,* 239–261.
Hopkins, K. M. (2002). Interactions of gender and race in workers' help seeking for personal/family problems: Perceptions of supervisor support and intervention. *Journal of Applied Behavioral Science, 38,* 156–176.
Hornung, S., Rousseau, D. M., & Glaser, J. (2008). Creating flexible work arrangements through idiosyncratic deals. *Journal of Applied Psychology, 93,* 655–664.
Jones, R., & Murrell, A. J. (2001). Signaling positive corporate social performance. An event study of family-friendly firms. *Business & Society, 40,* 59–78.
Judge, T. A., Livingston, B. A., & Hurst, C. (2012). Do nice guys-and gals-really finish last? The joint effects of sex and agreeableness on income. *Journal of Personality and Social Psychology, 102,* 390–407.
Kelly, E. L. (2010). Failure to update: An institutional perspective on noncompliance with the Family and Medical Leave Act. *Law & Society Review, 44,* 33–66.
Kelly, E. L., Ammons, S. K., Chermack, K., & Moen, P. (2010). Gendered challenge, gendered response: Confronting the ideal worker norm in a white-collar organization. *Gender & Society, 24,* 281–303.
Kelly, E. L., & Kalev, A. (2006). Managing flexible work arrangements in US organizations: Formalized discretion or 'a right to ask'. *Socio-Economic Review, 4,* 379–416.
Klerman, J. A., Daley, K., & Pozniak, A. (2013). *Family and medical leave in 2012: Technical report.* Washington, D.C.: Abt Associates.
Kossek, E. (2005). Workplace policies and practices to support work and families. In S. Bianchi, L. Casper, & R. King (Eds.), *Work, family, health & well-being* (pp. 97–116). Mahwah: LEA Press.
Kossek, E. E., & Distelberg, B. (2009). Work and family employment policy for a transformed work force: Trends and themes. In N. Crouter & A. Booth (Eds.), *Work-life policies* (pp. 1–51). Washington, D.C.: Urban Institute Press.

Kossek, E. E., & Michel, J. S. (2011). Flexible work schedules. In S. Zedeck (Ed.), *American Psychological Association handbook of industrial organizational psychology* (pp. 535–572). Washington, D.C.: American Psychological Association.

Kossek, E. E., Pichler, S., Bodner, T., & Hammer, L. B. (2011). Workplace social support and work–family conflict: A meta-analysis clarifying the influence of general and work–family-specific supervisor and organizational support. *Personnel Psychology, 64,* 289–313.

Kramer, A. (2008). Unions as facilitators of employment rights: An analysis of individuals' awareness of parental leave in the National Longitudinal Survey of Youth. *Industrial Relations, 47,* 651–658.

Li, A., & Bagger, J. (2011). Walking in your shoes: Interactive effects of child care responsibility difference and gender similarity on supervisory family support and work-related outcomes. *Group & Organizational Management, 36,* 659–691.

Liden, R. C., & Graen, G. B. (1980). Generalizability of the vertical dyad linkage model of leadership. *Academy of Management Journal, 23,* 451–465.

Lowen, A., & Sicilian, P. (2009). "Family friendly" fringe benefits and the gender wage gap. *Journal of Labor Research, 30,* 101–119.

Major, D. A., Fletcher, T. D., Davis, D. D., & Germano, L. M. (2008). The influence of work–family culture and workplace relationships on work interference with family: A multilevel model. *Journal of Organizational Behavior, 29,* 881–897.

Major, D. A., & Germano, L. M. (2006). The changing nature of work and its impact on the work-home interface. In F. Jones, R. Burke, & M. Westman (Eds.), *Work-life balance: A psychological perspective* (pp. 13–38). London: Psychology Press.

Major, D. A., & Lauzun, H. M. (July 2009). *An i-deals approach to coping with work–family conflict: Antecedents and consequences.* Paper presented at the III international conference of work and family, Barcelona, Spain.

Major, D. A., & Lauzun, H. M. (2010). Equipping managers to assist employees in addressing work–family conflict: Applying the research literature toward innovative practice. *The Psychologist-Manager Journal, 13,* 69–85.

Martenengo, G., Jacob, J., & Hill, E. (2010). Gender and the work–family interface: Exploring differences across the family life course. *Journal of Family Issues, 31,* 1363–1390.

Matos, K., & Galinsky, E. (2012). *2012 national study of employers.* New York: Families and Work Institute.

Matthews, R. A., Bulger, C. A., & Booth, S. M. (2013). Managing the work–family interface to the benefit of both subordinates and supervisors: Looking beyond supervisor support and focusing on leadership behaviors. In M. Paludi (Ed.), *Psychology for business success: Juggling, balancing, and integrating work and family roles and responsibilities* (pp. 153–170). Santa Barbara: Praeger.

Matthews, R. A., Mills, M. J., Trout, R. C., & English, L. (2014). Family-supportive supervisor, behaviors, work, engagement, and subjective, well-being: A contextually dependent mediated process. *Journal of Occupational Health Psychology, 19,* 168–181.

McCrate, E. (2005). Flexible hours, workplace authority, and compensating wage differentials in the US. *Feminist Economics, 11,* 11–39.

McMenamin, T. M. (2007). Time to work: Recent trends in shift work and flexible schedules. *Monthly Labor Review, 130,* 3–15.

McNamara, T. K., Pitt-Catsouphes, M., Brown, M., & Matz-Costa, C. (2012). Access to and utilization of flexible work options. *Industrial Relations: A Journal of Economy and Society, 51,* 936–965.

Morganson, V. J., Major, D. A., & Green, A. P. (Aug 2007). *Seeking work-life balance: Employees' requests and managers' responses.* Poster presented at the annual convention of the American Psychological Association, San Francisco, CA, USA.

Moss-Racusin, C. A., Phelan, J. E., & Rudman, L. A. (2010). When men break the gender rules: Status incongruity and backlash against modest men. *Psychology of Men and Masculinity, 11,* 140–151.

Neal, M. B., & Hammer, L. B. (2007). *Working couples caring for children and aging parents: Effects on work and well being*. Mahwah: Erlbaum.
Okimoto, T. G., & Heilman, M. E. (2012). The "bad parent" assumption: How gender stereotypes affect reactions to working mothers. *Journal of Social Issues, 68,* 704–724.
Parker, L. B., & Allen, T. D. (April 2002). *Factors related to supervisor work/family sensitivity and flexibility*. Paper presented at the Society for Industrial and Organizational Psychology Conference, Toronto, Canada.
Poelmans, S. (2012). The "triple N" model: Changing normative beliefs about parenting and career success. *Journal of Social Issues, 68,* 838–847.
Prentice, D. A., & Carranza, E. (2002). What women and men should be, shouldn't be, are allowed to be, and don't have to be. The contents of prescriptive gender stereotypes. *Psychology of Women Quarterly, 26,* 269–281.
Prottas, D. J., Thompson, C. A., Kopelman, R. E., & Jahn, E. W. (2007). Work-family programs: Factors affecting employee knowledge and accuracy. *Personnel Review, 36,* 163–189.
Raghuram, S., Weisenfeld, B., & Garud, R. (2003). Technology enabled work: The role of self-efficacy in determining telecommuter adjustment and structuring behavior. *Journal of Vocational Behavior, 63,* 180–198.
Raghuram, A., Luksyte, A., Avery, D. R., & Macoukji, F. (2012). Does your supervisor stress you out? How support influences sex differences in stress among immigrants. *Journal of Career Development, 39,* 99–117.
Rudman, L. A., & Fairchild, K. (2004). Reactions to counterstereotypic behavior: The role of backlash in cultural stereotype maintenance. *Journal of Personality and Social Psychology, 87,* 157–176.
Rudman, L. A., & Mescher, K. (2013). Penalizing men who request a family leave: Is flexibility stigma a femininity stigma? *Journal of Social Issues, 69,* 322–340.
Rudman, L. A., & Phelan, J. E. (2008). Backlash effect for disconfirming gender stereotypes in organizations. *Research in Organizational Behavior, 28,* 61–79.
Ryan, K. M., King, E. B., Adis, C., Gulick, L. M. V., Peddie, C., & Hargraves, R. (2012). Exploring the asymmetrical effects of gender tokenism on supervisor-subordinate relationships. *Journal of Applied Social Psychology, 42,* E56–E102.
Ryan, A. M., & Kossek, E. E. (2008). Work-life policy implementation: Breaking down or creating barriers to inclusiveness? *Human Resource Management, 47,* 295–310.
Sharpe, D. L., Hermsen, J. M., & Billings, J. (2002). Gender differences in use of alternative full-time work arrangements by married workers. *Family and Consumer Sciences Research Journal, 31,* 78–111.
Singh, P., Paleti, R., Jenkins, S., & Bhat, C. R. (2013). On modelling telecommuting behavior: Option, choice, and frequency. *Transportation, 40,* 373–396.
Singley, S. G., & Hynes, K. (2005). Transitions to parenthood: Work-family policies, gender, and the couple context. *Gender & Society, 19,* 376–397.
Society for Human Resource Management (SHRM). (2012). 2012 Employee benefits: The employee benefits landscape in a recovering economy. Retrieved from http://www.shrm.org/Research/SurveyFindings/Articles/Documents/2012_EmpBenefits_Report.pdf.
Stone, P., & Hernandez, L. A. (2013). The all-or-nothing workplace: Flexibility stigma and "opting out" among professional-managerial women. *Journal of Social Issues, 69,* 235–256.
Swanberg, J. E., Pitt-Catsouphes, M., & Drescher-Burke, K. (2005). A question of justice: Disparities in employees' access to flexible schedule arrangements. *Journal of Family Issues, 26,* 866–895.
Thomas, L. T., & Ganster, D. C. (1995). Impact of family-supportive work variables on work–family conflict and strain: A control perspective. *Journal of Applied Psychology, 80,* 6–15.
Thompson, C. A., Beauvais, L. L., & Lyness, K. S. (1999). When work–family benefits are not enough: The influence of work–family culture on benefit utilization, organizational attachment, and work–family conflict. *Journal of Vocational Behavior, 54,* 392–415.
United States Department of Labor. (2013). Family and Medical Leave Act: Overview. Retrieved from http://www.dol.gov/whd/fmla/.

Vandello, J. A., Hettinger, V. E., Bosson, J. K., & Siddiqi, J. (2013). When equal really isn't equal: The masculine dilemma of seeking work flexibility. *Journal of Social Issues, 69,* 303–321.
Van Giezen, R. W. (2013). Paid leave in private industry over the past 20 years. Pay and benefits, 2, U.S. Bureau of Labor Statistics. Retrieved from http://www.bls.gov/opub/btn/volume-2/paid-leave-in-private-industry-over-the-past-20-years.htm.
Villablanca, A. C., Beckett, L., Nettiksimmons, J., & Howell, L. P. (2011). Career flexibility and family-friendly policies: An NIH-funded study to enhance women's careers in biomedical sciences. *Journal of Women's Health, 20,* 1485–1496.
Vinkenburg, C. J., van Engen, M. L., Coffeng, J., & Dikkers, J. S. E. (2012). Bias in employment decisions about mothers and fathers: The (dis)advantages of sharing care responsibilities. *Journal of Social Issues, 68,* 725–741.
Waldfogel, J. (2001). Family and medical leave: Evidence from the 2000 surveys. *Monthly Labor Review, 124,* 17–23.
Wayne, J. H., & Casper, W. J. (2012). Why does firm reputation in human resource policies influence college students? The mechanisms underlying job pursuit intentions. *Human Resource Management, 51,* 121–142.
Wayne, J. H., & Codeiro, B. L. (2003). Who is a good organizational citizen? Social perception of male and female employees who use family leave. *Sex Roles, 49,* 233–246.
Williams, J. C., Blair-Loy, M., & Berdahl, J. L. (2013). Cultural schemas, social class, and the flexibility stigma. *Journal of Social Issues, 69,* 209–234.
Winfield, I., & Rushing, B. (2005). Bridging the border between work and family: The effects of supervisor-employee similarity. *Sociological Inquiry, 75,* 55–80.

Chapter 13
Shiftwork as Gendered and Its Impact on Work–Family Balance

Ryan M. Rosiello and Maura J. Mills

13.1 The Shift to Shiftwork

13.1.1 Standard and Nonstandard Shifts

Throughout history, the most common representation of a work shift has been the fixed day shift in which employees' work hours fall between the hours of 8:00 am and 5:00 pm, Monday through Friday (Perrucci et al. 2007; Presser 2006). Since this shift has been most common throughout history, it is often referred to as a 'standard' shift or schedule (Presser 2006). Although the standard shift has traditionally been the most common, there also exist other types of shifts worth exploring. In fact, it is because of these other shift types that the common fixed day schedule is considered to be a work shift and not just a typical work day. Any shift that operates outside of standard work hours or days is defined as a nonstandard shift (Albertsen et al. 2008; Barthe et al. 2011; Perrucci et al. 2007; Presser 2003; Wittmer and Martin 2010). Some types of work that are representative of nonstandard work schedules are part-time work, contract work, and self–employment (Presser 2003). Furthermore, nonstandard schedules are more likely to occur in service sector occupations such as protective community services or health care than in nonservice sectors with more predictable and less time-sensitive demands (Tuttle and Garr 2012). For employees in the former fields, likely subjected to shiftwork, the 40-hour (or more) work week is undoubtedly still manageable, but how it is managed by the employee and facilitated by the organization can make all the difference.

M. J. Mills (✉)
Departments of Psychology and Management, Hofstra University,
135 Hofstra University, Hempstead, NY 11549, USA
e-mail: maura.mills@hofstra.edu

R. M. Rosiello
Department of Psychology, Hofstra University, 135 Hofstra University,
Hempstead, NY 11549, USA
e-mail: rrosie3@pride.hofstra.edu

M. J. Mills (ed.), *Gender and the Work-Family Experience*,
DOI 10.1007/978-3-319-08891-4_13

Unlike standard shifts, which are characterized by one type of work schedule, nonstandard shifts can take several different forms. One type of nonstandard shift is fixed evening schedules, which involve working most days between 4:00 pm and midnight (Presser 2006). Another type is the fixed night schedule which involves working most days between midnight and 8:00 am (Presser 2006). In contrast to fixed schedules—and perhaps more problematically in terms of work–family needs—there is another type of nonstandard shift, the rotating shift, in which an employee's work hours change periodically from evenings or nights to days, and/or the employee has rotating days off between pay periods (Barthe et al. 2011; Perrucci et al. 2007; Presser 2006). Other types of nonstandard shifts include early-morning, late-evening, split-workday, and weekend work (Barthe et al. 2011).

Research has found that a substantial—and growing—percentage of Americans are working nonstandard shifts. Colligan et al. (1979) wrote that 26% of the American workforce was involved in shiftwork at that time, and Fenwick and Tausig (2001) noted that by the early 1990s this number had risen to 30%. A more recent estimation by Williams (2010) indicated that the number of people involved in shiftwork had further increased to 40%. More specifically, Wittmer and Martin (2010) noted that 36% of Americans are required to work weekends at least occasionally. Understandably, there is a higher incidence of shiftwork in some industries than in others, as well as in blue-collar work versus white-collar work, thereby potentially creating socioeconomic and/or racial considerations insofar as shiftwork's effect on work–family conflict.[1] For instance, Root and Wooten (2008) noted that 50% of employees working nonstandard hours work in restaurants and bars, while 25% work in hospitals and manufacturing.

13.1.2 *The Forces Behind Shiftwork*

There are some major forces behind the increasing number of employees working nonstandard schedules, including industry, demographic, and technological considerations (Presser 2006; Wittmer and Martin 2010). First, the recent shift in the industrial and economic landscape has influenced this. The economy in the 1960s appeared much different than it does today in a variety of ways, including that at that time many jobs were in large manufacturing organizations (Presser 2006; Wittmer and Martin 2010). Such jobs provided employees with greater job security and a more rigid, standard work schedule. Gradually, however, as new types of businesses started to emerge over time, the job market in the US started to shift from a primarily manufacturing economy to a more service-based economy. As opposed to manufacturing-based industries which are focused on making products for consumers, the service-based industries are more focused on providing services. Consequently, some of these services are required at all times of the day and night, such as medical care and transportation. Therefore, in order to meet the increasing demands of consumers and to effectively compete with other companies, organizations have

[1] For a more detailed discussion of socioeconomic and racial considerations in regard to work–family conflict, see chapters 3 and 4, respectively.

been forced to provide services at all hours in what has been labeled as the 24/7 economy. In order to accommodate this, organizations implemented varied shifts to staff all needed days and hours while not overburdening individual employees' quantity of work hours (Perrons et al. 2006; Presser 2006).

Another major force behind employees working nonstandard schedules is a change in workplace demographics. Over the past 50 years, there has been an enormous increase in the number of women who have entered the workforce (Barthe et al. 2011; Presser 2006; Rapoport et al. 2002). One of the reasons for this is the increasing availability of service-based jobs as a result of the changing economy (Perrons et al. 2006). Many of these jobs are subject to nonstandard scheduling since such services are needed either continuously or unpredictably. As such, with women spending an increasingly substantial proportion of their time working outside the home, the number of hours they have in the home to complete daily housework has declined. As a result, there is an increased need for services in order to help with daily in-home tasks, such as pre-made meals and household cleaning services. Some of these services may be required at nonstandard times, in turn further increasing the demand for jobs with nonstandard work schedules (Presser 2006).

Lastly, the increase in quality and quantity of readily-available technology is yet another major force behind employees working nonstandard schedules. The technology has made it possible for consumers to reach services they need at any time. For instance, smartphones and other mobile technologies have provided people with the opportunity to order goods or services online or over the phone at almost any hour throughout the day or night (Presser 2006). For those who work in a standard day shift, having the opportunity to obtain access to such services during the evening may be very convenient and therefore boost revenue for the providing service organization. As a result, the number of jobs requiring nonstandard hours has increased in order to meet this need.

13.1.3 *The Impact of Shiftwork*

The type of shift that an employee works can have a major impact on their life, including exacerbating typical work stressors as well as introducing new ones. Employees who work nontraditional and/or inconsistent shifts may experience a variety of negative outcomes, as explicated below.

13.1.3.1 Shiftwork and the Family

One of the major negative outcomes experienced by those working nonstandard shifts is increased work–family conflict (Akanni 2011; Haines et al. 2008).[2] For instance, employees working nonstandard night and evening shifts may be on

[2] It should be noted, however, that any such negative effects that nontraditional shiftwork may have on work–family balance are likely to be affected by the employee's degree of 'morningness' or 'eveningness', as found by Willis et al. (2008).

opposite sleep/wake schedules, thereby augmenting time-based work–family conflict. Additionally, their schedules are likely to cause fatigue and potentially result in moodiness and/or stress (Ǿamil et al. 2013), which may lead to increased strain-based conflict (Haines et al. 2008). Indeed, various researchers have found that employees who work night, split, and rotating shifts report higher levels of work–family conflict than those who work day shifts (e.g., Liu et al. 2011; Staines and Pleck 1984). Also, employees may be more likely to experience work–family conflict when they have to unexpectedly cover alternate shifts at short notice (Estryn-Béhar and Van der Heijden 2012). Interestingly, some initial research has found that it is not so much one's actual shift hours that lead to work–family conflict so much as it is one's perception of the fit between work and family that influences how shifts are related to outcomes (Tuttle and Garr 2012). It has also been found that shiftwork negatively impacts how employees balance their work and family roles. For instance, some initial research has suggested that employees' work–family balance may be more negatively affected by night and evening work than by rotating shifts (Albertsen et al. 2008). However, this is increasingly debated as rotating shifts are recognized as less predictable, and therefore more of a hindrance to day-to-day family planning considerations as well as employees' effective establishment of a consistent sleep routine. For example, Bambra et al. (2008) indicated that realignment to a new shift schedule can take between 8 and 12 days to adjust effectively, therefore leading to challenges when shifts are constantly rotating without consideration for such adjustment periods.

In addition to work–family conflict overall, shiftwork can also have serious negative repercussions on family relationships specifically. One of the major ways shiftwork can impact the family is by decreasing the degree of satisfaction a couple may feel in their marriage[3] (Perrons et al. 2006; Tuttle and Garr 2012). When partners work competing shifts, they may have little waking time to spend together. Therefore, spouses may no longer have time to partake in the activities that they would normally do together, such as eating meals together or participating in family or leisure activities with one another. Over time, this can cause partners to lose touch with one another and therefore feel more dissatisfied with their marriage (Albertsen et al. 2008; Presser 2006; Williams 2010).

Another way shiftwork can impact the family is by affecting parents' relationships with their children. Since shifts can occur at many different times, it may be possible for parents to adjust their schedules so that one parent cares for the child while the other is at work—often referred to as tag-teaming (Williams 2010). Tag-teaming can lead to some financial benefits and may make it easier for families to cope with their work and family responsibilities (Estryn-Béhar and Van der Heijden 2012; Lewis 2009; Williams 1999). Also, families may view this strategy as a way to avoid the cost and/or perceived risk of placing their children in daycare (Williams 2010). However, despite these benefits there may also be negative effects from a relationship standpoint. For instance, when children are passed from one parent to

[3] For a more detailed discussion of the impact of work–family conflict on marital relationship quality, see chapter 9.

the other, they only get to experience being with one parent at a time. Therefore, the child does not obtain the same family experience that they would if both parents and the child were all together at the same time (Lewis 2009). Furthermore, when parents work late afternoon and early evening shifts they often miss many of their children's extracurricular activities, which often take place during this time period (Presser 2006; Root and Wooten 2008). Notably, not only are they likely to miss the events themselves but they are correspondingly likely to miss opportunities to share their children's emotions immediately before and after the event. As a result, parents and children may feel less connected to each other and the quality of their relationship may decline. Lastly, when parents work different shifts, children may experience various mental and emotional issues. Some studies have shown that when parents work shifts, children are more likely to have poorer cognitive stimulation and increased odds of suffering from behavioral and emotional issues (Albertsen et al. 2008). However, although shiftwork may have a negative influence on children in the short term, a longitudinal study by White and Keith (1990) suggests that shiftwork may decrease child-related problems over time.

Beyond marital and parental roles, shiftwork can also have a major impact on the family dynamic as a whole. For instance, La Valle et al. (2002) found that when family members worked nonstandard shifts they had less time to spend together sharing evening meals, family holidays, and other family activities. These activities are similar to team-building in that they help to build and reinforce a sense of unity and togetherness (Presser 2006). Also, other negative implications of shiftwork on the employee (e.g., energy depletion, lack of quality and/or duration of sleep, moodiness) are likely to spillover to negatively affect the overall family dynamic. Such considerations have been supported by Grosswald (2003), who found that employees working nonstandard shifts tend to be less satisfied with their family lives than are employees working standard shifts.

Finally, while a step removed from family relationships, an employee's general social life and nonfamilial relationships are also likely to be compromised by shiftwork. That is, such an atypical work schedule is likely to present a challenge for employees in trying to find a common time to commiserate with friends, the majority of whom are statistically likely to work more standard schedules. As such, the shift worker's ability to participate in various social activities is threatened, therefore limiting time spent with friends and, often consequently, serving as detrimental to both the number and the quality of friendships. For instance, working nonstandard hours may make it more difficult for individuals to attend important life events such as weddings, baby showers, funerals, graduations, and the like (Fenwick and Tausig 2001). As a result, shift workers may experience compromised satisfaction with their social relationships in general, both within as well as outside of the nuclear family.

13.1.3.2 Shiftwork and the Experience of Work

Although shiftwork can have a major impact on an employee's familial and other social relationships, it can also have a major impact on the employee's day-to-day experience at work. For instance, such employees may have difficulty utilizing standard work–family policies or benefits, as they are typically framed with the traditional worker in mind. Furthermore, nonstandard schedules have been linked to decreased job satisfaction (Barthe et al. 2011) as well as to increased job-related burnout (Estryn-Béhar and Van der Heijden 2012). Moreover, those working rotating shifts may continually work with different people depending on the shift, which may prevent them from developing strong relationships at work and may impact their perceived (and actual) levels of coworker support, particularly during times of need or change, thereby negatively affecting the degree to which their needs for relatedness and affiliation are satisfied. Moreover, employees working the late night or "graveyard" shift, even on a consistent basis, may experience little customer interaction, again negatively affecting the satisfaction of their relatedness need in the workplace context.

Linked to this idea of the quality of employees' experiences at work is shiftwork's possible impact on absenteeism, although the research has been mixed in this regard depending on shift type. For instance, Colligan et al. (1979) found that nurses who worked the night shift took more sick leaves than those who worked afternoon shifts. Similarly, Sergean and Brierly (1968) found that British metal processers working the night shift were more likely to get sick than those working day and afternoon shifts. In contrast, Thiis-Evensen (1958), while dated, performed a longitudinal study of Danish employees over a 10-year period and found that fixed day shift workers were absent from work more frequently than those who worked in nonstandard hours. Other studies have found that while employees with rotating schedules get sick more often and develop more serious health problems, they generally take fewer sick leaves than those who work in fixed shifts, regardless of whether those shifts are day or night (Colligan et al. 1979; Costa 1996).

13.1.3.3 Shiftwork and Health

As implied above, shiftwork can impact the quality of employees' lives through its negative impact on both physical and mental health (Estryn-Béhar and Van der Heijden 2012; Fenwick and Tausig 2001; Wittmer and Martin 2010). Perhaps most obviously is shiftwork's detrimental impact on sleep. Indeed, major health issues can occur as a result of the employee sleeping during the day or on a variable schedule (Costa 1996; Fenwick and Tausig 2001). Evolutionarily, it is often suggested (e.g., Costa 1996) that humans have historically been conditioned to sleep during the nighttime (e.g., hunting was harder during darkness) and be awake during the daytime (e.g., without manufactured light, the natural light of daytime provided more opportunities for hunting, gathering, social interaction, etc.). Further, when we sleep at irregular times, we disrupt the production of melatonin, the hormone that regulates sleep cycles and strengthens the immune system. Consequently, when we force ourselves to sleep at such times, we do not sleep as long or as soundly (Costa 1996). Indeed, Øyane et al. (2013) found nighttime shift workers to be significantly more likely to suffer both insomnia and fatigue than employees working in traditional shifts, a finding also suggested by Estryn-Béhar and Van der Heijden

(2012). In addition, sleeping during the daytime is subject to more disturbances from typical daytime noises (e.g., telephone, doorbell, traffic, household noises, etc; Costa 1996). To compound these sleep problems, it is not unusual for shift workers to purposefully deprive themselves of sleep in order to spend more time with others who are normally awake during daytime hours (Presser 2006). Furthermore, when workers sleep at irregular or inconsistent times, they disturb their circadian rhythms and this can have many negative effects on their bodies (Albertsen et al. 2008; Costa 1996; Fenwick and Tausig 2001), a problem particularly relevant for employees working in biologically-insensitive shift rotation schemes. Some of the sleep-related symptoms that employees may suffer from working in these types of schedules include fatigue, insomnia, lethargy, poorer agility, decreased reaction time, and compromised productivity, performance, and safety-related behaviors (Costa 1996; Fenwick and Tausig 2001; Lindsey 2007; Pierce and Dunham 1992).

Beyond the sleep challenges that are perhaps the most obvious physical symptom associated with shiftwork, employees with nonstandard work hours may also experience gastrointestinal disorders resulting from variable eating habits and their bodies' difficulties adjusting to that inconsistency (Bambra et al. 2008; Costa 1996; Fenwick and Tausig 2001). Shift workers may have to eat in a hurry or away from home, and unless they plan and prepare healthy meals ahead of time, the types of food available at later hours is often of lower quality (e.g. fast food) (Costa 1996). These gastrointestinal challenges may be particularly pertinent for employees with rotating shifts, as Wyatt and Marriot (1953) found, with results indicating that both appetite and digestion were greatly disrupted when employees changed shifts from days to nights and vice versa (Colligan et al. 1979).

Another major health issue that employees working nonstandard schedules may experience is cardiovascular disorders, including heart attacks (Wilson 2002). In fact, Fenwick and Tausig (2001) found that the likelihood of coronary heart disease increased more than 200 % after 6 years of working a rotating night shift. It is thought that one of the reasons for this is the increased stress that shiftwork often causes (Lewis 2009; Williams 1999, 2010). That is, shiftwork—particularly rotating shifts—may make it difficult for employees to plan ahead from week to week, resulting in undue stress linked to perceived inability to successfully manage typical mundane chores and plans. For instance, an employee may experience increased stress if he or she schedules a doctor's appointment 6 months in advance only to find out that he or she is unable to keep the appointment due to work conflicts—a not uncommon situation that is further complicated by appointment cancellation fees as well as by the difficulty in trying to reschedule appointments with limited notice. This serves as only one example of why shiftwork can lead to increased stress, and others can be found throughout this chapter, in particular throughout the discussion of work–family challenges in particular.

Moreover, research has further suggested that shift workers are also likely to be at an increased risk for other physical health issues, although the evidence for these is less conclusive. For instance, a study by the World Health Organization (2007) found that an increased incidence of cancer might be linked to night shift work, and Fenwick and Tausig (2001) suggested that the same may be true for diabetes, elevated levels of uric acid, and high cholesterol. Most recently, Zhang et al. (2014) found that extended or inconsistent wakefulness may even lead to brain damage, as was evident in their study that subjected rats to inconsistent sleep schedules mirroring those of shift workers. Specifically, even after periods of recovery sleep, cognitive functioning and alertness remained compromised on a long-term basis, indicating damage to the area of the brain responsible for these functions—the locus coeruleus—via neuron loss that persists over time and, Zhang et al suggested, is likely irreversible. While this recent research obviously needs to be replicated with humans for more generalizable findings, Zhang et al.'s initial findings suggest that the overall health effects of shiftwork could be even more detrimental than previously believed.

13.2 Shiftwork and Gender

The literature presents some mixed results in regard to the proportions of men and women participating in shiftwork. According to Beers (2000) and Presser (2003), men are more likely to work in nonstandard shifts than women because the former generally choose occupations where shiftwork is found more frequently. Beers further notes that men are more likely to work nonstandard shifts than women, even when members of both sexes are working the same job type. In contrast, Tuttle and Garr (2012) more recently noted that shiftwork has risen in lower-paying service sector jobs that tend to be female-dominated, thereby yielding more shiftwork to women. Overall, however, the majority of the literature supports the notion that shiftwork tends to remain dominated by males, even if the pendulum is beginning to shift slightly to decrease that gap.

One of the major ways that men and women may differ in regard to shiftwork is the type of shift each gender is more likely to perform. Although in general, men are slightly more likely to work in nonstandard hours than women (Presser 2006), Estryn-Béhar and Van der Heijden (2012) found that female nurses generally work extended shifts more so than do men, while slightly more male nurses worked overtime than did female nurses. Other research (Presser 2006) has found that higher proportions of men work rotating hours and fixed nights schedules than women. Moreover, although few employees, regardless of gender, work exclusively weekend shifts, men are more likely than women to work weekend hours in addition to their weekly shifts. Women, on the other hand, are more likely to work only weekdays but less than 5 days a week. Barthe et al. (2011) found that all women with heavier responsibilities reported childcare being a major reason for their choice of shift, with two-thirds of women choosing their shift to accommodate familial responsibilities and homecare duties.

Men and women may also differ in their perceptions of gendered shiftwork. Marsh (1979) found some interesting results in how women and men view shiftwork and how others view them doing shiftwork; women were generally not in favor of working in the more committed types of shiftwork such as double-day shifts or weekend work. One of the reasons they tended to reject the notion of shiftwork is that they felt their lives were too complicated already and shiftwork would only make them more complicated and less manageable. In regard to how others view women working in nonstandard hours, Marsh noted that a majority of respondents in the study generally believed that women should have the opportunity to work evening shifts and overtime, especially if they are single. However, interestingly, a large majority of respondents believed that married women should not work night shifts, while a majority of male respondents saw no problem with working nonstandard schedules. Overall, Marsh noted, respondents indicated that male employees in particular should work as much as they desired, and that any issues arising from that decision are simply problems to be resolved within their respective families.

13.3 Gender and Work–Family Conflict

Despite growing similarities, there remain some important distinctions between how men and women may experience work–family tensions. For instance, women may arguably experience more work–family conflict as a result of their increased participation in the paid workforce. That is, there is reason to believe that in the past, when women spent most of their time solely looking after household and family responsibilities, they had fewer time constraints in accomplishing those duties. However, once women started to enter the paid workforce at increasing rates, they acquired extra work responsibilities in addition to their existing familial and household responsibilities. Compounding this problem is the consideration that despite women's increasing involvement in the paid work sphere, and despite men's increase in household involvement, the two have not increased at the same rate, with women still bearing the burden of the majority of the housework (Lewis 2009). This has kept women's workload in the family sphere at a very high level despite the additional burden of external employment, thereby increasing the likelihood and severity of felt work–family conflict.

Although research suggests that women tend to experience high levels of work–family conflict, there is also a research to suggest that men are also experiencing such conflict at increasing rates. Gerson (2009) reported that the amount of work–family conflict that men experience has risen by over 10 % since 1977, and when considering only men in dual-earner relationships, this increases to over 25 %. Nevertheless, although men are experiencing high levels of work–family conflict, they are also likely to experience such conflict somewhat differently than do women. In the past, when work and family-care responsibilities were separated by gender, being able to provide economically for the family, or breadwinning, defined males' identity insofar as their familial role. However, as more women entered the workforce and as cultural values shifted, men started to place a higher stake on their involvement in the home sphere in addition to their preexisting provider role.

Indeed, Root and Wooten (2008) reported that fathers have gone from spending about 30 to 45 % as much time with their children as did mothers in the 1970s and 1980s to about 65 % as much time on the weekdays and 87 % as much time on the weekends in more recent years. Interestingly, Gottzén and Kremer-Sadlik (2012) suggested that many fathers may prefer to be involved in their children's lives in ways that are different than mothers. While mothers generally become involved in their children's lives through general childcare, many fathers may prefer to be involved with their children's youth sports. This allows fathers to become more involved with their family without performing traditionally feminine activities, therefore not compromising their stereotypically masculine identity. However it is worth noting, as Gottzén and Kremer-Sadlik (2012) did, that since many after-school activities such as sports tend to occur in the afternoon or early evening, work obligations may often prevent fathers from being able to attend their child's sporting events, thereby threatening fathers' ability to care for their children and elevating their work–family conflict. This is certainly a consideration relevant to the varied temporal requirements of shiftwork, in addition to speaking to the necessity of gender-blind work–family policies available to allow for diminished conflict.

13.3.1 The Threat of Career Penalties

One of the major factors contributing to gender differences in work–family conflict is workplace policies and procedures. Such policies, such as parental leave and flexible scheduling, are typically designed to allow employees more control over how they balance their work and family lives with the idea of reducing work–family conflict (Gerson 2009; Lewis 2009). However, instead of increasing balance, many times such policies may be ineffective because they are often associated with substantial career penalties. That is, when an employee has less of a presence at work (either physically, mentally, or both) they may appear less committed than other employees who are regularly seen by key organizational members, a physical benefit commonly referred to as 'face time.' Therefore, management may be less inclined to offer workplace benefits or career advancement opportunities—such as raises and promotions—to employees who are less visible within the organization. Gerson (2009) wrote that although all employees may be subject to these types of career penalties, women may be more likely to accept them—voluntarily or otherwise—for the sake of their family. Thus, women may experience lower levels of job satisfaction as a result of being less likely to reach their desired career goals. Furthermore, even though men may be less likely to accept career penalties, they may still experience substantial work–family conflict since they miss out on using flexible policies which would help them spend more time with their family and on other nonwork commitments.

13.3.2 The Influence of Gender Norms

Another major reason why these policies may be ineffective is that there are often strong tacit norms against men using these policies. Williams (2010) writes that there is a stigma attached to men who make known their involvement in family care. Men who take time off for family purposes risk being viewed by others in the workplace as lacking in commitment, they may be openly ridiculed, and their 'manliness' may even be questioned (Levine and Pittinsky 1997; Williams 2010). Men who take even short family leaves may be penalized with both fewer rewards and lower performance ratings, as noted above. In addition, fathers who opt to serve as stay-at-home parents for any period of time are often viewed more negatively than fathers who are employed outside of the home. As a result, men are less likely to acknowledge and speak out about their need for work–family accommodations. It has even been reported that men are more likely than women to be fired because they had major work-life conflicts and were reluctant to seek employer help in managing them (Williams 2010). To cope with their reluctance toward utilizing official work–family policies, men often use a combination of vacation and sick leave to meet family demands (Levine and Pittinsky 1997). However, such reluctance can also lead to women experiencing heightened work–family conflict, since the more time men feel compelled to spend at work, the less availability they have to assist with home- and childcare responsibilities.

13.4 Gender, Shiftwork, and Work–Family Conflict

Compounding the various aforementioned research indications warrants consideration of how shiftwork may differentially impact each gender's perceptions and/or reality of work–family conflict. Indeed, there is evidence to suggest that there may be differential effects of work–family conflict for individuals working nonstandard schedules depending on gender.

13.4.1 Women, Shiftwork, and Work–Family Conflict

Several studies suggest that women who work nonstandard shifts experience greater work–family conflict than do men working such shifts (Fenwick and Tausig 2001; Haines et al. 2008; Tuttle and Garr 2012). Likewise, supplemental evidence supports the consideration that mothers' time is more affected by nonstandard hours than is fathers' time (Barnes et al. 2006; Craig and Powell 2011). One potential reason for this differential sense of conflict rests upon the fact that women are generally expected to shoulder more of the family responsibilities, therefore the same work complication (e.g., shift) may cause greater conflict with home roles for women than for men (Fenwick and Tausig 2001; Presser 2003). Furthermore, women are more likely to revolve their shift scheduling around their husband's shift, whereas the reverse is less likely (Presser 2003). Therefore, more women may get 'stuck' working shifts that they might perceive as conflicting with their family life because they have adopted such shifts based upon their husband's work schedule as opposed to their own preference.

In comparison to men, women may also experience greater health problems when they work nonstandard hours. Costa (1996) noted that women may experience greater stress due to time pressures that occur when they work at irregular times. Also, when women who are married and have children work nonstandard hours, they generally experience poorer quality sleep and more fatigue than do men (Costa 1996). Lastly, numerous studies have reported that problems of the female reproductive system—including increased menstrual cycle problems and miscarriages—can also be exacerbated by working nonstandard shifts (Axelsson et al. 1989; Barthe et al. 2011; Costa 1996).

However, although research suggests that women who work nonstandard hours generally experience higher work–family conflict than men working such shifts, when in the right situation, women may also experience greater work–family benefits. For example, Scheller (2011) noted that a bus driving profession allowed mothers to be home with their children at the times when their children needed them the most. However, this too rests primarily on the assumption that women may inherently feel (or be societally expected to feel) more responsibility to the home- and childcare domains of family life than do men, which is certainly a broad statement that fails to consider individual differences and other such contextual considerations.

13.4.2 Men, Shiftwork, and Work–Family Conflict

Although women may be experiencing greater work–family conflict than men as a result of working nonstandard schedules, men working such shifts may nonetheless experience relatively high levels of conflict. Perhaps one of the reasons it is reported that women experience higher levels of work–family conflict is that women are often more vocal about the conflicts they are experiencing, and those conflicts are more societally accepted from a woman than from a man. In fact, when Levine and Pittinsky (1997) interviewed men about their work and family conflicts, they found that men were experiencing more conflict than people thought but were reluctant to speak about it. One of the forces pressuring men to be more private and reserved about their work–family issues might be the negative, informal repercussions discussed earlier from using organizational policies to improve work–family balance.

Regardless of how open men are about their work–family issues, one of the reasons that they experience high levels of work–family conflict when working in nonstandard schedules is that many have expanding parenting responsibilities and these responsibilities may be more difficult to handle with a nonstandard work schedule. For instance, it was mentioned earlier that men often experience work–family conflict as a result of not being able to be involved in their children's lives to the extent that they would like. Since many fathers may prefer to be involved in their children's lives through their extracurricular activities, which often occur in the late afternoon or early evening, they may experience increased work–family conflict when they are assigned a shift during this time period. Moreover, men's responsibilities within the home are broadening as compared to past decades, so this alone is likely to yield such conflict, which is then exacerbated by the lack of societal acceptance of such responsibilities.

13.5 Recommendations for Improving Work–Family Balance for Shift Workers

13.5.1 Methods of Improvement

In summary, both men and women are likely to experience heightened work–family conflict as a result of working nonstandard shifts. However, there are some administratively controllable methods by which organizations can facilitate a reduction in such conflict for their employees. In particular, increasing the amount of flexibility and control that employees have over their hours, ensuring workers receive the support they need, and developing policies to support those who work nonstandard hours are all effective steps that organizations can take toward facilitating employees' improved work–family balance in the face of shiftwork.

13.5.2 Flexible Work Hours

One of the ways that organizations can help both men and women working nonstandard hours to improve their work-life balance is by offering them greater flexibility over when and how they perform their shifts. Both Levine and Pittinsky (1997) and more recently Gerson (2009) have suggested that allowing employees greater flexibility over their work hours may be an effective strategy for reducing work–family conflict. In fact, Williams (1999) noted that flexible work policies were some of the most preferred workplace benefits. There is also some evidence that mothers who have flexible work hours are significantly less likely to voluntarily turnover from their jobs. Lastly, Gerson (2009) suggests that flexibility is absolutely essential with nonstandard shifts because it helps families overcome interpersonal and economic uncertainties. Vila et al. (2002) discussed the importance of employee involvement in shift scheduling in relation to law enforcement officers in particular, a highly male-dominated shiftwork position. Vila et al. determined that excluding officers from scheduling and shift assignment decisions can trigger a vicious cycle that contributes toward employees' feelings of powerlessness in some of the most important aspects of their lives, as well as exacerbating the various other effects discussed herein, including fatigue, stress, and performance decrements.

Regardless of the extent to which employees are involved in scheduling decisions, if some flexibility is offered in work hours, employees can alternatively have control over how they utilize such options. Although some nonstandard shifts involve either fixed or rotating hours in the evening or at night, the employees may be allowed to use flexibility in order to vary their start and end times by an hour or two (Lewis 2009; Williams 1999). This may be especially helpful to those working in nonstandard shifts as it may allow them to take care of an errand, attend an event, or care for another when needed. Another way in which employees can utilize flexibility in their nonstandard hours is by telecommuting, which allows them to perform some or all of their work at home, although such an option is highly job-dependent. Some employees may alternately prefer to use flexibility to compress their work schedules, whereby they work for only 3 or 4 days a week but for longer-than-usual hours. Job sharing is another flexible work method whereby two part-time employees split the hours and the responsibilities of one full-time job. It is recommended that, to the extent possible, organizations allow employees one or more of these flexibility options to tailor to their needs, which will inevitably vary both within-person (over time), as well as between-person (wherein different employees will have different flexibility needs).

Although shiftwork may be viewed by some as a flexible work option in itself, the flexibility we are suggesting here is different in that it allows for some degree of employee control over the work demands, thereby reducing the sense of helplessness that can often exacerbate work–family conflict (Barthe et al. 2011; Fenwick and Tausig 2001; Gerson 2009). In fact, Lewis (2009) proposes that flexibility is only beneficial for nonstandard shift workers when the employee has some level of control over their hours. This is because employees who work in nonstandard shifts are often assigned to their shifts on short notice, therefore inhibiting the ability to attend preplanned appointments and events without using vacation time to do so. Thereby, having more control may be instrumental in helping parents who work in nonstandard shifts to be more consistently involved in their children's lives (Levine and Pittinsky 1997). For example, if a father who works a fixed, late afternoon shift can adjust his hours, he will have more ability to attend his child's extracurricular activity when his attendance is most desired (e.g., a game, recital, etc.). In addition, having more control over the scheduling of their nonstandard shift may help to reduce the anxiety that both mothers and fathers may feel over getting their child to and from daycare or other commitments (Levine and Pittinsky 1997). Having control over work hours would also help parents who opt not to use daycare: As Lewis (2009) notes, this is particularly likely to be the case for parents who are unable to afford the sharply rising and extremely high cost of full-time (or even part-time) daycare, an issue often pertinent to shift workers since nontraditional shifts tend to be more prevalent in lower-paying jobs.

As one might imagine, there exist differing viewpoints about how providing employees with flexibility options may differentially affect men versus women. Williams (1999) noted that there is evidence of flexibility options being utilized more by female employees than by male employees. Specifically, she suggests that because women may request flexibility more so than do men, flexible hours may reinforce the negative stereotype of women and caregiving. This stereotype may in turn make it more difficult for women to achieve work success if they are utilizing such flexibility options. In addition, Perrons et al. (2006) noted that flexible scheduling allows women to be able to better manage work and family responsibilities since they are the ones using the policies. However, this does not necessarily result in improved work–family balance for women because the responsibilities are not necessarily being shared with their spouses. Therefore, women are left with the same extent of nonwork responsibilities, they just have more control over when they can attend to them. In opposition to the idea that men do not make use of flexibility over their work hours when available, Levine and Pittinsky (1997) suggest that men may be more likely to use flexible schedules than other types of accommodations because such flexibility does not necessarily compromise family income, as opposed to other policies such as paternity leaves, which typically go unpaid. A third opinion suggests that giving both male and female employees the ability to have more flexible work schedules will allow them to coordinate their schedules so that they can better share household responsibilities. As a result, we firmly suggest that if increased schedule control is offered to employees, efforts must be made not only to make such policies available to both men and women, but also to encourage their usage equally amongst employees of both sexes.

Although organizations may view incorporating flexibility into shift workers' schedules with some skepticism as to its effects on organizational outcomes, there is some evidence to suggest that organizations may actually benefit from doing so (Lewis 2009; Williams 1999). Specifically, this added flexibility can allow employers to operate for longer hours without having to hire additional employees. For instance, if employees vary their start and/or end times by a few hours outside of normal business hours, it allows the organization to stay open longer without having to create new shifts, staffed by additional employees, to operate those hours. Lastly—but perhaps most importantly for long-term organizational success—flexibility (and its perceived usability) has been found to facilitate employee loyalty and commitment, as well as to enhance safety-related behaviors (via decreased fatigue and increased cognitive alertness) and overall performance (Eaton 2003; Kelliher and Anderson 2010; Ng et al. 2006).

13.5.3 Support of Employees

Another way that organizations can help shift workers to improve their work–family balance is by fostering an environment in which they are highly supported. Supportive environments can help employees because they can provide them with extra resources such as someone to cover a shift, help with extra work, or comfort them emotionally. These extra resources may compensate for those lost in working a nonstandard shift. Estryn-Béhar and Van der Heijden (2012) suggest that one of the ways that organizations can improve the support they offer to employees is to organize work schedules in a way that allows for social support from employees with similar familial responsibilities. A more revolutionary way that organizations can develop a more supportive environment is by fostering informal caretaking networks in which other employees can help each other with childcare responsibilities. These networks may allow employees who have different shifts to cover some childcare activities at times when other employees are working (Gerson 2009). Yet another strategy that organizations can employ to be supportive of employees' childcare needs is to provide on-site childcare which operates 24/7 so that employees working at all hours of the day are provided with a legitimate childcare option (Barthe et al. 2011).

On a much broader scale, organizations can also help to foster informal coworker support networks. As noted by Root and Wooten (2008), coworkers can serve as an extended kinship network to help provide each other with emotional support and instrumental assistance in coping with work responsibilities and family needs. For instance, coworkers can help to accomplish certain tasks when one employee needs to leave early to take care of a family responsibility. Of course, this type of support would have to be developed with reciprocity in mind so that employees do not take advantage of each other or create unnecessary interpersonal conflict within the organization.

A third type of support that organizations can foster is supervisor support, increasingly recognized in the literature as family-supportive supervisor behaviors (FSSB). Supervisors have a substantial influence over their subordinates in that they often serve as a gatekeeper to effective work–family management. Supervisors may choose to be extremely accommodating to an employee's desire for flexibility, or they can be very restrictive. As such, a lack of supervisor support can effectively render the aforementioned coworker support systems inoperable if they refuse to facilitate or allow for such work modifications. In addition to gatekeeping responsibilities, supervisors can also serve as an important source of emotional support for employees. As a result, organizations can foster supportive environments (and perceptions) a great deal though their supervisors, who serve as the 'front-line' contact for employees to organizational culture and policy.

There is some evidence to suggest that providing support as a work–family improvement may have differential effects dependent upon employee gender. For instance, some research has suggested that women may experience greater benefits from social and emotional support than men (Forbes and Roger 1999; van der Pompe and Heus 1993). However, other research has suggested that while women may receive more social support from nonwork sources than do men, they may not necessarily obtain more support from work sources (van der Pompe and Heus 1993). Hopkins (2002) suggested that a reason for this is that both men and women tend to have male supervisors, possibly leading female employees to feel less comfortable confiding in them than would male employees, who may enjoy more of a gender-fueled camaraderie, although this is certainly arguable. As a result, organizations would do well to consider gender in establishing and bolstering their social support programs so that both male and female employees are more likely to reap the benefits equally.

13.5.4 Strengthening Improvements Through Policies

Regardless of how organizations decide to facilitate work–family balance for employees working nonstandard shifts, it is imperative that they ground such improvements within formal organizational policies. Such formal policies facilitate employees' understanding of organizational culture and accepted accommodations. However, policies alone are grossly insufficient. As seen throughout this chapter, both men and women are often reluctant to utilize organizational policies in support of work–family balance for fear of negative perceptions and/or career implications. Therefore, it is crucial that any formal organizational policies be supported by upper management, that such support is evidenced through the trickle-down effect to middle- and lower-level managers who reinforce such a culture, and that employees are freely given the necessary information and encouragement to utilize such policies when necessary.

One of the most effective ways to assure employees of a supportive culture beyond formal policies is likely to be through the aforementioned FSSBs. Comprised of four different dimensions - emotional support, role modeling, instrumental support, and creative work–family management (Hammer et al. 2013) - FSSBs are expected to positively impact employees of both genders insofar as their comfort level in using work–family policies when they are available. In addition, FSSB has been shown to have a variety of positive effects on work–family outcomes, thereby enhancing the likelihood that such accommodations would enhance employees' work–family balance (Hammer et al. 2011; Odle-Dusseau et al. 2012).

13.6 Conclusion

In sum, the intersection between gender and the work–family domains, while intriguing, is widely complex, with a variety of supplemental issues affecting how the interplay between these domains presents itself in a variety of situations and contexts. Insofar as work structures go, the presence or absence—and the extent—of shiftwork for males versus females is one such contextual factor. This chapter has explored the various considerations underlying shiftwork's influence in this regard, with a hope toward sparking more extensive applied considerations of this work constraint and how it can best be managed in order to facilitate a more fulfilling experience of work–family balance for both male and female employees alike.

References

Akanni, A. (2011). *Shiftwork, job satisfaction and family life: An empirical study among nurses in Osun State Nigeria*. Lambert: Academic.

Albertsen, K., Rafnsdóttir, G., Grimsmo, A., Tómas-son, K., & Kauppinen, K. (2008). Workhours and worklife balance. *SJWEH Supplements, 5*, 14–21.

Axelsson, G., Rylander, R., & Molin, I. (1989). Outcome of pregnancy in relation to irregular and incovenient work schedules. *British Journal of Industrial Medicine, 46,* 393–398.
Bambra, C., Whitehead, M., Sowden, A., Akers, J., & Petticrew, M. (2008). A hard day's night? The effects of compressed working week interventions on the health and worklife balance of shift workers: A systematic review. *Journal of Epidemiology & Community Health, 62,* 764–777.
Barnes, M., Bryson, C., & Smith R. (2006). Working atypical hours: What happens to family life? London: National Centre for Social Research.
Barthe, B., Messing, K., & Abbas, L. (2011). Strategies used by women workers to reconcile family responsibilities with atypical work schedules in the service sector. *Work, 40,* S47–S58.
Beers, T. M. (2000). Flexible schedules and shift work: replacing the '9-to-5' workday? *Monthly Labor Review, 123,* 33–40.
Colligan, M. J., Frockt, J. I., & Tasto, D. L. (1979). Frequency of sickness absence and worksite clinic visits among nurses as a function of shift. *Applied Ergonomics, 10,* 79–85.
Costa, G. (1996). The impact of shift and night work on health. *Applied Ergonomics, 27,* 9–16.
Craig, L., & Powell, A. (2011). Non-standard work schedules, work–family balance and the gendered division of childcare. *Work Employment Society, 25,* 274–291.
Eaton, S. C. (2003). If you can use them: Flexibility policies, organizational commitment, and perceived performance. *Industrial Relations: A Journal of Economy & Society, 42,* 145–167.
Estryn-Béhar, M., & Van der Heijden, B. M. (2012). Effects of extended work shifts on employee fatigue, health, satisfaction, work/family balance, and patient safety. *Work, 41,* 4283–4290.
Fenwick, R., & Tausig, M. (2001). Scheduling stress: Family and health outcomes of shift work and schedule control. *American Behavioral Scientist, 44,* 1179–1198.
Forbes, A., & Roger, D. (1999). Stress, social support and fear. *British Journal of Health Psychology, 4,* 165–180.
Gerson, K. (2009). *The unfinished revolution: Coming of age in a new era of gender, work, and family.* New York: Oxford University Press.
Gottzén, L., & Kremer-Sadlik, T. (2012). Fatherhood and youth sports: A balancing act between care and expectations. *Gender & Society, 26,* 639–664.
Grosswald, B. (2003). Shift work and negative work-to-family spillover. *Journal of Sociology and Social Welfare, 4,* 31–56.
Haines, V. Y., Marchand, A., Rousseau, V., & Demers, A. (2008). The mediating role of work-to-family conflict in the relationship between. *Work & Stress, 22,* 341–356.
Hammer, L. B., Kossek, E. E., Anger, W. K., Bodner, T., & Zimmerman, K. L. (2011). Clarifying work–family intervention processes: The roles of work–family conflict and family-supportive supervisor behaviors. *Journal of Applied Psychology, 96,* 134–150.
Hammer, L. B., Kossek, E. E., Bodner, T., & Crain, T. (2013). Measurement development and validation of the family supportive supervisor behavior short-form (FSSB-SF). *Journal of Occupational Health Psychology, 18,* 285–296.
Hopkins, K. M. (2002). Interactions of gender and race in workers' help seeking for personal/family problems: Perceptions of supervisor support and intervention. *Journal of Applied Behavioral Science, 38,* 156–176.
Kelliher, C., & Anderson, D. (2010). Doing more with less? Flexible working practices and the intensification of work. *Human Relations, 63,* 83–106.
La Valle, I., Arthur, S., Millward, C., Scott, J., & Clayden, M. (2002). *Happy families? Atypical work and its influence on family life.* Bristol: Policy Press
Levine, J. A., & Pittinsky, T. L. (1997). *Working fathers: New strategies for balancing work and family.* Reading: Addison-Wesley.
Lewis, J. (2009). *Work-family balance, gender and policy.* Northampton: Edward Elgar.
Lindsey, D. (2007). Police fatigue. *FBI Law Enforcement Bulletin, 76,* 1–8.
Liu, H., Wang, Q., Keesler, V., & Schneider, B. (2011). Non-standard work schedules, work–family conflict and parental. *Social Science Research, 40,* 473–484.
Marsh, A. (1979). Women and shiftwork: The protective legislation survey carried out for the Equal Opportunities Commission. Office of Population Censuses and Surveys: Social Survey Division.

Ng, T. H., Butts, M. M., Vandenberg, R. J., DeJoy, D. M., & Wilson, M. G. (2006). Effects of management communication, opportunity for learning, and work schedule flexibility on organizational commitment. *Journal of Vocational Behavior, 68,* 474–489.

Øyane, N. M. F., Pallesen, S., Moen, B. E., Åkerstedt, T., & Bjorvatn, B. (2013). Associations between night work and anxiety, depression, insomnia, sleepiness and fatigue in a sample of Norwegian nurses. *PLoS ONE, 8 (8), 1–7.*

Odle-Dusseau, H. N., Britt, T. W., & Greene-Shortridge, T. M. (2012). Organizational work–family resources as predictors of job performance and attitudes: The process of work–family conflict and enrichment. *Journal of Occupational Health Psychology, 17,* 28–40.

Perrons, D., Fagan, C., McDowell, L., Ray, K., & Ward, K. (2006). *Gender divisions and working time in the new economy: Changing patterns of work, care, and public policy in Europe and North America.* Northampton: Edward Elgar.

Perrucci, R., MacDermid, S., King, E., Tang, C., Brimeyer, T., Ramadoss, K., et al. (2007). The significance of shift work: Current status and future directions. *Journal of Family and Economic Issues, 28(4),* 600–617. doi:10.1007/s10834-007-9078-3.

Pierce, J. L., & Dunham, R. B. (1992). The 12-hour work day: A 48-hour, eight-day week. *Academy of Management Journal, 35,* 1086–1098.

Presser, H. B. (2003). Race-ethnic and gender differences in nonstandard work shifts. *Work and Occupations, 30,* 412–439.

Presser, H. B. (2006). Employment in a 24/7 economy: challenges for the family. In Perrons, D., Fagan, C., McDowell, L., Ray, K., & Ward, K. (Eds.)*Gender divisions and working time in the new economy: Changing patterns of work, care, and public policy in Europe and North America.* (pp. 35–57). Cheltenham, UK: Edward Elgar Publishing.

Rapoport, R., Bailyn, L., Fletcher, J. K., & Pruitt, B. H. (2002). *Beyond work–family balance: Advancing gender equity and workplace performance.* San Francisco: Jossey-Bass.

Root, L. S., & Wooten, L. P. (2008). Time out for family: Shift work, fathers, and sports. *Human Resource Management, 47,* 481–499.

Scheller, L. (2011). How important is the liaison between professional work and family work? The case of women bus drivers. *Work, 40,* S5–S14.

Sergean, R., & Brierly, J. (1968). Absence and attendance under non-continuous three-shift systems of work. *Nature, 219,* 536.

Staines, G. L., & Pleck, J. H. (1984). Nonstandard work schedules and family life. *Journal of Applied Psychology, 69,* 515–523.

Thiis-Evensen, E. (1958). Shift work and health. *Industrial Medicine and Surgery, 27,* 493–497.

Tuttle, R., & Garr, M. (2012). Shift work and work to family fit: Does schedule control matter? *Journal of Family and Economic Issues, 33,* 261–271.

van der Pompe, G., & de Heus, P. (1993). Work stress, social support, and strains among male and female managers. *Anxiety, Stress & Coping: An International Journal, 6,* 215–229.

Vila, B., Morrisson, G. B., & Kenney, D. J. (2002). Improving shift schedule and work-hour policies and practices to increase police officer performance, health, and safety. *Police Quarterly, 5,* 4–23.

White, L., & Keith, B. (1990). The effect of shift work on the quality and stability of marital relations. *Journal of Marriage and the Family, 52,* 453–462.

Williams, J. (1999). *Unbending gender: Why family and work conflict and what to do about it.* New York: Oxford University Press.

Williams, J. (2010). *Reshaping the work–family debate: Why men and class matter.* Cambridge: Harvard University Press.

Willis, T. A., O'Connor, D. B., & Smith, L. (2008). Investigating effort-reward imbalance and work–family conflict in relation to morningness-eveningness and shift work. *Work & Stress, 22,* 125–137.

Wilson, J. L. (2002). The impact of shift patterns on healthcare professionals. *Journal of Nursing Management, 10,* 211–219.

Wittmer, J. L., & Martin, J. E. (2010). Emotional exhaustion among employees without social or client contact: The key role of nonstandard work schedules. *Journal of Business and Psychology, 25,* 607–623.

World Health Organization. (2007). Carcinogenicity of shift-work, painting, and fire-fighting. *The Lancet Oncology, 8,* 1065–1066.
Wyatt, S., & Marriott, R. (1953). Night work and shift changes. *British Journal of Industrial Medicine, 10,* 164–172.
Zhang, J., Zhu, Y., Zhan, G., Fenik, P., Panossian, L., Wang, M. M., et al. (2014). Extended wakefulness: Compromised metabolics in and degeneration of locus ceruleus neurons. *Journal of Neuroscience, 34,* 4418–4431.

Chapter 14
Gender Roles in a Masculine Occupation: Military Men and Women's Differential Negotiation of the Work–Family Interface

Ann H. Huffman, Satoris S. Culbertson, and Joseph Barbour

14.1 Introduction

Gender plays a key role in the attitudes and behaviors exhibited by individuals in both their work and family domains. Just as individuals can lie anywhere on a continuum from masculine to feminine, occupations can be similarly gender typed. For example, some occupations, such as construction, mining, and forestry, are often seen as highly masculine in nature, while others, such as nursing, early childhood education, and cosmetology are seen as highly feminine in nature, in part due to the sheer prevalence of men and women in the respective occupations. We argue that norms related to masculinity (vs. femininity) can influence one's self-selection into an occupation as well as one's work attitudes and behaviors once associated with an occupation. Since men and women associated with masculine occupations have unique work and family expectations, they also experience and negotiate the work–family interface differently than do individuals in more gender-neutral organizations.

In this chapter, we use the military as an example of a gendered (masculine) occupation. We provide a theoretical framework to guide an understanding of how the gender of employees in a gendered occupation can beget a unique set of work and family norms. We first provide a summary of the research on gendered occupations

A. H. Huffman (✉)
Department of Psychological Sciences and WA Franke College of Businesss, Northern Arizona University, P.O. Box 15106, Flagstaff, AZ 86011, USA
e-mail: ann.huffman@nau.edu

S. S. Culbertson
Department of Management, Kansas State University,
110 Calvin Hall, Manhattan, KS 66506, USA
e-mail: satoris@ksu.edu

J. Barbour
Department of Psychological Sciences, Northern Arizona University, 5 East McConnell Drive, P.O. Box 15106, Flagstaff, AZ 86011, USA
e-mail: jeb57@nau.edu

M. J. Mills (ed.), *Gender and the Work-Family Experience*,
DOI 10.1007/978-3-319-08891-4_14

and the work–family interface, followed by a theoretical overview of the proposed framework. We then provide a brief discussion of special populations (e.g., lesbian, gay, and bisexual [LGB] individuals) that may have diverse experiences within a gendered organization. Finally, we close with a section on application, emerging issues, and areas for future research.

14.2 Gendered Occupations

The term "Gendered Occupation" typically refers to an occupation that, for one reason or another, is comprised almost entirely of individuals of the same sex or individuals who self-identify as the same gender (Blackburn and Jarman 2006). Although gender (i.e., socially constructed) and sex (i.e., biological) are not synonymous in meaning or concept, a "gendered occupation" may be referring to either one depending on the specific context. An occupation might be considered gendered if it is comprised of a certain percentage of male or female employees, but it might also be considered gendered based on the degree of masculinity or femininity that society associates with it. Sex and gender are inevitably intertwined, and any attempt to completely tease them apart for the purposes of this chapter will surely prove futile. Because, however, the intent here is to eventually discuss work–family issues surrounding these gendered occupations, occupational segregation by sex (rather than gender) will be the primary focus. As such, "gendered occupations" in this chapter will be measured primarily by their percentage of biologically male and female employees.

Infantry soldiers in the United States military, for example, would certainly be considered an occupation segregated by sex, because women are not, as of now, permitted to hold this job, thus making the occupation 100% male[1]. Similarly, it would probably be safe to refer to medical transcriptionists as a gendered occupation, as 98% of the jobs are held by women (Bureau of Labor Statistics 2012). The case is slightly less clear, however, for many jobs. For example, detectives and criminal investigators are primarily male, with 75.2% of jobs held by men (Bureau of Labor Statistics 2012). This last example highlights the ambiguous lower limit for what might be considered a gendered occupation when measured by percent male and female. Currently, there does not seem to be a unanimously agreed-upon threshold for determining gendered occupations on the basis of sex prevalence.

14.2.1 *Gendered Occupations: Theoretical Perspectives*

Why is it that certain occupations are comprised almost entirely of one gender? Do men prefer different kinds of work than women? Do societal expectations for employment differ between the sexes? Do people, at some stage of development, learn that certain occupations are for men or women only (or primarily)? The following

[1] This exclusion of women in combat jobs is changing in 2016 with new Department of Defense policies that will allow women to hold combat positions.

section will address these and other questions by discussing some of the leading theories on why gendered occupations exist, and how they have changed over time.

Research investigating the potential sources of gendered occupations has focused heavily on gender role socialization and theories concerning learned social roles and norms (Aziz and Kamal 2012; DiDonato and Strough 2013; Feliciano and Rumbaut 2005; Jiang et al. 2010; Schuette et al. 2012; Vervecken et al. 2013; Wilbourn and Kee 2010; Wootton 1997). Nevertheless, there is certainly not a consensus on the issue. Multiple additional theories have been proposed that attempt to shed light on exactly why certain types of employment are so profoundly gendered; most notably, preference theory (Hakim 2000), social dominance theory (Sidanius and Pratto 1999), ascriptive inequality or biased hiring (Reskin 2003), professional role confidence and/or assessment of abilities (Cech et al. 2011), and workplace climate (i.e., certain workplaces seeming cold or unwelcoming toward either males or females; Sandler et al. 1996).

It is perhaps not surprising that such a large portion of the existing research and literature available on the subject is focused on gender role socialization. After all, from a very young age, males and females are treated differently by those around them, including parents, siblings, friends, and teachers. They are dressed differently, given different toys with which to play, introduced into different sports, and perhaps even spoken to differently (Thorne 1993). Moreover, children are capable, from a very early age, of picking up on the gender roles assumed by their parents. Children who observe their parents practicing an egalitarian division of labor are less likely to gravitate toward heavily gendered occupations than gender-neutral ones. Children who observe a more traditional and/or gendered division of labor are more likely to equate certain occupations and household duties with gender, and thus, choose their life course accordingly (Aziz and Kamal 2012). It is probably safe to state that the gender stereotypes to which a person is exposed, and the gender roles that they observe and assume in their youth, play a part in their vocational trajectory; the question is how much of a part do they play?

Along with children of all ages being exposed to certain stereotyped gender roles and expectations, many additional factors contribute to the segregation of occupations by sex. Preference theory (Hakim 2000) stresses, from a historical perspective, that women are faced with having to make very practical decisions regarding work and family, and that individual preference in those areas will largely determine the type and extent of work that a woman chooses to pursue. Social dominance theory (Sidanius and Pratto 1999), in this context, is referring to the notion that society at large is shaped by the gender stereotypes that we have created, and that subtle messages or wording in advertisements and job descriptions can be gender biased (Gaucher et al. 2011). Reskin's (2003) ascriptive inequality model posits that those in hiring positions within organizations may bias their decisions due to their own beliefs of performance and ability based on gender or the expectations of their profession.

Professional role confidence refers to the propensity of members of a particular gender to gravitate toward occupations in which they feel confident in their abilities to perform duties adequately (Cech et al. 2011). Historically, this source of occupational segregation by gender has been evident in the science, technology, engineering,

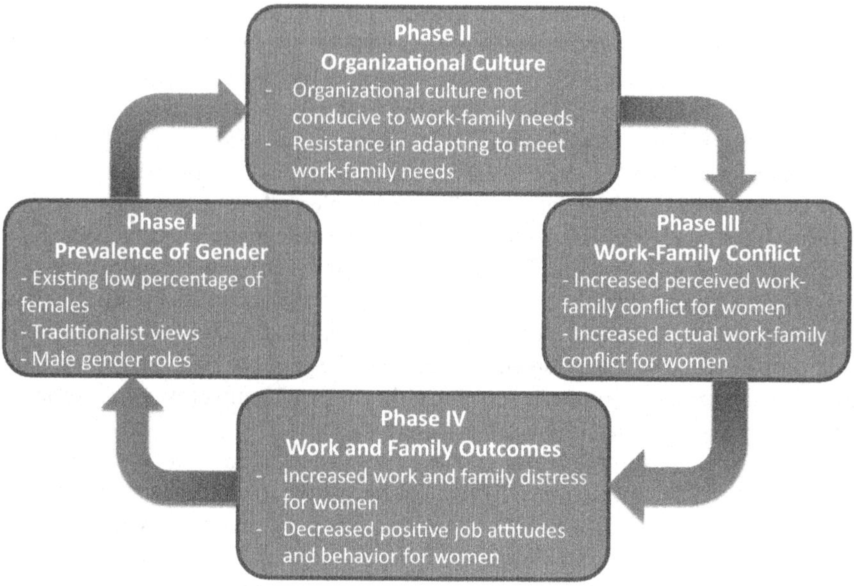

Fig. 14.1 Masculine occupations gender role model

and math (STEM) fields, where women have avoided employment largely based on their lack of confidence in their ability to perform in those jobs (Cech et al. 2011). Of course, any lack of confidence that they may have is at least in part the result of either gender role socialization or social dominance, not to mention the chilly climate experienced by women often associated with those traditionally male-held occupations. Development of an unwelcome or intolerant organizational climate, the last potential cause for gendered occupations that will be discussed here, refers to gendered segregation in occupations due a feeling on the part of one gender that they are unwelcome (Schneider et al. 2013). Each of these theories and possible explanations represent a piece to the puzzle that is occupational segregation by sex, and each must be considered when attempting to determine why a particular area of employment has evolved to become dominated by one sex or the other.

14.2.2 Masculine Occupations Gender Role Model

Now that the "what" and "why" of gendered occupations have been introduced, two new questions must be addressed: How do gendered occupational environments differentially affect the men and women who work in them, and how might these environments influence the work–family interface for women and men? In the following section we propose a comprehensive model to explain the gender disparity related to the work–family interface for occupations in which women represent the extreme minority. This Masculine Occupations Gender Role Model (see Fig. 14.1) provides an illustration of the cyclical nature of gender role influences within the masculine organization, beginning and ending with the high prevalence of men. This male prevalence not only affects organizational culture, but is also fueled by the consequences related to the organizational culture. The model suggests that certain, already existing, facets of masculine organizations combine to create a masculine culture. Further, the details of that culture encourage attitudes, beliefs, and experiences, such as perceived and actual work–family conflict, that are different for women than they are for men. Finally, these factors subsequently influence attitudes and behaviors such as organizational commitment, work performance, advancement, and retention. The Masculine Occupations Gender Role Model is explained in four distinct phases, and each is elaborated upon thoroughly in the following sections.

Phase I—Prevalence of Gender By definition, a masculine occupation is traditionally comprised of men. We propose two reasons why masculine organizations have a high prevalence of men, and are slow to change to more gender-neutral organizations. First, according to social role theory (Eagly 1987), men and women develop different skills, behaviors, and traits associated with their paid work roles. These skills, behaviors, and traits become the norm for the gender, and are adopted by society as indicative of what men and women are expected to do. These societal expectations perpetuate the presumptions that men play a more important role than women in masculine organizations. As such, men are more likely than women to join and stay with masculine organizations. Second, although change in gender prevalence is possible, change is slow due to the strength of attitudes that can affect organizational change. Attitudes toward social groups are key components in the development of discrimination (Fiske 1998; Glick and Fiske 2007). Whereas attitudes can indirectly influence group membership through factors such as an unsupportive supervisor, discrimination is an actual behavior (e.g., passing over for promotion, not allowing admittance to a specific job) that can directly affect the prevalence of a particular gender within a group. Unfortunately, "the power of gender stereotypes derives from their pervasiveness" (Eagly and Sczesny 2009, p. 24), with one of the most robust signaling cues for classification being simply whether someone is male or female.

The prevalence of one gender in an organization, of course, is not unique to a specific industry or occupation (Cabrera et al. 2009). In fact, noted researchers Carli and Eagly (1999) proposed that historical norms of women in domestic labor and men in paid work explain currently held gender stereotypes. The resulting consequence of this pattern of norms is gender typing, or the development of attitudes, behaviors, and interests that correspond to stereotypical masculine and feminine social roles (Liben and Bigler 2002). Gender typing is affected by both the prevalence of one particular gender in an occupation or job, and by the gender norms related to the tasks associated with the job (Lyness and Heilman 2006). Gender typing is the crux of gendered organizations, and can have effects on the minority sex through widespread organizational beliefs such as the organization's culture.

Phase II—Organizational Culture A high prevalence of men in an organization can create a general organizational culture not always conducive to the professional or personal needs and desires of female employees (and vice versa, although the focus here is on women en masse). According to Schein (1990), organizational culture is "(a) a pattern of basic assumptions, (b) invented, discovered, or developed by a given group, (c) as it learns to cope with its problems of external adaptation and internal integration, (d) that has worked well enough to be considered valid and, therefore (e) is to be taught to new members as the (f) correct way to perceive, think, and feel in relation to those problems" (p. 111). As evidenced by this definition, organizational culture encompasses all aspects of an organization and is a major influencer on organizational and employee behavior. The possibility should be noted that, because of the magnitude of effects of a majority male occupation, this culture is not one that is likely to adapt to make itself truly gender neutral, despite any expressed intentions to do so (Rothrauff et al. 2004). This is partly due to the fact that cultural beliefs are deeply ingrained (O'Reilly 1989), and therefore difficult to change (Haas and Hwang 2007).

Research has suggested that a high prevalence of one gender (in this case male) in an organization can affect the culture of the organization. Gender is a substructure of an organization's culture (Acker 1998), considered to be a foundational element of the organization's working structure. Research has shown that men and women value different qualities associated with an ideal organizational culture (Wicks and Bradshaw 1999), with women finding characteristics such as acceptance, emphasis on relationships, and cooperation as valued components of a healthy organizational culture. Conversely, men value objectivity, rationality, and problem-solving, and place less emphasis on friendliness and acceptance of authority in the workplace (Wicks and Bradshaw 1999). Based on social role theory (Eagly 1987), if people's views are not congruent with (fit) the organization's culture, then they are more likely to experience negative work outcomes. With conflicting values determining the culture, this is very likely the case for women in masculine organizations.

Phase III—Work–Family Conflict One negative work outcome that is common to employees is work–family conflict (Morgan and Milliken 1992). Work–family conflict is "a form of inter-role conflict in which the role pressures from work and family domains are mutually incompatible in some respect" (Greenhaus and Beutell 1985, p. 77). Work–family conflict is bidirectional, meaning that the work domain can interfere with the family domain and the family domain can interfere with the work domain (Greenhaus and Beutell 1985).

Haas and Hwang (2007) suggest that an organization's gendered substructure affects the degree to which an organization values the employee's family life, thus affecting the work–family interface. They introduce two related ideologies that help explain why organizational culture might affect fathers differentially than mothers. We put forth that this can be extended to understanding why organizational culture can be related to work–family conflict. The first ideology is the concept of *separate spheres*, which is based on the idea that work and family are two independent domains of influence. This assumption allows work organizations to run their businesses without concern for the role that organizations might have on the well-being of employees' families. Additionally, it devalues the skills and behaviors that are used in the family sphere, an area that is more likely to be filled by women. The second ideology is *masculine hegemony*, which is the idea that men should be in the primary position of power at work. Masculine hegemony helps to maintain the "maleness" in masculine organizations (Billing 2000), and sustains the ideas associated with the separate spheres ideology.

The existence of the ideologies of separate spheres and masculine hegemony manifests itself in the experiences of the minority sex, which can lead to work–family conflict. For example, because masculine organizations are less likely to adapt to meet female needs, women must make the choice of whether family or work will take priority in their lives. Some, of course, will choose work and some will choose family according to their individual needs and desires, and the result, inevitably, will be some degree of work–family conflict.

With regard to the work–family experiences for the minority gender in gendered occupations, there has been a fair amount of literature dedicated to the topic. The general consensus is that the minority gender will experience greater work–family conflict than their majority gender counterpart in their own workplace, and greater work–family conflict than they would if they worked in a gender-neutral setting (Cook and Minnotte 2008). With women in particular, striving for work–family balance in male-dominated professions is quite challenging, and can cause high attrition of the already few women in these jobs, as well as deter new women from seeking jobs within the organization (Glass and Estes 1997). Male-dominated professions are less likely to adjust their work schedules and expectation to fit the unique needs of females. This may be even more the case for women who are pregnant, nursing, or bearing the majority of the household labor burden, as male-dominated occupations have, over the years, demanded of their employees longer work hours and less time off, forcing women to either delay or forego childbearing in order to stay in their career, or leave for a more female-friendly work environment (Harris and Giuffre 2010). A particularly interesting and pertinent finding from Maume and Houston (2001) showed that longer work hours and tokenism (i.e., the perception that one is only present to fill a quota or represent some required or expected demographic criterion) for women in a male-dominated white collar profession were each positively associated with increased perceptions of work–family conflict.

Phase IV—Work and Family Outcomes One of the main concerns associated with work–family conflict is that it has been associated with many negative work and family outcomes (Allen et al. 2000). This relationship can be explained using the conservation of resources theory (Hobfoll 1989), which puts forth that "people strive to obtain, retain, foster and protect" (Hobfoll 2011, p. 117) those things in life that are valued most by them. These "resources," which can be personal, material, social, or energy resources, provide the foundation of support that both bolsters a person's positive affective state and sense of well-being and protects against negative psychological and health outcomes (Hobfoll 1989). The amassing of these resources will have positive outcomes for a person, while the loss of resources carries the potential for a cascade of negative outcomes ranging from depression to declined physical health and functioning. Moreover, resource loss spirals (Hobfoll et al. 2012) can occur, such that the pool of resources and support on which a person could normally rely to help reverse such a downslide is depleted, which of course is the cause of the downslide in the first place. Increased occupational stress alone can act as a catalyst for slow or possibly even rapid loss of resources, but when combined with additional sources of stress (e.g., marital conflict, parental needs, family time management issues) the potential for rapid resource loss is exponentially increased (Hobfoll et al. 2012)

Women in masculine occupations who experience increased work–family conflict can experience distress in the work domain, the family domain, or both. When the conflict in either or both domain builds to a certain point, the result is often the slow or rapid loss of centrally valued resources, which in turn may cause a mental or physical regression in either or both domains. This "breakdown" can vary widely in severity and may come in the form of increased depression and anxiety (Voydanoff and Donnelly 1989), often accompanied by decreased organizational commitment and increased turnover intentions (Jones and Butler 1980; Kelley et al. 1994).

The cyclical nature of the Masculine Occupations Gender Role Model culminates with the diminished performance, retention, confidence, and attitudes of distressed female employees, feeding back into the first phase and perpetuating the cycle. Recall that the cycle started with an organization built on a foundation of traditionalist views and gender roles and consisting of nearly all males. This primary phase is further exasperated by negative work and family outcomes, while the primary phase also feeds into subsequent phases. It does not appear advantageous to stay in an organization that makes it so difficult to manage one's work–family conflict. In the military, for example, the percentage of females in the military grows, yet grows very slowly (Mackenzie 2012). This slow growth of female service members can be attributed, in part, to the combined effects of resource loss outcomes and the cascade of obstacles deriving from the attitude and behaviors of male service members in a male-dominated profession. Additionally, the sense of military tradition as an all-male force, and the conscious or unconscious belief that women will not prosper in this setting (McSally 2011), is perpetuated as males in uniform notice the difficulty women experience trying to manage work–family conflict, and the wide-spreading ripple effects of this difficulty.

In the following section we build on the military example. First, we provide a context for the military organization as a gendered occupation. We then use the Masculine Occupations Gender Role Model to explain how employees in one specific masculine occupation (the military) deal with the challenges and demands associated with the work–family interface.

14.3 The Military as a Gendered Occupation

The US military organization provides an obvious example of a gendered occupation. As of 2011, women comprise roughly 15 % of the armed forces of the United States (Army, Navy, Air Force, Marines, and Coast Guard[2]), with 214,098 women

---

[2] Statistics on the Coast Guard were included in this discussion of the military, though they are no longer a branch of the Department of Defense.

in active duty components, 118,781 women in reserve components, and 72,790 women in the National Guard (Military Women in Service for America Foundation 2011). The fact, however, that over 80% of the current military is male only partially explains the gendered nature of military service. In order to fully grasp the heavily masculine, male-dominated culture that is the military, one must consider the military's historic and contemporary goals and how it has evolved over time, both in general and with regard to gender. Only then can the depth of the military as a gendered occupation be fully appreciated.

With the US armed forces being only 15% women, one could consider this as constituting occupational segregation by sex. Certainly a woman entering such an occupation cannot ignore the obvious demographic minority of which she has become a part. More important than the current numbers, however, is the lingering sense of tradition and gender expectations experienced by women in an institution that once allowed no females whatsoever (McSally 2011). Although women have aided the armed forces in varying capacities since the American Revolution, only since the turn of the twentieth century have they been allowed to serve in uniform; and then only in very limited occupations already deemed socially acceptable for women (McSally 2011).

The military is grounded in a sense of tradition, history, and pride. This sense is intentionally fostered by leaders who know that tradition strengthens morale during times of trial and tribulation and that, should tradition give way to pragmatism in the minds of service members, the ranks will falter (Schading 2007). Although some traditions have been identified as unfair, immoral, or unjust, the process of correcting certain immoral traditions while keeping all others intact while keeping moral high is a delicate issue. Hence, since 1901, when women were first allowed to serve in the Army and Navy Nurse Corps, women in uniform have been forced to work in a culture of tradition that seems disparagingly dominated by male-based pride and prejudice (McSally 2011). The rules have changed, and continue to change, but the climate remains arguably chilly for women.

Though the precise mission and scope of the military and its branches has changed and evolved over the course of the USA's history, the purpose of its very existence remains the same. The US military exists, first and foremost, as a fighting force, meant to defend the freedom and safety of its citizens. And whereas most jobs in the military are not of a combatant nature, they all exist to support the elements of the force created to make war (Schading 2007). Women are, at the moment, still not able to hold many of the more combat-related occupations within the military (Schading 2007). This point, in and of itself, highlights the gender inequality that must be perceived by most females in the military, regardless of whether or not they agree with the reasoning behind it. To be allowed to serve in the military in a support capacity, but not in the manner for which the military is, at its core, intended, may very likely promote perceptions of unwantedness or tokenism.

Virtually independent of the traditional atmosphere and subsequent gender-typed attitudes instilled in many young male service members is the strong possibility of an already existing overrepresentation of gender-biased males in the military (Young and Nauta 2013). Recall that gender role socialization in childhood and adolescence is theorized to be among the leading causes of occupational segregation by sex (Aziz and Kamal 2012; DiDonato and Strough 2013; Feliciano and Rumbaut 2005; Jiang et al. 2010; Schuette et al. 2012; Vervecken et al. 2013; Wilbourn and Kee 2010; Wootton 1997). The military, as an occupation, is likely more attractive to those who have been raised to believe that men should work in certain settings and women in others (Matthews et al. 2009; Young and Nauta 2013). The result is a force comprised largely of service members who believe that certain jobs are socially acceptable for women, and that the military is not one of them. Compounding that problem, of course, is the fact that, though they may be ever-so-slowly opening new doors for women, the military does not exactly discourage this traditional sex role manner of thinking. Rather, subtle and blatant forms of encouragement for this type of thinking and behaving are abundant, and evidence of social dominance theory can be found throughout the military (McSally 2011).

14.3.1 Work–Family Issues of Military Personnel

Of the nearly 2.2 million service members in the US military, roughly 53 % have dependents; a much higher percentage than service members in the past or current civilians in the same age brackets (Blaisure et al. 2012). Having a family (of creation, rather than a family of origin), as defined by the military, can mean one of several situations, and according to 2009 statistics regarding active military personnel, the precise familial breakdown is as follows: dual-military with children (2.8 %), dual-military without children (3.8 %), single with children (5.3 %), married to civilian [no children] (13.7 %), married to civilian [with children] (35.6 %), single [no children] (38.8 %) (Blaisure et al. 2012). The percentage breakdown for the reserve and National Guard components do not differ substantially from these figures and, for all components of the military, the majority of personnel comprising the single [no children] category fall in the junior enlisted (E-1 to E-4) and junior officer (O-1 to O-3) ranks (Blaisure et al. 2012).

Both men and women in the military commonly experience work–family conflict (Adams et al. 2006) since meeting the needs of the military as well as the needs of the family is quite challenging, particularly given the unrelenting "greediness" of both (Segal 1986). The military, being more of a lifestyle than an occupation, can be particularly unforgiving toward outside competitors for a service member's time, energy, focus, and dedication. The family, as in most cases regardless of occupation type, demands much time and devotion. The military has made, and continues to make, huge steps in the direction of a family-friendly force (e.g., family time, paternity leave; Adams et al. 2006), especially considering the core reasons for the very existence of these occupations. What has not changed throughout history, and likely never will, is that in the military the mission comes first meaning nothing supersedes the duties and obligations that these men and women have to their occupations (Adams et al. 2006). When it comes to properly caring for a spouse or family, this mentality affects men and women in uniform in ways large and small, long term and short term.

Work–family conflict in the military can potentially differ from work–family conflict in the civilian world in several key ways, not the least of which is the moderating role of the gender of military personnel. Other principal contributors to this difference include, but are not limited to, extreme lack of flexibility and/or predictability in work schedule; the possibility of being called into work at random and inconvenient times; frequent moves that may be inconvenient, stressful, or traumatic for service members, spouses, and children; hazardous duty assignments and unaccompanied tours of duty; long lengths of time away from family due to training or combat deployments; and the work-related stress that often accompanies both garrison life and combat (Adams et al. 2006; Blaisure et al. 2012). These represent some of the more pronounced influences on work–family conflict that the military can provide, and they are experienced by men and women alike.

Exactly how is work–family conflict influenced by these military-specific antecedents? Unfortunately there is no simple answer to this question due to the incredibly diverse nature of military work, the rank structure, and countless other variables which blur the picture. It can be stated with certainty, though, that the aforementioned points are largely absent from civilian occupations, and are present in most military family situations (Adams et al. 2006; Blaisure et al. 2012). There are certain special circumstances in which a service member might not experience some or any of these added stressors, but, generally speaking, they are part of life for most members.

So is work–family conflict actually different for women in the military than it is for men? After a thorough review of all of the pertinent literature (not military specific), Frone (2003) concluded that gender was not a significant (statistically or otherwise) moderator in the work–family interface. Indeed, this may be the case when the full spectrum of occupations is taken into account. Nevertheless, when the focus is on a gendered occupation, particularly one as deeply rooted in traditional sex roles as the military, work–family differences by gender become apparent. Would a stay-at-home wife and a husband as the sole breadwinner create the same sort of resentment, sexual confusion, or tension? Would having a second child have been as difficult? Would a male have needed to worry about his career by discussing his family with his chain of command? Would he have felt the need to discuss it? Only in 2008 was the first woman in the history of the US military promoted to the rank of General (Military Women in Service for America Foundation 2011). Advancement for women in the military has been and continues to be a hard-fought battle, and it is precisely the advancement dilemma that exacerbates the already present work–family conflict issue for women. As illustrated in the Masculine Occupations Gender Role Model, these increases in the potential for work–family conflict for women, as the minority gender, are directly and indirectly driving work and family distress, decreased functioning and performance, low retention, and the perpetuation of a male-centric organization.

14.4 Emerging Issues in the Gendered Military

Our discussion thus far of the Masculine Occupations Gender Role Model and the military as a gendered occupation has been tailored toward traditional familial situations, and has intentionally disregarded any subpopulations. In the following section we introduce some emerging issues and unique populations that require special attention. Many of these issues (e.g., LGB marriage in the military; women in combat) are related to policies that are currently, or have very recently been passed, and we do not know yet the unintended consequences (both positive and negative) associated with these changes. We do believe that it is beneficial, however, for future researchers to investigate work–family conflict with regard to these emerging issues, and the relationship that the military, as a gendered occupation, has with them.

14.4.1 Lesbian, Gay, and Bisexual (LGB) Populations

With approximately 4–17% LGB employees in the civilian workforce (4–17%, Gonsiorek and Weinrich 1991; 10–14%, Powers 1996), one can estimate that the military has a similar prevalence of LGB military personnel. These numbers are difficult to confirm with the military's longstanding policy of Don't Ask Don't Tell (DADT), which essentially forced LGB soldiers into the closet. In late 2010, DADT was repealed (Rich et al. 2012), and LGB service members were, for the first time ever, allowed to serve openly in the US armed forces. Even more recently, the government has taken steps to ensure that the spouses of homosexual and bisexual service members are eligible for full benefits, as is the case with any other military marriage (Secretary of Defense 2013). These are clearly large steps for occupational equality with regard to sex and gender, and the stamping out of discrimination in the armed forces.

To fully understand how work and family outcomes of LGB military personnel are affected by the gendered military organization, we need to examine processes related to the Masculine Occupations Gender Role Model. We noted earlier that a strong masculine culture leads to less acceptance of nontraditional gender identities. We propose that this masculine culture can stigmatize an LGB service member. A stigma is a very powerful phenomenon that has two dimensions—concealability and perceived controllability (Crocker et al. 1998). Individuals with concealable stigmas (such as LGB individuals) have to make a conscious decision regarding the degree of identity disclosure. Individuals with stigmas that are perceived to be controllability (such as being LGB[3]) can experience negative reactions if others believe it is their choice to have the stigmatized characteristics (in this case LGB status; Goffman 1963).

[3] We are not saying here that being LGB is a choice. We are merely noting that some individuals may see it as such, and therefore stigmatize LGB individuals accordingly.

Individuals who have a stigma are also potentially exposed to minority stress (Meyer 2003). LGB individuals usually live and work among non-LGB individuals (Waldo 1999), especially in the military environment. The LGB military personnel will experience the typical stressors that all military personnel might experience (e.g., separation from family, deployments), but will also experience additional stressors that are unique to their minority status (e.g., fear of being "outed", Ragins et al. 2007; discrimination, Kerrigan, 2012; identity management, Kerrigan, 2012). This accumulation of stress can affect both mental and physical health (Hobfoll, 1989), and could further exacerbate the consequences of work–family conflict (King et al. 2013).

Future researchers should consider two points when delving into work–family conflict in the military for LGB populations. The first is that recent research is showing evidence that the repeal of DADT is having an opposite effect on some service members, in that rather than allowing them the opportunity to serve openly, it has forced them further into the closet, and in some instances increased the level of workplace stress and anxiety with which they live (Rich et al. 2012). Researchers need to further probe this issue to understand why this effect might be occurring, and what the military can do to offset this unintended consequence. The second point worthy of consideration is the finding that LGB-specific social support can decrease negative work outcomes for employees (Huffman et al. 2008). The military organization (and other masculine organizations) might want to develop training programs that will teach supervisors how to provide support for this group. This is especially important since it is only recently that the military has formally recognized LGB personnel.

14.4.2 Women in Combat

In 2013, the Department of Defense announced that women would, for the first time in the history of the US armed forces, be allowed to serve in combat-related (combat arms) occupations (e.g., infantry, artillery, cavalry; Roulo 2013). Although the policy change has already been announced, the change itself will not take effect until 2016 at the earliest, due to the time it will take to reorganize the force to allow for such a drastic alteration to its established operating system. How will it change the nature of the military as a gendered occupation? And how will the inclusion of women in all jobs in the Army (and eventually every branch of the military) influence work–family conflict? To address these questions we can first return to our model. Although women make up approximately 14.4 % of military personnel, currently and historically, they have been entirely absent from combat arms jobs (Department of Defense 2011). This exclusion likely reinforces stereotypical views, such as beliefs that women are weak and are ill-suited for combat jobs (Young and Nauta 2013). Furthermore, men who are in combat arms jobs are less likely to have daily exposure to women, particularly within the workplace. As such, there are likely fewer opportunities for these stereotypes to be changed. Yet with the impending changes in rules concerning women in combat arms, some of these stereotypes may lessen. Pettigrew and Tropp (2011) suggest that intergroup contact by itself can decrease stereotypes. With the inclusion of women in combat arms jobs, the prevalence of women in the armed forces might increase overall, thereby allowing for more intergroup contact. This heightened contact could decrease stereotypes, and, with time, change the culture of combat arms units and the military as a whole.

Yet, we also have to examine the introduction of women into combat in the context of potential additional stressors for women, which could lead to work–family conflict and the resultant negative job outcomes. Although prevalence of women might introduce a more healthy culture, the exposure to combat could increase the likelihood of additional job stressors. To understand how women in combat might affect work–family conflict issues, we can extrapolate from research on military personnel in combat and its effect on such conflict. Vinokur et al. (2011), for example, provide some insight into the role that combat plays on work–family conflict. They assessed the exposure to war on military personnel's well-being. Their results showed that exposure to combat was related to increased conflict between work and family domains. Similarly, Hobfoll et al. (2012) examined exposure to trauma (which could occur for both combat arms and noncombat arms jobs) and work–family conflict as a source of stress and found that, together, these stressors led to lost resources, which led to outcomes such as posttraumatic stress disorder and perceived health outcomes. When taken together, the aforementioned theories would seem to predict a different, but not necessarily improved work–family conflict scenario for women in these combat arms occupations. The overall gendered culture of the military will have likely changed for the better, which, in theory, would create a decrease in work–family conflict for women within the military. However, for those women specifically in these combat arms professions, work–family conflict may not change, or may even increase, due to the ultra-male environment and more extreme gender-based beliefs of those who often work there.

14.4.3 Gender Stigmas for Injured Military Personnel

The subject of gender stigmas with regard to injury is particularly germane to today's military because of the recent wars and sheer number of physical and psychological injuries that have resulted from them (Fisher 2013). Although men are more likely to suffer combat-related injuries, women are significantly more likely to be injured in training, and both genders sustain injuries while off duty that then may impact their ability to perform their occupational duties and/or their readiness to deploy to combat (Tiesman et al. 2007). Additionally, research has suggested that women are more susceptible to the nonvisible wounds of battle (e.g., PTSD) than are men (Lutwak 2012). Recent research investigating the roots of this gender disparity in PTSD prevalence has identified combat related stressors, prior interpersonal victimization, and predeployment concerns about life and family disruptions during deployment as being differentially associated with PTSD for men and women (Polusny et al. 2014). Kline et al. (2013) further contributes that lower scores for women on predeployment military preparedness (i.e., lack of combat-specific training) and unit cohesion also predict the postdeployment PTSD gender disparity. Whether the injuries sustained are physical or psychological, the question then is whether these combat and noncombat-related injuries affect military men and women in the same way, and whether any differential treatment and/or expectations exist between the genders based on the gendered nature of military service.

Despite a growing body of literature exploring the individual and societal implications of traumatic brain injury, PTSD, and various other mental and physical injuries commonly found in those returning from deployments to Iraq and Afghanistan (Morissette et al. 2011), very little research has attempted to explore these issues through the lens of gender expectations. Given what is known regarding the gender-typed thinking in the military, it is perhaps not unreasonable to assume that those women who suffer physical and psychological injuries in the military do not feel comfortable talking about or displaying them in a manner that might otherwise be acceptable, for fear of being seen as weak or unsuitable for military work (Young and Nauta 2013). This places injured women in a rather precarious position because, while it is traditional "male" behavior to downplay the severity of physical and psychological hardship, as noted by Glick and Fiske (2001), when women in male-dominated occupations do not conform to traditional sex gender roles they may encounter various forms of resistance and negative attitudes form their male colleagues. Dealing with an injury in a masculine or feminine manner, it would appear, may bring additional distress to a female service member. This is an important area to consider and further explore when considering the implications, work–family related and otherwise, of work in a gendered occupation.

14.5 Conclusion

The United States military is simply one illustrative example of a male-gendered occupation. In every gendered occupation, the minority gender may face challenges that are unique to that specific occupation or organization (e.g., deploying to combat as a female), or challenges that are common to all occupations that are segregated by sex (e.g., tokenism). As such, some of the antecedents of work–family conflict mentioned in our example of the military as a gendered occupation may be more or less generalizable to other male-dominated professions. The same would be true if any other gendered occupation had been used as an example. We explicitly note this so that little doubt is left as to our intention with this chapter: to provide general knowledge concerning the potential for increased work–family conflict for those in the minority gender of a gendered occupation, and to provide specific examples from one of the most glaringly gendered organizations.

We proposed a model that can be applied to the military, or any other male-gendered profession, to help explain the cycle of gender segregation and the propensity for increased work–family conflict for women as the minority gender. In order to lay the groundwork for our model, a theoretical basis for the very existence of gendered professions was established to help bring to the forefront the reality of biological and social phenomena combining to form less than perfectly equitable occupational environments. Our model revealed how and why an occupation such as the military can be so heavily dominated by males (Phase I). Specifically, this was done by emphasizing the very facts and theory that provide support to the points that make certain occupations male-gendered. This prevalence of men create an occupational culture that is, both consciously and unconsciously, both actively and passively, supportive of the personal and professional needs of one sex (men), but neglectful to the needs of the other (women; Phase II). The translation of an unsupportive culture to the needs of women leads to the potential for increased work–family conflict (Phase III). Finally, conservation of resources theory highlights how increased work–family conflict for women in these male-dominated professions can instigate adverse psychological and physiological repercussions which, in turn, bring negative outcomes to both the work and family spheres (Phase IV). The cyclical nature of the model culminates, perpetuating the military, or any other male-gendered profession, to be dominated by men.

Stress or distress from the work domain spilling into and adversely affecting the family domain, and vice versa, is a possibility for any professional, of any gender, in any organization or industry. It is important to recognize, however, that certain groups and categories of people working in certain occupations may be naturally disadvantaged in this regard. Although women, as a minority group in the male-dominated military, provided an example of this phenomenon here, men could also experience minority status in another occupation (e.g., nursing). Remaining cognizant of the potential for inequitable conditions in and around work–family conflict should be a priority for researchers and employers alike.

References

Acker, J. (1998). The future of "gender and organizations". *Gender, Work and Organization, 5,* 195–206.

Adams, G. A., Jex, S. M., & Cunningham, C. J. L. (2006). Work–family conflict among military personnel. In C. A. Castro, A. B. Adler, & T. W. Britt (Eds.), *Military life: The psychology of serving in peace and combat* (pp. 169–192). Westport: Praeger.

Allen, T. D., Herst, D. E. L., Bruck, C. S., & Sutton, M. (2000). Consequences associated with work-to-family conflict: A review and agenda for future research. *Journal of Occupational Health Psychology, 5,* 278–308.

Aziz, S., & Kamal, A. (2012). Gender role attitudes and occupational aspirations of Pakistani adolescents. *FWU Journal of Social Sciences, 6,* 89–98.

Billing, Y. (2000). Organizational cultures, families and careers in Scandinavia. In L. Haas, P. Hwang, & G. Russell (Eds.), *Organizational change and gender equity*. Thousand Oaks: Sage.

Blackburn, R. M., & Jarman, J. (2006). Gendered occupations. *International Sociology, 21,* 289–315.

Blaisure, K. R., Saathoff-Wells, T., Pereira, A., MacDermid Wadsworth, S., & Dombro, A. L. (2012). *Serving military families in the 21st century*. New York: Routledge.

Bureau of Labor Statistics. (2012). *Employed persons by detailed occupation, sex, race, and Hispanic or Latino ethnicity*. http://www.bls.gov/cps/cpsaat11.pdf. Accessed 1 Sep 2013.

Cabrera, S. F., Sauer, S. J., & Thomas-Hunt, M. (2009). The evolving manager stereotype: The effects of industry gender typing on performance expectations for leaders and their teams. *Psychology of Women Quarterly, 33,* 419–428.

Carli, L. L., & Eagly, A. H. (1999). Gender effects on social influence and emergent leadership. In G. N. Powell (Ed.), *Handbook of gender and work* (pp. 203–222). Thousand Oaks: Sage.
Cech, E., Rubineau, B., Silbey, S., & Seron, C. (2011). Professional role confidence and gendered persistence in engineering. *American Sociological Review, 76,* 641–666.
Cook, A., & Minnotte, K. (2008). Occupational and industry sex segregation and the work–family interface. *Sex Roles, 59,* 800–813.
Crocker, J., Major, B., & Steele, C. (1998). Social stigma. In D. Gilbert, S. T. Fiske, & G. Lindzey (Eds.), *Handbook of social psychology* (pp. 504–553). Boston: McGraw-Hill.
Department of Defense. (2011). *Profile of the military community: 2010 Demographics.* Washington, D.C.: Office of the Deputy Under Secretary of Defense (Military Community and Family Policy).
DiDonato, L., & Strough, J. (2013). Do college students' gender-typed attitudes about occupations predict their real-world decisions? *Sex Roles, 68,* 536–549.
Eagly, A. H. (1987). *Sex differences in social behavior: A social-role interpretation.* Hillsdale: Erlbaum.
Eagly, A. H., & Sczesny, S. (2009). Stereotypes about women, men, and leaders: Have times changed? In M. Barreto, M. K. Ryan, & M. T. Schmitt (Eds.), *The glass ceiling in the 21st century: Understanding barriers to gender equality* (pp. 21–47). Washington, D.C.: American Psychological Association.
Feliciano, C., & Rumbaut, R. G. (2005). Gendered paths: Educational and occupational expectations and outcomes among adult children of immigrants. *Ethnic & Racial Studies, 28,* 1087–1118.
Fiske, S. T. (1998). Stereotyping, prejudice, and discrimination. In D. T. Gilbert, S. T. Fiske, & G. Lindzey (Eds.), *Handbook of social psychology* (pp. 357–411). New York: McGraw-Hill.
Frone, M. R. (2003). Work–family balance. In J. C. Quick & L. E. Tetrick (Eds.), *Handbook of occupational health psychology* (pp. 143–162). Washington, D.C.: American Psychological Association.
Gaucher, D., Friesen, J., & Kay, A. C. (2011). Evidence that gendered wording in job advertisements exists and sustains gender inequality. *Journal of Personality and Social Psychology, 101,* 109–128.
Glass, J. L., & Estes, S. B. (1997). The family responsive workplace. *Annual Review of Sociology, 23,* 289–313.
Glick, P., & Fiske, S. (2001). Ambivalent sexism. In M. P. Zanna (Ed.), *Advances in experimental social psychology* (pp. 115–188). Thousand Oaks: Academic.
Glick, P., & Fiske, S. T. (2007). Sex discrimination: The psychological approach. In F. J. Crosby, M. S. Stockdale, & S. A. Ropp (Eds.). *Sex discrimination in the workplace: Multidisciplinary approaches* (pp. 155–188). Malden: Blackwell.
Goffman, E. (1963). *Stigma: Notes on the management of spoiled identity.* Englewood Cliffs: Prentice Hall.
Gonsiorek, J. C., & Weinrich, J. D. (1991). The definition and scope of sexual orientation. In J. C. Gonsiorek & J. D. Weinich (Eds.), *Homosexuality: Research implications for public policy* (pp. 1–12). Newbury Park: Sage.
Greenhaus, J. H., Beutell, N. J. (1985). Sources of conflict between work and family roles. *Academy of Management Review, 10,* 76–88.
Haas, L., & Hwang, C. P. (2007). Gender and organizational culture. *Gender & Society, 21,* 52–79.
Hakim, C. (2000). *Work-lifestyle choices in the 21st century: Preference theory.* Oxford: Oxford University Press.
Harris, D., & Giuffre, P. (2010). "The price you pay": How female professional chefs negotiate work and family. *Gender Issues, 27,* 27–52.
Hobfoll, S. E. (1989). Conservation of resources: A new attempt at conceptualizing stress. *American Psychologist, 44,* 513–524.
Hobfoll, S. E. (2011). Conservation of resource caravans and engaged settings. *Journal of Occupational & Organizational Psychology, 84,* 116–122.

Hobfoll, S. E., Vinokur, A. D., Pierce, P. F., & Lewandowski-Romps, L. (2012). The combined stress of family life, work, and war in Air Force men and women: A test of conservation of resources theory. *International Journal of Stress Management, 19,* 217–237.

Huffman, A. H., Watrous-Rodriguez, K., & King, E. (2008). Supporting a diverse workforce: What type of support is most meaningful for lesbian and gay employees? *Human Resource Management, 4,* 237–253.

Jiang, X., Wang, P., & Wang, M. (2010). Relationship between college students' gender, gender-role identity and occupation-sex stereotype. *Chinese Journal of Clinical Psychology, 18,* 366–368.

Jones, A. P., & Butler, M. (1980). A role transition approach to the stresses of organizationally induced family role disruption. *Journal of Marriage and the Family, 42,* 367–376.

Kelley, M. L., Herzog-Simmer, P. A., & Harris, M. A. (1994). Effects of military-induced separation on the parenting stress and family functioning of deploying mothers. *Military Psychology, 6,* 125–138.

Kerrigan, M. F. (2012). Transgender discrimination in the military: The new don't ask, don't tell. *Psychology, Public Policy, and Law, 18,* 500–518.

King, E., Huffman, A., & Peddie, C. (2013). LGBT parents and the workplace. In A. E. Goldberg & K. R. Allen (Eds.), *LGBT-parent families: Possibilities for new research and implications for practice* (pp. 225–237). New York: Springer.

Kline, A., Ciccone, D. S., Weiner, M., Interian, A., St. Hill, L., Falca-Dodson, M., Black, C. M., & Losonczy, M. (2013). Gender differences in the risk and protective factors associated with PTSD: A prospective study of National Guard troops deployed to Iraq. *Psychiatry: Interpersonal & Biological Processes, 76,* 256–272.

Liben, L. S., & Bigler, R. S. (2002). The developmental course of gender differentiation: Conceptualizing, measuring, and evaluating constructs and pathways. *Monographs of the Society for Research in Child Development, 67,* vii–147.

Lutwak, N. (2012). The negative effects of MST and combat injuries among female soldiers: A major concern. *Journal of Psychiatric Research, 46,* 691–723.

Lyness, K. S., & Heilman, M. E. (2006). When fit is fundamental: Performance evaluations and promotions of upper-level female and male managers. *Journal of Applied Psychology, 91,* 777–785.

Mackenzie, M. H. (2012). Let women fight. *Foreign Affairs, 91,* 32–42.

Matthews, M. D., Ender, M. G., Laurence, J. H., & Rohall, D. E. (2009). Role of group affiliation and gender on attitudes toward women in the military. *Military Psychology, 21,* 241–251.

Maume, D. J., & Houston, P. (2001). Job segregation and gender differences in work–family spillover among white-collar workers. *Journal of Family and Economic Issues, 22,* 171–189.

McSally, M. E. (2011). Defending America in mixed company: Gender in the U. S. armed forces. *Daedalus, 140,* 148–164.

Meyer, I. H. (2003). Prejudice, social stress, and mental health in lesbian, gay, and bisexual populations: Conceptual issues and research evidence. *Psychological Bulletin, 129,* 674–697.

Military Women in Service for America Foundation. (2011). Statistics on women in the military. http://www.womensmemorial.org/PDFs/StatsonWIM.pdf. Accessed 1 Sep 2013.

Morgan, H., & Milliken, F. (1992). Keys to action. *Human Resource Management, 31,* 227–248.

Morissette, S. B., Woodward, M., Kimbrel, N. A., Meyer, E. C., Kruse, M. I., Dolan, S., & Gulliver, S. B. (2011). Deployment-related TBI, persistent postconcussive symptoms, PTSD, and depression in OEF/OIF veterans. *Rehabilitation Psychology, 56,* 340–350.

O'Reilly, C. (1989). Corporations, culture, and commitment: Motivation and social control in organizations. *California Management Review, 31,* 9–25.

Pettigrew, T. F., & Tropp, L. R. (2011). *When groups meet: The dynamics of intergroup contact.* New York: Psychology Press.

Polusny, M. A., Kumpula, M. J., Meis, L. A., Erbes, C. R., Arbisi, P. A., Murdoch, M., Thuras, P., Kehle-Forbes, S., & Johnson, A. K. (2014). Gender differences in the effects of deployment-related stressors and pre-deployment risk factors on the development of PTSD symptoms in National Guard soldiers deployed to Iraq and Afghanistan. *Journal of Psychiatric Research, 49,* 1–9.

Powers, B. (1996). The impact of gay, lesbian, and bisexual workplace issues on productivity. In A. Ellis & E. Riggle (Eds.), *Sexual identity on the job: Issues and services*. New York: Haworth.
Ragins, B. R., Singh, R., & Cornwell, J. M. (2007). Making the invisible visible: Fear and disclosure of sexual orientation at work. *Journal of Applied Psychology, 92,* 1103–1118.
Reskin, B. F. (2003). Including mechanisms in our models of ascriptive inequality. *American Sociological Review, 68,* 1–21.
Rich, C., Schutten, J. K., & Rogers, R. A. (2012). "Don't drop the soap": Organizing sexualities in the repeal of the U.S. military's 'don't ask, don't tell' policy. *Communication Monographs, 79,* 269–291.
Rothrauff, T., Cable, S. M., & Coleman, M. (2004). All that you can be: Negotiating work and family demands in the military. *Journal of Teaching in Marriage & Family, 4,* 1–25.
Roulo, C. (2013). Defense department expands women's combat role. *U.S. Department of Defense News*. www.defense.gov/News/NewsArticle.aspx. Accessed 1 Sep 2013.
Sandler, B. R., Silverberg, L. A., & Hall, R. M. (1996). *The chilly classroom climate: A guide to improve the education of women*. Washington, D.C.: The National Association for Women in Education.
Schading, B. (2007). *A civilian's guide to the U.S. military: A comprehensive reference to the customs, language and structure of the armed forces*. Cincinnati: Writer's Digest Books.
Schein, E. H. (1990). Organizational culture. *American Psychologist, 45,* 109–119.
Schneider, B., Ehrhart, M. G., & Macey, W. H. (2013). Organizational climate and culture. *Annual Review of Psychology, 64,* 361–388.
Schuette, C. T., Ponton, M. K., & Charlton, M. L. (2012). Middle school children's career aspirations: Relationship to adult occupations and gender. *Career Development Quarterly, 60,* 36–46.
Secretary of Defense. (2013). Extending benefits to same sex domestic partners of military members. http://www.defense.gov/news/same-sexbenefitsmemo.pdf. Accessed 1 Sep 2013.
Segal, M. (1986). The military and the family as greedy institutions. *Armed Forces & Society, 13,* 9–38.
Sidanius, J., & Pratto, F. (1999). *Social dominance: An intergroup theory of social hierarchy and oppression*. New York: Cambridge University Press.
Thorne, B. (1993). *Gender play: Girls and boys in school*. Piscataway: Rutgers University Press.
Tiesman, H. M., Peek-Asa, C., Zwerling, C. S., Sprince, N. L., & Amoroso, P. J. (2007). Occupational and non-occupational injuries in the United States Army: Focus on gender. *American Journal of Preventive Medicine, 33,* 464–470.
Vervecken, D., Hannover, B., & Wolter, I. (2013). Changing (s)expectations: How gender fair job descriptions impact children's perceptions and interest regarding traditionally male occupations. *Journal of Vocational Behavior, 82,* 208–220.
Vinokur, A. D., Pierce, P. F., Lewandowski-Romps, L., Hobfoll, S. E., & Galea, S. (2011). Effects of war exposure on air force personnel's mental health, job burnout and other organizational related outcomes. *Journal of Occupational Health Psychology, 16,* 3–17.
Voydanoff, P., & Donnelly, B. W. (1989). Work and family roles and psychological distress. *Journal of Marriage & Family, 51,* 923–932.
Waldo, C. R. (1999). Working in a majority context: A structural model of heterosexism as minority stress in the workplace. *Journal of Counseling Psychology, 46,* 218–232.
Wicks, D., & Bradshaw, P. (1999). Gendered organizational cultures in Canadian work organizations: Implications for creating an equitable workforce. *Management Decision, 37,* 372–383.
Wilbourn, M., & Kee, D. (2010). Henry the nurse is a doctor too: Implicitly examining children's gender stereotypes for male and female occupational roles. *Sex Roles, 62,* 670–683.
Wootton, B. H. (1997). Gender differences in occupational employment. *Monthly Labor Review, 120,* 15–24.
Young, L. M., & Nauta, M. M. (2013). Sexism as a predictor of attitudes toward women in the military and in combat. *Military Psychology, 25,* 166–171.

Chapter 15
Women in STEM: Family-Related Challenges and Initiatives

Vanessa A. Jean, Stephanie C. Payne, and Rebecca J. Thompson

15.1 The Problem

Women represent more than 50% of the population and capacity for innovation in the USA, but they earn less than 25% of the doctoral degrees in engineering, computer science, and physics, and are underrepresented in almost all science technology, engineering, and math (STEM) careers (National Science Foundation 2013). Despite relatively equal proportions of boys and girls enrolled in STEM courses during grade school, women are significantly underrepresented in STEM degrees and occupations around the world (Hill et al. 2010). Advances in STEM are critical to our health and security, and diversification of the STEM workforce is believed to enhance creativity, innovation, and quality of STEM contributions (Burke 2007).

It is important to increase the representation of women in STEM for various reasons. First, women have relevant knowledge and skills to contribute which has the

The authors express their appreciation to José Bermúdez and Nate Keiser for their assistance with the childcare data and to Mindy Bergman, Laura Lomeli, Kathi Miner, Xiaohong (Violet) Xu, and Carla Zimmerman for their feedback on earlier versions of the chapter. This chapter is based upon work supported by the National Science Foundation under NSF Cooperative Agreement No. HRD-1008385.

V. A. Jean (✉)
Department of Psychology, Texas A&M University,
College Station, TX 77843, USA
e-mail: vjean@tamu.edu

S. C. Payne
Department of Psychology, Texas A&M University,
College Station, TX 77843, USA
e-mail: scp@tamu.edu

R. J. Thompson
University of Baltimore, Baltimore, MD 21201, USA
e-mail: rthompson@ubalt.edu

M. J. Mills (ed.), *Gender and the Work-Family Experience*,
DOI 10.1007/978-3-319-08891-4_15

potential to extend our accomplishments in these areas. Second, women offer additional perspectives, which can facilitate problem solving and generation of solutions. More perspectives tend to challenge preexisting assumptions, thereby leading to innovation. Third, having more women in STEM creates more role models and mentors for future generations of STEM workers.

Extensive research has been conducted on sex differences focusing particularly on the underrepresentation of women in STEM (for a review see Ceci and Williams 2007). This research examines genetic differences, environmental influences throughout the lifespan beginning even before birth (i.e., prenatal), and the combination of the two. Although relatively equal proportions of boys and girls enroll in STEM courses during grade school, the distribution is not equal thereafter. The phrase "leaky pipeline" has been used to describe statistical trends concerning women in STEM reflecting a "sex-based filter that removes one sex from the stream and leaves the other to arrive at the end of the pipeline" (Blickenstaff 2005, p. 369).

In the current chapter, we highlight the influence that family-related challenges have on STEM academic and nonacademic careers. The objectives of this chapter are fourfold: (1) briefly review gender-related theories used to explain underrepresentation of women in STEM, (2) summarize some of the empirical evidence of work–family challenges that STEM women in academia and industry experience, (3) present some new data about the importance of childcare to STEM women's careers, and (4) identify various initiatives, including family-friendly policies and practices, that have been implemented to alleviate work–family challenges and in turn retain women in STEM.

15.2 Theories About Underrepresentation of Women in STEM

There are a number of theories that have been offered to explain why women are underrepresented in STEM. We briefly review gender-related theories, focusing particularly on the theories that explain why women disproportionally experience family-related challenges. These include social role theory (Eagly 1987; Eagly et al. 2000), role congruity theory (Eagly and Karau 2002), stereotype threat (Steele and Aronson 1995), and implicit bias (Greenwald and Banaji 1995).

One theory proposed to explain the underrepresentation of women in STEM is social role theory (Eagly 1987; Eagly et al. 2000). Gender roles are common beliefs about what men and women *tend* to do (descriptive norms) as well as what men and women are *supposed* to do (injunctive norms; Eagly 1987). Historically, men have been the breadwinners, providing financial support for the family, while women have been cooks, homemakers, and the caretakers of the children and the elderly. Further, STEM fields are historically male-dominated (Kanter 1977). Thus, history and tradition contribute to gender based stereotypes about *who should be* scientists, technology professionals, engineers, and mathematicians.

These normative expectations influence boys and girls from the day they are born—through the toys people give them to play with and the reactions people had when they expressed their preferred interests and career-aspirations. These stereotypes continue to have an impact on men and women well beyond their developmental years, as stereotypes influence many people who play important roles in their lives. For example, family members frequently expect women to adopt caretaking roles and responsibilities in the home. Organizational decision makers may be more inclined to hire men for STEM positions (e.g., Steinpres et al. 1999) and give men more developmental opportunities, raises, and promotions than women. Students may take gender roles into consideration when evaluating professors in the classroom (Bennett 1982).

Gender roles not only influence how people perceive others, but they also influence how people perceive themselves. Correspondingly, gender roles can influence women's identity and the decisions they make concerning both their personal and professional lives. Beyond the decision to pursue a career in STEM, gender roles can influence decision making about taking a break from one's career, bearing children, and prioritization of a partner's career.

A related theory concerning women's perceptions of themselves, decisions that they make, and their performance is stereotype threat, or a fear of confirming stereotypes about one's groups (e.g., "girls aren't good at math"; Steele and Aronson 1995). This theory has been used to explain lower levels of performance on math tests by women than men (e.g., Spencer et al. 1999).

A third theory that has been used to explain sex differences in STEM is role congruity theory. This theory extends social role theory to explain what happens when women (or men) violate gender roles (Eagly and Karau 2002) or when there is an incongruity between characteristics of an individual and the requirements of another role they are taking on. It is tempting to discount traditional gender roles as old-fashioned and question how much they still exist today. Unfortunately, a number of recent studies suggest that such views are still perpetuated in the media (e.g., Collins 2011) and in work-related decisions (e.g., Correll et al. 2007). For example, researchers at Ohio State University recently manipulated the authors listed next to abstracts of scientific studies and asked graduate students to rate the quality of the study. Sadly, the abstracts of studies with male authors were rated as higher quality than identical abstracts of studies with female authors (Knobloch-Westerwick et al. 2013).

Some people react negatively to violations of gender roles (Eagly and Karau 2002) especially if those people have developed a bias, implicit or explicit, in favor of people conforming to traditional gender roles. Implicit biases are unconscious and automatic preferences that people make based on stereotypes (Greenwald and Banaji 1995). Implicit bias is not the same as explicit bias, which is likely to be manifested in more blatant discrimination. Implicit bias is much more subtle, unintentional, and unconscious. It influences how we perceive people and the decisions that we make.

At first, implicit biases may not seem to make much of a difference, but scientists argue that subtle slights accumulate over time and result in larger disparities (i.e., a multiplier effect): As Valian (1999) noted, "Mountains are molehills piled one on top of the other" (p. 4). This is evidenced by the relatively small number of women who achieve some of the highest ranks within STEM within education, academia, and industry. While implicit biases are unconscious, they still have negative consequences. For example, implicit biases have been revealed in hiring recommendations based on gender stereotypes conveyed in letters of recommendation (Madera et al. 2009; Trix and Psenka 2003). Disadvantages accrue and have a major impact on salary, promotion, prestige, and advancement (Martel et al. 1996).

15.3 Work–Family Challenges in STEM Occupations

Many interventions designed to increase the percentages of women in STEM fields focus on supporting and educating *undergraduate* women on the virtues of these majors. There have been some increases in women in these majors, the number of women in STEM occupations has not increased correspondingly (Fouad et al. 2011; Preston 2004). While women and men are earning undergraduate degrees in STEM fields at similar rates, consistent with others (e.g., Preston 2004), we posit that family-related challenges pose significant hurdles for STEM women's careers. Fundamentally, the more roles people take on, the more opportunities there are for role conflict. Work–family conflict (WFC) is broadly defined as the interrole conflict that occurs when strains from the work and family domains are in some way mutually incompatible, making involvement in each role more challenging as a result of the other (Greenhaus and Beutell 1985). The following section describes six family-related challenges faced by many women in STEM: (1) overlap of biological clock and the timeline for career advancement, (2) pregnancy and childbirth, (3) quality childcare, (4) eldercare challenges, (5) dual-career couple challenges, and (6) balancing critical career experiences with family demands.

15.3.1 Overlap of Biological Clock with the Timeline for Career Advancement

One family-related challenge to a STEM career is overlap of the biological clock with the timeline for career advancement. A woman's biological clock conveys the time period in which it is biologically optimal for her to conceive and reproduce. During this time she is fertile—regularly releasing eggs and also physically capable of bearing children. For American women, this time period is between the ages of 15 and 44, with the most babies in the USA born to women between 20 and 24 years of age in both 2007 and 2009 (Sutton et al. 2011). This timeframe directly overlaps with the critical timeframe for career advancement.

In academic occupations, the timeline for career advancement is somewhat prescribed. Postsecondary teachers or college/university professors are typically required to have a doctorate (Bureau of Labor Statistics 2012). A 4-year degree must be obtained prior to an approximately 6-year doctorate. Thus, a direct path to an academic career means most tenure-track professors start the tenure track around 28, which is already beyond the most common age range for human reproduction in the USA (20–24 years; Sutton et al. 2011). Tenure can take up to 7 years to obtain, making most women 35 by the time they achieve tenure. If they deviate from a direct path, they could be well into their 40s by the time they achieve the milestone of tenure. In fact for many STEM-related fields, earning a doctorate is followed by a postdoctoral position that lasts anywhere from 1 to 7 years and sometimes longer, further extending time devoted to training for one's career.

The tenure clock schedule coincides with the biological clock of a woman, such that a woman who chooses to not have a child because she is striving for tenure may not be able to physically have a child after completion of the tenure process due to risk factors associated with age. Although the age when fertility begins to decline is different for each woman, the chance of conceiving drops considerably after age 35 and even more prominently after age 40 (National Center for Biotechnology Information 2013). The rates of miscarriage and fetal chromosomal abnormalities increase with maternal age after 35 years, as do the risks of developing complications during pregnancy, such as gestational diabetes (Cleary-Goldman et al. 2005).

While most women working in nonacademic STEM careers do not face the specified career goal of tenure, their career advancement frequently overlaps with family demands (e.g., new projects, promotions). In a US study of women in mid-level information technology (IT) occupations, nearly one-third of women reported delaying their career goals in order to have children (Simard et al. 2008). Additionally, mid-level women in IT reported being more likely than their male colleagues to sacrifice marriage/partnership and/or having children altogether in order to accomplish their career goals. While this group was in the minority, these career pressures were also coupled with stress-related health issues (Simard et al. 2008), revealing additional difficulties experienced by women in STEM occupations when trying to have a family.

Many STEM organizations are either unaware or uninterested in the extent to which family demands hinder career advancement. In a study of German IT firms, Menez et al. (2001) found that roughly 60% of the firms interviewed did not identify obstacles to the professional advancement of women, despite the fact that only 27% of the employees in IT firms were women. "Temporary interruptions of the career because of family obligations are the most important obstacle" for women in IT fields (Menez et al. 2001, p. 8). The authors attributed these findings to the domain-specific knowledge which often evolves quite rapidly in STEM fields, making any leave, however short, particularly difficult on an individual's career (Menez et al. 2001). In other words, when women take leaves to have children, they are often penalized simply by the constantly progressing nature of the work of which they are a part. Additionally, because of the manner in which STEM professionals are trained, many have few alternative career options if and when they choose (or are forced) to leave.

15.3.2 Pregnancy and Childbirth

A second family-related challenge to a STEM career is pregnancy and childbirth. Working in some STEM disciplines can be dangerous, and this may be problematic for women who are planning to conceive in the near future, women who are pregnant, or women who are breastfeeding a newborn. As an example, chemists and chemical engineers could be exposed to toxic chemicals and substances that could be detrimental to a pregnancy or a newborn via breast-feeding. Further, some fields, like anthropology, are physically demanding, requiring women to crawl around in tight spaces or endure miles of outdoor hiking for fieldwork. Thus, some women may not be able to do all of their job-related tasks when they are pregnant. In addition, physicians may impose additional restrictions (e.g., bed rest) during the pregnancy due to the pregnancy being classified as "high risk" or because of other medical complications. These job requirements and restrictions could interfere with the woman's ability to make adequate progress in her career during the pregnancy. Further, independent of other medical complications, travel is usually prohibited in the late stages of pregnancy.

In order to maximize their time with their newborns, women may feel compelled to try to time their deliveries around peak times in their annual work schedules. In fact, "May babies" are common enough among female faculty to have warranted this label (Armenti 2004). Some female professors intentionally attempt to schedule their pregnancies such that they can give birth to a child in the month of May allowing them to recuperate and care for their newborn child over the summer, or even hide their pregnancy from others if they are pretenure (Armenti 2004). Unfortunately, women have valid reasons for believing that they may be discriminated against if they disclose their pregnancy to others in the workplace. For example, in a recent study investigating discrimination toward pregnant women, researchers found that pregnant job applicants in the USA experienced more interpersonal hostility compared to nonpregnant applicants and this was attributed to stereotypic beliefs about their commitment to the job and flexibility (Morgan et al. 2013).

Having May babies typically provides female faculty with a reprieve from their teaching load following the birth or adoption of a child because classes are out for the summer, although it is common for professors to conduct research during the summer months (Armenti 2004). In universities nationwide, academics can be found mentoring graduate students, attending meetings, conducting research, and sometimes teaching classes during the summer months. Thus, a professor's workload during the summer months is not likely to change dramatically from the traditional school year. A lack of participation in these activities due to childbirth and childcare would be noticed because summer is often about catching up rather than resting.

15.3.3 Quality Childcare

A third family-related challenge to a STEM career is obtaining quality childcare. Reliable and affordable childcare is essential to any working parent, as the ability to manage and focus on work demands is greatly hindered when childcare is unavailable and/or inadequate. This is particularly salient for female faculty, who have a short window of time to prove themselves to the academic community. Female STEM faculty may be further disadvantaged by the university's geographical location. It is common for top tier research universities to be located in rural areas of the country and for faculty members to relocate to the university town. As a result, faculty may live far from their families and have less support for childcare than those in other fields. Further, childcare options are not always optimal or convenient to faculty in rural areas.

In order to determine how childcare issues affect STEM women in academia, we recently conducted a brief childcare needs analysis of all faculty at a large, southern US university. We asked the following open-ended question: "In what ways have good, reliable childcare facilitated your career and/or in what ways have inadequate, unreliable childcare interfered with your career?" A number of themes emerged in the 93 responses received to this question from STEM female faculty[1] and were systematically coded into one or more of the categories that emerged. Most respondents reported more than one theme in their narrative answer. Three themes emerged the most frequently: (1) childcare is critical to one's career, (2) childcare permits peace of mind/psychological focus on work, and (3) childcare is difficult to find/insufficient childcare options available. It is interesting to note that although our sample consisted of only STEM women in academia (faculty), none of these themes appear to be unique to academic careers. The frequency with which these themes were mentioned and an example quote for each of them is displayed in Table 15.1.

It is clear that the STEM female faculty in our sample experienced considerable challenges locating childcare options. This theme emerged in the responses from STEM women faculty more than any other theme. The comments coded for this theme included concerns related to the unavailability of infant care, after hours care, and care for sick children. There were also comments pertaining to the difficulty they experienced trying to find convenient childcare. Additionally, STEM women faculty reported that reliable, adequate childcare is critical to their careers, with some noting that they are unable to work if it is not attainable. Comments classified under this theme indicated that childcare is a career necessity, not an optional benefit. Lastly, many STEM women faculty reported that having adequate childcare allows them to focus on their work, freeing them from worrying extensively about their children during their work time. As highlighted in our brief needs analysis, affordable, convenient, quality childcare is imperative to the careers of female faculty in STEM fields. Future research should directly examine the influence of childcare challenges on the leaky pipeline to both academic and nonacademic careers.

[1] In order to keep the assessment brief, respondents were asked to indicate their college but not their department. As such, STEM classification was determined by college rather than department. Because two of the colleges include both STEM and non-STEM departments as defined by the National Science Foundation, our STEM classification is likely over-inclusive, containing some responses from faculty belonging to non-STEM departments.

Table 15.1 Three most common responses by STEM women faculty as to how childcare has impacted their career

Frequency	Type of impact on career	Description/definition	Example respondent quotes
44	Inadequate/ difficult to find	Childcare reported to be inadequate in terms of convenience, quality, or availability	I was on the waitlist for (the campus childcare center) for 1 year. I struggled to find good daycare in the town, but that information was difficult to obtain (i.e., there are no lists of recommended daycare providers). The daycare resulted in added time commuting. In addition, the daycare days of operation were not always consistent with the university schedule
30	Critical to career	Affordable, adequate childcare is a key element to have successful career	If my kids are not properly taken care, work cannot be done.
			I could not have gone back to work—period—without good, reliable childcare as I do not have family anywhere in [this state]. So having a reliable, good daycare has been critical.
9	Psychological focus/peace of mind	Childcare provides peace of mind and freedom from worry, allowing for focus on job tasks	High quality, reliable childcare allows me to concentrate on my job when I am at work so that I am not distracted worrying about my child.

Ongoing family obligations have been frequently identified as an obstacle for women in nonacademic STEM careers as well (Preston 2004). In a recent national study examining why women in the US leave engineering, Fouad and Singh (2011) identified that one quarter of women left their engineering career because they wanted more time with family. Caretaking obligations, particularly for children, are consistent concerns for STEM women in nonacademic careers (Fouad et al. 2011). "Predictably, women with childcare responsibilities experienced greater interference between their work and nonwork roles than those without such responsibilities" (Fouad and Singh 2011, p. 42). It appears that the lack of adequate childcare is a considerable obstacle to the advancement and retention of women in STEM careers.

15.3.4 Eldercare Challenges

A fourth family-related challenge to a STEM career is eldercare. Due to the aging population of baby-boomers, eldercare presents a challenge for many employed caregivers. The number of persons older than 85 years of age in the USA will grow to more than 18 million by 2050 (U.S. Census Bureau 2009). Further, some employees serve as caregivers to both children and elders, a cohort of individuals sometimes referred to as the "sandwich generation" (Hammer and Neal 2008). Women caring for elders could be perceived as being less committed to their work than their male counterparts if the caregiving interferes with work (Morgan and Milliken 1993).

Additionally, according to a recent report from the Sloan Center on Aging and Work that examined nine US workplaces as part of their Age & Generations study (Pitt-Catsouphes et al. 2009), the experiences of women with eldercare responsibilities differed significantly from those with other dependent care responsibilities, such as childcare. Specifically, women who provided care to an elder reported having less access to flexible work options, receiving less support from their supervisors, and having less job security than did those who provided childcare or dependent care other than eldercare. Although there are similarities between childcare and eldercare and both present challenges, eldercare has several differences that lead to unique effects in the workplace. As noted by Wagner (1991), childcare is more predictable than eldercare, mainly because the intensity and duration of eldercare needs vary. Eldercare-giving may result in more work interruptions because sudden medical issues such as strokes, heart attacks, or other episodic conditions are more prevalent in older adults than young children. To our knowledge, no research has systematically examined the influence of eldercare responsibilities or how supportive STEM organizations are of these challenging responsibilities on STEM women's careers. Future research is needed on this differential responsibility to determine the extent to which eldercare contributes to the leaky pipeline.

15.3.5 Dual-Career Couple Challenges and Benefits

A fifth family-related challenge to a STEM career is dual-career considerations. There is an upward trend of dual-earner couples in the USA such that in 2010, 58% of married-couple families with children under 18 years of age were classified as dual-earner status (Bureau of Labor Statistics 2010). It has been estimated that 83% of female scientists in academia in the USA are partnered with another scientist in academia (Schiebinger et al. 2008). Likewise, women in nonacademic STEM occupations experience similar partnership dynamics. For example, a study of midlevel IT employees in the USA found that nearly 70% of women who have full- or part-time working partners have partners working in IT. In contrast only one third of men had partners in the same field (Simard et al. 2008).

Dual-career couples have the unique challenge of finding equally satisfying positions in the same geographical location, which has been referred to as the "two-body problem" (Li 2009) and the "co-location problem" (Wolf-Wendel et al. 2004). The dual-career situation often leads to a compromise, with one partner putting his/her career on hold or settling for a less prestigious position for the benefit of the other's career. According to the Cornell Couples and Careers study, 12% of men and 39% of women regard their spouses' career as more important than their own

(Moen et al. 1999). In fact, a study of 13 leading research universities in the USA found that 40 % of academic women refused outside offers due to their partner not receiving an adequate offer in the area, making it the top reason why women refused, compared to only 27 % of academic men (Schiebinger et al. 2008). Based on these findings, STEM women faculty who are married or partnered to STEM men may be more inclined to sacrifice their careers for their spouse or partner, which further contributes to the leaky pipeline effect.

In a study investigating the "two-body problem" at one university in the USA, researchers found support for their hypothesis that joint hire faculty members (both the primary hire and partner) in STEM fields are just as statistically productive than their colleagues, if not more so, thus alleviating concerns about the productivity of joint hires in STEM (Woolstenhulme et al. 2012). This hypothesis was based on the premise that couples in academia will likely accept positions at less prestigious universities in order to be in the same location together. Additionally, joint hires in STEM were found to be 22 % more likely than their colleagues to obtain a grant, and the joint hire in STEM produced on average 0.73 more publications than their mean nonjoint hire colleague (Woolstenhulme et al. 2012).

Although women in STEM fields with families face numerous challenges when juggling work and family, there are many benefits associated with having a supportive family. For instance, one study in the western USA found that female university employees with supportive spouses or partners experienced significantly less WFC than unmarried or unpartnered employees, and this effect was five times larger for women than men (Elliott 2003). This WFC should lead to women staying in STEM fields as opposed to leaking from the pipeline. Additionally, married faculty members have the benefit of similar yearly work schedules, which makes planning vacations and sabbaticals less complicated.

In another study of dual-career academic couples in the USA, the couples reported they were "more successful" due to their partner and cited several reasons for their increased success (Schiebinger et al. 2008). Fifty-eight percent of the dual-career academic couples in the sample said that they benefit from shared professional networks, colleagues, and friends, compared to only 25 % or less of the faculty members with spouses employed elsewhere or stay-at-home spouses. Interestingly, 35 % of the faculty in the sample with spouses who were nonacademic or stay-at-home reported gains in research productivity due to their partner, whereas 44 % of the dual-academic career faculty reported research gains due to their partner (Schiebinger et al. 2008).

15.3.6 Balancing Critical Career Experiences with Family Demands

A sixth family-related challenge to a STEM career is simultaneously managing critical career experiences and family demands. Attending conferences is important for professors to disseminate their research and establish their reputations in their fields. It fosters networking with colleagues with similar interests who could become collaborators on research projects and grant applications and facilitates new relationships with potential students and postdoctoral candidates as well as senior colleagues who may serve as external reviewers of tenure packages. Similarly, attending conferences and professional development workshops is advantageous for individuals in nonacademic STEM careers in order to learn about up-to-date knowledge and best practices in their field as well as to facilitate networking opportunities with potential clients and/or business associates.

A potential effect of having children and breastfeeding on women in STEM is the reduced availability and comfort with extended conference travel, particularly international travel. In a study of presenters at the European Society for Evolutionary Biology (ESEB) Congress 2011, female scientists declined invitations to speak half of the time, compared to only about a quarter of the time for men (Schroeder et al. 2013). Women were significantly underrepresented as presenters at the symposia (15 %), as well as among the oral presenters (41 %), plenary speakers (25 %), and all presenters (46 %), although all abstracts submitted were accepted. The authors of this study surmised that this disparity is due to a number of reasons, including childcare responsibilities (Chesley and Moen 2006; Schroeder et al. 2013). Taken together, these findings demonstrate that further research should examine the possibility that family and childcare responsibilities preclude women from having the availability to travel to speak at conferences and other important networking opportunities. Presenting at and attending conferences is essential, particularly during the first few years of career establishment, and this lack of availability could stymie the success of women in STEM fields.

A recent study by Casadevall and Handelsman (2014) examined symposia at two meetings held by the American Society for Microbiology and found that having at least one woman on the convening team was associated with reduced likelihood of having an all-male presentation by approximately 70 %. When organized by all men (who were perhaps influenced by gender roles), an average of 30 % of the sessions were held by all-male speakers, compared to an average of only 8.9 % when organized by a team that included at least one woman. Although this study is correlational and does not identify the cause of these findings, it nonetheless supports the importance of having women on STEM conference committees as a way to promote the inclusion of women on conference programs.

Along those lines, grants are extremely important and necessary in STEM fields as evidenced by some university policies that require evidence of a history of extramural funding prior to consideration for hire and when awarding tenure. Not attending conferences may also result in lack of access to funding opportunities that are imperative to employment at a research university or national laboratory. A recent study found that among married tenure-track faculty with young children, women are 21 % less likely than men to have their work partially or entirely funded by federal grants or contracts (Goulden et al. 2009). Additionally, among married tenure-track women, those with young children were found to be 26 % less likely than those without young children to have their work funded partially or completely by federal grants or contracts. These small setbacks early on can accumulate to form a larger disadvantage that lingers for the length of the career.

15.4 Organizational Barriers to the Success of STEM Women with Family Demands

Several organizational barriers can also impede STEM women's success. Specifically, contextual factors such as an unsupportive or "chilly" climate, historical underrepresentation of women in STEM careers, long-term career consequences for those who choose to have children, and a lack of successful female role models who effectively manage work and family demands have all been linked to the lack of women in STEM careers. These barriers are discussed in the next section.

15.4.1 Chilly Organizational Climates

Another fundamental explanation for the leaky pipeline is believed to be the lack of work–family support for individuals in these job domains (Fouad and Singh 2011). As these occupations have been historically male, the culture surrounding STEM careers has developed in a manner that is not conducive to the careers of individuals also managing extensive family-demands. As a result, STEM organizations offer fewer programs and policies that enable schedule control or the ability to take breaks in one's career trajectory than non-STEM organizations (Fouad and Singh 2011). Similarly, the culture that has evolved is one in which attending to family obligations (or even considering this) is not supported or encouraged. Fouad and Singh (2011) found that women engineers in the USA with high levels of work-demands working in environments with negative climates for women experienced high-levels of WFC. Finally, some STEM occupations (e.g., IT) require employees to be available during nontraditional work hours as well as have unpredictable schedules (Major et al. 2003). While STEM careers have become renowned for innovation in numerous arenas, due to the stagnation of family-supportive leadership, as well as lack of initiatives to enable employees to manage competing role demands, women frequently leave STEM careers.

A recent meta-analysis of family-friendly policies examined how the availability of policies and family-supportive organizational perceptions (FSOP; Allen 2001) influence work attitudes and found that FSOP yielded stronger relationships with positive job attitudes and a stronger negative relationship with work-to-family conflict than the availability of policies (Butts et al. 2013). This study indicates that perceptions of family-supportiveness matter, and simply having family-friendly policies does not guarantee their effectiveness at improving employee attitudes and decreasing work–family conflict.

Further, a recent study of faculty members at a Tier I research institution in the USA found that women reported significantly less FSOP than men (Jean et al. 2014). In addition, both male and female STEM faculty reported less FSOP compared to non-STEM faculty. These results showed that STEM departments were lagging behind non-STEM departments in family-friendliness, which may contribute to women being less attracted to or ultimately leaving positions in STEM fields. Some researchers have pointed to the "old-boy network" defined as "managers' preference to interact with other managers of similar status rather than with line employees, and intentional exclusion by managers who have negative stereotypes about women's and minorities' abilities, motivation, and job preferences" (Noe 2013, p. 437) as a possible explanation for the "chilly climate" experienced in STEM departments.

Some researchers argue that initiatives designed to increase the family supportiveness of work cultures may ultimately be of limited effectiveness, as work cultures do not reduce the family demands women experience due to their primary caregiver role (Fouad and Singh 2011). Programs that provide women with the ability to successfully manage family demands around work demands and vice versa may be more effective at increasing the retention of women in the STEM workforce. For many women with resources, this means outsourcing some household chores including cleaning, laundry, and cooking.

15.4.2 Motherhood Penalty

Data from the Perceptions of Women in Academic Science study demonstrate that US female scientists have fewer children than desired compared to their male counterparts, and they are more likely to attribute having fewer children than desired to their careers as scientists (Ecklund and Lincoln 2011). A number of researchers have speculated about the effects of parenting on careers. Unfortunately, researchers have consistently demonstrated a "motherhood penalty" in which women experience more negative effects of parenting than men and sometimes men actually benefit (Correll et al. 2007). This has been demonstrated when examining salaries, hierarchical positions within academia (non-tenure track vs. tenure track and associate vs. full), and retention in academia with even stronger effects for women in STEM (Mason et al. 2013). The motherhood penalty also occurs outside of academia. For example, Budig and England (2001) found a 5 % wage penalty per child after controlling for job experience in a longitudinal study of a US sample of 5000 women employed in a wide range of occupations. In addition, women in nonacademic STEM careers describe experiencing a "motherhood penalty" or "family penalty" as an important obstacle to their career success (Simard et al. 2008).

15.4.3 Underrepresentation of STEM Women in Leadership Positions

Family-related challenges discouraging women from remaining in STEM careers have led to a dearth of women in STEM leadership positions. Since Valian's (1999) influential work examining gender inequities in various occupations, little has changed with regard to the underrepresentation of women in executive leadership roles in organizations, particularly STEM companies. Although gender schemas have begun to change, STEM careers and organizations have been particularly slow to accept women's roles in management as well as recognize how family supportive organizational culture can influence the attraction and retention of capable female employees (Soe and Yakura 2008).

As STEM domains have been historically male-dominated (Kanter 1977), the culture of STEM workplaces has been heavily defined by issues of gender inequality and sexism (Fouad et al. 2011). STEM job domains and organizations have remained predominantly populated by men and thus sustained cultural norms and expectations of what is an "ideal" STEM employee. Because the need to balance career and family remains a primary factor pushing women out of STEM careers, relatively few women have attained senior or leadership positions in STEM careers (Rossler and Taylor 2009). Sociological examinations of the culture of engineering have identified that stereotypically "masculine" characteristics of technical obsession, territorialism, and aggressive self-promotion were distinguishing features of engineering cultures (Fouad et al. 2011; Robinson and McIlwee 1991). While both men and women associate characteristics of their own sex as relating to managerial ability, men do not identify female traits with managerial characteristics (whereas women classify traits from both sexes as managerial characteristics; Schein and Mueller 1992). Thus, leadership in STEM fields has perpetuated a schema of masculine characteristics associated with leadership (Eagly and Karau 2002). Correspondingly, the individuals who are most likely to succeed are those who display traits typically associated with maleness, leading to the marginalization and underrepresentation of women in STEM leadership roles. As a result, women in STEM careers have relatively few examples to look toward when trying to navigate their career paths while simultaneously maintaining family obligations.

These findings suggest that a lack of women in organizational leadership, particularly in STEM industries, has led to the perception that the best model of leadership is the male model. While many STEM leaders have families, this model suggests that in order to succeed, one cannot be the primary caregiver. As a result, relatively few examples of executive women leaders exist, and even fewer who have managed to effectively balance work and family demands. Therefore, a lack of female role models in STEM industries appears to be an additional barrier facing women seeking successful careers in STEM. While both career and psychosocial (i.e., social support) mentorship have been associated with career mobility in the USA (Scandura 1992), relatively few studies have examined how psychosocial mentorship or specifically having a mentor provide guidance on how to manage work and family demands can benefit women, particularly women in STEM careers. Thus, more research is needed examining the ways in which organizations can provide guidance for women regarding how to be successful in managing a STEM career and family demands.

15.5 Initiatives to Facilitate the Promotion and Retention of Women in STEM Careers

Despite the upsetting trends in STEM academic and nonacademic jobs, many promising initiatives have recently launched in order to assess the underlying causes of the leaky pipeline effect and implement programs to help women overcome the obstacles to success in these fields. These initiatives are targeted at women of all age groups, including young children. Trends supported by federal government research grants alongside organizational efforts suggest that women in STEM disciplines and careers will have brighter futures.

Companies have begun actively attempting to change the perceptions of what STEM fields look like by encouraging girls and young women to become and remain interested in STEM careers (Starnes 2013). One particularly exciting effort to facilitate the increase of interests in STEM in young girls is by a company called Goldie Blox based in the USA. These construction sets are designed to increase girls' interest in STEM subjects. The goal behind these and similar efforts is to engage girls in STEM at an early age, potentially mitigating the societal gender expectations of these career interests. Another noteworthy partnership began in 2010 between the Fortune 500 company 3M and the University of Minnesota's *STEM Education Center* to train elementary and secondary school teachers to successfully integrate STEM subjects into their courses in order to increase students' interest in STEM disciplines and careers (University of Minnesota 2013). Through these efforts, the University of Minnesota has trained thousands of graduates to go on to work at 3M. Numerous similar efforts are underway across the country, many of them funded by the National Science Foundation (NSF) and by corporations. In fact, each year Catalyst, a leading nonprofit organization with a mission to expand opportunities for women and business, gives the Catalyst Award to one or more companies that demonstrate innovative organizational approaches to the recruitment and advancement of women (Catalyst.org).

The NSF's ADVANCE-IT program provides funding to academic institutions with the goal of promoting research and interventions to improve outcomes of STEM women faculty members and to better understand the unique issues they face (National Science Foundation n.d.). The NSF has awarded over $ 130 million to over 100 institutions in support of proposed research and initiatives aimed at increasing and retaining faculty in STEM disciplines. As a result, research and programs developed by these institutions have shed light on the experiences of women in STEM fields and the factors that lead to the leaky pipeline effect. Additionally, many tools have been developed that can be utilized to support similar objectives in other academic and nonacademic settings. For example, Rice University developed a career workshop for postdocs and late stage PhD students from underrepresented minority groups in STEM disciplines to help prepare them for academic careers (Rice University n.d.). Another notable ADVANCE initiative is Michigan's Strategies and Tactics for Recruiting to Improve Diversity and Excellence (STRIDE) training for recruitment and retention (University of Michigan 2013). The NSF also has a career-life balance initiative and the National Institute of Health (NIH) has a number of family-friendly initiatives including parental leave stipends, developmental supplements following time off to attend to family, and the requirement to identify childcare resources when hosting a conference funded by NIH.

Although women in STEM careers have relatively few examples to look toward when trying to navigate their career paths, there are some resources available that may help them succeed in leadership roles while meeting family demands. For example, a recent book describes the experiences and success of 10 women US university presidents, 9 of whom have children (Madsen 2008). Additionally, a book of personal narratives was recently published that focuses on the ways in which female scientists can be successful in both their careers and motherhood, and underscores the need for organizations to assist with and adapt to the needs of scientists with children (Monsson 2008). Likewise, other compilations of success strategies for STEM women have been published as well (e.g., Pritchard 2006).

Recognizing the overlap between the biological and tenure clocks, universities have attempted to accommodate by allowing faculty members to take extension(s) on their tenure clock in order to provide care for a newborn. Flexible tenure clock policies, also referred to as "stop clock policies," are defined as policies that provide tenure-track faculty with the option of postponing their tenure review if events occur that are likely to negatively impact their research productivity. Extensions are usually granted in increments of 1 year (Manchester et al. 2013) and were originally adopted to attract women to academia, to develop equity, and to facilitate work–family balance (Manchester et al. 2010). For these reasons, tenure clock extensions are common, particularly amongst female faculty for the purpose of childbirth or childcare. Nonetheless, some recent research revealed a wage penalty associated with extending the tenure clock for family reasons as opposed to nonfamily reasons (Manchester et al. 2010). This finding highlights the persistent disadvantage associated with the alignment of tenure and biological clocks for women. Certainly some female faculty choose to have children before earning tenure and given the ticking biological clock, one can certainly appreciate why.

In addition to fostering a family-supportive climate, there are specific work–family support policies which are aimed at providing employees the ability to balance work and nonwork role demands that are being adopted with increasing prevalence (e.g., tenure clock extensions, flextime; Matos and Galinsky 2012). Work–family support policies are defined broadly as policies organizations implement that are designed to reduce WFC (Butts et al. 2013). While at least some work–family support policies exist at most universities and organizations, the climate at each university/organization, and even within each department, may not support their use, thereby rendering them less useful to employees. Therefore, it is important to have *both* a supportive climate and formal policies in place.

Workplace flexibility has been cited as an organizational tool enabling employees to navigate between work and family roles while meeting the needs of employers and clients (Kossek et al. 2014). In a study of best practices of IT supervisors in the USA, Major et al. (2003) identified that high-performing supervisors offered some form of flexible scheduling to their employees due to the highly demanding nature of IT work schedules, despite the fact that the policies were often informal and on case-by-case bases. Correspondingly, because of the detrimental role that WFC plays in STEM women's careers (Fouad and Singh 2011), researchers have identified the importance of family-friendly policies for the retention of women in STEM (Villablanca et al. 2011).

In support of these trends, in 2009, President Obama signed an Executive Order establishing the White House Council of Women and Girls to identify and confront issues of inequality and resulting challenges for women of all ages (whitehouse.gov n.d.). In response, many STEM companies, groups, and agencies have initiated efforts to actively recognize examples of women in STEM careers as well as target and address issues that lead girls and women to drop out of the STEM pipeline. The National Aeronautics and Space Administration (NASA) launched the Women@NASA website, celebrating the success of women throughout NASA's history through a collection of 64 videos and essays describing the many roles that women play across the agency (NASA 2013). In addition, the National Institutes of Health (NIH) supports work–life balance by providing grantee institutions with policies and practices to support family-friendly environments (NIH n.d.). Similarly, the NSF launched the Career-Life Balance Initiative to promote family-friendly policies with the goal of clearing the path for women in STEM from graduate education to careers in STEM (White House 2011).

15.6 Conclusion

In summary, there are a number of family-related challenges that likely contribute to underrepresentation of women in STEM, especially at the higher ranks. Overall, there is considerable overlap between the time periods in which critical career-related development and experiences are expected and required to occur (e.g., academic tenure) and when women are at the optimal age to conceive and bare children. Additional challenges include dependent care (both child and elder) and dual-career considerations. Theoretically, many of these challenges come about because traditional gender roles and stereotypes result in (implicitly) biased decision making by women themselves as well as many important others. Fortunately, there are many national and organizational/university initiatives directed at repairing the leaky pipeline, as well as individual strategies. Continued efforts to educate key decision makers and alleviate these challenges will hopefully result in fewer disparities between men and women in STEM careers.

References

Allen, T. D. (2001). Family-supportive work environments: The role of organizational perceptions. *Journal of Vocational Behavior, 58,* 414–435.

Armenti, C. (2004). May babies and posttenure babies: Maternal decisions of women professors. *The Review of Higher Education, 27,* 211–231.

Bennett, S. K. (1982). Student perceptions of and expectations for male and female instructors: Evidence relating to the question of gender bias in teaching evaluation. *Journal of Educational Psychology, 74,* 170–179.
Blickenstaff, J. C. (2005). Women and science careers: Leaky pipeline or gender filter? *Gender and Education, 17,* 369–386.
Budig, M. J., & England, P. (2001). The wage penalty for motherhood. *American Sociological Review, 66,* 204–225.
Bureau of Labor Statistics. (2010). Employment characteristics of families. http://www.bls.gov/news.release/archives/famee_03242011.pdf. Accessed 1 April 2014.
Bureau of Labor Statistics. (2012). Postsecondary teachers. http://www.bls.gov.ooh/education-training-and-library/postsecondary-teachers.htm. Accessed 1 April 2014.
Burke, R. J. (2007). Women and minorities in STEM: A primer. In R. J. Burke & M. C. Mattis (Eds.), *Women and minorities in science, technology, engineering and mathematics: Upping the numbers* (pp. 3–27). Northampton: Edward Elgar.
Butts, M. M., Casper, W. J., & Yang, T. S. (2013). How important are work–family support policies? A meta-analytic investigation of their effects on employee outcomes. *Journal of Applied Psychology, 98,* 1–25.
Casadevall, A., & Handelsman, J. (2014). The presence of female conveners correlates with a higher proportion of female speakers at scientific symposia. *mBio, 5,* 1–4.
Ceci, S. J., & Williams, W. M. (2007). *Why aren't more women in science? Top researchers debate the evidence.* Washington, DC: American Psychological Association.
Chesley, N., & Moen, P. (2006). When workers care: Dual-earner couples' caregiving strategies, benefit use, and psychological well-being. *American Behavioral Scientist, 49,* 1248–1269.
Cleary-Goldman, J., Malone, F. D., Vidaver, J., Ball, R. H., Nyberg, D. A., Comstock, C. H. et al. (2005). Impact of maternal age on obstetric outcomes. *Obstetrics & Gynecology, 105,* 983–990.
Collins, R. L. (2011). Content analysis of gender roles in media: Where are we now and where should we go? *Sex Roles, 64,* 290–298.
Correll, S. J., Benard, S., & Paik, I. (2007). Getting a job: Is there a motherhood penalty? *American Journal of Sociology, 112,* 1297–1338.
Eagly, A. H. (1987). *Sex differences in social behavior: A social-role interpretation.* Hillsdale: Erlbaum.
Eagly, A. H., & Karau, S. J. (2002). Role congruity theory of prejudice toward female leaders. *Psychological Review, 109,* 573–598.
Eagly, A. H., Wood, W., & Diekman, A. B. (2000). Social role theory of sex differences and similarities: A current appraisal. In: T. Eckes & H. M. Trautner (Eds.), *The developmental social psychology of gender* (pp. 123–174). Mahwah: Erlbaum.
Ecklund, E. H., & Lincoln, A. E. (2011). Scientists want more children. *PLoS One, 6*(8), e22590.
Elliott, M. (2003). Work and family role strain among university employees. *Journal of Family and Economic Issues, 24,* 157–181.
Fouad, N. A., & Singh, R. (2011). Retention and attrition: The impact of workplace climate on women in the engineering field. *Marine Technology, 48,* 9–11.
Fouad, N., Fitzpatrick, M., & Liu, J. (2011). Persistence of women in engineering careers: A qualitative study of current and former female engineers. *Journal of Women and Minorities in Science and Engineering, 17,* 69–96.
Goldie Blox. (n.d.). http://www.goldieblox.com/. Accessed 1 April 2014.
Goulden, M., Frasch, K., & Mason, M. A. (2009). *Staying competitive: Patching America's leaky pipeline in the sciences.* Berkeley: Berkeley Center on Health, Economic, & Family Security and the Center for American Progress.
Greenhaus, J. H., & Beutell, N. J. (1985). Sources of conflict between work and family roles. *Academy of Management Review, 10,* 76–88.
Greenwald, A. G., & Banaji, M. R. (1995). Implicit social cognition: Attitudes, self-esteem, and stereotypes. *Psychological Review, 102,* 4–27.
Hammer, L. B., & Neal, M. B. (2008). Working sandwiched-generation caregivers: Prevalence, characteristics, and outcomes. *The Psychologist-Manager Journal, 11,* 93–112.
Hill, C., Corbett, C., & St. Rose, A. (2010). *Why so few? Women in science, technology, engineering, and math.* Washington, DC: AAUW.

Jean, V. A., & Payne, S. C., & Thompson, R. J. (June 2014). Are STEM departments family-supportive work environments? Paper presented at the work family researchers network conference. New York, USA.

Kanter, R. M. (1977). *Men and women of the corporation*. New York: Basic Books.

Knobloch-Westerwick, S., Glynn, C. J., & Huge, M. (2013). The Matilda effect in science communication: An experiment on gender bias in publication quality perceptions and collaboration interest. *Science Communication, 35,* 603–625.

Kossek, E., Hammer, L., Thompson, R., & Burke, L. 2014. *Leveraging workplace flexibility: Fostering engagement and productivity*. Alexandria: SHRM Foundation report.

Li, J. (2009). Academic couples and the economics of the co-location problem (Unpublished doctoral dissertation). University of Minnesota, Minneapolis, Minnesota.

Madera, J. M., Hebl, M. R., & Martin, R. C. (2009). Gender and letters of recommendation for academia: Agentic and communal differences. *Journal of Applied Psychology, 94,* 1591–1599.

Madsen, S. R. (2008). *On becoming a woman leader: Learning from the experiences of university presidents*. San Francisco: Wiley.

Major, D. A., Davis, D. D., Germano, L. M., Fletcher, T. D., Sanchez-Hucles, J., & Mann, J. (2003). Managing human resources in information technology: Best practices of high performing supervisors. *Human Resource Management, 46,* 411–427.

Manchester, C. F., Leslie, L. M., & Kramer, A. (2010). Stop the clock policies and career success in academia. *American Economic Review, 100,* 219–223.

Manchester, C. F., Leslie, L. M., & Kramer, A. (2013). Is the clock still ticking? An evaluation of the consequences of stopping the tenure clock. *ILR Review, 66,* 3–31.

Martel, R., Lane, D. M., & Willis, C. (1996). Male-female differences: A computer simulation. *American Psychologist, 51,* 157–158.

Mason, M. A., Wolflinger, N. H., & Goulden, M. (2013). *Do babies matter? Gender and family in the ivory tower*. New Brunswick: Rutgers University Press.

Matos, K., & Galinsky, E. (2012). 2012 National study of employers. New York: Families and Work Institute. http://familiesandwork.org/site/research/reports/NSE_2012.pdf. Accessed 1 April 2014.

Menez, R., Munder, I., & Töpsch, K. (2001). Personnel recruitment and qualification in the IT sector–first results of the on-line study BIT-S. In Proceedings of the conference «Innovations for an e-society: challenges for technology assessment, ITAS Karlsruhe.

Moen, P., Harris-Abbott, D., Lee, S., & Roehling, P. V. (1999). The Cornell couples and careers study. Cornell Employment and Family Careers Institute.

Monsson, E. (2008). *Motherhood, the elephant in the laboratory: Women scientists speak out*. Ithaca: Cornell University Press.

Morgan, H., & Milliken, F. J. (1993). Keys to action: Understanding differences in organizations' responsiveness to work-and-family issues. *Human Resource Management, 31,* 227–248.

Morgan, W. B., Walker, S. S., Hebl, M. R., & King, E. B. (2013). A field experiment: Reducing interpersonal discrimination toward pregnant job applicants. *Journal of Applied Psychology, 98,* 799–809.

NASA. (2013, November). Women and girls initiative. http://women.nasa.gov/. Accessed 1 April 2014.

National Center for Biotechnology Information. (2013). Infertility: Inability to conceive; Unable to get pregnant. http://www.ncbi.nlm.nih.gov/pubmedhealth/PMH0002173/. Accessed 1 April 2014.

National Institute of Health. (n.d.). NIH family-friendly initiatives. http://grants.nih.gov/grants/family_friendly.htm. Accessed 1 April 2014.

National Science Foundation. (n.d.). ADVANCE at a glance. http://www.nsf.gov/crssprgm/advance/. Accessed 1 April 2014.

National Science Foundation, National Center for Science and Engineering Statistics. (2013). Women, minorities, and persons with disabilities in science and engineering: 2013. Special Report NSF 13-304. Arlington, VA. http://www.nsf.gov/statistics/wmpd/. Accessed 1 April 2014.

Noe, R. A. (2013). *Employee training and development*. New York: McGraw Hill.

Pitt-Catsouphes, M., Matz-Costa, C., & Besen, E. (2009). *Age and generations: Understanding experiences at the workplace (Research Highlight 6)*. Chestnut Hill: The Sloan Center on Aging and Work at Boston College.

Preston, A. E. (2004). *Leaving science: Occupational exit from scientific careers*. New York: Russell Sage.

Pritchard, P. A. (Ed.). (2006). *Success strategies for women in science: A portable mentor*. Boston: Elsevier.

Rice University. (n.d.). Rice University's future faculty workshop. http://advance.rice.edu/futurefacultyworkshop/. Accessed 1 April 2014.

Robinson, J. G., & McIlwee, J. S. (1991). Men, women, and the culture of engineering. *The Sociological Quarterly, 32,* 403–421.

Rossler, S. V., & Taylor, M. Z. (2009). Why are we still worried about women in science? Academe. American Association of University Professors. http://www.aaup.org/article/why-are-we-still-worried-about-women-science#.Uvjq7vldXzg. Accessed 1 April 2014.

Scandura, T. A. (1992). Mentorship and career mobility: An empirical investigation. *Journal of Organizational Behavior, 13,* 169–174.

Schein, V. E., & Mueller, R. (1992). Sex-role stereotyping and requisite management characteristics: A cross-cultural look. *Journal of Organizational Behavior, 13,* 439–447.

Schiebinger L., Henderson, A. D., & Gilmartin, S. K. (2008). *Dual-career academic couples: What universities need to know*. Stanford: The Michelle R. Clayman Institute for Gender Research.

Schroeder, J., Dugdale, H. L., Radersma, R., Hinsch, M., Buehler, D. M., Saul, J., et al. (2013). Fewer invited talks by women in evolutionary biology symposia. *Journal of Evolutionary Biology, 26,* 2063–2069.

Simard, C., Henderson, A. D., Gilmartin, S. K., Schiebinger, L., & Whitney, T. (2008). *Climbing the technical ladder: Obstacles and solutions for mid-level women in technology*. Michelle R. Clayman Institute for Gender Research, Stanford University, Anita Borg Institute for Women and Technology, Stanford, CA.

Soe, L., & Yakura, E. K. (2008). What's wrong with the pipeline? Assumptions about gender and culture in IT work. *Women's Studies, 37,* 176–201.

Spencer, S. J., Steele, C. M., & Quinn, D. (1999). Stereotype threat and women's math performance. *Journal of Experimental Social Psychology, 35,* 4–28.

Starnes, A. (2013, Jun). Eight organizations promote women in STEM. http://stemwire.org/2013/06/04/eight-organizations-promote-women-in-stem/. Accessed 1 April 2014.

Steele, C. M., & Aronson, J. (1995). Stereotype threat and the intellectual test performance of African-Americans. *Journal of Personality and Social Psychology, 69,* 797–811.

Steinpres, R. E., Anders, K. A., & Ritzke, D. (1999). The impact of gender on the review of the curricula vitae of job applicants and tenure candidates: A national empirical study. *Sex Roles, 41,* 509–528.

Sutton, P. D., Hamilton, B. E., & Mathews, T. J. (2011). *Recent decline in births in the United States, 2007–2009 (NCHS data brief, no. 60)*. Hyattsville: National Center for Health Statistics.

Trix, F., & Psenka, C. (2003). Exploring the color of glass: Letters of recommendation for female and male medical faculty. *Discourse and Society, 14,* 191–220.

University of Michigan. (2013). Committee on strategies and tactics for recruiting to improve diversity and excellence (STRIDE). http://sitemaker.umich.edu/advance/STRIDE_Committee. Accessed 1 April 2014.

University of Minnesota. (2013, October). Future STEM innovators. Discover. http://discover.umn.edu/news/teaching-education/3m-supports-us-stem-education-efforts-prepare-future-leaders. Accessed 1 April 2014.

U.S. Census Bureau. (2009). *Projections of the population by selected age groups and sex for the United States: 2010 to 2050*. Washington, DC: U.S. Census Bureau, Population Division.

Valian, V. (1999). *Why so slow? The advancement of women*. Cambridge: MIT Press.

Villablanca, A. C., Beckett, L., Nettiksimmons, J, & Howell, L. P. (2011). Career flexibility and family friendly policies: An NIH funded study to enhance women's careers in biomedical sciences. *Journal of Women's Health, 20,* 1485–1496.

Wagner, D. L. (1991). Eldercare: A workplace issue. In B.B. Hess & E.W. Markson (Eds.), *Growing old in America* (pp. 377–387). Piscataway: Transaction Publishers.

White House (2011). The White House and National Science Foundation announce new workplace flexibility policies to support America's scientists and their families. Retrieved August 5,2014 from: http://www.whitehouse.gov/thepress-office/2011/09/26/white-house-and-national-science-foundation-announce-new-workplace-flexi. Accessed 1 April 2014.

Wolf-Wendel, L., Twombly, S. B., & Rice, S. (2004). *The two-body problem: Dual-career-couple hiring practices in higher education*. Baltimore: Johns Hopkins University Press.

Woolstenhulme, J. L., Cowan, B. W., McCluskey, J. J., & Byington, T. C. (2012). *Evaluating the two-body problem: Measuring joint hire productivity with a university*. Unpublished manuscript.

Chapter 16
Examining the Work–Family Experience of Workaholic Women

Malissa A. Clark, Angela A. Beiler, and Lauren M. Zimmerman

16.1 Introduction

Evidence from a variety of sources suggests that employees in the USA are working increasingly long hours, both in terms of annual hours worked (Murphy and Sauter 2003; Schor 2003) and average hours worked per week (Brett and Stroh 2003; Kuhn and Lozano 2008). Several factors may be contributing to these trends, including advances in technology (e.g., smart phones) which have the potential to blur the boundaries between work and home (Wajcman et al. 2008) and facilitate working outside the traditional 9–5 workday. Furthermore, there have been steady increases in women's participation in the workforce over time (Jacobs and Gerson 2004; U.S. Department of Commerce 2011), the percentage of dual-earner households (Galinsky et al. 2009), and the number of households where mothers are the sole or primary provider (Wang et al. 2013). These trends have caught the attention of researchers, leading to a number of studies examining the impact of increased work involvement on work–family conflict.

Work–family conflict is a form of interrole conflict that occurs when role pressures from the work and home domains are mutually incompatible in some respect (Greenhaus and Beutell 1985). This conflict can be bidirectional in that one's work may interfere with one's family or home (work-to-family conflict; WFC) and one's family or home may interfere with one's work (family-to-work conflict; FWC).

M. A. Clark (✉)
Department of Psychology and Institute for Women's Studies,
University of Georgia, Psychology Building, Athens, GA 30602, USA
e-mail: clarkm@uga.edu

A. A. Beiler
Department of Psychology, University of Georgia, Athens, GA 30602-3013, USA
e-mail: aabeiler@uga.edu

L. M. Zimmerman
Department of Psychology, University of Georgia, Athens, GA 30602-3013, USA
e-mail: lzimm@uga.edu

M. J. Mills (ed.), *Gender and the Work-Family Experience*,
DOI 10.1007/978-3-319-08891-4_16

This interference may manifest in a number of forms, including time-based (when time spent in one domain makes it difficult to fulfill responsibilities in the other domain), strain-based (when strain experienced in one domain hinders performance in the other domain), or behavior-based (when behaviors performed in one domain are incompatible with behaviors in the other domain). Examinations of overall work–family conflict have strongly supported a relationship between work hours and increased work–family conflict (Adkins and Premeaux 2012; Hughes and Parkes 2007; Matthews et al. 2012). For example, Adkins and Premeaux (2012) examined the relationship between work hours and both WFC and FWC at a variety of organizational levels, as well as examining potential moderators. They found a positive linear relationship between hours worked and WFC, and a curvilinear relationship between hours worked and FWC. These findings suggest an ability to adjust family roles to minimize interference with work after conflict exceeds a certain point, although that same flexibility does not exist in the opposite direction for work roles. Additionally, the study found that number of children moderates this relationship, such that individuals with more children experience greater levels of WFC, yet families with fewer children experience a stronger relationship between the number of hours worked and levels of WFC. Hughes and Parkes (2007) also found a positive relationship between work hours and work–family conflict, as well as support for the moderating role of work-time control. Individuals with higher work-time control experienced lower levels of conflict, which in turn was negatively related to family satisfaction outcomes.

Although the relationship between work hours and work–family conflict has been examined in a number of contexts, conspicuously absent from the work–family literature is an examination of the role of workaholism (a dispositional form of heavy work investment; see Snir and Harpaz 2012). Given that a key characteristic of workaholics is that they often spend excessive time at work or thinking about work (Scott et al. 1997), it is not surprising that research has found that workaholics tend to experience a variety of negative outcomes, such as greater work–family conflict (e.g., Bakker et al. 2009) and poorer psychological and physical well-being (Andreassen et al. 2007; Taris et al. 2005). While workaholism may yield negative outcomes overall, the basic premise of this chapter is that workaholic women may experience a greater number of negative work–family outcomes compared to their male counterparts, due to such factors as societal pressures suggesting that women should be more heavily invested in their families (Blair-Loy 2001) and the fact that women typically have more family responsibilities than men (Carli and Eagly 2012).

In this chapter, we first review the concept of workaholism, as well as its relationship with work–family conflict. Next, we review the literature on gender roles and societal norms, and how these will uniquely impact work–family outcomes of workaholism for women. Specifically, we propose that workaholic women face extra pressures compared to workaholic men, and may in fact suffer even greater negative consequences as a result of their workaholic behavior. These extra pressures are largely due to the conflict that women experience between their inner drive to work and traditional gender role expectations, which expect women to be primarily devoted to their families. We then present empirical data which tests some possible emotional mediators in the relationship between workaholism and work–family conflict for working women. Finally, we discuss overall conclusions and an agenda for future research.

16.2 Workaholism

Workaholism can be defined as "an internal drive to work, in which an individual is consumed with thoughts and feelings about work, and he/she spends excessive time working and/or thinking about work (even when it is not required of them) to the exclusion of other important life roles" (Clark et al. 2014). Workaholics are driven to work because of internal factors such as an obsession with working or feelings that one "should" be working (Oates 1971; Schaufeli et al. 2008a), rather than external factors such as organizational requirements or financial needs (Sussman 2012). Contrary to what is often discussed in the popular press, workaholics are *not* driven to work because of an internal passion or love of working (Clark et al. 2014; Mudrack 2006). That particular group of individuals is more appropriately called engaged workers (Schaufeli et al. 2008b) or devoted workers (Snir and Harpaz 2012). Instead, we (and others) argue that it is more appropriate to conceptualize workaholics as individuals who are essentially addicted to work, and that are consumed by feelings of guilt that one "should" be working as opposed to working because of a love or passion for work (Clark et al. 2014; McMillan and O'Driscoll 2006; Schaufeli et al. 2008b). Workaholics often continue working even when their behavior leads to negative outcomes (Sussman and Sussman 2011). They often miss family events, work evenings, and blur the lines between work and home by bringing their work home with them or choosing recreational activities that advance or complement their work (Bonebright et al. 2000; Ng et al. 2007).

Given that workaholics tend to spend an exorbitant amount of time at work at the expense of their family obligations (Scott et al. 1997; Sussman and Sussman 2011), it is not surprising that workaholism has been linked to greater work–family conflict. This relationship between workaholism and work–family conflict can be explained by both resource drain theory as well as spillover theory (see Edwards and Rothbard 2000). Resource drain theory suggests that when individuals expend personal resources (e.g., time, energy) in one domain (e.g., work), this depletes the available resources in another domain (e.g., family). Thus, workaholics may be more likely to experience WFC because they are expending a large amount of personal resources at their job. For example, a workaholic parent who spends a large amount of cognitive resources focusing on work tasks and projects during the day may be too exhausted to help their children complete their homework in the evening. Spillover theory, on the other hand, suggests that one's mood, skills, values, and behaviors experienced in one domain may spill over and impact (either positively or negatively) one's functioning in the other domain. Thus, negative emotions felt at home (e.g., guilt felt by workaholics when they are not working) may spill over and negatively affect them at work. Conversely, negative emotions felt at work (e.g., anxiety due to a workaholic's compulsive nature) may spill over and negatively affect them at home. Several studies have supported these ideas that workaholism is related to greater work–family conflict (e.g., Aziz et al. 2010; Bonebright et al. 2000; Taris et al. 2005). Furthermore, the positive relationship between workaholism and work–family conflict has been found in many different countries which have varied cultural norms and expectations toward work, including the USA (Aziz et al. 2010), Norway (Andreassen et al. 2013), the Netherlands (Bakker et al. 2009), Spain (del Libano et al. 2012), Italy (Guglielmi et al. 2012), and Japan (Shimazu et al. 2011).

Workaholism has also been shown to negatively affect the family unit. Specifically, research has shown that workaholism results in work–family crossover, where stress experienced by one individual crosses over to his or her spouse (Westman 2001). For example, Bakker et al. (2009) found that partners of workaholics reported receiving less social support, which in turn was related to lower partner relationship satisfaction. Additionally, a recent meta-analysis found that workaholism is related to lower family satisfaction and functioning and greater marital estrangement (Clark et al. 2014). Taken together, these studies suggest that not only does the workaholic individual suffer negative consequences, but the family of the workaholic also suffers.

Recent meta-analytic evidence (Clark et al. 2014) as well as primary studies (Burke 1999; Graves et al. 2012) have found little to no evidence for gender differences in self-reported workaholism. In other words, men and women may be equally likely to be workaholics. However, it is interesting to note that gender has been found to moderate the relationship between age and workaholism, suggesting that men and women may have different lifespan trajectories of workaholic behaviors (Clark et al. 2014). Specifically, using meta-analytic data and assessing gender as the proportion of women in the sample, Clark et al. found that in samples with the highest proportions of women, there was a positive correlation between age and workaholism, whereas in samples containing the largest proportions of men, there was a negative relationship between age and workaholism. This suggests that for men, workaholic behavior may decrease over one's lifespan, while for women, workaholic behavior may increase over one's lifespan. However, a direct test of this has not been conducted to date. Unfortunately, there has been little research on gender differences in workaholism, and no known studies have examined the relationship between gender role and workaholism.

In the next section, we propose that because of existing societal pressures suggesting that women should be more heavily invested in their families (Blair-Loy 2001), coupled with the fact that women typically have more family responsibilities than men (Carli and Eagly 2012), women will experience more negative work–family outcomes from their workaholic behavior than will men. We now turn to theory supporting this proposition.

16.3 Gender Roles and Societal Norms

To date, studies of workaholism have focused primarily on how someone's workaholic nature impacts various outcomes (e.g., personal, family, work). However, a basic premise of this chapter is that men's and women's *experiences* as a workaholic may differ in consequential ways. Specifically in regard to work–family conflict, we argue that the research to date has focused exclusively on how the noticeable characteristics of workaholism (e.g., the excessive number of hours worked or the persistent compulsion to work) influence work–family conflict. To our knowledge, one factor that has not been considered to date in the workaholism and work–family literature is whether a workaholic's perceptions and experiences of work–family conflict may be due to pressures from gender role expectations (Blair-Loy 2001).

According to traditional gender role expectations, men are responsible for acting as the main financial contributors for the family, allowing for a greater amount of attention to be paid directly to the work role rather than splitting time and resources between work and family roles. For men, being largely devoted to work may be viewed as an expected behavior and part of the "good provider" role, wherein men work to provide a stable income for the family (Bernard 1981). Because paid work has been traditionally viewed as men's main contribution to the family unit, a high investment in work is not likely to be viewed by men as having a strong impact on their perceived levels of work–family conflict (Gutek et al. 1991). Women, on the other hand, face unique struggles as they strive to balance their inner drive to be heavily involved in work, while also conforming to traditional gender role expectations that women should be intensely committed to their families. Further support for these differing gender expectations has been offered by Groysberg and Abrahams (2014), whose surveys of executives found that—regardless of gender—these employees felt that the responsibility of handling tensions between work and home to be primarily a women's problem. In addition to the internal struggle between their devotion to work and the pressures of gender role expectations, women may also be chastised by family, friends, and individuals in the community for their heavy involvement in work at the expense of their families (Gutek et al. 1991; Ridgeway 2011). All of these factors combined may lead to higher perceived levels of work–family conflict for women.

In her book, *Competing Devotions: Career and Family among Women Executives,* sociologist Mary Blair-Loy (2003) presents a fascinating description of the struggles faced by executive women, framing their struggles in terms of a clash between cultural work and family devotion schemas. According to Blair-Loy, cultural work and family devotion schemas are frameworks that individuals utilize to view, filter, understand, and appraise the present reality. Through time, schemas are developed by societies and become internalized within individuals to shape their personal goals, identities, and desires. In addition to fostering individual aspirations, cultural schemas are collectively shared to shape social structures within organizations and families. Specifically, Blair-Loy's (2001) work and family devotion schemas represent "ideal types" of individuals that influence how individuals spend their time, energy, and passion, that is particular either to their work or family.

The devotion to work schema emerged during the twentieth century when the pressure of capitalism encouraged men to immerse themselves in their professional careers, in order to secure a good income that allowed their wives to stay home and devote themselves to caring for the family. In addition to providing financial rewards, the work devotion schema promised individuals a sense of competence, identity, belonging, and meaning from their work (Blair-Loy 2003). On the other hand, the family devotion schema ascribes women to care for the home and family, while demanding complete allegiance to the role of being a mother. Additionally, this schema mandates a heterosexual marriage in which wives rely on their husbands for social status and financial sustenance, while husbands rely on their wives for physical and emotional support for themselves and their children (Blair-Loy 2001). In return for complying with these mandates, the family devotion schema provides women with a sense of fulfillment, meaning, creativity, and intimacy from raising their children. At the work and family devotion schemas' inception, these schemas were complementary; they prescribed husbands to care for the family financially through an intense devotion to their work, which allowed women to embrace the family devotion schema by staying at home with the children, and since women cared for the home and children, it also enabled husbands to fully embrace the work devotion schema (Blair-Loy 2003). However as more women embrace the work devotion schema by dedicating themselves to their work, the work and family devotion schemas have shifted from complementary devotion schemas to competing devotion schemas (Blair-Loy 2003).

As the number of dual-earner (Jacobs and Gerson 2004) and female-as-breadwinner (Wang et al. 2013) households continue to steadily increase, women are increasingly likely to experience competing work and family devotions. Specifically, competition between the work and family devotion schemas arises when women embrace the traditionally masculine work devotion schema to pursue professional careers, which is in opposition to the traditionally feminine family devotion schema that women are expected to embrace. This illustrates a violation of Eagly's (1987) social role theory of sex differences, which asserts that individuals tend to engage in activities that align with their culturally defined gender roles, due to external social pressures and individual internalized cultural gender expectations that intrinsically motivate individuals to engage in gender role congruent behaviors. However, when women immerse themselves in their work, they are engaging in behaviors that are incongruent with traditional gender role behaviors requiring women to devote all their time to their children in order to be "good" mothers.

One implication of women investing heavily in the work devotion schema is that they will likely experience higher levels of both WFC and FWC due to expectations that they are active and perform effectively in both work and family roles. Their male counterparts, however, may not experience the same pressure to take on responsibilities in the family domain, allowing them to invest more heavily in their work role. From a gender role perspective, women's experience of work–family conflict can be conceptualized at a deeper moral level as the conflict between what it means to be a good employee and what it means to be a good parent (Blair-Loy 2003). Specifically, WFC is likely to arise when workaholic women first have child(ren), which evokes the family devotion schema to fully devote oneself to caring for the home and children, even though they have previously embraced the work devotion schema due to their inner drive to work (Ridgeway 2011). However, men who are workaholics are not as likely to experience the same level of WFC as women because upon the arrival of children, the masculine work devotion schema of providing financially for the family is reemphasized, which mandates a contribution to the family by working as opposed to physically caring for the children (Ridgeway 2011). Accordingly, studies have shown that men tend to work more hours upon the arrival of children, while women tend to work fewer hours once they have children (Paull 2008). Therefore, as workaholic women juggle competing work and family demands, their long work hours and persistent inner drive to work may not allow them to fulfill all of their responsibilities in their family roles, resulting in WFC.

In addition to experiencing higher levels of WFC in comparison to men, workaholic women are also likely to experience increased levels of FWC. As noted by Ridgeway (2011), working women encounter "the maternal wall" in the workplace when they have children and are no longer viewed by the organization as the "ideal" worker who is agentic and assertive. Instead, they are now identified also as a mother who is communal and sensitive, which clashes with the "ideal" worker. One result of the "mother" image in the workplace is that working mothers tend to be viewed by organizations as lower-status, less valued, and less competent employees, due to the demands of motherhood impeding their effort to perform at work. Therefore, women experience inner conflict between conforming to the ideal worker, who is fully committed to and available for work, and the ideal mother, who is completely dedicated to and always there for her family and children. At the same time, women are also being held to higher standards by organizations to prove their ability and commitment to their work, since they are undermined as working mothers (Ridgeway 2011). Once again, men who are workaholics are not subject to opposition in the ideal worker and father roles, because the father role prescribes men to care financially for the family by working (Ridgeway 2011). Collectively, these experiences that women encounter, particularly the higher commitment and ability standards set by organizations, may hinder workaholic women's abilities to fulfill all of their responsibilities in their work roles since they have to work harder to meet the higher standards, leading to greater FWC.

An additional contributing factor to workaholic women's heightened experiences of WFC and FWC in comparison to men emanates from the increasing prevalence of organizations' "gendered" cultures (Cahusac and Kanji 2014; Lovejoy and Stone 2011). As more organizations promote the traditional linear career model by encouraging continuous work and upward mobility, organizational cultures are becoming more gendered with greater advantages for men. Specifically, men typically ascribe to the traditional linear career model due to their stable devotion to work, even upon the arrival of children. This consistency provides men with greater power in the organization in comparison to women, who may forgo the traditional linear career model by taking a break from employment to have children. Men's greater organizational power is reflected in increased opportunities for advancement, expansive social networks, and up-to-date skills due to their continual work, while women who have taken employment breaks (e.g., due to children) may have fewer advancement opportunities, smaller social networks, and greater skill deterioration, contributing to this deficit in power (Cahusac and Kanji 2014). Furthermore, as organizations encourage their employees to adopt the traditional linear career model that emphasizes long work hours to attain success, women experience conflict between the organization's push to work countless hours and the gender role expectation for women to devote time to the family. Therefore, women experience greater WFC and FWC due to the push and pull between work and family expectations as organizations promote the traditional career model that discourages women's employment breaks and results in diminished organizational power as women seek to return to work.

In addition to the inner conflict that workaholic women experience from their own competing work and family devotion schemas, these women are also likely to experience opposition from family, friends, and individuals in the community for their devotion to work at the (perceived) expense of their families. These external pressures arise when other individuals hold gender beliefs that are incongruent with the employee's gender beliefs and they express their disapproval (Ridgeway 2011). For example, even when someone has a supportive partner, individuals outside of the immediate family unit may still hold traditional work and family devotion schemas (Blair-Loy 2001), which prescribe men to care for the family by working and women to care for the family by managing the home and raising the children. Therefore, if a workaholic woman leaves her husband in charge of caring for the children in the evening so that she can complete a project for work, individuals outside of the immediate family unit may chastise her (whether confrontationally or more subtly) because it violates traditional work and family devotion schemas. Thus, workaholic women not only experience pressure and conflict from their internal struggles with work and family roles, but they also experience external pressure from other individuals.

Workaholic women face general societal norms that encourage greater participation in the home rather than work domain, potential inner conflict regarding their role as a "good parent" versus a "good employee", and possible outside pressure from individuals who do not agree with their decision to immerse themselves in the work environment. For these reasons, we propose that workaholic women will experience higher levels of negative outcomes than workaholic men, including greater work–family conflict. These negative outcomes may include both self-inflicted outcomes (via guilt) and negative outcomes inflicted by others (including guilt, societal pressures, etc.). In order to further understand the emotional experiences of workaholic women, we conducted an empirical study exploring the discrete emotions experienced by women both at work and at home, and how these discrete emotions mediate the relationship between workaholism and work–family conflict.

16.4 An Empirical Examination of Mood Spillover for Workaholic Women

Recall that work–family mood spillover theory (see Edwards and Rothbard 2000) suggests that the negative emotions that individuals experience at work or home may spill over and negatively impact functioning in the other domain. For example, after a frustrating day at work, this negative mood may influence one's mood at home and in turn negatively affect one's ability to interact in a positive and fulfilling way with one's spouse or children. In addition to traditional sources of negative moods at work or home (e.g., job demands, angry customers, family demands, conflict with spouse), we propose that workaholic women may experience additional stressors (e.g., pressure from her family members to devote more of her time and energy to family, self-imposed expectations of conforming to societal expectations of what it means to be a good mother), which may trigger a variety of negative emotions that her male counterparts may not experience to the same degree. For example, a woman who is a workaholic may experience a great amount of guilt and anxiety while she is at work because she is choosing not to adhere to the family devotion schema (Blair-Loy 2003). Men, on the other hand, are encouraged to contribute to the family via financial support. Therefore, they may not experience these same emotions when they are working.

To test these ideas, we conducted an empirical study involving 215 working women that explores the mediating role of negative emotions in the relationship between workaholism and work–family conflict. Specifically, we tested a model which examines whether negative emotions (i.e., guilt, anxiety, anger, and disappointment) at work and home mediate the relationship between workaholism and WFC/FWC.

The women involved in this study had an average age of 45 years (SD = 10.1) and worked an average of 37.7 hours (SD = 8.1) per week. Ninety-two percent of the women were married or in a serious committed relationship and 84 % had at least one child. Turning to the results of the two models, we first discuss the WFC model in which women's experience of negative emotions at work (i.e., guilt, anxiety, anger, and disappointment) mediate the relationship between workaholism and WFC (Fig. 16.1). Overall, this model fit the data very well [χ^2 (9) = 14.30, $p = 0.11$; CFI = 0.99; TLI = 0.96; RMSEA = 0.05; SRMR = 0.03] and accounted for a significant amount of the variance in WFC ($R^2 = 0.38$, $p < 0.001$).

Next, we discuss the specific relationships between workaholism, negative emotions at work, and WFC. First, there was a positive relationship between women's workaholic behaviors and WFC ($\beta = 0.23$, $p < 0.001$). Therefore, women with higher levels of workaholism experienced higher levels of WFC as compared to women with lower levels of workaholism. Next, we examined the mediating role of women's negative emotions experienced at work in the relationship between workaholism and WFC. Mediation results revealed that workaholism was positively related to work guilt ($\beta = 0.17$, $p < 0.05$), work anxiety ($\beta = 0.31$, $p < 0.001$), and work

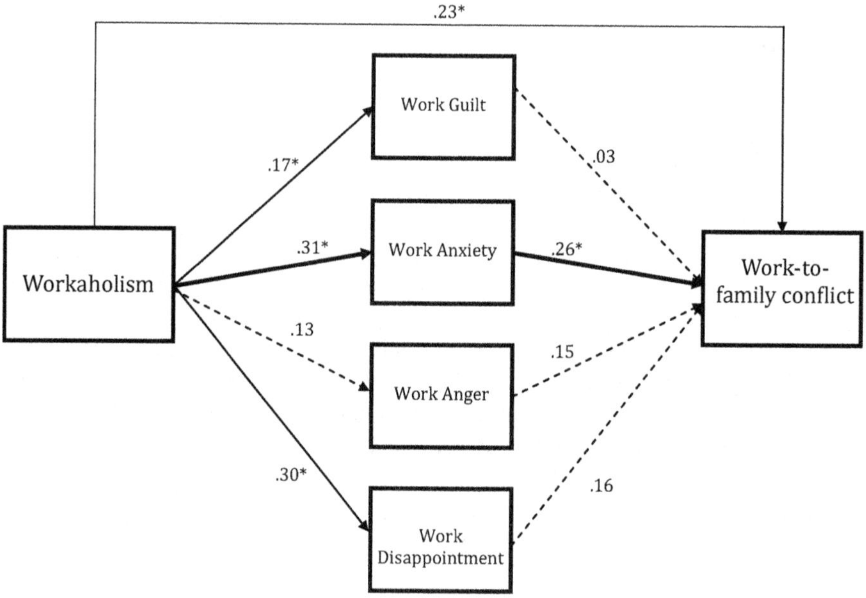

Fig. 16.1 Multiple-mediation model of workaholism on work-to-family conflict through negative emotions at work

disappointment ($\beta=0.30$, $p<0.001$); however, the relationship between workaholism and anger experienced at work was not significant ($\beta=0.13$, $p=0.07$). Only work anxiety ($\beta=0.23$, $p<0.001$) was positively related to WFC. Additionally, specific indirect effect analyses indicated that work anxiety (*indirect effect*=0.08, $CI_{0.95}=0.03, 0.13$) mediated the relationship between workaholism and WFC. Therefore, women's experience of anxiety at work is one mechanism through which workaholism can spill over and negatively impact women's functioning at home.

Moving on, we now discuss results from the FWC model, in which women's experiences of negative emotions at home (i.e., guilt, anxiety, anger, and disappointment) mediate the relationship between workaholism and FWC (Fig. 16.2). In general, this model fit the data well [χ^2 (9)=20.65, $p<0.05$; CFI=0.97; TLI=0.91; RMSEA=0.08; SRMR=0.04] and accounted for a significant amount of the variance in FWC ($R^2=0.29$, $p<0.001$). There was a positive relationship between workaholism and FWC ($\beta=0.27$, $p=0.001$), which suggests that women exhibiting higher levels of workaholism experience higher levels of FWC, compared to women exhibiting lower levels of workaholism.

We next examined the possible mediating effects of negative emotions in the relationship between workaholism and FWC. Results show that workaholism was positively related to home anxiety ($\beta=0.17$, $p=0.05$), home anger ($\beta=0.18$, $p=0.01$), and home disappointment ($\beta=0.16$, $p=0.01$); however, workaholism was not significantly related to home guilt ($\beta=0.12$, $p=0.14$). Only home anger ($\beta=0.21$, $p<0.05$) was positively related to FWC, indicating that the greater a woman's anger

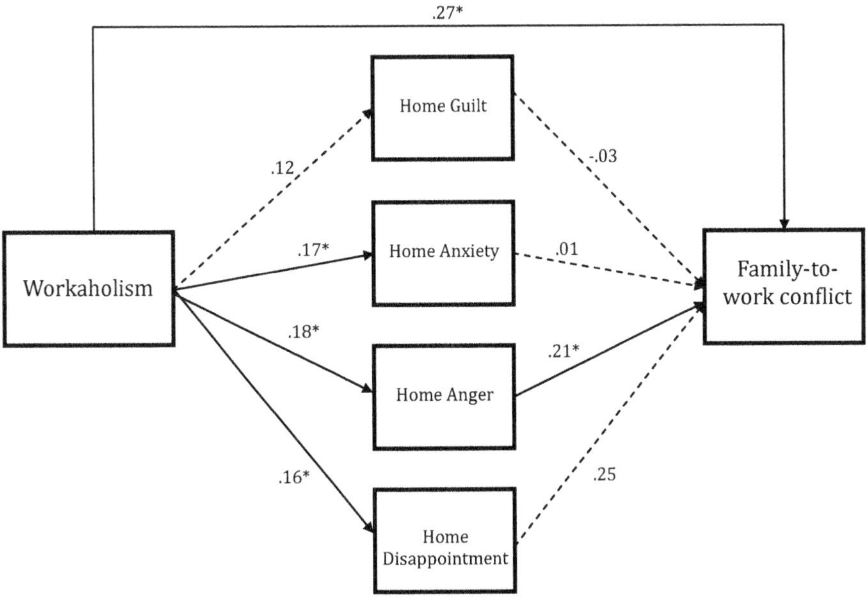

Fig. 16.2 Multiple-mediation model of workaholism on family-to-work conflict through negative emotions at home

at home, the higher her levels of FWC. However, the indirect effect for home anger was not significant (*indirect effect*=0.04, $CI_{0.95}$=−0.01, 0.09).

Collectively, these results provide important insights into the relationships between workaholism, negative emotions experienced at work and home, and work–family conflict. In regard to the work-to-family model, women's workaholism exhibits a direct and positive relationship with WFC. Furthermore, when examining women's experiences of negative emotions at work as an underlying mechanism of this relationship, women's anxiety is an important mediator. Therefore, as women engage in more workaholic behaviors they tend to experience more anxiety at work, which in turn relates to greater amounts of WFC, possibly through mood spillover. Specifically, negative moods experienced in one domain can spill over and negatively influence performance and produce negative moods in another domain (Edwards and Rothbard 2000). Women may feel anxiety while at work because they are not adhering to the family devotion schema (Blair-Loy 2003). However, because we assessed anxiety at work in general, rather than anxiety specifically about being at work and not at home, future research is needed to further understand this relationship.

Similarly, results from the family-to-work model indicated a direct and positive relationship between women's workaholism and FWC, while the inclusion of women's experience of negative emotions at home also served as a mechanism underlying this relationship. Specifically, as women display higher levels of workaholism they tend to experience more anger at home, which then relates to higher levels of FWC. One reason for our findings regarding anger at home could be that workaholic women are more severely impacted by resource drain than their male counterparts, due to the fact that women have more responsibilities in the home than men (Carli and Eagly 2012). This in turn may lead to resentment and anger, possibly toward one's spouse, who does not have as many family obligations, or anger about societal expectations that the majority of family responsibilities falls firmly on the woman's shoulders. Again, future research is needed in order to further examine this finding. One surprising finding from the family-to-work model is that women's workaholism was not significantly related to their experience of guilt at home, which is a prominent characteristic of workaholism (Ng, Sorenson, and Feldman 2007). However, it is important to note that the model examined the role of each mediator in the context of the other mediators in the model. Examinations on the bivariate level revealed that workaholism was significantly related to higher levels of guilt experienced at home ($r=0.15$, $p<0.05$), which suggests that it is still important to consider the role of guilt when investigating the emotional experiences of workaholic women.

16.5 Conclusion

In this chapter, we have proposed that workaholic women experience specific and unique work–family outcomes as compared to workaholic men. Specifically, we argue that workaholic women face extra pressures and may in fact suffer from even greater negative consequences as compared to workaholic men, due to the conflict between their inner drive to work and traditional gender role expectations. Men, on the other hand, are expected to be devoted to work and the providers for their families based on traditional gender role expectations. Thus, a man's experience as a workaholic is likely to be very different than a woman's experience. The current empirical study examined the relationships between workaholism, discrete emotions, and work–family conflict with a sample of women. Our findings provide evidence that workaholism directly impacts work–family conflict, and that this relationship is mediated by anxiety at work and, to some extent, anger at home. Additionally, this is the first known study to specifically examine the emotional mechanisms through which workaholism influences work–family conflict specifically for women. However, additional research is needed to fully understand the internal and external factors underlying these negative emotions. In a society where working hours are extending and dual-earner family dynamics are becoming more prevalent, it is important for future research to more closely examine these relationships to minimize the unique negative impact felt by workaholic women.

There are a number of future research directions that could aid in the study of workaholic women. More specifically, qualitative studies or experience sampling (ESM) studies specifically targeting the experiences of women who are workaholics could allow for much greater insight into their perceptions and experiences by examining the dynamic nature of their experiences over time. Additional research could parse out specific examples of self-inflicted (e.g., personal guilt) and other-inflicted (e.g., gender and societal norms) pressures to see how the type of pressure influences the manner in which workaholic women experience negative emotions.

In addition to pursuing future research on the unique experiences of workaholic women, it is vital to address the ways in which these women may cope with their workaholic behaviors, especially in regard to reducing work–family conflict. From a general managerial perspective, Haas (1991) urged managers to assist their employees in altering their workaholic behaviors by referring them to employee assistance or recovery programs for treatment, which includes encouraging workaholics to delegate their work and take scheduled breaks from work. As workaholic women endure the tug-of-war between work and family demands, as well as gender role and societal pressures, we encourage women to seek out support groups for women balancing work and family. These specialized groups for women should expand beyond Workaholics Anonymous groups (e.g., www.workaholics-anonymous.org) by providing women with a network of support that targets the unique pressures women experience as they strive to balance their work and family. Another avenue that workaholic women may pursue to reduce work–family conflict is family involvement and counseling, to determine if family life is contributing to their workaholic behaviors (Burke 2000). Furthermore, family initiatives may enhance satisfaction with time spent with the family, thus reducing work–family conflict.

In sum, more research is needed in order to understand the relationship between workaholism and work–family conflict, particularly research that focuses on the unique experiences of workaholic women. Research on workaholic women and their experiences of work–family conflict is particularly important given that both work hours and levels of work–family conflict are on the rise (e.g., Brett and Stroh 2003; Siegel et al. 2005), coupled with the increase in dual-earner households and households with women as the sole or primary provider (Galinsky et al. 2009; Wang et al. 2013). We encourage researchers to apply some of the sociological theories discussed in this chapter to the study of work and family, including (although certainly not limited to) thinking about work–family conflict as a moral dilemma involving competing work and family devotions (see Blair-Loy 2003). This alternative conceptualization of work–family conflict is relevant not only to understanding the specific experiences of workaholic women, but also to understanding the experiences of any working woman.

References

Adkins, C. L., & Premeaux, S. F. (2012). Spending time: The impact of hours worked on work family conflict. *Journal of Vocational Behavior, 80*, 380–389.

Andreassen, C. S., Ursin, H., & Eriksen, H. R. (2007). The relationship between strong motivation to work, "workaholism", and health. *Psychology and Health, 22*, 615–629.

Andreassen, C. S., Hetland, J., & Pallesen, S. (2013). Workaholism and work–family spillover in a cross-occupational sample. *European Journal of Work and Organizational Psychology, 22*, 78–87.

Aziz, S., Adkins, C.T., Walker, A.G., & Wuensch, K.L. (2010). Workaholism and work–life imbalance: Does cultural origin influence the relationship? *International Journal of Psychology, 41,* 72–79.

Bakker, A. B., Demerouti, E., & Burke, R. (2009). Workaholism and relationship quality: A spillover-crossover perspective. *Journal of Occupational Health Psychology, 14,* 23–33.

Bernard, J. (1981). The good-provider role: Its rise and fall. *American Psychologist, 36,* 1–12.

Blair-Loy, M. (2001). Cultural constructions of family schemas: The case of women finance executives. *Gender and Society, 15,* 687–709.

Blair-Loy, M. (2003). *Competing devotions: Career and family among women executives*. Cambridge: Harvard University Press.

Bonebright, C. A., Clay, D. L., & Ankenmann, R. D. (2000). The relationship of workaholism with work–life conflict, life satisfaction, and purpose in life. *Journal of Counseling Psychology, 47,* 469–477.

Brett, J. M., & Stroh, L. K. (2003). Working 61 plus hours a week: Why do managers do it? *Journal of Applied Psychology, 88,* 67–78.

Burke, R. J. (1999). Workaholism in organizations: Gender differences. *Sex Roles, 41,* 333–345.

Burke, R.J. (2000). Workaholism among women managers: Personal and workplace correlates. *Journal of Managerial Psychology, 15,* 520–530.

Cahusac, E., & Kanji, S. (2014). Giving up: How gendered organizational cultures push mothers out. *Gender, Work, and Organization, 21,* 57–70.

Carli, L. L., & Eagly, A. H. (2012). Leadership and gender. In J. Antonakis & D. Day (Eds.), *The nature of leadership* (2nd ed., pp. 417–476). Thousand Oaks: Sage.

Clark, M. A., Michel, J. S., Zhadnova, L., Pui, S., & Baltes, B. B. (2014). All work and no play? A meta-analytic examination of the correlates and outcomes of workaholism. *Journal of Management*. Advance online publication. doi: 10.1177/0149206314522301

del Libano, M., Llorens, S., Salanova, M., & Schaufeli, W. B. (2012). About the dark and bright sides of self-efficacy: Workaholism and work engagement. *The Spanish Journal of Psychology, 15,* 688–701.

Eagly, A.H. (1987). *Sex differences in social behavior: A social-role interpretation*. Hillsdale: Erlbaum.

Edwards, J. R., & Rothbard, N. P. (2000). Mechanisms linking work and family: Clarifying the relationship between work and family constructs. *Academy of Management Review, 25,* 178–199.

Galinsky, E., Aumann, K., & Bond, J. T. (2009). *Times are changing: Gender and generation at work and at home*. New York: Families and Work Institute.

Graves, L. M., Ruderman, M. N., Ohlott, P. J., & Weber, T. J. (2012). Driven to work and enjoyment of work: Effects of managers' outcomes. *Journal of Management, 38,* 1655–1680.

Greenhaus, J. H., & Beutell, N. J. (1985). Sources of conflict between work and family roles. *Academy of Management Review, 10,* 76–88.

Groysberg, B., & Abrahams, R. (2014). Manage your work, manage your life: Zero in on what really matters. *Harvard Business Review, 92*(3), 58–66.

Guglielmi, D., Simbula, S., Schaufeli, W. B., & Depolo, M. (2012). Self-efficacy and workaholism as indicators of the job demands-resources model. *Career Development International, 17,* 375–389.

Gutek, B. A., Searle, S., & Klepa, L. (1991). Rational versus gender role explanations for work–family conflict. *Journal of Applied Psychology, 76,* 560–568.

Haas, R. (1991). Strategies to cope with a cultural phenomenon—workaholism. *Business and Health, 36,* 4.

Hughes, E. L., & Parkes, K. R. (2007). Work hours and well-being: The roles of work-time control and work family interference. *Work & Stress, 21,* 264–278.

Jacobs, J. A., & Gerson, K. (2004). *The time divide: Work, family, and gender inequality*. Cambridge: Harvard University Press.

Kuhn, P., & Lozano, F. (2008). The expanding workweek? Understanding trends in long workhours among U.S. men, 1979–2006. *Journal of Labor Economics, 26,* 311–343.

Lovejoy, M., & Stone, P. (2011). Opting back in: The influence of time at home on professional women's career redirection after opting out. *Gender, Work, and Organization, 19,* 631–653.
Matthews, R. A., Swody, C. A., & Barnes-Farrell, J. L. (2012). Work hours and work–family conflict: The double-edged sword of involvement in work and family. *Stress and Health, 28,* 234–247.
McMillan, L. H. W., & O'Driscoll, M. P. (2006). Exploring new frontiers to generate an integrated definition of workaholism. In R. J. Burke (Ed.), *Research companion to working time and work addiction* (pp. 89–107). Northampton: Edward Elgar.
Mudrack, P. E. (2006). Understanding workaholism: The case for behavioral tendencies. In R. J. Burke (Ed.), *Research companion to working time and work addiction* (pp. 108–128). Northampton: Edward Elgar.
Murphy, L. R., & Sauter, S. L. (2003). The USA perspective: Current issues and trends in the management of work stress. *Australian Psychologist, 38,* 151–157.
Ng, T.W.H., Sorensen, K.L., & Feldman, D.C. (2007). Dimensions, antecedents, and consequences of workaholism: A conceptual integration and extension. *Journal of Organizational Behavior, 28,* 111–136.
Oates, W. E. (1971). *Confessions of a workaholic: The facts about work addiction.* New York: World Publishing.
Paull, G. (2008). Children and women's hours of work. *The Economic Journal, 118,* F8–F27.
Ridgeway, C.L. (2011). *Framed by gender.* New York: Oxford University Press.
Schaufeli, W. B., Taris, T. W., & Bakker, A. B. (2008a). It takes two to tango: Workaholism is working excessively and working compulsively. In R. J. Burke & C. L. Cooper (Eds.), *The long work hours culture: Causes, consequences and choices* (pp. 203–225). Bingley: Emerald.
Schaufeli, W. B., Taris, T. W., & van Rhenen, W. (2008b). Workaholism, burnout, and work engagement: Three of a kind or three different kinds of employee well-being? *Applied Psychology: An International Review, 57,* 173–203.
Schor, J. (2003). The (even more) overworked American. In de Graaf, J. (Ed.), *Take back your time: Fighting overwork and time poverty in America* (pp. 6–11). San Francisco: Berrett-Koehler.
Scott, K. S., Moore, K. S., & Miceli, M. P. (1997). An exploration of the meaning and consequences of workaholism. *Human Relations, 50,* 287–314.
Shimazu, A., Demerouti, E., Bakker, A. B., Shimada, K., & Kawakami, N. (2011). Workaholism and well-being among Japanese dual-earner couples: A spillover-crossover perspective. *Social Science & Medicine, 73,* 399–409.
Siegel, P. A., Post, C., Brockner, J., Fishman, A. Y., & Garden, C. (2005). The moderating influence of procedural fairness on the relationship between work–life conflict and organizational commitment. *Journal of Applied Psychology, 90,* 13–24.
Snir, R., & Harpaz, I. (2012). Beyond workaholism: Towards a general model of heavy work investment. *Human Resource Management Review, 22,* 232–243.
Sussman, S. (2012). Workaholism: A review. *Journal of Addiction Research and Therapy, S6,* 4120.
Sussman, S., & Sussman, A. N. (2011). Considering the definition of addiction. *International Journal of Environmental Research and Public Health, 8,* 4025–4038.
Taris, T. W., Schaufeli, W. B., & Verhoeven, L. C. (2005). Workaholism in the Netherlands: Measurement and implications for job strain and work–nonwork conflict. *Applied Psychology: An International Review, 54,* 37–60.
U.S. Department of Commerce (2011). *Women in America: Indicators of social and economic well-being.* Prepared by the U.S. Department of Commerce Economics and Statistics Administration, for White House Council on Women and Girls.
Wajcman, J., Bittman, M., & Brown, J. E. (2008). Families without borders: Mobile phones, connectedness and work–home divisions. *Sociology, 42,* 635–652.
Wang, W., Parker, K., & Taylor, P. (2013). Breadwinner Moms. Pew Research Center. http://www.pewsocialtrends.org/2013/05/29/breadwinner-moms/.
Westman, M. (2001). Stress and strain crossover. *Human Relations, 54,* 717–751.

Chapter 17
Family Life on the Fast Track? Gender and Work–Family Tradeoffs Among Highly Educated Professionals: A Cross-Cultural Exploration

Maria Stanfors

17.1 Introduction

During recent decades, the progress women have made in education and the labor market has been comprehensive throughout most industrialized nations. Not least does this apply to their inroads into the professions. Today, both men and women are attaining high-status degrees and entering fast-track professions such as law, medicine, and academia. This has changed the conditions for both family formation and pursuing a career. Generally, high levels of education and career orientation among women are associated with delayed and reduced involvement in family life, indicating that professional gains may be offset by familial losses (cf. Bertrand et al. 2010). One reason for this is that higher education, getting a degree, and starting a career takes time. Also, childbearing and career breaks are considered costly for the highly educated. Perhaps more important; however, is that while women have made substantial inroads into the professions, the career paths of some jobs have changed little. They are still inflexible and are arguably therefore largely incompatible with having a family, especially for women who tend to take on more caregiving responsibilities than men do.

Although there is an extensive literature documenting the negative relationship between education and fertility, there is evidence of change. A recent study on the case in Sweden showed that couples where both partners were highly educated professionals were more likely to continue childbearing and less likely to separate than were other couples (Dribe and Stanfors 2010). Sweden has been in the forefront internationally when it comes to gender equity and work–family policies targeting men as well as women, so there are clearly more opportunities to combine career and family in Sweden than in many other countries. However, there is also evidence from the USA indicating that highly educated women nowadays have more children (Shang and Weinberg 2013). This does not extend to the same degree to all the

M. Stanfors (✉)
Centre for Economic Demography, Lund University, P. O. Box 7083, 220 07 Lund, Sweden
e-mail: maria.stanfors@ekh.lu.se

M. J. Mills (ed.), *Gender and the Work-Family Experience*,
DOI 10.1007/978-3-319-08891-4_17

highly educated (Herr and Wolfram 2011; Wolfinger et al. 2010), and reports that have attracted a lot of media attention have suggested that highly educated women are "opting out" due to work–family conflicts, choosing family over career (Belkin 2003; Stone 2008; Story 2005).[1]

The current chapter focuses on how fast-track professionals fare with respect to family life (more specifically continued childbearing). Given the long-term increasing trends in women's education and labor force participation, fast-track professionals are highly relevant to study from a work–family perspective since they put work–family support systems to the test. The career structures of many fast-track jobs were designed for men with stay-at-home wives and few family responsibilities, but these have not changed much over time. It should be noted that the work–family issues that men and women in fast-track professions face are different from those faced by men and women in other jobs. For many fast-trackers, family formation coincides with defining moments on the job with respect to career growth, so the question arising is whether and how to build a family. As parents, the work–family conflicts facing this group relate to scheduling and shortage of time rather than money. It is also relevant to document whether gender has an impact on family life among fast-trackers, because it puts into perspective the investments in education and career that women make nowadays. The demands of a professional career, the asymmetries of male–female relationships, and the difficulties of conceiving later in life are supposed to undermine the combination of career and family for women but not for men. In this chapter, evidence from Sweden is explored and contrasted with the experiences from the USA. Sweden has been a precursor in terms of various aspects of gender equality, partly through its longstanding, strong orientation toward work–family policies that target men as well as women. While Sweden has introduced extensive policies alleviating parents from work–family conflicts, such policies are limited in the USA. If there is a certain pattern emerging in the combination of career and family among highly educated professionals, Sweden is one of the places where this should be noticed first, while indicating what might be emerging elsewhere.

17.2 Background

17.2.1 Women's Changing Economic Roles

During the twentieth century, women became increasingly engaged in labor market activities, with the most dramatic increase in maternal employment taking place during the 1970s (Goldin 1990; Stanfors 2003). Today the dual-earner household model has overtaken the traditional male breadwinner model in Europe as well as in the USA (Bianchi and Raley 2005 on the USA; Drew et al. 1998 on Europe). Although

[1] These reports have; however, been contested by scholars like Goldin (2006), who claims that facts speak against the "opting out" story and that greater fractions of college-educated women today are combining family and career than ever before.

female employment rates and the time spent by women, especially mothers, in paid work have increased substantially, it has been argued that their time in unpaid work has not declined enough to compensate for this (Bianchi 2000; Gauthier et al. 2004). Men have increased their time in unpaid activities, but this has also failed to compensate for the changing employment status of women since this increase over time has been small and has started from a very low level (Coltrane 2000; Gershuny and Robinson 1988). Quite commonly, it is argued, women are doing a "second shift" of unpaid work and they are more often short of time and have less of it to devote to leisure than do men (Berk 1985; Hochschild 1989; Sayer 2005). Another view has challenged the second shift, claiming that men's and women's work patterns have converged over the past 40 years, with women now performing more paid work and less unpaid work than before, and men performing more unpaid work and less paid work (Bianchi et al. 2006; Gershuny 2000). These changes have been facilitated by household technology and various services that have reduced unpaid domestic activities. The proponents of convergence have argued that the gender revolution set off in the 1970s has not stalled at all. Quite contrary, change will, according to this view, go on because younger men and women, especially those with a higher education, are likely to adopt more gender-equal ideals and adapt to a less traditional division of labor. The predictions as to whether experiences of work–family conflict will extend to men are, however, not clear.

17.2.2 Work–Family Conflict

Although many men and women had experienced conflicts between work and family life before 1970, the rise in dual-earner households at this time sparked substantial interest in this question, both academically and politically, putting work–family issues on both the research and political agendas in many countries. That work interferes more with family commitments than vice versa may reflect the idea of the "ideal worker," who prioritizes work over family (cf. Acker 1990; Hochschild 1997; Williams 2000). The image of the ideal worker stems from the era of the male breadwinner model but still lives on in the minds and visions of employers and a variety of organizational features and practices sustains the notion that work should trump other commitments (Ely and Meyerson 2000). It also lives on in the minds of many workers, especially in the fast-track professions where career structure rigidity and work demands such as long working hours compete with home demands. Having a fast-track career and a family is thus often seen as incompatible, not least for women.

Work–family conflicts occur when both work and family demand commitment, time, and energy. Quite commonly, periods when demands are the strongest in each domain—peaks of family formation and career growth—may coincide. Reconciling the demands of work and home is thus a challenge for many, but experiences of work–family conflict are certainly most common among men and women belonging to dual-earner couples with (young) children at home (Bellavia and Frone

2005; Moen and Yu 1999). Parenthood is often considered a major cause behind gender differences in time allocation, especially between paid work and housework (Bianchi 2000; Sayer 2005 on the USA; Hallberg and Klevmarken 2003 on Sweden). The extent to which men's and women's time allocation is affected by parenthood varies according to individual, household, and contextual factors (Craig and Mullan 2010; Neilson and Stanfors 2014).

Work–family conflict mainly occurs in three respects stemming from time demands, scheduling demands, and work–family spillover (Greenhaus and Powell 2003). To a certain extent work–family conflict apply to all workers, but in some respects more to fast-track professionals than to others. Many workers feel stressed when they try to accommodate the demands of both work and family. A common strategy for solving this problem among women is to limit work demands by, for example, working part-time. Part-time work is, however, seldom compatible with having a career. Moreover, time shortage does not only occur as a result of work demands; people also face time demands at home because the basic upkeep of the household and the maintaining of personal relationships demand time.

Scheduling is another problem, which arises when a worker needs to be in two places at the same time. Late meetings or overtime when the child care center is closed are such examples, but activities relating to children, household maintenance, and personal care that occur during standard working hours also create a conflict. Lack of control over work schedules is a source of stress among working parents, especially mothers, and for this reason they seek flexible work schedules (Barnett and Rivers 1996; Goldin and Katz 2013). Scheduling demands are also the result of inflexible child care arrangements (Hofferth 1999).

One way of reconciling work and family demands is to bring work home. This has become more prevalent with the erosion of the male breadwinner model. In the heyday of the male breadwinner model, men were responsible for earnings and women were responsible for the family and home, and the concerns of each domain tended to stay separate. Today, both men and women have responsibilities in both the work and family domains. Advances in information technology have increased the ability of some workers to work from home, providing them with the flexibility to accommodate child care schedules. While many professionals find this option an advantage (Epstein et al. 1999), especially when they are parents with young children at home, it is double-edged in that it has increased the pressure on them to be constantly available outside the office (Glass 2000; Hochschild 1997; Hymowitz and Silverman 2001).

17.2.3 Responses to Work–Family Conflict

Combining work and family is a pertinent issue. There is considerable variation across countries in terms of policies and institutions that affect the opportunities of combining work and family. When it comes to policy, attempts to resolve work–family conflicts tend to center on the practical problems of combining work and family, particularly child care. More recently there have been attempts through collective agreements and the provision of technical services to facilitate flexibility and work at home for many groups of workers. Institutions differ between countries when it comes to parental leave schemes, income replacement, the working conditions of parents, the provision and pricing of child care, and whether families or individuals are the subjects of benefits and taxation. All these components are important, but most likely it is the combined effect of all these factors taken together that determines the degree of work–family compatibility.

Almost every country provides its own specific set of solutions for the issue of combining work and family. In many countries policies only deal with the reconciliation of women's double roles, whereas in other countries, like Sweden, institutional arrangements have a broader scope and address gender equality issues alongside the work–family balance for all parents (Kimball 1999; McDonald 2000). Sweden is often seen as a forerunner when it comes to family and work-related policies (Ruhm and Teague 1997). Part of the reason why countries differ in their responses to work–family conflict is ideological.

In Sweden and the other Nordic countries, work–family reconciliation is a public concern. There is a strong belief that society bears the responsibility for family well-being in that it will gain from investing in the next generation. At the other ideological endpoint, in the USA, work–family reconciliation is a private concern; the responsibility for family well-being and finding ways to accommodate both work and family roles has first and foremost fallen on individuals. Thus Nordic policies are universalistic and general, and are in contrast to the USA where government-sponsored programs are rare and minimalistic and employer-sponsored programs only apply for some groups of employees, which does not solve work–family conflict for most workers. Despite the fact that managers and professionals are among those privileged workers who most commonly have access to family benefits, assistance with child care, and flexible scheduling, they seem to have more problems combining work and family than do their Nordic counterparts (Jacobs and Fanning Madden 2004). Due to its universalistic and general design, all workers potentially benefit from the Swedish welfare state and its opportunities to combine work and family. In reality, however, the combination of work and family is a result of choices concerning both career and childbearing that have been made at the individual and couple level. For example, highly educated couples are more likely to make use of publicly provided child care and other services provided by the welfare state than are other couples (Stanfors 2003). This may be explained by their stronger work orientation, better information, and the fact that highly educated individuals have more gender-equal attitudes (Bernhardt and Goldscheider 2006). Parental leave, child benefits, and subsidized child care reduce the negative price effect of parents' and especially of women's wages on fertility, making it independent of education, and instead boost the income effect. In Sweden, public child care is of a high quality and fees are greatly subsidized, especially for high income earners.[2] Higher income

[2] Child care fees are based on the total gross income of the household in which the child resides. Fees are only income-dependent up to the equivalent of a gross monthly income of 42,000 SEK (in 2009; equivalent to 5,250 USD at the time in question). After that, the same fee applies to all households, irrespective of income, which is especially beneficial for high income earners. Coverage is

also enables people to buy goods and services in order to cope with both career and family (cars, housing, home services, etc.).

17.3 Work–Family Tradeoffs among Highly Educated Professionals

17.3.1 Education and Fertility

Much interest has been devoted to the association between education and fertility, especially educational attainment and fertility (see Brand and Davis 2011, for a review). Typically, a negative relationship between education and fertility has been assumed. This assumption is based on standard human capital theory, which predicts that better-educated women will have their first births later in life and ultimately fewer children compared to less educated women. Women with a higher education postpone family formation because enrollment in education and earning a degree is demanding and not compatible with childbearing. After finishing their degrees, women with a higher education face higher opportunity costs of childbearing than do women with a lower education because they usually have better jobs, career prospects, and wages (Becker 1991; Mincer 1963). They are also, and more often than is the case with women with less education, in occupations with steeper earnings profiles and potentially faster depreciation rates (Polachek 1981). High opportunity costs in both real economic and career terms depress fertility among highly educated women, especially among those in fast-track professions. Whereas the opportunity cost of childbearing is supposed to outweigh the income effect of earnings potential among women, this is not the case among men. As long as fathers are not expected to give up the same amount of their working time for child care as mothers are, men's education and professional careers will not conflict with childbearing to the same extent as women's; instead they are expected to be positively rather than negatively related to fertility.

Whereas several studies have shown that women's educational attainment has a negative effect on various childbearing outcomes, others have more recently found positive relationships between educational attainment and fertility after first birth (e.g., Dribe and Stanfors 2010; Joshi 2002; Kravdal 2001, 2007; Kreyenfeld 2002). This challenges the idea that opportunity costs outweigh a positive income effect among highly educated women. The emergent positive association between education and fertility may be explained by a strengthening of the income effect in more gender-equal contexts, where childbearing and employment are made more compatible, women are not primarily caregivers but workers, and highly educated

extensive—about 85 % of all children aged 1–6 were in public day care in 2005—and therefore dual-career couples are able to spend more of their income on other goods and services that may help them combine career and family.

women contribute substantially to household income. The income effect may be reinforced by assortative mating based on education. A positive association between education and higher order births may also be a result of self-selection when modeling birth intervals separately (Kravdal 2001).

17.3.2 *Occupation and Fertility*

It has been shown that educational orientation may be an even more important determinant of fertility than educational level (Hoem et al. 2006; Lappegård and Rönsen 2005; Stanfors 2003; Van Bavel 2010). Educational orientation works through occupational choice since these are closely related, especially for the professions. Should there be systematic differences when it comes to career tracks, work demands, and perceived work–family conflict between occupations, the investment in different kinds of higher education will not only determine professional life but also choices with respect to personal life.

Few studies have considered how career choice affects fertility. Existing studies deal mainly with the USA. Examples are studies of gender differences in childbearing among academics (Mason and Goulden 2004) and doctors (Boulis 2004) that conclude that women in the professions analyzed are less likely to have children than are other women or their male peers. Cooney and Uhlenberg (1989) analyzed the situation in 1980 for women only, finding that doctors felt more of a family commitment and were more likely to have children than were lawyers and post-secondary teachers. Wolfinger et al. (2010) built on Cooney and Uhlenberg by using data from the 2000 Census for both men and women. They confirmed that physicians had the highest rate of birth events, followed by attorneys, and academics. Men had, within each profession, more birth events than did women. The factors that explain fertility variation by profession for men (i.e., marital status, income, and spousal employment) only partially account for differences by profession for women. This may be related to the more complex relationship between family and career for women as documented by many (e.g., Avellar and Smock 2003; Budig 2003; Goldin and Katz 2008; Hewlett 2002; Noonan and Corcoran 2004).

17.3.3 *Career and Family Compatibility*

The reason why a career and family may be seen as incompatible, at least for women, is because they both demand commitment, time, and energy, thereby inherently implying a tradeoff. Although women have increased their education and labor force participation, they have largely retained responsibility for child care and domestic work. For women on the fast track, family formation is often associated with taking up a second career as "supermom" and assuming the main responsibility of housework. For men, on the other hand, both paid and family work is usually less influenced by their role as fathers. However, during the last decades the effects of parenthood on time allocation in Scandinavia have started to converge between men and women (Dribe and Stanfors 2009). As seen above, there exists considerable variation across countries when it comes to policies and institutions which may affect the combination of work and family. On an aggregate level, it seems as if the institutional arrangements in Sweden, and its Scandinavian neighbors, are most favorable for dual-earner households (Blossfeld and Drobnic 2001) and are more supportive of combining employment and childbearing (e.g., Billari and Kohler 2004) than are conservative and liberal models with more traditional approaches to family and gender roles. In a universalistic and general welfare state, like Sweden, all parents potentially benefit from the opportunities to combine work and family. Parental leave, child benefits, and subsidized quality child care reduce the negative price effect of parents'—especially women's—wages on fertility, making it independent of education, and instead they boost the income effect. Once parenthood and employment are no longer alternatives at odds with one other but are instead possible to combine, the negative effects of women's education, labor force participation, and wages are expected to be greatly reduced, and even reversed, to produce a positive income effect. Thus, women's as well as men's education and earnings may impact positively on continued childbearing, although perhaps not equally across the professions.

In some occupations the career structure is rigid and the job inflexible (cf. Goldin and Katz 2011). In these the workload is high, hours are long, and production in a given number of (early career) years is most important. Moreover, skill depreciation is more of a problem in some occupations than in others. Expertise, firm-specific, and technological skills tend to depreciate faster than general skills, and this aggravates career interruptions. In some occupations the career structure is less rigid and working conditions are more flexible. This implies that those who work longer hours and produce more will be promoted at a faster pace than others, but it is possible to adjust the workload and reduce hours through part-time work, or even stop the "career-clock" in order to take time off for caring. Public sector work is generally more flexible than private sector employment and provides greater employment security. Steeper earnings profiles among private sector employees exacerbate the negative effects of career breaks on lifetime earnings in relation to the public sector. Thus, in order to cope, (potential) parents may choose occupations and careers that accommodate family responsibilities and reduce earnings punishment (cf. Polachek 1981).

Career structure rigidity and work inflexibility are likely to affect men and women in the professions differently. They are the legacies of organizational norms that were developed in times when men, married to full-time homemakers, were the only ones to be fast-track professionals. The norms that establish which time in life specific career goals should be achieved rest upon expectations about work-related productivity applying to a worker who does not have the responsibility to care for a home and a family. If different social norms and practices apply for men and women with respect to parenting, putting more pressure on women to be primary caregivers, and to take on more responsibility for housework than men, women will face more difficulties in combining a career and family.

17.3.4 *Differences Between Professions*

The current chapter contrasts the patterns of continued childbearing among lawyers with those of medical doctors and PhDs working as post-secondary teachers and researchers in academia (i.e., higher education institutions). They are all high-status professions that demand higher education, specific degrees, and long training programs. By tradition, these professions have been male-dominated but are now becoming increasingly feminized. They are, to varying degrees, examples of a career model that is not conducive to childbearing if that implies assuming more childrearing responsibilities and greater involvement in parenting. There is thus the anticipation that occupational differences in childbearing will be stronger for women than for men. Primary evidence from Sweden is explored and contrasted with experiences from the USA, as documented by Wolfinger et al. (2010). While Sweden has launched extensive policies alleviating parents from work–family conflicts, these are limited in the USA. There is thus the anticipation that occupational differences in childbearing will be more articulated in the USA than in Sweden.

A few words are warranted here regarding the professional development of lawyers, doctors, and academics, and the extent to which there are differences between the professions and between Sweden and the USA.

In Sweden, law school is a 4-year program and medical school comprises 5 years. Entry into these vocational programs is highly restricted. After graduation, an essentially compulsory 2-year training period as a clerk or an intern follows. It is often seen as a defining moment in terms of career opportunities as to when and where this internship takes place. The majority of law and medical school graduates are in the age range of 25–29, the average age being slightly higher for men than for women, which means that they are around 30 when they finish as clerks or interns.

A law graduate has several career options, one being to join a law firm and spend 5–10 years to make partner, which is challenging. It implies a less secure position in the company hierarchy. Failure to make partner implies a significantly slower career development and perhaps a change of law firms. Not all law graduates aspire to such a career, choosing instead alternatives routes such as to work in administration elsewhere. One alternative is the career track in the national courts administration with the aim of becoming a district attorney or judge. This is competitive, as are all professional careers, but different in character because of a more bureaucratic and standardized schedule for promotions long-standing in the public sector. There is no up-or-out decision. It is possible to slow down or stop one's career for a period of time when, for instance, caregiving demands are pressing. This means that mothers and fathers may become district attorneys and judges at a later point in life than colleagues that do not have similar family responsibilities, but they are not excluded from the competition. There are, however, wage differences that follow with the career choices, with law practitioners in the private sector earning considerably more than those working in the public sector.

Medical school graduates who finish their internships may follow additional specialist training or work as internists. All doctors—even interns—are regularly employed during their residencies, the overwhelming majority being in publicly run hospitals or health care centers. Wages improve with each step up the hierarchical ladder. Due to the limited supply of doctors and a high demand for their competence, medical graduates can expect to rank among the top earning professional groups, not only among those employed in the public sector but also more generally. Medical school graduates achieve a fairly secure position with respect to both career and income at around age 30, which is conducive to childbearing. Job stability is good, although terms of contracts may vary. Irregular hours and night calls may be demanding, especially for parents with young children, but are solved partly through the provision of child care that is available for parents who work at odd hours of the day.

Becoming an academic is different from the other professional tracks. Doctoral-level education follows bachelor's and Masters degrees,[3] which means that PhDs are older than lawyers and doctors when they graduate. PhD candidates are formally employed on fixed-term contracts. After receiving a PhD, they may either stay in academia (commonly on fixed-term contracts) or seek work elsewhere. Since the Swedish academic system has no tenure track, there is great variability among academic careers, and the challenge to publish or perish within a limited time period does not apply to all (cf. Wolfinger et al. 2010). It may take time until a PhD is in a position that is conducive to childbearing. For many, graduate school seems to be a better time to have children than the post-doctoral period, given work load and income stability. Academics receive, on average, less pay than lawyers and doctors. On the other hand, academics enjoy more flexibility when it comes to working hours and the opportunity to work at home than the other professions do. Like other public sector employees, there is no up-or-out decision with respect to an academic career in Sweden.

The most obvious differences between the professions studied in Sweden and the USA relate to academics. The career structure of academia in the USA offers no good time for childbearing. Academics who want to reduce working hours get reduced pay and generally resort to lower status jobs. Only a few universities offer employer-sponsored programs with a beneficial scheme for prospective parents. It seems that in the USA both medicine and law offer more opportunities for flexibility than academia (Goldin and Katz 2011, 2013; Wolfinger et al. 2010). Another obvious difference between Sweden and the USA is that many more fast-trackers are in public sector employment in Sweden, and generally this sector offers more family-friendly working conditions than does the private sector.

Based on differences in working conditions, career structures, and professional demands between the professions, doctors are expected to be the most likely to have a second or a third birth once they have started childbearing, irrespective of gender. In Sweden, they are expected to be followed by academics and law practitioners in the national courts system (i.e., public sector employees). Lawyers working in the private sector are expected to be the least likely to continue childbearing, especially

[3] Men and women who opt for a PhD are generally 25–29 years old. Only about 10% of all PhDs in Sweden are awarded to people under 30. In 2007, 41 % of all male PhD recipients and 37 % of all female PhD recipients were in the age range of 30–34.

if they are women. Differences with respect to type of profession are expected to be stronger among women than among men, especially in professions where the career structure is unpredictable and not very flexible, and where there is more likely to be an "up-or-out" decision than in other professions. Differences according to profession and gender are thus expected to be fewer among medical doctors and greater among lawyers.

17.4 Continued Childbearing Among Highly Educated Professionals

In order to establish whether there are differences by profession in continued childbearing among highly educated men and women, multivariate analyses have been performed. The focus is set on what happens after the birth of the first child among individuals who, already at the time of their first birth, have a degree and have started a career in medicine, law, or academia.[4] The analysis is thus conditional on having a career and on the partnerships formed whereby at least one child has been born. The fast-track professionals studied have all made considerable career investments, yet follow professional routes that are not equally compatible with family life. The scope of the analyses is to determine which fast-track professions facilitate higher order childbearing for men and women.[5]

17.4.1 Data

The data analyzed comes from the Swedish population registers maintained by Statistics Sweden.[6] From a dataset consisting of all the individuals in the birth cohorts 1942–1989 who resided in Sweden at any time from 1961 onwards, individuals in heterosexual couples (married or cohabiting without being formally married) who were in their first partnership have been selected and followed from the birth of the first child, beginning in 1989 and up to the time of either the woman reaching the age of 45, the dissolution of the partnership, emigration, or the end of the study period in 2009. The analytical sample is limited to include individuals in couples who were in their first partnership and wherein either the man or the woman belonged to one of the professions studied. The sample is also truncated at 8 years since the

[4] Thus there is per definition not much of a problem of reverse causality.

[5] The analyses do not allow for any strictly causal inferences and do not deal with selection, whether this be into professions based on family orientation or into larger family sizes.

[6] The data derive from the multigenerational register (*Flergenerationsregistret*), which contains information on biological and adopted children to all index persons in the sampling frame (all individuals in birth cohorts 1942–1989 who resided in Sweden at some point in time after 1960). Due to frequent cases of missing information on adoption dates, only biological children are included in the analysis.

previous birth. The analytical sample consists of 13,334 focal persons (7,428 men and 5,906 women).

The professions of interest are identified using a combination of educational and occupational codes (highest educational level attained the field of that education and branch of employment). Profession is a variable divided into lawyer working in a private law firm, law practitioner employed in the national courts and taxation system, medical doctor; and PhD in academia (e.g., post-secondary teacher and/or researcher belonging to any academic field).

The dependent variable in all analyses is a higher order (more specifically a second and third) birth event. Independent variables are used to explain the relationship between profession and a higher order birth. Although the register data cover the entire population and are very reliable, they mostly include crude measures of demographic and economic indicators, few social and job-related indicators, and do not include any attitudinal variables. Independent variables used here include age, union status, partner's educational status and professional orientation, income,[7] duration since last birth, age of woman at first birth, cohort, country of birth, and urbanicity.

More than half of the men and women studied were medical doctors. It is more common for men to be PhDs employed in academia. Among law professionals, men are equally distributed between private law and the national courts and taxation system, while women are to a larger extent employed in the courts administration than in private law firms.

As for the empirical analysis, logit models are estimated separately for men and women at each birth interval (i.e., second and third births). The results from the multivariate analysis are reported as odds ratios and displayed graphically, net of controls, for an intuitive yet statistically correct interpretation.[8] It should be noted that there is a very strong two-child norm in Sweden, which is reflected in the data where a large majority of the births studied are second births.

[7] Total income includes wages for employees and self-employed and benefits paid in connection to work (i.e., parental leave, pensions, unemployment benefits, and payment from sickness insurance). To enable comparisons over time, annual income is related to the so called price base amount (hereafter simply called base amount) of the year. The base amount is set for each year on the basis of changes in the consumer price index (CPI). Its main purpose is to adjust different kinds of public benefits (pensions, student aid, sickness insurance, etc.) to account for inflation. A variable measuring the income share earned by the woman proxies her relative position in the partnership.

[8] An odds ratio is a measure of effect size. It describes the strength of association between data values (for example x and y). If the odds ratio is greater than 1, then there is an association in the sense that having some properties, such as x) (relative to not having x) increases the odds of having y. It should be made clear that we are talking about associations since the causal link has not necessarily been established.

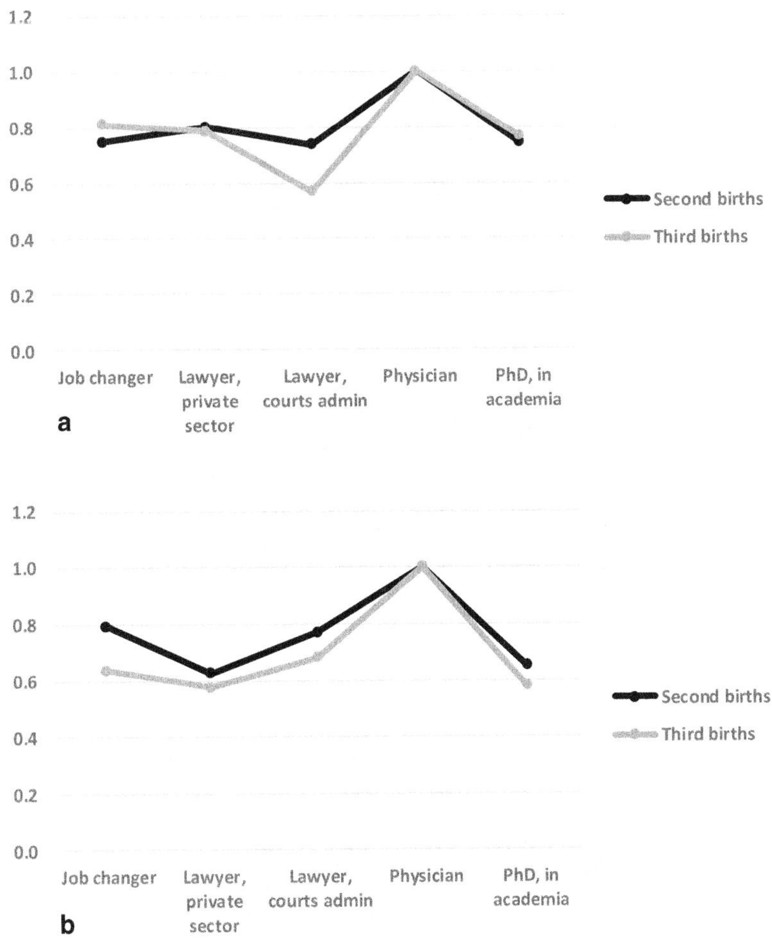

Fig. 17.1 The patterning of experiencing a second or third birth among fast-track professionals in Sweden 1991–2009, by gender. Odds ratios from logit estimates are indicated on the *y*-axis (1 = reference category). **a** Men. **b** Women. (Note: regressions control for own profession, partner's education and professional orientation, own age, partner's age (and their square terms), age of woman at first birth, couple income (and its square term), woman's share of couple's income, time since last birth, cohort, country of birth for both partners, civil status, and place of residence. Source: Statistics Sweden, see text)

17.4.2 Empirical Findings

Empirical results displayed in Fig. 17.1 establish that doctors have the highest chances of having a higher order birth in relation to the other professional groups. This is true for both second and third births, and for women as well as for men. The patterning of second or third births by profession is stable for both men and women,

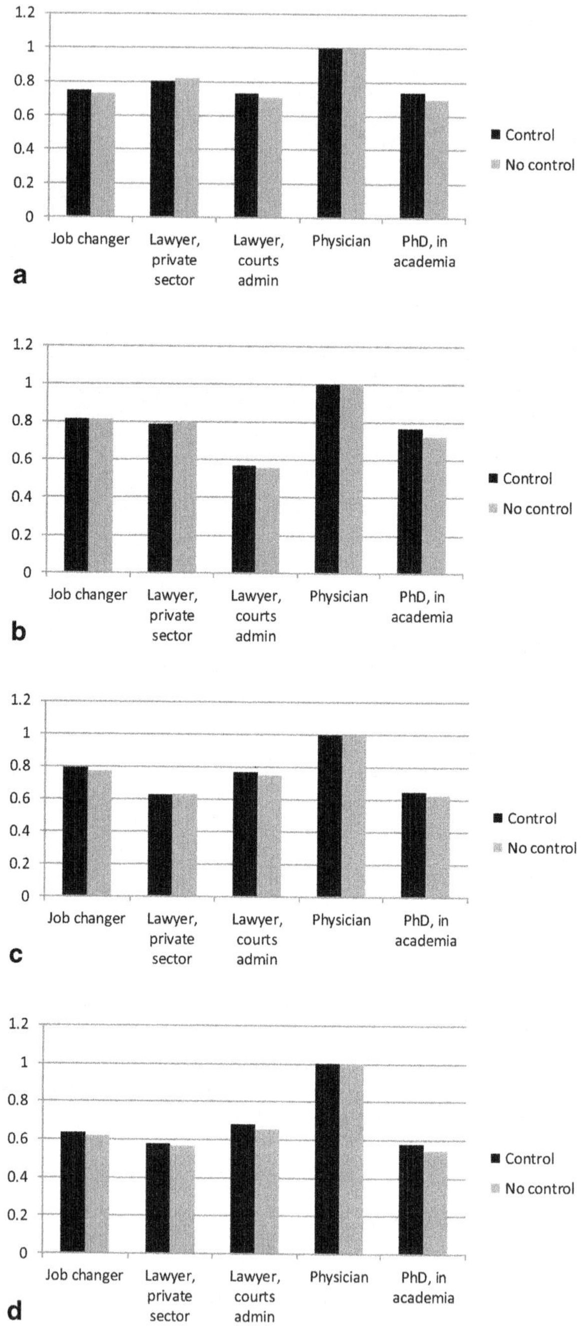

Fig. 17.2 Model comparisons of the patterning of experiencing a second or third birth among fast-track professionals in Sweden, 1991–2009. Odds ratios from logit estimates of experiencing a birth, with and without controlling for couple income and woman's share of couple income. (1=reference category). **a** Men, Second births. **b** Men, Third births. **c** Women, Second births. **d** Women, Third births. (Note: Based on model estimates controlling for all other variables, cf. Fig. 17.1; Source: See Fig. 17.1)

yet there is a difference in pattern by profession and gender. Among women, lawyers in private law firms are the least likely to experience a second and third birth. For women in law, employment in the public sector seems to be more conducive to continued childbearing, all else equal. This is not the case for men who work as law professionals. Women in academia also have less chance of continued childbearing, having almost equally low odds ratios as women working in private law firms. Men, too, who work in academia have lower odds ratios of experiencing a second or a third birth as compared to both doctors as well as to lawyers in the private sector. The members of the group of "job changers", which consists of professionals who belonged to one of the four professional categories at the time of their first birth but have since then changed professional status, have quite consistently medium-low odds of experiencing a birth at both intervals, among men as well as among women. There is generally more variation according to profession among women than among men, but the main result is that doctors as a group stand out in relation to the other professional groups.[9] The pattern by profession observed for second births is attenuated, particularly among women, for third births.

One interesting finding to note is that the relationship between professional orientation and continued childbearing is not driven by income. This is made visible in Fig. 17.2. Should the impact of professional status be felt through income; i.e., the fact that physicians as a group are more likely to have a second and a third birth because they earn more money, and thus can afford more children, then the exclusion of the income controls would make the impact of own profession a stronger one. The results indicate that virtually no differences in continued childbearing among fast-track professionals relate to income. When the odds ratios for second and third births of two separate models (one including income controls and one without such controls) are compared, there is only a slight change in odds ratios for academics and lawyers working in the national courts administration. This is understandable since academics and lawyers in the public sector earn on average less than medical doctors. Accordingly, they have somewhat lower chances of experiencing a second and a third birth than do physicians. The patterns are highly robust, so the main explanation for the observed patterns according to (1) profession and (2) profession and gender combined seems to come from underlying differences between the professions regarding, for example, career structures and flexibility.[10]

[9] This is corroborated by sensitivity tests where the model is estimated with different professions as reference categories.

[10] The results hold up for a number of sensitivity tests including stepwise modeling with a gradual inclusion of independent variables, and the estimation of logit models of the probability of having a second or a third birth within 5 years, to see if the results are driven by a subgroup with a specific temporal fertility behavior. Also, logit models where the covariates refer to the situation at the time of the previous birth are estimated in order to obtain a counterfactual that renders similar results. Since the original analysis is based on a select group consisting of men and women who have attained their professional status and started their careers at the time of their first birth, logit models are estimated for individuals who ever attain the professional status in question. None of these sensitivity checks alters the pattern observed.

These results may be compared with results reported for the USA by Wolfinger et al. (2010), who use data from the 2000 Census to examine the likelihood of a birth event (defined as having a child younger than 2 years in the household) for men and women belonging to the same professions as studied above. In the USA too, doctors have the highest rate of birth events, followed by lawyers and academics. The patterning is similar for men and women, but within each profession men have more birth events than do women. Although the patterning of childbearing among fast-track professionals in Sweden and the USA is similar, there are interesting differences relating to couple characteristics. While doctors in Sweden are very likely to belong to a dual-earner household, not seldom consisting of two medical doctors, male doctors in the USA more often have spouses who are out of the labor force. They therefore have higher fertility in part because they have wives who see to child care and domestic work. Male professionals whose wives are academics do not have higher fertility, which is an indication that the low fertility among female academics can affect the fertility of men in these professions.

17.5 Concluding Discussion

There are obvious differences with respect to continued childbearing within the group of highly educated professionals, not only in Sweden, but also in a contrasting context such as that in the USA. Doctors emerge as being more likely to go on to having a second or third child once they have started a family compared to law professionals and academics. Doctors are clearly different compared to the rest, a result that holds for both men and women. There are, however, differences in the variation across professions by gender, indicating that public sector employment is conducive to Swedish women's continued childbearing. Moreover, the tendency among the other professional groups to be less likely to go on to a second birth compared to doctors is attenuated when it comes to third births, especially among women.

The evidence at hand gives general support to the hypothesis that differences in the working conditions, career structures, and professional development that follow upon occupational choice generate differences in continued childbearing within the professions studied. In line with expectations, those who are in a rigid fast-track hierarchy, with the constant pressure of producing measurable results and output, obviously face more difficulties combining work and having more than one child than do those who work in organizations where it is possible to step out of the rat race temporarily, and who enjoy greater job protection and fewer career penalties. In line with this reasoning, it is found that, in the case of women, lawyers working in the private sector are the least likely to have either a second or a third birth once they have started childbearing, when compared to doctors. Women in academia are, however, not very different from lawyers working in the private sector when it comes to their chances of continued childbearing, whereas women working in the courts administration are somewhat more likely to experience higher order births than are the two aforementioned groups. Yet they are all less likely to continue childbearing in relation to physicians, all else equal.

It is perhaps not surprising that the results indicate a sharper tradeoff between career and continued childbearing for women working in private law firms than for women working as doctors and in the national courts system, but it is somewhat more challenging to understand why academics have similarly low chances of experiencing a second and third birth in relation to physicians. In the light of the career structure rigidity and work demands that are important in all fast-track professions, the lower chances of continued childbearing among academics could be understood in the sense that, even though there is no formal tenure track in Swedish academia, PhDs have invested to a high extent in their careers through undergoing a lengthy training period and facing a competitive environment after graduating. This is especially the case if they are research-oriented and aim for an academic career and not just a teaching position. There is a *de facto* tenure track for the career-oriented that puts pressure on Swedish academics to perform in a way similar to the US system (cf. Mason and Goulden 2004; Wolfinger et al. 2010). There is also a long-standing shortage of academic positions, in stark contrast to the great demand for physicians, which adds to the competitive pressure. This puts academics in a relatively disadvantaged position compared to other professional groups, not least doctors. When it comes to family building, these disadvantages seems to net out the advantages of flexibility that the academic profession is characterized by.

Another explanation could be that academics systematically have different preferences regarding family building as compared to doctors; i.e., that there is occupational selectivity with respect to personality, meaning that career-oriented individuals choose certain professions such as academia and law, whereas more family-oriented individuals choose other professions such as medicine. If there is a selection of individuals into different professions due to different work–family orientations, the result will be more of continued childbearing among those in professions that are more compatible with childrearing. If there is a selection of individuals at risk of having a second and a third child, those who have started childbearing will have already revealed a preference for having children, which may make them more willing to have an additional child. Individuals in professions where it is more difficult to combine parenthood and caregiving responsibilities with a career, who nevertheless did become parents, might be a select group with strong family preferences. The result then would mean lower bound estimates of differences according to profession.

With this in mind, the results indicate that continued childbearing is facilitated among doctors who corroborate selection into profession. The results also indicate that continued childbearing is facilitated among public sector employees, confirming selection into family-friendly public sector employment of which Sweden is well-known. Yet continued childbearing is not facilitated to the same extent across the professions, not even in Sweden. Since a similar pattern is observed for both men and women, selectivity with respect to personality and career-family orientation seems to be gender-neutral, although this is not indicated by other labor market outcomes.

The pattern observed also indicates that medical doctors are different compared to other professionals irrespective of gender and country context. Physicians are more likely to continue childbearing in both Sweden and the USA, although the countries offer very different employment conditions and work–family support systems. Overall the opportunities to combine work and family are good in Sweden compared to elsewhere, particularly the USA. Parents have statutory rights to take time off on parental leave for more than a year, to work part-time until the child is 12, and they receive generous compensation during their parental leave, even if they belong to the upper tail of the earnings distribution. Quality child care services are available at low cost through government subsidies, which facilitates the combination of work and family for all parents. Yet, despite its many pros, the Swedish model has limitations in some respects, especially for fast-track professionals who may need more flexible solutions in order to accommodate work demands. The lack of alternatives may be more of a compatibility issue in the Swedish context, especially for fast-track professionals, and so may be the lack of home care services that make people devote more time and energy to housework and maintenance on a do-it-yourself basis and thereby spend less time and effort on market work and careers. Lately, there has been a tendency among private companies to accommodate workers who are also parents with family-friendly policies and flexible solutions. This does not, however, eliminate the fact that fast-track jobs in rigid hierarchies are inflexible; the volume of work produced is still vital for achieving promotion, and the common response to this is longer work hours. There are norms regarding the time in life when certain career goals should be achieved, and these are designed not around the primary caregiver but rather around the full-time breadwinner with support from within the home. All else equal, workers who spend more hours on the job and devote more effort to their careers will produce more, while mothers (and fathers) who have family responsibilities, and perhaps also a partner who has a demanding profession, will be disadvantaged.

Compatibility issues are found in the workplace and the career structure of the professions investigated in this study, but in many senses the degree of career-family compatibility also depends on the relationship between partners. Contrary to other contexts, couples in Sweden where both partners have a higher education are more likely to continue childbearing compared to couples where one partner has a lower education. In line with this, and in contrast to the US experience, it is also the case that couples where both partners belong to one of the professional groups studied here are more likely to continue childbearing compared to others. It thus seems as if the assumed disadvantages and pressures of pursuing a professional career are mediated by shared interests and networks and a mutual understanding of each other's situation. The higher rate of continued childbearing among professional couples can probably also be explained by more egalitarian attitudes and practices toward the household division of labor made by these couples. In dual-career households, in which both spouses have a high level of career involvement, both partners have access to economic resources that serve as a basis for negotiation and therefore mutual goals can be achieved. Moreover, competing preferences and stress can be mediated through having a higher degree of understanding for each other's workload, and this may facilitate work–family issues, especially for women. When it comes to childrearing, couples with higher educational status and skills share more of the total parental leave benefits than do those with lower educational status and skills, and they make more use of public child care.

To conclude, in the current chapter it has been made clear that continued childbearing varies by profession and also by profession and gender. These differences are smaller in Sweden than in the USA, but cannot be explained by income and the fact that some professionals, including doctors earn more than others, such as academics. Rather, the results indicate that working conditions and career structure contribute to making it easier for some groups than for others to combine a professional career and children. The patterns that emerge for men and women reflect the facts that they are not equally involved in childbearing and are not equally sensitive to career structure, especially not those hierarchies presenting them with up-or-out decisions implying a tradeoff between career and children at an early stage in their career. The results presented indicate that the way professional careers are structured and how flexible jobs are matter a great deal for the combination of work and family. Among fast-track professions, there still exist differences as to whether jobs are flexible (at least temporarily during childbearing years), even in a supposedly family-friendly country like Sweden where the same rights to leave schemes and part-time work apply to all workers. These differences make the combination of work and family more difficult for some workers than others. On the other hand, flexibility on the job often comes with sacrifices in regard to both salary and career advancement—prices that, up until now, more women than men have been willing to pay. This puts policies promoting work–family compatibility for all into perspective, especially as increasingly many women and men are opting for higher education and careers and when the prestigious professions are feminizing.

References

Acker, J. (1990). Hierarchies, jobs, bodies: A theory of gendered organizations. *Gender & Society, 4,* 139–158.

Avellar S., & Smock, P. J. (2003). Has the price of motherhood declined over time? A cross-cohort comparison of the motherhood wage penalty. *Journal of Marriage and Family, 65,* 597–607.

Barnett, R. C., & Rivers, C. (1996). *She works/he works: How two-income families are happier, healthier, and better off.* New York: Harper Collins.

Becker, G. S. (1991). *A treatise on the family.* Cambridge: Harvard University Press.

Belkin, L. (October 26 2003). The opt-out revolution. *New York Times Magazine*, p. 42.

Bellavia, G., & Frone, M. (2005). Work-family conflict. In J. Barling, E. K. Kelloway, & M. R. Frone (Eds.), *Handbook of work stress* (pp. 113–147). Thousand Oaks: Sage.
Berk, S. F. (1985). *The gender factory: The appointment of work in American households*. New York: Plenum.
Bernhardt, E., & Goldscheider, F. (2006). Gender equality, parenthood attitudes, and first births in Sweden. In *Vienna yearbook of population research* (pp. 19–39). Vienna: Vienna Institute of Demography.
Bertrand, M., Goldin, C., & Katz, L. F. (2010). Dynamics of the gender gap for young professionals in the financial and corporate sectors. *American Economic Journal: Applied Economics, 2,* 228–255.
Bianchi, S. (2000). Maternal employment and time with children: Dramatic change or surprising continuity? *Demography, 37,* 410–414.
Bianchi, S. M., & Raley, S. (2005). Time allocation in working families. In S. M. Bianchi, L. M. Casper, & R. B. King (Eds.), *Work, family, health, and well-being* (pp. 21–42). Mahwah: Lawrence Erlbaum.
Bianchi, S. M., Robinson, J. P., & Milkie, M. A. (2006). *Changing rhythms of American family life*. New York: Russell Sage.
Billari, F. C., & Kohler, H.P. (2004). Patterns of low and lowest-low fertility in Europe. *Population Studies, 58,* 161–176.
Blossfeld, H. P., & Drobnic, S. (Eds.), (2001). *Careers of couples in contemporary societies: From male breadwinner to dual earner families*. Oxford: Oxford University Press.
Boulis, A. (2004). The evolution of gender and motherhood in contemporary medicine. *Annals of the American Academy of Political and Social Science, 596,* 172–206.
Brand, J. E., & Davis, D. (2011). The impact of college education on fertility: Evidence of heterogeneous effects. *Demography, 48,* 863–887.
Budig, M. (2003). Are women's employment and fertility histories interdependent? An examination of causal order using event history analysis. *Social Science Research, 32,* 376–401.
Coltrane, S. (2000). Research on household labor: Modeling and measuring the social embeddedness of routine family work. *Journal of Marriage and the Family, 62,* 1208–1233.
Cooney, T., & Uhlenberg, P. (1989). Family-building patterns of women professionals: A comparison of lawyers, physicians, and post-secondary teachers. *Journal of Marriage and the Family, 51,* 749–758.
Craig, L., & Mullan, K. (2010). Parenthood, gender and work–family time in USA, Australia, Italy, France and Denmark. *Journal of Marriage and Family, 72,* 1344–1361.
Drew, E., Emerek, R., & Mahon, E. (1998). *Women, work and the family in Europe*. London: Routledge.
Dribe, M., & Stanfors, M. (2009). Does parenthood strengthen a traditional household division of labor? Evidence from Sweden. *Journal of Marriage and Family, 71,* 33–45.
Dribe, M., & Stanfors, M. (2010). Family life in power couples: Continued childbearing and union stability among the educational elite in Sweden, 1991–2005. *Demographic Research, 23,* 847–878.
Ely, R. J., & Meyerson, D. E. (2000). Theories of gender in organizations: A new approach to organizational analysis and change. In A. Brief & B. M. Staw (Eds.), *Research in organizational behavior* (pp. 103–151). New York: Elsevier.
Epstein, C. F., Seron, C., Oglensky, B., & Sauté, R. (1999). *The part-time paradox: Time norms, professional lives, family, and gender*. New York: Routledge.
Gauthier, A., Smeeding, T., & Furstenberg, F. (2004). Are parents investing less time in children: Trends in selected industrialized countries. *Population and Development Review, 30,* 647–671.
Gershuny, J. (2000). *Changing times: Work and leisure in post-industrial societies*. Oxford: Oxford University Press.
Gershuny, J., & Robinson, J. P. (1988). Historical changes in the household division of labor. *Demography, 25,* 537–552.
Glass, J. (2000). Envisioning the integration of family and work. *Contemporary Sociology, 29,* 129–143.

Goldin, C. (1990). *Understanding the gender gap: An economic history of American women*. New York: Oxford University Press.
Goldin, C. (15 March 2006). Working it out. *New York Times*, p. A27.
Goldin, C., & Katz, L. (2008). Transitions: career and family life cycles of the educational elite. *American Economic Review: Papers and Proceedings, 98,* 363–369.
Goldin, C., & Katz, L. F. (2011). The cost of workplace flexibility for high-powered professionals. *Annals of the American Academy of Political and Social Science, 638,* 45–67.
Goldin, C., & Katz, L. F. (2013). The most egalitarian of all professions: Pharmacy and the evolution of a family-friendly occupation. NBER Working Paper No 18410.
Greenhaus, J. H., & Powell, G. N. (2003). When work and family collide: Deciding between competing role demands. *Organizational Behavior and Human Decision Processes, 90,* 291–303.
Hallberg, D., & Klevmarken, A. (2003). Time for children: A study of parents' time allocation. *Journal of Population Economics, 16,* 205–226.
Herr, J. L., & Wolfram, C. (2011). Work environment and "opt-out" rates at motherhood across high education career paths. NBER Working Paper No 14717.
Hewlett, S. A. (2002). Executive women and the myth of having it all. *Harvard Business Review, 80,* 66–73.
Hochschild, A. R. (1989). *The second shift: Working parents and the revolution at home*. New York: Penguin.
Hochschild, A. R. (1997). *The time bind: When work becomes home and home becomes work*. New York: Metropolitan Books.
Hoem, J. M., Neyer, G., & Andersson, G. (2006). Educational attainment and ultimate fertility among Swedish women born in 1955–59. *Demographic Research, 14,* 381–403.
Hofferth, S. (1999). Child care, maternal employment, and public policy. *The Annals of the American Academy of Political and Social Science, 563,* 20–38.
Hymowitz, C., & Silverman, R. E. (16 January 2001). Can work stress get worse? *Wall Street Journal*, p. B1.
Jacobs, J. A., & Fanning Madden, J. (2004). Mommies and daddies on the fast track: Success of parents in demanding professions. Special issue of *The Annals of the American Academy of Political and Social Science*, 596.
Joshi, H. (2002). Production, reproduction and education: Women, children and work in a British perspective. *Population and Development Review, 28,* 445–474.
Kimball, G. (1999). *21st century families*. Chico: Equality.
Kravdal, Ø. (2001). The high fertility of college educated women in Norway: An artefact of the separate modelling of each parity transition. *Demographic Research, 5,* 187–216.
Kravdal, Ø. (2007). Effects of current education on second- and third-birth rates among Norwegian women and men born in 1964: Substantive interpretations and methodological issues. *Demographic Research, 17,* 211–246.
Kreyenfeld, M. (2002). Time-squeeze, partner effect or self-selection? An investigation into the positive effects of women's education on second birth risks in West Germany. *Demographic Research, 7,* 15–48.
Lappegård, T., & Rönsen, M. (2005). The multifaceted impact of education on entry into motherhood. *European Journal of Population, 21,* 31–49.
Mason, M. A., & Goulden, M. (2004). Marriage and baby blues: Redefining gender equity in the Academy. *Annals of the American Academy of Political and Social Science, 596,* 86–103.
McDonald, P. (2000). Gender equity in theories of fertility transition. *Population and Development Review, 26,* 427–439.
Mincer, J. (1963). Market prices, opportunity costs, and income effects. In Christ, E., et al. (Eds.), *Measurement in economics*. Stanford: Stanford University Press.
Moen, P., & Yu, Y. (1999). Having it all: Overall work/life success in two-earner families. In T. Parcel (Ed.), *Research in the sociology of work* (pp. 107–137). Greenwich: JAI.
Neilson, J., & Stanfors, M. (2014). It's about time! Gender, parenthood and household divisions of labor under different welfare regimes. *Journal of Family Issues, 35*, 1066–1088.
Noonan, M. C., & Corcoran, M. E. (2004). The Mommy track and partnership: Temporary delay or dead end? *Annals of the American Academy of Political and Social Science, 596,* 130–150.

Polachek, S. W. (1981). Occupational self-selection: A human capital approach to sex differences in occupational structure. *Review of Economics and Statistics, 63,* 60–69.

Ruhm, C., & Teague, J. L. (1997). Parental leave policies in Europe and North America. In F. D. Blau & R. G. Ehrenberg (Eds.), *Gender and family issues in the work place* (pp. 133–156). New York: Russell Sage.

Sayer, L. (2005). Trends in women's and men's paid work, unpaid work and free time. *Social Forces, 84,* 285–303.

Shang, Q., & Weinberg, B. A. (2013). Opting for families: Recent trends in the fertility of highly educated women. *Journal of Population Economics, 26,* 5–32.

Stanfors, M. (2003). *Education, labor force participation and changing fertility patterns. A study of women and socioeconomic change in twentieth century Sweden.* Stockholm: Almqvist and Wiksell International.

Stone, P. (2008). *Opting out? Why women really quit careers and head home.* Los Angeles: University of California Press.

Story, L. (20 September 2005). Many women at elite colleges set career path to motherhood. *New York Times*, pp. A1, A18.

Van Bavel, J. (2010). Choice of study discipline and the postponement of motherhood in Europe: The impact of expected earnings, gender composition and family attitudes. *Demography, 47,* 439–458.

Williams, J. (2000). *Unbending gender: Why family and work conflict and what to do about it.* New York: Oxford University Press.

Wolfinger, N. H., Mason, M. A., & Goulden, M. (2010). Alone in the ivory tower. *Journal of Family Issues, 31,* 1652–1670.

Index

M. J. Mills (ed.), *Gender and the Work-Family Experience*,
DOI 10.1007/978-3-319-08891-4

CPSIA information can be obtained
at www.ICGtesting.com
Printed in the USA
LVOW03*1113210316
480070LV00011B/77/P

9 783319 088907